THE LOST HISTORY
of the Little People

"Tales and legends of the wee folk, or little people, are numerous around the world. At times they are reportedly meddlesome, but always very mysterious. Through her extensive research into the subject matter, Susan Martinez, Ph.D., establishes the little people as the progenitor of civilization and one of the ancestors of the people of today."

JACK CHURCHWARD, AUTHOR OF
*LIFTING THE VEIL ON THE LOST CONTINENT
OF MU, MOTHERLAND OF MEN*

THE LOST HISTORY
of the Little People

Their Spiritually Advanced
Civilizations around the World

Susan B. Martinez, Ph.D.

Bear & Company
Rochester, Vermont • Toronto, Canada

Bear & Company
One Park Street
Rochester, Vermont 05767
www.BearandCompanyBooks.com

Text stock is SFI certified

Bear & Company is a division of Inner Traditions International

Library of Congress Cataloging-in-Publication Data

Martinez, Susan B.
   The lost history of the little people : their spiritually advanced civilizations around the world / Susan B. Martinez.
      p. cm.
   Includes bibliographical references (p.   ) and index.
   ISBN 978-1-59143-145-9 (pbk.) — ISBN 978-1-59143-804-5 (e-book)
   1. Pygmies—Civilization. 2. Civilization, Ancient. 3. Pygmies—History. 4. Stature, Short—History. 5. Stature, Short—Social aspects—History. 6. Spirituality—Social aspects—History. 7. Kindness—Social aspects—History. 8. Pygmies—Folklore. 9. Stature, Short—Folklore. I. Title.
   CB281.M37 2013
   930—dc23

                                                                2012029463

Printed and bound in the United States by Lake Book Manufacturing, Inc. The text stock is SFI certified. The Sustainable Forestry Initiative® program promotes sustainable forest management.

10 9 8 7 6 5 4 3 2 1

Text design by Virginia L. Scott Bowman and layout by Priscilla Baker
This book was typeset in Garamond Premier Pro with AlParma Petit, Helvetica Neue, Legacy Sans, and Papyrus used as display typefaces

The author wishes to heartily thank her editor, Mindy Branstetter, for supplying excellent section titles. Thanks, Mindy.

Figures 2.1a, 2.5, 2.6b, 2.17, 2.34, 3.3, 6.1, 6.2, 7.7, 7.8, 7.12, 7.13, 7.22 by Jose Bouvier
Figures 2.19 and 2.31 courtesy of Loren Coleman
Figures 3.5 and 3.6 courtesy of Marvin E. Herring, M.D.
Figures 3.1, 3.8, and 5.7 courtesy of J. B. Newbrough

To send correspondence to the author of this book, mail a first-class letter to the author c/o Inner Traditions • Bear & Company, One Park Street, Rochester, VT 05767, and we will forward the communication, or visit the author's website at **earthvortex.com** or contact the author directly at **poosh8@gmail.com**.

For Mary Elizabeth Fisher,
friend for life

Do the Pygmies hold the answer?

CARLETON COON,
THE ORIGIN OF RACES

Contents

APPENDICES

Word Derivations and Their Geographic Relationships and Historic Themes

Note to Reader

Most damaging to the study of history was the deification of the little people. This sort of development actually has a name: *euhemerism,* wherein mortals (usually the ancestors) were converted, over time, into beings of the Other World—gods and spirits. I have bolded all such names and words throughout the book, so the reader can follow this theme.

I am also using shorthand for time counts: "BP" means "years before present."

Preface

It is only within recent time, relatively speaking, that we have begun to understand the high civilizations of antiquity. Yet, as historians have long noted, they seem to have sprung up suddenly and without precedent. What then lies *behind* the greatness of the Maya, Inca, Egyptians, Sumerians? Eighty years have elapsed since George C. Vaillant said:

> The great civilizations of the Aztecs and the Mayas are like flowers, but of the stalk, which bore them and gave them nutriment, we have scant knowledge. Who knows what discovery awaits us that may alter our entire conception of the unfolding of Middle American civilization?[1]

That missing discovery—especially for those who believe in the Original Unity of mankind—will account not only for the Maya of Mexico, but for all the high cultures of the hidden past, all over the world.

In most of those mysterious high cultures, it is little people whom we will find behind the scenes—yet, there is no literature on them; one has to paste together their story from bits and pieces, a thousand fragments. In tackling this much-neglected subject it is my aim to identify *Homo sapiens pygmaeus* as that lost race that brought humanity to the heights, not only of its material culture, but also of its spiritual potential. You may wonder why you have not heard of them before. Well, they are below the radar for a number of reasons:

1. They are extinct.

2. They were endogamous, reclusive, keeping their habitation, writing, and rites secret. And they were, in time, driven off to some of the most remote parts of the world.

3. They were deified out of existence (see below).

4. Cremation burials, general to the Bronze Age, are sometimes found without weapons; this is a sign of the peaceful little people. The Wisconsin and Tennessee mounds, for instance, "afford ample evidence of cremation,"[2] as do crematoriums found at North American mound sites such as Davenport or Hopewell. Nevertheless, in Tennessee, are also found extensive "pigmy graveyards." The high civilizations of North America were in general cremators, therefore leaving no fossils. Mexico's Teotihuacan culture burned the dead. The Cocle of Panama cremated in urns. The "delicately built" fossil men of Australia at Lake Mungo also cremated.

5. Finally, the little people upset the charter myths of both biblical and evolutionary schemes (Christianity and Science), and perhaps for this reason archaeologists sometimes don't bother to note the *height* of skeletons. The swarthy little people (Negritos), frets M. Stewart, have been airbrushed from history, those in Australia expunged from popular memory, suggesting "an indecent concurrence between scholarly and political interests."[3]

Body size . . . has been overlooked by physical anthropologists.

W. E. le Gros Clark,
The Fossil Evidence for Human Evolution

But:

Civilizations rarely die without leaving any trace.

Georges Roux, *Ancient Iraq*

Fig. P.1. Anthropologist Joseph Birdsell standing with a twenty-four-year-old Australian aborigine of the Kongkandji tribe. The Australian pygmies, charges one online critic, a Mr. Stewart, have been totally obliterated from public memory. Even when they are listed in tribal studies, not a word about their stature is mentioned.

Thus, in today's world, "we may look upon the Andamanese, the Aetas, and the Semangs [Negritos], as living fossils; and by their aid, conjecture the condition of the whole population of the land in ancient times."[4]

Many of our clues to the past do indeed come from living societies with keen memory of the Ancestor. Among some Slavic peoples, for example, their forebears are remembered as tiny, about the size of a six-year-old. They were called "Grandfather." In other parts of Europe they are remembered simply as the "Old Ones."

Anyone can have a brush with the little men, as did Loren Eiseley, anthropologist-raconteur, who happened to come across a diminutive mummy at a "bone camp" in the American West. After declining the pleasure of purchasing said mummy, Eiseley went on to muse: "I never expected . . . to live to hear my little man ascribed an extraplanetary origin," as books were then coming out on flying saucers and such. "There is a story back of him, it is true," Eiseley reckoned, "but it is a history of this earth."[5]

Very much the history of this Earth—indeed, a lost history that corroborates the Original Unity of mankind. Ours will be a journey back in time, as far back as 24,000 years, before the "Tower of Babel," here introducing Panology—the study of the Flood and the lost lands of Pacifica, herein called Pan. "The Sumerians like the Hebrews . . .

believed in the existence of a universal speech prior to the period of the confusion of languages."[6] This speech is the common language of Pan, called "Panic," whose vocabulary we will explore at length.

God said: Now the world was of one language and one speech; in all the places . . . they spoke alike, person to person.

OAHSPE, THE LORDS' FIRST BOOK 1:74

Back, back, back we go—to a time in history that is not about heroes and conquerors, kings and despots, but about the first civilizers and holy men—the sacred tribes who were saved from the Flood, a people no taller than three and a half feet in height. Not "dwarfs," for they were perfectly proportioned and remembered in aftertime as a delightfully handsome and splendidly refined race.

Fig. P.2. Sakai Negritos of Perak, Malaysia

Their mixed descendants today reside mostly in isolated mountains, jungles, and islands. They are the living remnant of the little people, and they have been around longer than we have. They are called, for the most part, Negritos and Negrillos—the Aeta, Batek, Andamanese, Bushmen, Twa, Vedda, Semang, Sakai, and so forth.

By the time we get even to the thirteenth century, the fairies had been euhemerized.

KATHARINE BRIGGS, *THE VANISHING PEOPLE*

The Flemish little people, for example, seemed so strange that "they became changed in the imagination of the dreamy Germans into mysterious beings, a kind of ghosts or gods."[7] Another example: "In the beginning," says Iroquois myth, "there was only the primordial waters. . . . The **Ongwe** lived in the heavens." Ah, but the **Ongwe** (First Indians) lived right here on Earth.

Indeed, Manetho thought that all the gods of Egypt had once been mortals who lived on Earth. Just as the powers of nature were often deified, so were the ancestors. In general, that which befell before living memory tends to be attributed to the supernaturals. Even some of our modern, dominant religions can barely distinguish between God, prophet, and Creator—and even scholars have made gods of the little people! Andrew Lang, for example, discussing the "pygmy theory," concluded that the "inhabitants of the *sidhes* (see chapter 7) were not a real dwarfish race. . . . [but] a lingering memory of the chthonian beings, chthonian meaning gods or spirits of the Underworld."

CHAPTER 1

The Old Ones

THE DISAPPEARANCE OF
THE LITTLE PEOPLE

The day after Christmas in 2004, a gigantic tsunami broke over the coast of northwestern Sumatra following a 9.0 earthquake that violently lifted the floor of the Indian Ocean. Spreading in all directions, the energy released by the quake was the equivalent of 10,000 atomic bombs. The deadliest tsunami in recorded history, the 2004 disaster inundated coastal communities, from Indonesia to Somalia, with waves up to 100 feet high. Estimated death toll hovered around 200,000 human beings. Some reports claimed that no *animals* lost their lives to the great Indian Ocean Earthquake of 2004: one can almost believe that the animal kingdom is hardwired with some sort of early warning system, alerting them to imminent danger in the rumblings of Mother Earth.

The human kingdom, however, is not so well equipped, or so it seems; even after Sumatra was hit early in the morning, reluctant tourist industries, "diplomatic protocol," and assorted dilatory responses left little time for at-risk communities to head for the hills. Nevertheless, the Pacific Tsunami Warning Centre dispatched timely advisories to many countries in the path of the deluge. The only problem: many islands in the Indian Ocean are not connected to the Centre. This is especially true of the small and isolated areas of insular Southeast Asia, which we sometimes refer to as Sundaland. Some of these island nations were the worst hit. No body count was possible in places like North Sentinel

Island—a pancake-flat land, conceivably the most isolated place on Earth. The coastal villagers of the Nicobars also suffered major losses, "if not near extinction"—at least half of their population was engulfed.

And yes, numerous of these insular groups are (or were) of Negrito stock, designating the race of brown-skinned, pint-size folk—hunters, gatherers, simple horticulturalists, among the last of Earth's Paleolithic (Old Stone Age) tribes, some believed to have inhabited those distant isles as long ago as 60,000 years. The tsunami decimated the little Andaman people of the Bay of Bengal; almost all of the inhabitants drowned or went missing after the Boxing Day disaster. Reports are scant: Did the tsunami wipe out the last of these little people—already decimated by nineteenth-century smallpox? Indeed, whole tribes of Andamanese Negritos perished; earlier rogue waves having long since devastated the aboriginal inhabitants of low lying islands, wiping out anyone not living upland or in tree huts or caves. Whole colonies of the little people have gone missing in Ceylon as well.

THE ISLAND OF FLORES

The Earth gives and the Earth takes away. Philosophically stirring, in the same year (2004) that so many of Earth's wee people were swept away, a media sensation erupted, centered on the little people in the Indonesian arc of that tsunami, between Bali and Timor. Here lies the island of Flores, where a discovery of tiny human skeletons was made in the Liang Bua Grotto. Dubbed "hobbit" (officially *Homo floresiensis*), these little men and women had been remarkably skilled hunters, despite being very small-brained. Experts who examined these finds called them "totally unexpected," a scientific event of seismic proportions. After all, this exceptionally primitive creature—long-armed, chinless, weighing hardly more than fifty pounds—was (supposedly) "completely new to science." But not really: Dutch anthropologists *fifty years before,* in 1955, had found on Flores six skeletons of the very same type![1] Besides, there are (or were?)[2] Negritos on Flores!

Here, simply, was one type of *Homo sapiens pygmaeus:* the little people. But how could this small-brained hobbit have lived on Flores as recently as 13,000 years ago, if all the primitive versions of *Homo sapiens* were supposed to be gone from the Earth, extinct, at least 28,000 years ago? Something was amiss in the "evolutionary" scheme of things.

A bit over three feet in height and well proportioned, this little Flores man who hunted Komodo dragons had an extraordinary mixture of primitive and advanced traits. To a point, he resembled *Homo erectus,* one of the early, rough-hewn, hominids; but hobbit is way too recent and his stone tools too "sophisticated." We will, further on, take a closer look at these all-important mixings, for they are the pith of man's ascent—and key to the genesis of humankind.

Indulging in a hearty round of back-slapping, scientists involved in the hobbit discovery saw their find as "spectacular," "astonishing,"* claiming it to be "the smallest human species ever discovered." Not true, as we will soon see. Invoking the spirit of Charles Darwin, one celebrated paleontologist boasted, "This is a splendid example of evolution." Is it? Or is it *devolution*? Or is it neither? Hobbit man triggered a heated scientific shoot-out centered on his origins and the ultimate question—why is he so small? In a pose of scientific humility, another member of the hobbit team allowed, "This find shows us how much we still have to learn about human evolution."[3]

Or—unlearn . . .

A GENTLE VOICE

And what about human *nature?* Humankind, opined the learned anthropologist Ashley Montagu, during a 1946 interview with Albert Einstein, was not innately aggressive; "There was no such thing as a drive toward destruction . . . as Freud had postulated. . . . Indeed, human beings had no instincts at all." Though I completely agree with Montagu on this point, Einstein begged to differ, recalling Freud's personal reply to him, to the effect that man is incapable of suppressing his aggressive tendencies; but with this codicil: "In some happy corners

---

*Astonishing? Local legend (doesn't that count?) long remembered the tiny people of the Sunda Islands. Besides, there are still Negritos and little people on Flores—the Rampasas.

of the earth, they say . . . there flourish races whose lives go gently by, unknowing of aggression. . . . This I can hardly credit; I would like further details about these happy folk."

As far as Montagu was concerned, Freud had not done his homework: "The details were available in Freud's day for the Australian aboriginies, the Veddas of Ceylon, the Hopi and Zuni, the Pygmies of the Congo. Many such gentle, unwarlike peoples do exist."[4]

Interesting that Montagu should have cited the Veddas ("a kind and affectionate people," according to the Victorian prehistorian John Lubbock), as well as the pygmies and aborigines, for in each of these places can be found the little people, short of stature: *Homo sapiens pygmaeus;* while in America, the missions called the Hopi "The Little People of Peace." The Pygmaioi of ancient Greece all loved to show kindliness, according to early mythographers. Ditto in Scotland where the fairies are "The People of Peace," and in Africa, where the pygmies are known to be a "gentle, peaceful people"—Armand de Quatrefages, in *The Pygmies,* recalls the "gentleness of their voice"; and in southern Africa, where the Bushmen (San) call themselves *zhu twa si,* "the harmless people," and "speak very softly," rather like the Scand Ellefolk (four feet tall) whose voices, legendarily, are mellow and gentle.

Colin Turnbull thought the pygmy world was one that is "still kind and good . . . and without evil."[5]

God said: I preserved the Ihin race [*H. pygmaeus*] to be without evil, as the foundation of my light, from whom I could reach forth to the tribes of darkness.

OAHSPE, BOOK OF APH 4:1

The little Menehune of Hawaii had "friendly eyes." Many of the Filipino Negritos are on the "shy" side. The Semang Negrito of Malaysia is said to be a modest soul: "his gaiety is restrained and muted. . . . The Semang are by no means warlike," observed Father Paul Schebesta, adding that their "psychological attitude . . . makes them unfit for war. . . . Even during the time of persecution by the Malays, nothing is known of any resistance by the Semang; they protected themselves by flight."[6]

All the little people were originally nonresistants, which helps to explain the absence of weapons in those Bronze Age burials.

Worldwide folklore gives us tales of diminutive people who merge (euhemistically) into the gentle and fairylike **denizens** of Nature's hidden niches. The Eskimo describe *silam inua** ("soul of the universe") as "a gentle voice, like a woman."[7] This is quite analogous to the ancestral Sri Vede of India, the mild and merciful little people, "that is, the sacred tribes," wrote Vernon Wobschall who "were called Sri-vede-iyi, People of the true light; they were womanlike. In other words, the spiritual aspect is feminine, meaning, the Ihins* were a feminine race, receptive to spiritual teachings."[8] Various languages have the Tahitian **Hina** as First Woman and *all-good* wife of Creator (hina is a variant of ihin).

Known as "the Good People," Europe's fairy folk sometimes help householders with their chores, though their own abode is at retired spots, perceived as "gentle" places, softly haunted. For the Irish, these habitués are called the Sidhe or the Daoine Shi, which (Gaelic) translates as "Men of Peace." Here in Ireland, the legendary home of the little *grogachs,* Clough-na-murry, is said to be a "gentle place."

Of the Welsh fairies, it was said that their beauty was equaled only by their courtesy and affability. French *fées,* say the peasantry, were "altogether most kind and obliging." On the Baltic Isle of Rugen, inhabitants remember the little underground people (the White Dwarfs) as the most delicate and beautiful of all human beings, and of an innocent and gentle disposition.

Across the sea, the Mandan Indians on the Great Plains of North America impressed nineteenth-century travelers as "mild and sweet,"

---

*Eskimo *inua* (from "Ihin," as we will see in appendix D) recalls their small-size ancestor, who—focused on the feminine—is Mother of All. The Papuans of southwestern New Guinea call "woman"—*aina;* on Ceram, she is *mahina;* and in other parts of Indonesia, she is P*ina*-lungao, the goddess of birth. In Polynesia, "mother" is *ina.* First Mother is H*ina*marou or H*ainu*wale. The queen, in the Society Islands, is Mah*ina*-vahine. The *ine* of the Irish Daoine is in the same family of names as *inua, aina, hina, ihin,* and so forth. The root is universal (Panic), especially among Negritos who are one-part Ihin themselves: *ina* is "mother" in the Philippines, western Indonesia, and the Andamans. Mother Earth is *Ina* in Central Asia as well (*Ino* to the Pelasgians). The Chaldean Earth goddess is Damk*ina,* and Sun Goddess for the Celts is Gre*ine.*

a particularly gracious people, possessed of "moral superiority . . . and a mild expression of countenance not usually seen among Indians . . . They were noted for their virtue."[9] And when we meet them again we will find their customs and characteristics akin to the little people.

Among the Cherokee, the Nunnehi, the "Little People," are well remembered. These gentle and minute forest-dwellers, the Cherokee storyteller will recount with muted awe, are "here to teach lessons about living in harmony with nature and with others." Like the fairy folk of the Irish, "with their immaterial charm,"[10] the Nunnehi happily help out in a jam and take care of corn crops while the farmers sleep. The Nunnehi (and the related Yunwi Tsusdi) inhabited the scenic wilds of the Great Smokey Mountains, time out of mind, long before the arrival of the tall Cherokees. These elflike beings—moon-eyed, with white skins, bearded faces, and blue eyes—were sometimes seen firsthand by the Cherokee, but more often, only their distant drums could be heard. They were "kind to lost ones," especially to Cherokee children who, at age seven, would stand at the same height as a full-grown Nunnehi or Yunwi.

CONNECT THE DOTS

In 1828, ten years before the infamous Exile of the Eastern Cherokee (the Trail of Tears, a calamity the prescient little people had foretold), Tennessee newspapers began reporting the discovery of remarkable burial grounds in both Sparta and White counties. "Very little people," according to a later account in *Harper's Magazine* (July, 1869), "had been deposited in coffins of stone . . . the bones were strong and well set, and the whole frames were well formed." Then, Smith County joined the controversy, with more finds of well-formed skeletons measuring three feet in length.

In light of these unusual burials (found almost two hundred years before the touted "hobbit" of Java), isn't it time for archaeologists and folklorists to get together and connect the dots? For we have every reason to believe it was the remains of the early moundbuilders whom they found in those southern tombs. Yet these diminutive sarcophagi were dismissed out of hand as the graves of "newborn infants" or small children—or even small animals (*American Antiquarian,* 1901)! How about that! A race of small children! Or stone coffins—for animals.

By 1980, though, a controversial Harvard paleontologist named Barry Fell, reconstructing thousands of these Tennessee cranial fragments (acquired from 600 burials), found that the teeth showed "complete development and severe wear," proving the skulls to be from middle-aged adults. Fell, moreover, was able to match these Tennessee skulls with look-alikes in the Philippines—a good hint of *Homo pygmaeus'* once-widespread distribution in the world. Indeed, another writer linked up these Tennessee (plus related Kentucky and Ohio) specimens to similar ones in Malaysia, Fiji, and the Sandwich Islands: their common artifacts "clearly of a Polynesian character. . . . The North Americans, Polynesians, and Malays were formerly the same people, or had one common origin."[11] That common origin, orbiting Polynesia, will be a major thread of this book, as we move toward the rediscovery of Pan—the lost homeland of the little people—in the Pacific.

Nevertheless, writers like Joseph Jones in his 1901 book, *Exploring the Aboriginal Remains in Tennessee,* thought he "thoroughly refuted . . . the pigmy theory." His opinion, however, didn't stop the White, Sparta, and Smith County finds from being joined now by a far vaster "pigmy graveyard" at Hillsboro, Tennessee (Coffee Country). A man had been plowing his field and turned up a small skull and other bones. Further investigation revealed six acres of graveyard, with skeletons either in a sitting or standing position. "The bones show that they were a dwarf tribe . . . about three feet high. It is estimated that there were about 75,000 to 100,000 buried there."[12]

So let's connect the dots: One of the Sparta County skeletons, lying on its back with hands on chest, had about its neck ninety-four pearl beads. We might suppose he was the spiritual head or priest of these little people; for in aftertime, the Cherokee shaman, *adawehi,* adorned himself with a like pectoral of shining river pearls,* symbolizing the secrets of the stars, the spirit-helpers, and the Immortals (Nunnehi).

---

*In Ohio, at the acclaimed Hopewell mounds, pearl ornaments were again found in profusion, thousands of pearl beads and magnificent mantles of freshwater pearls. Dubbed "The Great Pearl Burial," it was assumed to be the tomb of a royal family, or at the least, to contain occupants of high standing.

Adawehi is an interesting word that denotes not only the shaman himself (Cherokee), but all that is divine, encompassing the invisible world that permeates and empowers the living. The term applies as well to the shaman's familiar spirits who can be invoked for assistance; but all men, animals, plants—all tribes of the living—are infused to some

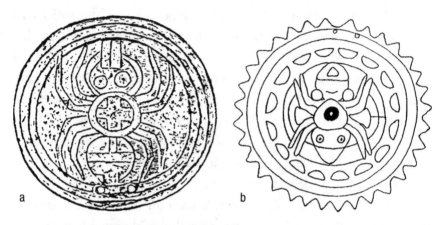

Fig. 1.1. Pectorals. A shell-gorget from Tennessee (a) rather resembles a scarab tablet found in an Egyptian tomb (b). (Also see analogous scarabs from Ohio in fig. 7.9c, p. 232).

Fig. 1.2. Part of a gorget, carved in shell, found in an Oklahoma mound. Note the dwarfishness of the figure, which evokes "Gnome-dale" (valley of the gnomes) mentioned on Oklahoma's "Heavener Stone." Why have authors systematically failed to note the short stature of these iconographic figures?

degree with adawehi. The eagle is a great adawehi, and his feathers may only be carried by the most acclaimed medicine men. The Nunnehi people were abundantly adawehi. These little men could assume various shapes at will, or even become invisible.

PROPHECIES AND MIRACLES

Were they magical beings? "An ignorant people," wrote John Lubbock in *Pre-historic Times,* "living by the side of a more civilized race . . . attribute their superiority to magical arts." Just so, magical Little Men were remembered, as recorded in that famous volume, *Corps of Discovery,* detailing the Jeffersonian expedition to the unknown West. On August 25, 1804, Meriwether Lewis and William Clark happened to camp on a hill near the Teton River (Kansas). The "hill" was actually a mound, man-made. Here, the explorers learned that the Dakota Indians called the place Mountain-of-the-Little-People, or Spirit Mound. The original inhabitants were, according to the elders, People-of-Another-World, so enlightened, so spiritual in nature—not unlike the fairies of European lore.

And so it is, inevitably, to Ireland that we turn for light on the fairies—the wee people. Like their congeners in Cherokee country, the grogachs or brownies (at Ulster, Ballycastle, and Shetland) work diligently helping the farmers in their cornfields. In Northeast Antrim, the supernatural ways of the grogachs are well known; while the Sidhe, the fairylike Tuatha De Danaan, were renowned for their wizardry and magic; their very name implies "enchanted." Said to know the secrets of heaven, they could cause storms and cast spells; they are witches' familiars, tutoring them in all the magical arts. The romance of Lancelot calls all those women fays or fées—who had to do with enchantments and charms, who knew the power and virtue of words, stones, and herbs. Fées can take the shape of bats, moles, and small animals; banshees can foretell disasters and epidemics. The *korrigan,* another type of these phantasmagorical little people, can predict the future, assume any form they please, and move from place to place with the rapidity of thought.

Europe's dwarfs are also reputed to see into the future and make themselves invisible. The *dvergar* (dwarfs) of the Norse Eddas possessed

Fig. 1.3. Depiction of a Germanic dwarf from *Voluspa* by Lorenz Frolich, 1895. The Norse dvergar were of such divine power that even the gods of Aesir must rely on them for their inventory of magical items.

enviable supernatural knowledge and are frequently associated with luck, craft, and wisdom, rather matching Chinese tales of magical dwarfs.

The Swiss dwarf is so endowed (with adawehi), he can divert the course of a devastating landslide.* In both Irish and Swiss traditions, "gifted" dwarfish people dwell in mountain caves or man-made souterrains. In Grimm's, as well as other bodies of folklore, the dwarf has the uncanny power to grant wishes and other aids to help people in distress. Indeed, from Iceland to Italy to India, there are countless stories of their benevolence, practical wisdom, and otherworldly powers. The Queen of Elfland had "a grip on all the Craft." The elves of Iceland, it was said, caused equipment to malfunction and workers to be injured when a new construction project in 1962 threatened their habitation; because of all the trouble, Reykjavik learned to route roads *around* hallowed boulders and other spots believed to be inhabited by the elves.

---

*In Bernese Oberland, a story was recorded concerning the destruction of the village of Burglauenen; all the cottages were inundated by the flood, except one little hut that had given shelter to a dwarf, who was seen seated on a stone, directing the moving mass away from the abode of his friends.

These magical powers are not confined to Europe or America, or even to folklore, for that matter, for very real little people like the Malay Negrito are also "gifted": they can direct a spear to point to an unknown malefactor, or they can summon the tiger. This is true for the little people of southern Africa as well—a Bushman's spirit can go out-of-body and talk to the lions in the veld, convincing them to go away and not trouble them; there was "something uncanny" about the Bushman's symbiotic relationship with the lion. And in the Congo, where cannibalism has been going on in the north Kivu province, pygmies are regarded as sub-human and besides, some say eating their flesh confers magical powers.

The sacred little people in the wilderness . . . [could] charm even the great serpents and savage lions and tigers, to be their friends and worshipers.

OAHSPE, BOOK OF WARS 21:3

Fig. 1.4. Eighteenth Dynasty Egypt: worshipping baboons of morning. Even the apes were induced to worship the Higher Power.

The little Bushmen are strongly adawehi: without radio communication, they can tell in advance when "bush pilots" would be landing in their territory, and when—at a great distance—an eland has been killed by their hunters, the camp immediately knows of it "by psychic wire." In camp, before the hunters return home with their kill, one could hear the sounds of the song that was used to celebrate such occasions.

The Ihins were capable of prophecies and miracles to such an extent that all other people called them the sacred people.

OAHSPE, BOOK OF DIVINITY 11:13

The "miraculous little people," the Menehune of Hawaii, are also adawehi: they give magic to the fire-thrower, and have power over the winds. Sometimes the supernal light (adawehi) may be quite literal: In the Mangrove Swamps of Durham, South Africa, some visitors were hiking and came upon a clearing with a natural amphitheater. They saw fire lights all around, and then a small person appeared, just over three feet in height. Presently, more than twenty little people were seen; the hikers described the light and forms as ethereal, far less dense than regular light. "We were shocked and frightened. . . . We turned and ran." That ethereal light has been seen by others, other times, other places: nineteenth-century fairies encountered in England (three feet high) seemed light and shadowy, "not like solid bodies" (for they are spirits, not mortals, but ex-mortals).

It is something like the *kemoit* (shade of the Negrito dead), which "glows with light, like a firefly." Too, the Polish little people are called Iskvzycki, meaning "spark," comparable to the "fairy sparks" of Europe, being the phosphoric shine from decaying trees, but thought to be the light of fairy revels. All these sparks emanate from the adawehi that spiritual beings may possess: angels with the power to shape-shift and take on any form. In October 2003 in Greensburg, Pennsylvania, a woman looked out on her land and saw a little man sitting on the stone wall. "The area looked different somehow . . . shimmery is the first word that comes to mind . . . [the] little elf-looking man [was] peering right at me." When she startled, "Ooh!" it just disappeared into thin air.[13]

Such are the ways and capacities of discarnate spirits; we do not need to invent "devas" or "elementals," but only to understand the transformative powers possessed by the spirits of the dead, living on the Other Side. (The Irish call fairy people—the Others.) Among myriad spirits visiting the nineteenth-century ghost house of the Eddy's in Vermont, it is curious that "young girls with lithe forms, yellow hair, and short stature"[14] would manifest; the angels of the Ihins (with their yellow hair) indeed act as guardian spirits once they leave the Earth. "The angels of heaven remained with corporeal man, but not in the semblance of mortals, but as spirits; and by virtue of their presence, strove to make man wise and upright . . . being guardian angels over them."[15]

TRIBES OF LIGHT

My colleague, Vernon Wobschall, has written: "The Ihins of ancient times, with their light and purity, become earth-ized and conceptualized in myth as gnomes, dwarfs, leprechauns, and the like, with earthly desires and common frailties; they retain impressions of their high estate . . . in having magical properties." These special powers belong more particularly to beings of Light; but even the flesh-man may attain the higher degrees of adawehi. Another friend, author Paul Eno, had a chance encounter in Australia with a little man. Paul was waiting for his ride out of a rural area near Melbourne when he got talking with a little guy (four feet high) called Mindiluwi. This wrinkled and cheerful aborigine, thought Paul by the time their conversation ended, "was a giant." Mindiluwi talked about *guruwari,* the seeds of life planted in the Dream Time by their ancestors. One must realize that guruwari (rather like adawehi) is a mustard seed within each and every self. Paul discussed his own "paranormal" theories with Mindiluwi, who not only understood it all, but also "shed much light on it. I think I learned more in my few hours of talk with him than I did in years of reading books."[16]

Following that invisible Light, that life force, that guruwari, and moving north of the Australian landmass into the Malay Peninsula, we come upon a great number of Negrito tribes. Little People. Despite the Malaysian's ingrained prejudice against Negritos, they do retain "a certain amount of superstitious respect" for them, believing these little men and women to be "in league not only with the wild beast, but with all the supernatural and inhuman powers of the forest."[17]

Now if the reader will indulge me in a brief linguistic foray, we might detect a trace of the earliest tribes of light among these wee folk relict though they be: Negritos, no doubt, are some of the most primitive people in the world today. Some Aetas eat ants, some Negritos, like the Andamanese,

Fig. 1.5. Onge Andamanese women

know not how to make fire; many go naked and unclothed, like their part-ancestor, the *druk* who did not hide his nakedness. Thus is Negrito heritage a perfect mixture of the dark and light, as language now reveals: The Onge people of the Andamans have an intriguing name. Onge is a very, very early form (Panic), which—like guruwari and adawehi—signifies "spiritual light" both in Algonquin and in Hebrew (frequently the "o" sound gives way to "a"). Here we list a few words incorporating this ancient root, all based on the concept of Receptacle of Light:

onge	men, people, Little Andaman
ang	mankind, Algonquin[18]
ongwe	person, Mohawk*
ongji	window, Algonquin
ang'hoi	medicine man, Algonquin
angakoq	Eskimo shaman
Anguta	**supreme being** of the western Eskimo
s'angutu	priestly chamberlains, Chaldean
s'angoma	Zulu medicine man or woman
ganga	priest, Mongo tribe, Congo
m'angku	Bali high priest, shaman
pawang	priest, Sakai

*See fig. 9.4, (p. 307): ongwee = Indian. Sometimes the Mohawk sachem, like the eighteenth-century Kayender-ongwe, carried this name.

poyang	shaman, Malay Binouas
kaang	heavenly chief, Bushman
mong	chief, foremost/Hopi
Korong	man possessed by a god/Pelew Islands
bonga	nature spirit, Santal, northeast India
Bong	"Light Girl," Japanese myth
Morongo	Evening star, Rhodesia
bong	night, Malekula
Qong	night, Banks' Island
sa'ang	star, Panic
Koong	the moon, Haida
ang'ji, yang	Light, China
ang'ni	light, Vedic
angal	"The Great Above," Sumerian
dang	infinite and formless, Tibetan
Kongoro	spirit of dawn-light, Andamanese
yong	daylight, Hebrew
Rangi	space; Sky Father/Maori
rangi	sky, Polynesian
rangit	sky, Zambal
Rongo	and Tangaroa Gods of Polynesia
Tonga	divinity, Pacific Islands
Shango	Sun god, Yoruba
Tanga-tanga	a South American principal deity
Xaratanga	moon goddess, Tarascan
benang	gift of spirits,[19] Panic

In North America, Onga or Ho'anga was he who stood as leader of the mysteries, under the Brotherhood of Prophets (see fig. 7.16, p. 243). "And Gitchee raised up Honga . . . And Honga went into the

Fig. 1.6. "Sang or Sa'ang (Panic), stars. The small shining that sendeth forth the twinkle. Anga (Algonquin), the far-off worlds."[20] The Sumerian ideogram for "deity" was a star; bint-ang = star/Malay; hy'ang = stars/Vedic, India; orang = light/Fonece (forerunner of Phoenician, see Language Tree fig. 4.1, p. 110); jong = pole star/Batek; yope'ang = sacred star/Algonquin.

mountains of Ghiee (Rocky Mountains) . . . and the Voice of the Great Spirit remained with the tribes of Honga, and it came to pass that he who heard the Voice, who was always the chief high prophet for the tribe, was called Hoanga."* (Pronounced almost the same as Hoanga, *Wanga,* in the folk religion of the African Igbo and Fon, as well as their West Indies offshoots, is a magical charm, the words proper to magic.) Is it not curious that among the first inhabitants of Malaysia (the "merry and cheerful little people"[21]), their ancestress is called T'angoi, while *anghoi,* hardly different, is the Algonquin medicine man? T'angoi it was who taught these Negrito women magical engravings (on combs), and who built the first *pano,* the "séance hut." These little people call themselves Or'ang asli—meaning "original people"—the name Or'ang ("people"†) taken also by related groups, such as the Orang Selitar, Orang Darat, Orang Laut, Orang Bukit, Orang Kuba, Orang Rimba, and Orang Sabun.

The earliest meaning of *ong* and *ang* is, simply, "light from above," and by extension, it came to represent Intelligence or People of Light, in touch with angelic beings, their ancestors, their teachers—who are called Orang Hidap, "the Immortals." Malaysia is chock full of Ang/Ong-named places and tribes.‡ So much that contains guruwari (the seed of life) is found in ang words in Malaysian languages:§ Ang-lah,

---

*Are "angel" and "Anglo" also derivative of this root? And what about the countless Asian, African, and Oceanic towns and peoples: Angkor Vat, Bangkok, Bangalore and Ganges (India), Tonga, Gangtok, Pedong, Hong Kong, Angyang (China), Tsangpo, Kalang (Java), Tamang, Mongolia, Angara River (Russia), Chepangs, and others. And Orongo, the sacred ceremonial village on Easter Island where the most important religious festival is held.

†Or'ang, freely translated, means "creatures of light," that is, human beings.

‡Names and places imbued with this life force abound also among Africa's pygmy groups: Kolongo, Ubangi, Ekianga, Toangbe, Ishango, Congo, Nyange, Ageronga, Masimongo, Kibanga, Mulanga, Angola, etc. They are prevalent also among the little people of the Philippines: Lango, Ogong, Bayombong, Bangued, Mangatarem, Ilongot, Fatanga, and others.

§Some of these are: the Semang, Pahang, Selangor, Penang, Jeransang, Batang, Teliang, Tampang, Mekong, Langka (ancient name of Ceylon), Kenderong, Temangor, Trang, Mahang, Sadang, Pangan, Kangsar, Kupang, Hangat, Lenggong, Kampong, Belong, Tiong, Siong, Ruong, Chong, Bong, Gunong, Yong, and others.

a thunder god; Klang, hawk god; *angin,* wind, life-soul; *wong,* child; *tukang,* craftsman; *tangkel,* talisman; *menang,* lightning; *moyang,* a smith or ancestor (who was a smith).

Now here's the crux of it: Orang asli gives us a linguistic clue to Negrito origins—"people of mixed light." The combination of or'ang, "human beings with spiritual light," plus *asli* (var. *asuri* var. *asu*), "original," i.e., aborigine; of the Earth only, *without* the light of heaven—asu man.

ASU MAN

In India, the Veddic word *asu* (later changed to "Adam" in Persian) meant "without spirit" or "earth-born" (aboriginal). This is seen also in Hebrew, where *adam* means "red earth," and in *meshe'adam,* the Azerbaijani Yeti or Bigfoot, the most animal-like version of man. In Akkadian, *adami* meant "red clay," the material from which the first man was legendarily fashioned. This first man (Tiki), agreed the Maori, was made of red clay. He was earth-made. Tahitians also say that humankind was created out of red earth, *araea*—as do the Siberians and the Kenta Negritos, the latter relating that Creator drew the first ancestors from the Earth. In the Batek version, the soil was molded into manikins ("little men") by Allah and Ta'allah; hence the red-brown color of Batek skin.

This "earth man" (asu) also seems to be embedded in the old Egyptian term for the dark (earth-toned) races: N-ahsu, related perhaps to Apsu, **the first Egyptian divinity,** unfruitful and inert, devoid of personality (read: before the spirit part was added). Even Egypt's Aswan (after which the Dam was named), is otherwise spelled Assuan, probably after that primordial person or divinity: the first man on Earth. *Su* by itself means spirit or spiritual, appearing in Latin as *sui* ("self"); thus *suta* means "people" (Nabaloi/Philippines). Sukkal, in Sumerian texts, meant angel-like beings; other variants of "su" appear in a great variety of languages.

The Senoi Negritos actually have a deity named Asu, represented as a bird, while in the Nabaloi dialect of the Philippines, *asu* means "dog."

Fig. 1.7. Left: The icon of *su:* The spirit part; the interior bright, spark of spirit, the immortal self, an enlightened man with the gift of prophecy*; spirit-man: su-gan. Right: The icon of su'is: a seer, one who sees the Unseen.[22]

Asua is also the name of a pygmy tribe in the Congo, and some Amazonian groups remember U-assu in their myths.†

Long, long ago, Asia (called *Assuwa*), was covered with the "original people," the aborigines of Earth, the autochthonous race. "In all parts of the earth there lived ground people."[23]

---

*Su: tribal names in Africa and South America include the Sumu people of South America, the Chacha city of Suta and the Supe River (Peru); the Chibcha/Muysca high god Bochica had an alternate name: Sua, "The White One" (meaning, the "pure" one?); Supay, the Peruvian ruler of the Shades and god of rains; the ancient Sus tribe in Egypt, the sacred mountain of the ancient Orient—Su-meru. Plus Susa, in Elam, with imposing tell and wheel-cross on pottery; Kara Su, old Phoenicia; *sua* also meant "sun," indicating the highest spirit. The Wasusu tribe in Brazil is a 12,000-year-old culture with shamanistic cave carvings and sacred traditions about the "first inhabitant." Not to mention Suyuyoc, prefect of Inca village and the Sumus people of Honduras; as well as the Subis Mountains, Borneo, Sulu Sea in Philippines, Suuna Rii, Sudan, Sumatra, and the Suku little people in Sudan.

†In Koita (Melanesian), *sua* means "soul"; in Algonquin *shu* means "enlightened"; *su-* means "good" in the Gaelic language. In Chinese *su* means "prophetic"; in Hottentot, *surri* means priest, while *isu* denoted "child prophet" in Aham (the sacred language of Arabinya; see Language Tree fig. 4.1, p. 110, the word leading to *iesu* and *Jesus* and possibly also to Sunni/Islam). Among Negritos, *su'ara* is voice, while *su'nyi* means wind (hissing sharply like *su'nyi,* it sends a petition to the heavens). *Su* in Sanskrit is "beautiful" and, as a verb, means "stimulate, inspire"; Suria is the Hindu Sun God. Among the *Su*cubti people of Panama, *sua-mi* means "The Great Spirit," just as the Quetzalcoatl of Brazil was *su-me.*

Fig. 1.8. A stylized depiction of asu man, similar to archaeology's *Australopithecus* and *Ardipithecus*, who lived a partly arboreal existence. In Polynesian myth, this first man is widely associated with tree tops. The early hominids had long brachiating arms and powerful grasping hands, ideal for climbing trees. The Nittevo of Ceylon, with more asu genes than most of us, were Asia's most spectacular tree-climbers.

When man first became widely diffused, he was not a speaking animal.

CHARLES DARWIN, *THE DESCENT OF MAN*

To the Veddas of India, asu meant "he who lives and moves in the great phenomena of nature." On a par with this creature is the "Early Atlantean" as envisioned by Max Heindel:[24] the classic feral man, possessed of long arms and small blinking eyes. Of course, the asuans of old were long armed, like our ancestors (*Australopithecus afarensis, Homo habilis,* the druks and Neanderthals, "hobbits," and Teutonic dwarfs), a trait retained by some of today's little people: Andamanese, Malaysian Negritos, Aeta, and Veddas. Sasquatch has arms reaching almost to the knees. Being only partly bipedal, long arms helped early man knuckle-walk, like some of the great apes. This creature of the Atlantean Age had scarcely any forehead (no frontal development of brain), just a slope from eyes to pate. And he was without light (ong).

THE GROUND PEOPLE

Though asu man is long extinct, his genes live on in all of us, but especially in the barbarian druks (their mixed descendants, a.k.a. *Homo erectus*) and in atavistic groups who, not intermarrying, kept recycling some of this ancestor's ancient genes. "The second race was the druks, incapable of inspiration, save for their stomach's sake."[25] Remnants of hairy, brutal, and cannibalistic people still exist in remote parts of the interior of South America, and they are greatly dreaded. They are known to the Spanish as Cabelludos ("Hairy People"), and to the Portuguese as Morcegos ("Bats"), from their custom of hiding during the day and hunting by night. The Indians call them Tatus, or "Armadillos," from their way of burrowing in the ground, in holes about twelve feet in diameter, roofed over with branches.* "The ground people had long arms and were naked and not ashamed, for which reason they were called druks . . . [and there are] sufficient tribes unto this day who dwell in darkness, even cannibals . . . possess[ing] no desire for evolution."[26] Indeed, relict creatures answering this description are found on almost every continent. Some Negritos in Malaysia tell of a group called "Batak," said to live around the headwaters of the Plus, who are cannibals, and dwell in "burrows in the ground."

The ground people of South America were visited in the 1920s, when Colonel Percy H. Fawcett, the "Brazilian Livingstone," boldly explored the wilds of Matto Grosso, looking for lost cities but unexpectedly encountering the Bats:[27] These large hairy men with exceptionally long arms whom Fawcett found north of Maxibus, lived on a diet of four-inch peanuts. He found other tribes, great apelike brutes that "looked as if they had scarcely evolved beyond the level of beasts, hairy, emitting grunts as if human speech was beyond their powers."

When Fawcett's party suddenly came upon a village of the Bats, two hundred of them were sleeping in their holes.[28] Fawcett was struck with fear, but also with an inspired ploy to dance with a lighted torch, shouting at the top of his voice a chorus from a famous music-hall song of the late 1890s: *Ta-ra-ra-boom-de-ay!* The effect was magical. The creatures came out of their holes in the ground, regarding him as some strange white god, and bowed low to the ground.

---

*Even the Bushmen (with an asu gene or two) sometimes sleep in hollows, shallow depressions in the sand, lined with tufts of soft grass, like the scooped nests of shore birds on a beach; here the people can lie curled just below the surface of the plain to let the cold night wind blow across the veld and pass over them.

Fig. 1.9. Bats and explorers, drawn by Brian Fawcett, Percy's son, in 1925.

Such relict groups are no doubt the mixed descendants of asu man and his ground-burrowing offshoot—the druks (*Homo erectus*). When asu was vaguely remembered in the Old Testament, the term *asui* was employed, meaning "animalistic." So it was that Jacob's brutish twin was named Esau*—"And the *first* [emphasis added] came out red, all over like a hairy garment; and they called his name Esau" (see Gen. 25:30–1, 14:5, 16:25, 35:31). Esau "the barbarian" even tried to slay his twin Jacob while still in the womb; later, his sons were notorious for bestiality and incest. These old legends portray the asu race as the first on Earth, followed by Ihin (Abel), just as Esau was the first twin born of Isaac. Esau spent his time hunting, while Jacob, refined and thoughtful, spent his time learning the ways of the Lord. The Sumerian Asag may also be cognate of Asu and Esau: he was a demon, cursed in a manner not unlike Jacob's son Esau.

---

*Gaulish barbarians of ancient times were called by a similar name, Esus, indicating those born with a thick and shaggy reddish lanugo. Gaulish idols in old France probably share provenience with the French *farfadets* who lived in underground tunnels, some of these people described as hairy dwarfs: a sort of creature of Middle Earth.

Fig. 1.10. European conception of wild man: note his short stature and coat of hair.

SHAGGY MAN

In Africa, Livingstone's Stanley met pygmies with "fell" over their body, almost feathery; just as the first white men to meet the Twa in the nineteenth century said their whole body was covered by thick, stiff hair, almost like felt. To this day there are pygmy tribes among whom infants are born with a reddish lanugo. Were they akin to the hairy black dwarves (farfadets) featured in the folklore of France and the British Isles? In Mesoamerican, Hindu, and biblical reckoning, these hairy ones were of malignant character. The Nittevo pygmies who once inhabited the high mountains of southeastern Ceylon were a fierce people, between three and four feet high, with very hairy legs; indeed a reddish "fur" over most of their bodies. There are rumors of "hairy pygmies" in other parts of Southeast Asia and Sundaland such as Laos and Burma—very small wild-men with reddish body hair.

We are aware of some strange creatures of this type quite a bit closer to home: Jacko, for example, seen by a huntsman in British Columbia, was a four-feet-seven-inch fellow who "resembled a human being" but was covered with reddish-brown glossy hair and had unusually long arms.[29] Bernard Heuvelmans (Mr. Cryptozoology) reported on a wild type known as *didi* in Venezuela and British Guiana, who, asu-like, answers to the description of Jacko: short, with human features and reddish brown fur. Didi resembles, in turn, the Sisemites of Central America who are covered in black hair that grows almost to the ground. These creatures must somehow be cousin to the Irish grogach, hairy and naked (unlike the clothed and civilized leprechauns).

These "LHMs" (little hairy men), hirsute, swift, and strong, are in fact known everywhere from southeast Asia to the Pacific, and Africa to the Americas. A kind of "Little Foot," his names are various: *sedapa, shiru, sehite, agogwe, ikal, the-lma*. Slender with thick fur, often red, these are the true wild men of the world, carryovers or throwbacks from the days of the druk. That some of them have survived to this day in isolated pockets should not come as too great a surprise or scientific bombshell. For there is often a viable continuum from folktale to fact, the strong little man of Gaelic lore, Lapanach (thick-set, like the Scots highland dwarfs, muscular and of immense strength) clearly resembling First Man of the Chukchee, with his powerful arms (a Neanderthal type), as well as the Nisqualli dwarf, the Crow little people, and the Menehune. Finally, this archaic type manifests in specimens such as Sumatra's very real Orang Pendek with huge chest, powerful arms, and enough sheer physical power to uproot small trees.

FAIRIES OR FALLEN ANGELS?

Orang Asli (lit. "man-original") is the proper name for the Negritos of Malaysia, who do not care for the name Semang. It is a pejorative term used by the Malays, meaning a species of long-armed tree monkey (var. *siamang*). Despite the insulting tone of it, Semang remains the accepted name for most of Malaysia's "pygmies." Yet, if mankind did indeed develop out of monkeys or apes, as evolution holds, shouldn't our pongid ancestors be held in great esteem?

But mankind did *not* issue from the pongids—although earliest man (asu) was *like* a beast—long-armed, slope-headed, splay-footed, inarticulate. "And man [asu] was dumb, like other animals; without speech and without understanding, even less than any other creature."[30] Yet he was a man—but in his lowest form, not *quite* a human being, not a sapient being. As the oldest traditions hold, it was for this very reason that the gods set about raising up that rude creature to the light. Thus do the Sumerian tablets attribute the creation of true humanity to God Ea, who engineered a hybrid race by combining savage earth-man with the seed of the gods. Indeed, this idea of humanity as child of the stars is one of the most persistent legends among the tribes of man. And there is truth in it. Variations on the theme of this extraordinary amalgam, this hybrid of heaven and Earth, are found in every form: God Mars fathered the man Romulus by mating with a vestal virgin; the mortal kings of India were procreated by gods and goddesses (the woman Kunti, for example, was impregnated by the Sun God); Marduk of Babylonia fertilized a mortal maiden,[31] and so on.

Too, there are the Han-Dropa pygmies of Tibet in the Bayan-Kara-Ula mountains whose hieroglyphics read: "The Dropa came down out of the skies"; or as the Chinese told it—"from the clouds," echoing, in turn, the legend of the Tuatha De Danaan who arrived in Ireland on May first* "on dark clouds"; just as the Kickapoo culture hero Wisaka "fell from the sky." As we go on, we will find that these myths somehow resemble the legend of the Fallen Angels, also with its hidden kernel of truth. For there is no shortage of this universal tale of a Divine Person lending his seed for the creation of the human race. Ranginui, Sky Father of the Maori, mates with Earth Mother (Papatuanuku) and has "divine children" (the holy Ihins). Myths of much the same character fill the cosmogonies of Native American tribes. In ancient Greece, Heaven and Earth were the parents of a

---

*In addition, the ancient astronaut theory postulates the intermarriage of space-faring gods with nubile Adamic (earthly, asuan) females. Spacemen, it has been suggested, artificially fertilized female members of the species and kept up this breeding experiment until producing an intelligent creature.

great brood of mortal children, randy Sky Father Zeus having impregnated the maiden Danae with a "shower of gold," their most celebrated offspring—the hero Perseus. Even the Christian Virgin's "immaculate conception" repeats the old idea of the divine impregnation of an Earth woman.

It was the same in the apocryphal legend of Enoch: When Noah, hair white as snow, was born, the village people whispered about the mysterious origin of this strange baby—was it from the holy beings, the Watchers? Distraught, his father Lamech went to *his* father Methuselah and pleaded for an answer. Methuselah, in turn, went to *his* father Enoch, who told him: "To be sure, in the days of my father Jared, heavenly beings did indeed come down to earth and seduce mortal women"[32] (timeframe—wrong, concept—right). Another Hebrew legend has it that two hundred angels descended to the summit of Mount Hermon, defiling themselves with the daughters of men.

Although the divine parent myth has a germ of truth, in the marvelous confusion of time, tongues and tradition, these children of the stars came to be cast in the *fairy kingdom*. But who, really, are the fairies? Linguistically, the word "fairy" translates as *hada* in Spanish (*fadas* in Portugal and *fadhas* in Switzerland). There are interesting cognates here: "hada" is the Panic word for the intermediate world, later giving way to English "Hades." *Haden* in Chinese means "sky, heaven," just as "sky" in Phoenician is *aden*. Some believe the word "heaven" itself comes from this Phoenician root: "Eden, Aden, Haden, Jeden are of the same meaning in the Vedic, Phoenician, and Chinese languages."[33]

Now Hades is the abode just beyond our plane of matter, which some might call the astral plane. The reason mythology placed fairyland in this intermediate zone is because the fairies (at least according to medieval notions) are the fallen angels: too good for hell, but too mischievous and vain for heaven. They fell to Earth and dwelt there for a season, the "first gods of earth." The story, moreover, avers that they were cast out of heaven along with Lucifer, and condemned by God to remain in the elements of the Earth. But this is myth . . . no, it is dogma, created, as we will see, to strike a blow at the "heathen."

SPIRITS OF THE DEAD

Supposedly part of Lucifer's apostasy, the Irish fairies are clearly pre-Christian and un-Christian, hence with no hope of salvation—the Bible and other holy objects are often used as a charm against their influence. Turning them into an object lesson for lapsed Christians, doctrine held fairies as the souls of the pagan dead, caught betwixt heaven and Earth because they were not baptized.

Iberian and Russian traditions hold that the fairies are spirits of the dead, or more to the point, of the *premature* dead—for it is said that *nixes* are girls who committed suicide because of a broken heart. Alternatively, fairies are the ghosts of venerated ancestors: their magical powers, their "shimmering," and other supernatural aspects certainly align them with well-known ghostly prodigies coming from the discarnate world of spirits. They are none other than revenants of the dead, known to revisit their earthside haunts. Many of "these fairies," owned author Katharine Briggs, "were indubitably the dead. . . . It is a common thing for underground fairies to live under human dwellings. It may be that they were the spirits of former inhabitants."[34]

And one more thing: like ghosts of the departed, the fairies can make themselves visible to humans if they so desire—but usually only to those with clairvoyant sight, the Seeing. The little people, in an American example, are never actually seen by the common Choctaw; only their prophets and herb doctors claim the power of seeing them and communicating with them. In the same vein, in northern Europe "it is not everyone that can see the Elves"[35]—usually only Sunday Children can do so.*

So, again, who are the fairies? In a word, they are, often enough, simply spirit people. The fairy, to my thinking, is neither a fallen angel, nor "elemental," nor "deva," nor any other kind of psychic fauna from

---

*The British seer Tom Tyrrell sees them, the little people, "only when I do a little fasting," as told to Arthur Conan Doyle.[36] Said the great writer Robert Louis Stevenson, some of his best work came from the "little people" who entered his mind, his being, supplying wonderful plots and characters. He watched their efforts as if from a stage box.

some unknown parallel world. Considering recurrent butterfly myths, we find the fairy unmasked—as the human soul! Some tribes believe the soul can leave the body in the form of a butterfly. As the Solomon Islanders say, when a person dies, his soul flies to heaven in the form of a butterfly; the liberated soul in Burma, too, appears as a butterfly. And if the Negritos believe that winged butterflies are the souls of non-Negritos (and that souls of the dead are *small*), the Irish also believe in fairies as the souls of the Wee People: the spirits of a race of tiny beings who inhabited Celtic lands long ago—that is, the ancestors. Thus were Italian sprites (*folleti*) "little butterflies," about the size of small children with many magical powers. And on the Isle of Rugen, it was thought that the white dwarfs frequently fly about "in the shape of butterflies, showing kindness and benevolence to the good who merit their favor."[37] Too, most of Mexico's ancient people used the butterfly as symbol* of the dance of death;[38] elsewhere, mummies were decorated with butterflies as a symbol of the departed. From all this, then, we can surmise that the winged wraith, especially the fairy, is a conceit, a metaphor, invented by fertile imagination to portray the very *real* powers of the invisible domain above, of the Immortals who we shall all become, after this earthly sojourn is done.

The fairies are sprung from the feared and venerated dead.

LEWIS SPENCE, QUOTED IN
BRIGGS, *THE VANISHING PEOPLE*

Fairies are, in reality, nothing more than one type of earthbound entity (EB). One must appreciate the skills that spirits may attain, assuming any name or form; celestial beings known to the Malay Batek, as an example, can assume any embodiment they wish—a person, a snake, a rhinoceros, a tiger, or any flying (winged) creature. But both Kirk Endicott and Father Schebesta (their ethnographers) think these beings are simply the ghosts of dead shamans. And I agree. The Malaysian Hantu (which instantly reminds us of "haunt") are spirits that can take the form of animals, as is also the case in certain parts of

---

*Used in Mexican funeral rites as a symbol of the soul.

Brittany, where villagers are afraid of evil (human) spirits, called *teurst*, which appear in the likeness of domestic animals. Similarly, in Yorkshire, the *barguest,* barn spirit, is a type of "fairy" who was known to appear in animal form. God-animals, wise animals, talking animals, jaguar/feline cults have all come about as the result of EBs entering the bodies of animals, as a place to "stay" on Earth. Thousands of years ago the world was so overrun with these unprogressed earthbound (EB) spirits (like tuerst and baguest), that the kings issued edicts prohibiting familiar spirits and forbidding workers of magic: "And these spirits continued to dwell with man on the earth. So that in the course of time the world was overrun by spirits of darkness. . . . [Thus did] mortal kings issue edicts against magicians and prophets . . . and the consultation of spirits."[39]

Biblical injunctions followed suit: "Regard not them that have familiar spirits, neither seek after wizards to be defiled by them. . . . And the soul that turneth after such . . . I will even set my face against that soul, and will cut him off from among his people" (Leviticus 19:31, 20:6).

And now there was no place left for familiar spirits to obsess mortals. In desperation, then, these disembodied souls distributed themselves—some going into swine, and living with them; others dwelling in fisheries and slaughterhouses; and still others, in kennels, with dogs and cats.[40] Yet others hugged the Earth in among her gardens and flora, pretending to be elementals or members of the (nonexistent) deva kingdom.

One man who wandered into the fairy hills in the British Isles says he saw there three people he knew who had died. Can spirits of the dead impersonate fairies? Yes, I think so. When obsessing spirits overran Egypt (in the time of Osire), Osire decreed to his Lords: "Ye shall not permit spirits to inhabit deserted houses; nor permit them to form habitations on the graveyards, on the earth. Ye shall not permit spirits to inhabit caves nor *waterfalls* [emphasis added] on the earth."[41]

Indeed, fairies are commonly associated with waterfalls, streams, and mists, like the leprechauns or the *Geow-lud-mo-sis-eg,* often seen near water places, or Mexico's *chaneques,* legendary dwarfs, who live in waterfalls. Those beings who live under waterfalls, say the Cherokee, are always plotting mischief (they are our troublesome EBs, ghosts, really). One of the three tribes of little people known to the Seneca lives "under the falls" of the Genesee River, and are called Stone Throwers.[42] (And isn't paranormal stone-throwing one of the oldest tricks of the EBs, the disgruntled discarnates?) Europe calls them wraiths or elementals—those nymphs and misty spirits usually found in forest pools and waterfalls. Oh, how the pitiful earthbound have been romanticized!

I listened to the voice of spirits, the [lowest order of] angels travelling with the earth . . . the fairies, the butterfly angels, the triflers, that forever look in crystal waters to behold their own forms . . . the rollicking, deceiving angels . . . the vampire angels, that nestle in the atmosphere of mortals, largely living on their substance.

OAHSPE, BOOK OF CPENTA-ARMIJ 2:3

Even a thousand years before Osire's decree against these infesting spirits, a great clean-sweep had been ordered by the gods to efface the Earth of all such deceiving EBs, whether dressed up as fairies or speaking through animals.

God sent pruners around about the lower heaven of the earth [hada] . . . saying to them: "Find all the evil spirits dwelling with mortals . . . and gather them into one place. Then find the spirits and fairies who have taken up caves and *waterfalls* [emphasis added] . . . as their abode, and bring them to the same place . . . Then find the lusters, who dwell in old castles* and ruined cities . . . When they are going out for raids on mortals, seize them and bring them to the same place [to rehabilitate them].

OAHSPE, BOOK OF AH'SHONG, CHAPTER 7

---

*Prowling old castles is a particular activity of EBs; the Welsh Tylwyth Teg are especially fond of hanging out in ruined castles, much like the "White Ladies" of northern Europe or the Weisse Frauen (a.k.a. Fainen and Sibille) who attended the old pagan priestesses; often taken as ghosts (which they are!), they are generous with mortals, but can be angered easily and turn vicious.

Nevertheless, many did escape the dragnet: one old man averred he often saw fairies at waterfalls, especially at the Vale of Neath, enjoying the music of their harps. France also has its Fee du Grand Cascade (waterfall), while Andvari, the Germanic dwarf, still hides under the waterfall. "Some of the dispossessed went into the forests to dwell and some to the fountains and mists in waterfalls."[43]

This we know: there is the world of the living, and there is the world of the departed. Both are real. But sorting one from the other, in search of the little people, is a devil of a job. Absorbed by and into fairy lore, as well as into doctrine (fallen angels) and ancestor cults, the original little people, now extinct, faded away—but not entirely. Join me now, chapter 2, in our world tour of the *real* living little people.

CHAPTER 2

Where Are the Little People?

BETWEEN GODS AND MORTALS

A golden race of humans, according to Hesiod, was created in the time of Kronos' reign, but later hidden away in the Earth to become beneficent spirits. And, often enough, this is how the little people are remembered: their works conceived as the "creative" output of the *gods*—or at best, the invisible beings. Without the Sumerian "god" Enlil, for example, "no cities would be built, no settlements founded, no stalls would be built."[1]

This is euhemerism: the deification of man. For these cities and settlements, canals and roads, tunnels and earthworks were built by men—not gods.

Yet this apotheosized ancestor is nearly universal. Archaeological work in Mexico indicates that their **sculpted gods** "indeed depict humans and not deities."[2] In South America, the Tupis of Brazil were named after their first ancestor "who is now their highest divinity, maker of all things."[3]

No wonder the little people have been lost and forgotten!

Too often, a gray area clouds the difference between "god and heroes," between real humans and true celestial beings, between fairies and mortals.

In Europe and Egypt also, the dwarf people got mixed up with **spirits and gods**; Egypt's dwarf gods include Bes and Ptah, the latter being the creator deity who made the world with his heart and tongue, chief god of the capital, Memphis (First Egyptian Dynasty), and father (*ptah* var. *piter* var. *pater* means "father") of pharaoh Rameses II; the high priesthood of Egypt was reserved for the Memphite temple of Ptah. Egypt's other dwarf god, Bes (like the Italian dwarf Lars), is a *protective* deity. Yet the translation of Bes, "initiated," tells us this was a man, not a god. Other dwarf celestials of Egypt include Anhuri, Aha, and Hity (var. Haty) who overcome the forces of evil.

As we learn more of the little people, the Good People, we will come to understand why they are remembered as protectors, a force of righteousness and justice. God*like* they were, but myth took over and turned them into divinities. There is one other reason the sacred little people got mixed up with the celestial realm: they were intermediaries, as it were, in constant communication with the spirit world!

Fig. 2.1. Left: The Egyptian god Bes, squat and bearded, worshipped as a protector and defender of all that is good. Drawing by Jose Bouvier. Right: Bronze Anhuri, an Egyptian sky-god, Saite period, a deification, it seems, of the Good Little People.

There is a class of Breton fairies, though, who are not like ephemeral sprites but live a life rather like mortals. Indeed, Great Britain's "elf-arrows" were artifacts of the *aborigines*. Plentiful in Scotland, where they were manufactured by the fairy people, these flint points came to be called "arrow of the Gods," though originally simply known as "arrow of the Elves." See how easily the two realms have been confounded?

In the good day, the Little People [were] most impudently called fairies when they were more frequently seen than they are in this unbelieving time.
                                    "THE LEGEND OF BOTTLE HILL"[4]

One occupational hazard of the antiquarian is the great muddle made when history and dogma intertwine. There is no better example of this than the fairy tales of Ireland. Thus does Ireland give us the fairy kingdom as an Otherworld of little people living "behind the world of men"—like divinities of Earth, some accounts giving the "Others," the "wee bodies," a phantasmagorical height of two inches!

That said, we perceive through the blur a historical race of small men. The leprechauns of Ulster, say locals, were indeed the Gentry who built the (sidhe) mounds and circles of stones, which abound. In many places have the little people left tangible signs of their presence, most notably the sidhes, built by and for a race of small-bodied people, identifiable as the Picts, a pre-Celtic and matrilineal "dwarf race," who early seized on the Scottish Lowlands, such as the Cruithin of Scotland, corresponding also to the "dwarfs" who inhabited the Orkneys until the ninth century. Whether Pecht, Pict, Pixie, or Pisgy, these now-extinct little people are also part of Ulster, Devonshire, and Cornwall history.

EGYPTIAN BRITS

"The Sidhe," commented Robert Graves, "are now popularly regarded as fairies; but in early Irish poetry they appear as a real people—a highly cultured and dwindling nation . . . living in the raths . . . They were, in fact, Picts."[5] In both Scotland and Ireland, tradition has the

Picts migrating to the British Isles from—Egypt! This is the reason blue Egyptian beads are found in Salisbury Plain burials. Indeed, the great prehistorian V. Gordon Childe saw "striking parallels" in the pottery of Egypt, the Iberian Peninsula, and the British Isles. In addition, Egyptian-style mummification is found in the British Isles.

Iberia was the link, the midpoint. Observing the same link, Laurens van der Post likened the small Paleolithic hunters of Iberia to the ancient Egyptian and Libyan little people who, in his view, "formed the prototype of the little man in European folklore."[6] "They sailed west from there [Egypt] . . . to Ireland, out of Spain.* Everyone knows it here in Scotland."[7] The Irish hero Tuan MacCairill, for one, was a royal immigrant from Spain, just as the oldest British "barrows" (mounds) were inhabited by a Neolithic race of Iberians, so small in stature that a man five and a half feet in height was a giant among them (these ancient Iberians standing only about four feet ten inches high). These colonizers from Spain (and some from Greece) became the Fir Bolgs of Ireland: a race of little people.

From North Africa to Iberia to the British Isles: Some say these race founders started out from the Gulf of Sirte in Libya.† Indeed, the North African (Aurignacian) tool kit is found at several sites in southern Spain. Europe's adventurous Count de Prorok, who knew both cultures, detected a great similarity between the Basque and (North African) Berbers. Rows of menhirs appear at both Carnac in Brittany and Karnac in Egypt, reminding us of similar standing stones in Cornwall and Iberia (Pyrenees). In fact, Brittany's little *korreds* (who are, in some traditions, considered the builders) are still occasionally seen in the Basque Pyrenees.

Not only are Basque sun temples found in England,‡ but the technique and shaping of Stonehenge's sarcens are identical to Egyptian obelisks. The use of inches in the "year-circle," according to writer Tom Valentine, "was utilized by both the builders of the Great Pyramid and

---

*The highly curious cup-and-ring marks (petroglyphs) of Galicia, Spain, are duplicated in the British Isles (see fig. 9.2 on p. 300).

†Indeed, the cluster-type housing of Libya and the Orkneys make a match!

‡The Basque are rather short, not Aryan, and possess a rare blood type—nor is their language Indo-European.

Fig. 2.2 (right). Map and arrows showing the path from Egypt and North Africa to Malta and Gibraltar to the Pyrenees and finally to the British Isles.

Fig. 2.3. Illustration from a Basque folktale. The ancestors of the Basque people of the French and Spanish Pyrenees were great builders and engineers in antiquity, as well as cave artists. Today they retain some of the shortness of their forebears. In Basque folklore, it is the "fairy Laminaks" who built bridges for them "in a single night." "Long, long ago, one was apt to meet a good fairy at any turn in the highway," says one Basque tale.[8]

the builders of the monument at Stonehenge, England."[9] Some have argued that Stonehenge was actually built by Egyptians or people from Crete. Too, Malta's standing stones (trilithons) are of the same stamp as Stonehenge's—all of which dovetails with Joseph Campbell's observation of "diffusion of the megalithic mound [culture] . . . through Gibraltar to Ireland."[10] Carleton Coon, of anthropological fame, points out the presence in Spain of a North African tool industry, "by way of Gibraltar," accounting in the same breath for Europe's "curly hair, freckling, blood type B, and the so-called African Rh blood type . . . [all of which suggest] very ancient contacts across the Strait of Gibraltar." The measurements of North African Riffians, he found, put them close to the British type.[11]

Scottish chronicles trace their own "Scota, the daughter of Pharaoh" through the Milesians, a people who came to their land via Spain. An old Irish manuscript traces the "wee-bodies" to the race of Ham (Kham or Khem), after which Khemet (Egypt) itself was named: "they fared from Africa." Following these links, Sir John Morris-Jones discovered remarkable ties between the Welsh tongue and Hamitic languages of Egypt, publishing a list of no less than 3,000 cognates. Strengthening this connection, one Col. MacPherson uncovered a strong resemblance between the North African Berber language and Gaelic. Yet another line of research uncovered the migration of hundreds of thousands of Egyptians after the fall of that great empire, settling in western Europe where they intermarried with the aborigines—and "their offspring were called Druids, Picts, Gaelics, Welsh, Galls. . . . These are all Egyptian names, preserved to this day."[12]

THE HOUSE OF DAN

The "mythological tribes" arriving after the Deluge, according to the Irish *Book of Invasions,* include: the Nemedians (var. Neimhead, indicating a "noble, sacrosanct, worthy" people—the king's poets); the Fir Bolg (those little Iberians); and the great Tuatha De *Dan*aan (*De* meaning "god"), being the People of Light, children of the goddess *Dan*u (*Dan* itself meaning Light, as in "dawn"). These Danaan people were later fitted out as some sort of **divine race**, the heroic fairies; we can include in the family of Dan-names the Greek *Dan*ae and the river Don, for though the Tuatha were matrilinear, "the Goddess Danu was eventually masculinized into Don."[13]

The spiritual nature of Dan was also known in America: for the Algonquins, the temple of Egoquim, their Great Spirit, "is the sacred house of Dan." Its builders were the equivalent People of Light in Guatama.*

In the Old World, Dan was of course a tribe of Israel, which came from the fifth of Jacob's twelve sons; the Phoenician sailors—great navigators and merchants—were mostly Israelites from the tribes of Dan; these sea people were called Danites (Judges 5:17). Most interesting, the Irish name Tuatha De, meaning People of God, was used to refer to the Israelites in early Christian texts! In the Holy Bible, we learn of skilled engravers among the people of Dan, sent from Tyre to King Solomon (see also Chronicles 2:13–14). "Craftsmen" named Dan are to be found in the Irish annals as well: Tri De Dana were their "three gods of craftsmanship." Not only do Israelite and Irish dovetail on this point, but both seem to spring ultimately from an Indic source: the name of Creator (or god of blessings) in Abraham's time was Shaddai or Shidi (Exodus 6:2–3) corresponding to the Irish Sidhe ("people of God"). This Sidhe in turn, resembles the Sanskrit Siddhi. And like the Irish (and the Celts, to whom Dana was the "Mother of mankind"), the Hindu named their goddess Danu. The Irish Sidhe, (i.e., the learned Tuatha De Danaan), suggest an irresistible connection to India's Danavas people, with their siddhi, which are the "magical powers" possessed by the siddha, "perfected master."

These gifted people also produced the *Dan*es: "the Tuatha De Danaan . . . reached Ireland by way of Denmark."[14] The tall Danes,

---

*Guatama is an ancient name for the Americas, 24,000 years old, and believed to be the source of the name "Guatemala." Unchanged, the name appears at Mt. Shasta in California, whose mysterious inhabitants honored the "time when their forbears were saved from the great catastrophe . . . of Lemuria [Pan] as it was submerging." The name of this particular ceremony is "Adoration to Guatama."[15] All along the coast of Peru, before the Conquest, stone statues of a god called "Guatan" could be seen in the temples.

OLD WORLD DAN

THE ELECT OF PROTOHISTORY, BUILDERS, AND CRAFTSMEN

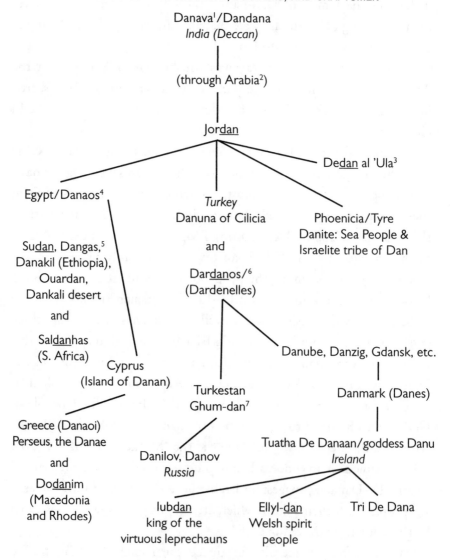

Danava[1]/Dandana
India (Deccan)

(through Arabia[2])

Jordan

Dedan al 'Ula[3]

Egypt/Danaos[4]

Turkey
Danuna of Cilicia

and

Dardanos/[6]
(Dardenelles)

Phoenicia/Tyre
Danite: Sea People &
Israelite tribe of Dan

Sudan, Dangas,[5]
Danakil (Ethiopia),
Ouardan,
Dankali desert

and

Saldanhas
(S. Africa)

Cyprus
(Island of Danan)

Danube, Danzig, Gdansk, etc.

Turkestan
Ghum-dan[7]

Danmark (Danes)

Greece (Danaoi)
Perseus, the Danae

and

Dodanim
(Macedonia
and Rhodes)

Danilov, Danov
Russia

Tuatha De Danaan/goddess Danu
Ireland

Iubdan
king of the
virtuous leprechauns

Ellyl-dan
Welsh spirit
people

Tri De Dana

1. First priests and scientists in India, ca 20,000 BP, according to the Ramayana
2. Iram (Hiram) of the Pillars, great builders of Arabia
3. Great temple builders in Trans-jordan
4. Greek ancestor who migrated to Greece from the Nile delta
5. Egyptian dwarfs
6. Dardanus was the Samothracian Noah; while Dardania was the original name of Troy,
   with great craftsmen and carvers on the Plain of Troy.
7. 20-story high Ghum-dan was said to be the world's first skyscraper

Fig. 2.4. Dan people: the chart professes not necessarily the migratory paths of these
tribes but simply shows some relationship among Dan-named people.

probably of Celto-Slavic stock, are known to be of much later date than the *little* Danes; it was Sir John Lubbock who first reconstructed a Stone Age "race of small men . . . on the low shores of the Danish Archipelago."[16] In Danish folklore are many adventures of a tiny fellow, like Tom Thumb who, along with the Picts, skillfully built the raths and souterrains of Ireland, while the rest of Europe was living in caves.

Inhabiting the "hollow hills" or sidhe mounds, these pint-sized people eventually provided Europe with its ethereal fairy kingdom, though for long ages the Sidhe were as mortal as you or me, as recorded in the oldest Celtic histories. One English scholar wrote that he was "thoroughly persuaded of the former existence, all over the United Kingdom, of a race of men who were smaller in stature than the Celts, yet agreeing in all essential features with the fairies." If, in fact, the fairy kingdom is based on a real historical race, it would be, as Jacque Vallee once remarked, "crucial to any theory concerning the nature of the humanoids."[17]

LEPRECHAUNS

Kin to the fairy, the leprechaun has an awesome pedigree. This little man is also called *luchorpan* (var. *lucharman, lurican, lubberkin, lurikeen, lurigadaun, leipreachan*—depending on the county). They are the Irish "wee bodies" (Fir Bolg) said to have arrived from Hamitic North Africa via Spain.* Indeed, these small Iberians left an alphabet not unlike that of the British Druids, using the Arab device (some say, taken from the Egyptian-Hyksos) of naming letters after trees. Originating in North Africa, this short-statured Celto-Iberian stock, which spread throughout France and Spain and ultimately to the British Isles, left their genes to the short Welshmen, mostly in the southern counties; the Welsh ancestors are called Y Dynon Bach Teg, the Little Fair People—or simply Ellyll.

---

*Reminding us of James Churchward's humorous stories of "pure Gaelic" spoken in the Basque country of the Pyrenees.[18]

The Ligurians (var. Luighne), another member of this diminutive stock, occupied sections of France; Ireland itself was settled by some of these "Laigin," from northwest France, a people who also entered Belgium and Switzerland. The name Ligerian also seems to link up with Lygtemand—Scandinavia's will-'o-the-wisp, whose *mortal* counterparts are the Scand Ellefolk, four feet tall and said to be young and beautiful with loose blond hair. Their ancestors, we might surmise, are the Lykos, for Lykos was one of the four famous Telkhines who sprang from Ge and Pontos, the original Mother and Father of mankind. And they were little people.

Another permutation of leprechaun is Luchrabain (var. *luchchromain*), the name of Scotland's Isle of Pygmies, which the poet Collins in 1749 mentioned as the "Herbid Isle [Hebrides] in whose small vaults a pigmy folk is found." And yes, miniature human bones have been dug up in this Isle of Pygmies. "The pigmies," declared one Irish scholar, "were *Spaniards* [emphasis added] who originally came to Lewis [in Hebrides]." Their roofed lanes were only four feet high, and a kind of mound was built around the whole village.*

European archaeology has other little people hiding in its folds: Around 12,000 years ago, a very small people mixed with a tall race. France's Magdalenian period finds:

1. Cro-Magnon's stature "diminished" to 5 feet 1 inch, "no longer 6 feet and 6 feet 4 inches (based on skeletons found at Les Hoteaux, *Ain*)[19]

2. The related "Chancelade" type† standing at only 4 feet 7 inches[20]

---

*This ingenious architecture is sometimes compared to that of the Tuatha De Danaan's gods of craftsmanship, most notably, Luchta (from Luchrabain?), which name, in turn, reminds us of the Celtic god Lugus (var. Lug, resembling the type of leprechaun called *logh*eryman). Lugh, the leader and high king of the Tuatha De Danaan, was husband of Eriu (Erin, i.e., Ireland itself), and father of Cuchul*ainn,* the great hero of Ulster, a favorite among the Sidhe.

†Example: in 1954, a French miner walking down a country road met a man of "small height and bulky figure . . . and fur-covered body. The midget, less than four feet tall, had a large head . . . the eyes protruded."

There are still enclaves of very short people in parts of France, such as Saint Mathieu.[21]

Indeed, late Neolithic man of Italy and Switzerland, as paleontology attests, was only about five feet two inches. The skeleton of a "little man" was found in a Tuscan coal mine in 1956. "Neolithic pigmies" of Europe, including two very small specimens found in a cave at Dachsenbiel (standing at about three and a half feet tall and buried in close proximity to men of normal height), are well known from excavations by researchers Nuesch at Schweizersbild and Kollman of Basle. Matching these diminutive finds are legends of Swiss dwarf races, called trolls, in Switzerland, Albania, and Sweden. Sometimes the Swiss troll acts as a household helper who puts everything in order in the small hours. Here too, the Alpine folleti is an elf with hypnotic powers; while other gnomes of the high Alps (named *barbegazi* after their heavy beards) are very shy but sometimes help people, giving prophetic warnings of avalanche or snow drifts. There are also living (still?) representatives of little people in Switzerland: "Small people were found in isolated Alpine valleys a century ago."[22]

Add to this catalog the Slavic ancestor, called "Grandfather," remembered as being the size of a six-year-old, and possessing the power to bless homes. *Ludki* are their Serbian counterparts, while folklore speaks of similar creatures (*vily, domovoy,* etc.) in Poland and Hungary, with occasional folktales of dwarf-kings. (There are still pockets of extremely short people in Poland, near Grodno.) All these mythological types are ultimately relevant to the archaeological record: at Spy, Belgium, for example, Prof. Fraipont examined the skeletal remains of a race of small stature "contemporary with the mammoth," nicely approximating Grimm's dwarfs (*wichtlein*) who live deep in the German forest.

LITTLE PEOPLE OF THE CLASSICAL AUTHORS

Turning to the classical authors, we have Homer, Aristotle, Juvenal, Pliny, and Herodotus all writing of pigmy races. Pliny the Greek, in *Natural History,* referred to the little people of Thrace, called the Catizi dwarfs, inhabiting the region of the Black Sea coast, matched perhaps by later Greek stories of beings the size of small children—the

Fig. 2.5. Bronze statue of diminutive Etruscan woman in cloak; classical writers spoke of these Etrurian dwarfs. Like the Basque, their language was non-Indo-European; though cultured, they had the archaic traits of enormous, bulging eyes, pronounced eyebrow ridges, and sloping forehead. Drawing by Jose Bouvier.

kallikantzaros who ride dog-size horses; they are best known in the vicinity of Mt. Parnassus. Other sources direct us to diminutive men along the Mediterranean, at the Canary Islands, Cyprus, Lycia, Abyssinia, Sicily, Italy. Each town and village of Italy has its own native elf, up to three feet tall, like the garden gnomes so prominent at Pompeii.

Aristotle firmly believed in the existence of small people, a race of short stature inhabiting the marshes of Upper Egypt toward the sources of the Nile. Additionally, Philostratus the Elder wrote of their prophetic powers, such as heralding the coming of the great floods of the Nile. Is this, then, the same stock of clever little people who migrated from Egypt to become the Picts and leprechauns? Recently, a Georgetown University Hospital pediatrician, Dr. Chahira Kosma, became intrigued with these "dwarfs" (*nmie*) seen in Egyptian art. Digging into ancient records and ruins, she discovered fifty tomb-covers depicting little people, as well as vases and statues showing them as personal attendants, overseers of linen, animal tenders, jewelers, dancers, and entertainers. According to Kosma, the earliest biological evidence of dwarfs in ancient Egypt dates to the Baderian period, 4500 BCE; the Baderians were a small, delicate people of the Neolithic—not really dwarfs (see fig. 2.25 on p. 68). She also tracked down several tiny skeletons from the Old Kingdom (2700–2200 BCE).[23]

Judging from folklore alone, and moving now north and east of Egypt, we might discover some Mesopotamian dwarfs in such characters as King Oberon, the "Fay" found along the road from Syria to Baghdad. He was only three feet high, and had an angelic face, though his body was "humpy," and his behavior a bit mischievous: Oberon likes to snare old wayfarers. Icongraphically, ninth-century Babylonian tablets do indeed show little people worshiping Shamash, the Sun God; while herders of Ur are also depicted as dwarfs. At Khafeje (Sumer), the first Temple of Sin had chambers of diminutive proportions, and their pit houses had doorways no taller than five feet.

Asia Minor (Turkey) will be of the greatest interest in these discussions. It was here that Homer's *Iliad* was vindicated, when nineteenth century excavations turned the legend of Troy into real history. It was a history that changed the face of Europe: A twelfth-century account reminds posterity that the English were in fact once called Trojans and "Britons," after Troy's leader Brito, who was actually Brutus, Aeneas' great-grandson (and refugee from Troy);[24] hence—"Brit"-ain.* Indeed, the founders of England are said to have come "from the East," one legend crediting Lady Albine with settling Britain and naming it New Troy, which later was changed to London, in honor of Lud, a royal Trojan, the king who built London. Prehistorians tend to attribute not only English but also Greek and Roman civilization to the Trojans, through Aeneas, just as Herodotus traced Rome's Etruscans to the coast of Turkey, a fact now vindicated by genetics. A seventeenth-century BCE manuscript refers to England as the land of *Albi*on—probably a permutation of Turkey's Lady Albine. One tradition of deluge survivors relates to "Albion's Pillars," while the school of Theosophy alludes to "seven sons of Albion, the white land in the north," and "the seven on board the ark."

As we encounter other flood legends from Turkey, we hear that Noah's son Iapetos† (Jaffeth) escaped to Mt. Ida (var. Ina) in a boat of skins; this Iapetos went on to found the great city of Troy, a celestial

---

*Pandrasus, a king of Greece, persecuted Trojan exiles under Brutus, until they fought back and Brutus took the king's daughter as wife, and emigrated to Albion (later called Britain), according to Bullfinch.

†Early writers referred to Europe as "Japetia."

Fig. 2.6. Alabaster statuette of a small Chaldean lady (above). Note the short stature of the bearded priest of Sumer (left), as well as of these attendants of the Assyrian god Shamash (below); the rayed disk appears as a modified ball-and-cross (also see figs. 4.11, p. 126; 7.9a, p. 232; 7.20, p. 250).

name: "Five heavenly places will I build . . . one Troy . . . [ruled by] Foebe, Lordess of Troy."[25] Phoebe indeed was the goddess and tutelary spirit who stood as the Mother of Troy. The city, legend holds, was built by Apollo, whose reign began 18,000 years ago. Hence it became the domain of "Phoebus Apollo." This decidedly Paleolithic date for the settlement of Troy by one of Noah's great sons accords well with James Churchward's timeframe, which establishes the occupation of Asia Minor and the Caucasian Plains "many thousands of years before 14,000 BC."[26]

When Heinrich Schliemann in the late nineteenth century dared to discover "fabled" Troy (today's Hissarlik, Turkey), he found among the crown jewels a woman's bracelet of such small size as to fit a nine-year-old. Notably, cases of Laron syndrome (populations with a genetic difference causing short stature) are reported in Turkey (and in nearby Israel), matching folk memory, which holds that a race "smaller than normal people" once lived in Turkey's Taurus Mountains. This may be corroborated by Pliny the Elder's notice of "a race of Pygmae . . . living in the region of Phrygia in Asia Minor" as well as by Aristotle, who places little people in Asia Minor at Caria.

In digging out the ancient city of Troy, Schliemann also came upon the great emblem of Creator—the ball-and-cross—(see fig. 2.6) the original logo of the sacred tribes.

> *Trojans be of eldest, noblest race.*
>
> VIRGIL, *THE AENEID*

Caesar himself claimed to be descended of the Ilians of the Troad, where mysterious mounds on the Plains of Troy are one more sign of the long-ago little people.

Were the Hebrews once a smaller (and paler) people, as strands and snippets of these histories suggest?* According to the diligent research

---

*Populations with Laron syndrome are also found in Israel. At the Mt. Carmel archaeological site, a small race of Natufians, no taller than five feet, was found. Possessed of "vastly superior" tools (Childe, *The Most Ancient East,* 18, 28), they appear to be the precursors of the Neolithic Revolution.

Fig. 2.7. Left: Oahspe, Tablet of Kii, Plate 80, indicating that Troy was a holy sanctuary during the fifth millenium BCE. Right: Tennessee pot from grave mounds with central design of ball-and-cross, as also found at Troy (note the drawing of a mound in the tablet at the bottom right, the large rotunda-like hill). This tablet and its ceremonies belonged not only to Troy and the Algonquin tribes, but also to Persia, Arabia, and Greece 5,400 years ago. Further linking Troy and the Tennessee moundbuilders (through a common homeland), both people knew the sacred rites and signs and produced exquisite pottery. The finest ceramics found in North America, with very unusual sculptural decoration, were in those Tennessee mounds.

of my colleague Martha Helene Jones,[27] the tale of David and Goliath connotes a smaller race vanquishing a pack of "giants," that is, the larger Canaanites (see Psalm 119:141 and Psalm 68: 27, 30): "There Benjamin *tzoir rdm* [little rulers of Judah] pelted . . . the Zebulun chiefs." The verse refers to the men of Benjamin as small in size, and comments on how singular it was to see these little fighters of Judah pelting their large adversaries, the men of Zebulun. *Tzoir* translates as "small," the root *tzo-* appearing also in the name of the city Tzoar or Zoar (Genesis 19:20–3), whose inhabitants, the Israelites, were "little ones." Jones flushes out other permutations of Zoar: Tsoar, Tsawar, and Tsaur, which are often translated as "Israelite" in old texts, but mean literally, "small people."

Why are we not surprised, then, when other languages of Western Asia portray the Israelites as little people? Assyrian and Babylonian names for Israel were, respectively, Kumri and Ghimri. Pointing out the boastful scenes of conquest carved on the Persian Behistun Rock (see fig. 6.9, p. 198), Jones infers that these captives, grown men, with full beards, "were of much shorter stature than their captors, only coming up to their waists! The mention of the Ghimri on the Behistun Rock illustrates that the ancient Israelites were a people of small stature." *Ghimri* or *gamir,* in turn, are quite possibly the linguistic parent of gamin and gnome, the dwarflike earth-dwelling spirit; just as Ezekial in the Bible speaks of the Gammadims as valorous men, "pygmaei" or "Pygmenians."[28] "There is," Jones adds, "still another ancient rock carving [depicting] the slaughter of a tribe of these little people, namely, the stele of Naram."[29]

Where did these small Persian Semites come from? Shem, to which the word "Semite" owes its origin, is a word for "land" in the Middle East, which can be traced back to the ancient name of India itself. Let us turn to Mother India then, the land of Shem.

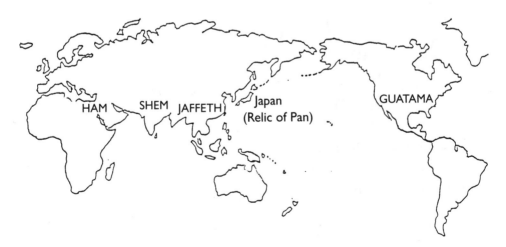

Fig. 2.8. Map showing names of the continents peopled by the sons of Noah after the Flood.

DWARF TRIBES OF INDIA

At the dead city of Mohenjo-Daro, along the Indus, a 1922 excavation unearthed the remains of a small-statured people. Shortness was indicated in their architecture, too: "the houses were built for quite small men."[30] This acclaimed but enigmatic Indus Valley civilization, with many modern amenities, predates the historical culture of India. It was a Bronze Age civilization of huge cities with mixed population. Mentioned by Pliny the Elder, Aristotle, and Eusebius, the region south of the Ganges (Baluchistan), coming toward the Indus, was populated by mountain tribes, "a race of Pygmaei" (some said to not exceed three spans in height, i.e., twenty-seven inches!) Today there are still "lean and meager" people living near the Indus.

Mohenjo-Daro as well as her sister-city Harappa in Pakistan were large metropolises with populations over a million inhabitants—but no one knows their true names or what race built them. The mystery only deepened when scholars discovered a startling resemblance of Indus hieroglyphics to those of Easter Island. As we go on, the "mystery" will lighten, for we will probe and find their common origins in a land beneath the sea.

Fig. 2.9. India's Aditya "Romeo" Dev, at just two feet nine inches, is the world's smallest bodybuilder and strongest "dwarf." Even smaller is Gul Mohammed of New Delhi, twenty-two inches, the world's shortest man, born in 1957.

Throughout the subcontinent of India there are tales of dwarf tribes descended from the monkey-god Hanuman. Well, we have seen this sort of ludicrous reckoning before—in Malaysia, for example, where myth has the Semang Negritos descended from siamang (gibbon; "simian" in English is cognate), an obvious racial slur. In legend, Hanuman, acting as native host of the incoming Aryans, is really a figure representing the indigenous Negrito population of India.

Ctesias, after Herodotus, knew of pygmies in the heart of India, describing them as black and only four feet in height (Negritos), skillful archers in the train of the Indian King. A remnant, situated near the Indus, are the Bandra-Loks dwarfish people (which may be now extinct). Surviving into modern times are the little Bhils hunters in Gujarat, an aboriginal people with dark skin and straight hair; as well as the Chenchus (of the Farhabad Hills); and the Pulaiyans and Kadar aborigines of Central and South India (Cochin), their men only four and a half feet tall and the women much shorter. These chocolate-brown folk have wavy hair. The Negrito strain in India increases as we move south, where the Dravidian tribes (Kanikar, Kurumba at Malwar, etc.), shy and primitive, are short and dark skinned.

The Cochin type is closely allied to the Veddas of northern Ceylon

Fig. 2.10. A Vedda archer, descendant of the Kings' bowmen of Ctesias' time. In Sri Lanka, the pure, unmixed Vedda is almost extinct (though Vedd*oid* tribes on the mainland are legion). Vedda women of the ninth century measured an average of 4 feet 6 inches.

(Sri Lanka) in the forested interior. Yet some of these clans are very pale skinned, the men barely five feet tall, the women usually four feet ten inches. Of mixed ancestry, they are classed as Caucasian, and are well-built, with wavy to straight hair, their feet unusually flat; the men sport chin-beards. But the little people of Sri Lanka that have captured the most attention are the wild Nittevo, to be discussed in later chapters.

LITTLE PEOPLE OF THE FAR EAST

Even more controversial than the atavistic (and now extinct) Nittevo are the pygmy tribes inhabiting Sichuan province in the mountainous frontier of China-Tibet. Barely exceeding four feet in height (the smallest adult measuring two feet one inch!), and answering to no known ethnic taxon, the Han-Dropa people of the isolated Bayan-Kara-Ula range look neither Chinese nor Tibetan. Weighing about fifty pounds, these blue-eyed, large-headed semi-troglodytes are certainly some of the most unusual-looking folks on Earth. And while puzzled experts simply label them "a mystery," an even greater enigma is presented by the remarkable artifacts excavated from surrounding caves. For here were unearthed the now-celebrated (originally banned!) 715 stone discs, nine inches in diameter and shaped something like a phonograph record with a hole at the center. Scattered about the area's extensive cave system, the discs contain a form of grooved writing, which, once deciphered, declares a celestial origin of these little people who "came down out of the skies."

Mythic as it may sound, the account resonates with Tibetan and Chinese folklore recalling small, pygmylike people, sky-people, no larger than an eight-year-old, who came among them eons ago by dropping from the sky; read: one part heaven, one part Earth. Discovered in 1938, the cobalt-laden granite discs in these Han-Dropa caves curiously resemble the acclaimed Phaistos Disk of Crete, which is also imprinted in a spiral, as is the Disk of Dendera, Egypt. Engraved with a writing code evidently 12,000 years old, the Sichuan discs were only partially translated in Beijing in 1962.

Miniscule people are not altogether unknown in that part of the world. Since the early twentieth century, reports have been filed regarding a pygmy tribe of Tibeto-Burman speakers called the T'rung, inhabiting a remote spot in Mt. Hkakabo Razi, where China, India, and Tibet meet. The T'rung stand at approximately four and a half feet, and are said to be the only pygmies of "clearly East Asian origin."

Well, not quite: Japan has legends of three-foot-tall sprites, dressed in pale yellow; perhaps a version of the Neolithic Yamato (meaning "dwarf"), a white-skinned ancestor with fine ceramics. Japan's haniwa, clay figures of curious little people, are called Jomon Dogus; their noble Caucasian (not Mongoloid) features have surprised archaeologists.

We might also note a Negrito skeleton found in a cave in Indo-China, at Minh-Cam. Nor should we ignore figures of dwarfish stature carved on Cambodia's monumental ruins. Indeed, there are *living* Negritos in Cambodia, the Saoch, a tribe of men no taller than five feet one inch. This region is not well studied; if it were, we might find, all over Indochina, quite a few little-people enclaves, like the Krabi in southern Thailand.

We would also meet with Burmese folktales of little men, short, dark, and fuzzy haired, some of them cannibals. In Vietnam, too, "the oldest known human population has unquestionably been Negrito."[31] As these chapters unfold, we shall find the substratum of humanity, the aborigines of the world, were little people of mixed color.

Negrito types are also said to inhabit the Kun-lun mountains of China and Northern Tibet, and, according to James J. Y. Liu, professor of comparative literature, the term Kun-lun in Chinese actually means "Negrito." Judging from theosophical rumors concerning the Kun-lun, the disc records of the Han-Dropa (above) might prove to be confirmation of secret "library caves" installed by the old masters and carved out

Fig. 2.11. These characters literally mean the Kun-lun Mountains but also "slave."

of solid rock in the high mountains of the Kun-lun.* Here, a vast underground complex is said to conceal clay tablets and ancient books in hidden sanctuaries directly linked to Pan, the lost land in the Pacific.[32]

THE LITTLE PEOPLE OF SOUTHEAST ASIA AND OCEANIA

Continuing our search for little people beyond the Asian mainland, heading to points south, we reach the true cradle of the world's Negritos, where the Philippine basin gives way to insular Southeast Asia.

Once called Sundaland by archaeologists, this vast and geographically confusing region of higgledy-piggledy archipelagoes stretches from Sri Lanka in the west to New Guinea in the east, and from the South China Sea in the north to Australia and Tasmania in the south. Borneo, Malaysia, Java, Sarawak, Sumatra, and Indonesia are all part of this great tropical region sprawled out between the Pacific and Indian Oceans.

Surely it is no coincidence that here along the fringes of Oceania (the lost homeland) are ensconced the majority of today's Negritos. They have been here for a long, long time and there is reason to believe they have always been here. Most live in isolation from the outside world, though evidence points to their once having been widespread. Linguistics alone tells this tale: the number of indigenous languages still spoken in the Philippines, Indonesia, Malaysia, Papua New Guinea, and Australia has been estimated at over 1,400, which is more than a quarter of all the world's languages![33] Diversity of languages, if nothing else, betrays a formerly far-flung, archaic, and indigenous population. Though once widespread, the Negritos were driven back, back, back—to the ends of the Earth; just look at the tips of the continents: people there are "small and undersized."[34]

New Guinea tribes of little folk (averaging four and a half feet in height) are tucked away in mountainous refuge areas. Such are the Tapiro of the Nassau Range.

---

*A California-based group called the Lemurian Fellowship says a school of Muvian adepts relocated to Kun-lun mountains of western Tibet after the "sinking of the Pacific continent about 24,000 years ago." The group was later known as the Great White Brotherhood.

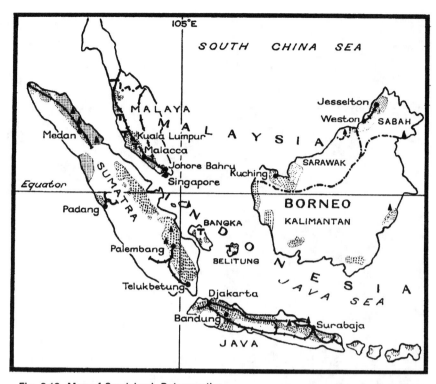

Fig. 2.12. Map of Sundaland. Between the Bay of Bengal and the Melanesian islands spreads out a grand arc of Negrito peoples. Nineteenth-century ethnologists knew of such populations "in Formosa, the interior of Borneo, Sandalwood Island (Sumba), Xulla, Bourou, Ceram, Flores, Solor, Lomblem, *Pan*tar, Ombay, and Celebes."[35]

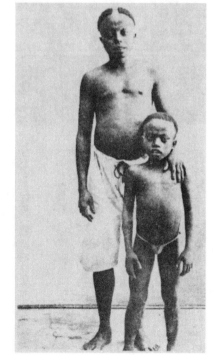

Fig. 2.13. Andamanese Negrito and his son. The man stands at 4 feet 8 inches.

Fig. 2.14 (above). Barrineans. In the remote jungles of Queensland, Australia (out from Cairns), are the Tjapukai people, sometimes called Barrineans. In 1960 R. R. Gates found these "dwarfs" near Cairns, on the Atherton Plateau.[36] Some of Australia's aborigines remember the "Tuckonie," a race of little men living in thickly timbered country.

Fig. 2.15. Left: Two Tapiros with a Papuan at center. Below: Tapiro bamboo penis-cases. The Tapiro Negritos of New Guinea are extremely modest, and treasure their handsome penis-guards.

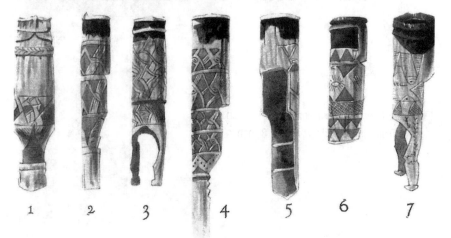

1   2   3   4   5   6   7

LITTLE PEOPLE IN SUNDALAND

Location	Tribal Group	Comment
Andaman Islands	Jarawa, Mincopie, Onge, etc.	all of these people are about the same size, the tallest men 4'10"
Malacca	Pangyan, Petani, Tumior	note *Pangyan*
Malaysia	Semang, Senoi, Pleh, Menrik, Jehai, Siong, Jembe, Kensieu, Kintak Bong, Tonga, Batek, Menik Kaien, Lanoh, Sabubn, and others	most living in small family groups
Sumatra	Semang and Orang Rimba	Semang in ninteenth century standing at average of 4'5"
Celebes	Toala	note Toa, var. Tua
Java	Kalang and Mbuti	also early "hobbit"* here
New Guinea	Tapiro Timorini Aiome, Karon, Mafulu; others along the Sepik, Gogol and Ramu rivers	in Nassau Mountains in Torricelli Mountains average height of Ramu: 4'8"
New Britain	Negrito groups	
Fergusson Islands	Negrito groups	men in 1906 averaged 4'7"
Bismarck Archipelago	little people	in the interior islands
Bougainville	little people in the mountains	men: 4'7"
Marianne Islands	fossil man	Negrito type
Admiralty Islands	fossil man	4'5"
New Ireland	fossil man	extremely small skulls

---

*Hobbit, whom we have already met and will meet again, is the name assigned to those tiny fossil men and women discovered on the Indonesian isle of Flores. One of the smallest human species ever discovered, *Homo floresiensis* occupied caves in the rain forest at least 18,000 years ago, and still figures in the legends and stories of island tribes. Today's light-skinned, short-statured Rampasas people on Flores are likely mixed descendants of this original hobbit man.

LITTLE PEOPLE OF THE WESTERN PACIFIC

Moving right along and reaching the western Pacific (Micronesia's Caroline Islands), we come upon a rich vein of prehistoric cave remains bearing an extinct population of little people: twenty-five miniature humans who lived perhaps some 2,000 or 3,000 years ago on the rock islands of Palau. With more than 1,500 bones excavated by a National Geographic team in 2006, Palau's Little Men are thought to resemble "hobbit" of Flores, though with larger brains. These little Palauans, together with their hobbit cousins, have been the center of a hot scientific debate since their recent discovery.

Micronesia's fantastic ruins tell a tale—Panape's (var. Ponape) *Nan* Madol, by its very name, is suggestive of dwarf races (*nanus* meaning "small" in Latin). Here, artificial islets rest in a shallow lagoon, making up a Venice-like city, which was once the capital of an oceanic empire: the "mythical lost continent of Mu." Panape's enormous stone ruins, built by a forgotten race, are all that remains, according to legend, of the continent of Kalu'a: "Our motherland rests at the bottom of the Ocean." Considered the oldest of the Caroline Islands, Panape has no shells, suggesting the true Pan Mountains.

A sacred and royal enclave, its temple was called *Nan* Zapue. Tradition on Panape asserts that the land was originally inhabited by a race of little people, and their graves (if not their descendants) are still to be found here and there around the island. But no one knows for sure the origin of the cyclopean stones that adorn the island-city of Nan Madol lying off the eastern shore of Panape. Abandoned, these ruins speak of an ancient religious center; one has to crouch down to pass through their (dwarf-size) entryways.*

Fanciful legend aside, let us zero in on the meaning of Nan: the founders of *Nan* Madol established worship of *Nan*isohrsapu, "Hon-

---

*One scrap of local legend (dubiously) attributes the megalithic feat to the black magic of a dwarf race who "flew" the stone logs into place from the quarry to the site of construction. (Peruvians, when asked about their own cyclopean ruins, replied, in kind, they had been "built by the gods" who caused the enormous rocks to "fly into position." Yeah, right.)

Fig. 2.16 (above). Chaldean temple servants shown with King Ur-*Nan*she (var. Urnina) on 4,600-year-old limestone wall plaque. Nana, too, was the name of the **Chaldean goddess** while Ash*nan* was the grain goddess of the Sumerians.

Fig. 2.17 (right). Teteoin*nan* "Mother of the gods," primeval Earth-mother in the Basin of Mexico; she was worshipped at the feast of Och*Pan*itztli. Drawing by Jose Bouvier.

ored of the Land"; *Nan*dauwas was the royal mortuary here, and district chiefs were called *Nan*mwakis (after a Panape dynasty). The name provides a wonderful clue—for "Nan" here denotes distinction or royalty. A world away, in old Iraq, Ur-*Nan*shem was the founding dynast of Lagash (Sumer), reminding us, too, of the *Nan*da dynasty of India. Nan carries a similar meaning in Europe as well, where Lusig*nan,* France, was named after the Compte de Lusignan—nobility of Luxembourg. And Melus*ine* (with the –ine appendage of the Ihin) was a fairy woman and ancestress of the Counts of Lusignan.

This line of royalty, of course, was ultimately **deified**—as in *Nan*ihehecatl, Aztec God of the Four Winds, and Nanhuatzin, another Aztec hero-god, as well as tinki*nan*tah, the Mayan term for our psychic relation to the cosmos. This euhemeristic Nan follows suit in: Nan-chi Hsien-weng (of the Chinese pantheon) and Tin Hi*nan,* goddess, queen, and ancestor of the North African Tuareg. In Ireland, too, A*nan* is the title of Goddess Danu, "good Mother" of the Danaan gods, which ties the people of Dan to the Nans; while Craig-el-*nan* is the name of a fairy mound and la*nan*shi is a fairy woman of the Scots.

The ubiquitous mother goddess Nan trickles down in the language of today with "nanna" and "nanny" as maternal figures. Her counterpart Ti-nan means mother in the New Hebrides. Nana is also mother in the Aeta language of the Philippines (with their Para*nan* Negritos and Pangasi*nan* Province). Other places in and bordering the Pacific Ocean reflect this ancient honorific that can only have originated in the Motherland of Pan.

- Peru: A*nan* Yauyas were the "Upper" members of Lima's high Quechua lineage (ha*nan* meant "upper districts," i.e., of the Cuzco aristocracy).
- Chi*nan* is one of the seven sacred lakes of Peru in the Vilcabamba region where the lost city of the Chachapoyas is guarded by the *short-statured* Machiguengas.
- Te*nana* was an eighteenth-century king of Huahine, Tahiti; the Tahitian king's house is called *Nan*u, 397 feet long!

Nan-places along the Pacific rim may once have been cultural centers established by this ancient elect:

- Nanaimo, Vancouver, where were found "skeletons all over" of little people; Ta*nana* River in Alaska; A*nan*gula Island (Aleutian) on the Alaskan Peninsula. The Klamath Indians knew of a dwarf race called na'hni'as.
- Nanumanga and Nanumea in Melanesia (east of Solomon Islands), where Negrito tribes abound. Here in Melanesia, their "Adam" is named To Kabi*nana*.
- Nandi on Fiji, where the exclusive men's society is called *Nan*ga.
- Nanumea Island in South Pacific.
- Kaulleo-*nana*-hoa in Hawaii.
- Nanango and Nannine in northern Australia.
- Nantou on Taiwan.

- Binan-Gonan Negritos on Luzon in Philippines.
- Nankoku, Shi*nan*o, Nansei and Nanao in the Japanese isles.
- Pramba-*nan* in central Java, with its monumental architecture, the great temple of Shiva, built by a sophisticated and well-organized society.
- Penesta*nan* and Tenga*nan* in Bali.
- The Pe*nan* people of Borneo.

With the preponderance of Nan-named cities and towns situated in the Far East,* we wonder if this linguistic clue does not actually point us yet further eastward to the great Oceanic emptiness, and its lost horizon. Writers such as James Churchward, David Hatcher Childress, and others (including myself) tend to view Panape's Nan Madol as a remnant of a submerged continent; Childress has collected first-hand legends of a sunken city at the bottom of Metalanim Bay (on Panape).

Owing to the worldwide diaspora of deluge survivors, this theme carries over to other lands: in Africa, culture hero A*nan*si (var. Nany) on the Upper Guinea coast and Gold Coast, made the first men at the command of god; however, says legend, they were ungrateful, so he made instead a *small* man and he became the hero of the race. Oddly, we find an echo of this in South America: Mo*nan* was the name of the Author of All among the Brazilian Tupis, but seeing the ingratitude of men, he caused a conflagration of fire, which then filled him with such pity that he sent a "*deluging* rain on the earth."[37]

Nan- people, as we follow this Ariadne thread, are often associated with a great flood of waters (see Nan- chart in appendix A). Tir-nan-noge, Nana, Nene, Nanabozho, Nanih Wayah ("we emerged wet and

---

*Far East: Funan, Cambodia (earliest known Cambodian civilization; Nan in Thailand, Nanam, Sinan, Cheonan, and Nangnim in Korea, Nandu of Vietnam, Nanshan in Tibet and numerous towns and parts of China: Nanchang, Nancheng, Nanda Devi, Nanking, Nan Ling, Nankang, Nanning, Nan Shan, Nanping, Nantong, Nanxiang, Nanxiong, Honan, as well as Hainan (a major language of South China), Nanaitsi (a Siberian people), Yunnan province in China (pyramid there), and Punan (a people of Borneo).

breathing"), and Ma*nan*nan, the Irish hero who carried the "Treasures of the Sea" in a special bag of skin.

If the fading memory of the Great Little People (a "nan" people) is captured in Old World place-names like *Nan*garhar Province (Afghanistan), Wadi Fay*nan,* Poz*nan* (Poland), Perpig*nan* (France), Ky*nan* (Wales), Iat*nan*a (ancient name of Cyprus), A*nan*atuba (East of French Guiana), Ka*nan* (Kenya), Pen*nan*y (near Calcutta)—we may also look to Latin *nanus,* French *nain,* and Spanish *enano*—all representing the figure of a dwarf.

In fact, *na-* means "little" or "young" in Algonquian; and with their culture hero *Nan*abozho, we find a well-remembered ancestor, survivor from the sunken land. Nanabozho (var. Nanabush) is the legendary ancestor of human beings; the saga speaks of a destroyed land, "the first land," an island beyond the great ocean. After Nanabozho emerged and "crossed a great ocean,"[38] he started a new race. This nan-, this ancestor, is also embedded in North American tribal names such as Ta*nan*os, Nise*nan*, *Nan*ticoke, *Nan*ohiganset, *Nan*tucket, *Nan*tahala (forest stronghold of the Nunnehi), Ma*nan* (off Maine), A'a*nan*ine, and Sali*nan* (California).

To the woodlands people (including the Ojibwa and Cree) and also among the eastern Algonquin, this spiritually endowed predeces-

Fig. 2.18. Nanabozho in the Flood

sor, Nanabozho, was sent to Earth by the Creator (Gitchi Manito) to teach the people.* He named all the plants and animals and founded the Midewiwin society; he also invented fishing and hieroglyphics. And he was a builder, like the great Nan ancestor of Panape and the industrious Menehune (var., *Nen*ehune) of Hawaii.

LITTLE PEOPLE OF THE ISLANDS

Spend a little time in Hawaii and soon you will be hearing about the Menehune (*ka poe Nenehune*), the "Small Sacred Workers." Best known of Oceania's legendary little people, they nonetheless kept to themselves, secluded in the forested uplands. Described as almost three feet tall, stout and strong, the Menehune were reddish-skinned with big eyes overhung by long bushy eyebrows.

As we discover in almost every part of the world that has little people, the Menehune were the first race in their region; according

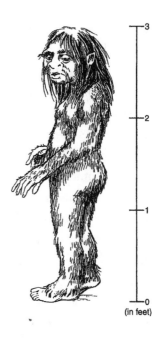

Fig. 2.19. The Menehune might deserve a more refined portrayal than this. Master architects, they were renowned for their engineering and temple-building. Drawing courtesy of Loren Coleman.

---

*The well-known Indian spokesman the late Russell Means mentioned the little people in a recent talk, saying: "They help us mend the sacred hoop of life, connecting mind and heart."

to Hawaiian history, these little folk were already there on the islands when the Hawaiians first arrived in their migrations from Tahiti. The Menehune covered all the islands before being driven back to the mountains of Kauai, and are credited with the preexisting canals and irrigation tunnels, as well as the petroglyphs found carved on rocks. Most especially are the Menehune remembered today as the builders of the great Alekoko fishpond, the island's largest aquaculture reservoir.

Likewise were the little people on Easter Island renowned builders, said to have raised stone houses four and a half feet high.[39] Similar though less-known folk inhabit (or inhabited) the islands of Micronesia, including Fiji, where natives say the little people were the original islanders. Even in modern times have there been encounters and reports of hairy dwarfs, one dated July 19, 1975, in the *Fiji Times:* Six eyewitnesses one fine day saw eight small figures—no taller than two feet, covered with black hair—run and disappear behind some bushes.

On the Philippines are the Luzon, Mindoro, Panay, Negos, and Mindanoa Negritos, totaling about 20,000 Filipino little people. Generally known as Aetas, their women average four feet nine inches, some much shorter, and the men average four feet ten and a half inches. In 1903, the shortest Aeta man measured four feet two inches. Other Aetas, though, are barely three feet tall, the true height of the ancient Ihin ancestor. Mountain-dwellers like so many of the world's little people, these small-framed, brown-skinned folk have inhabited the upland jungles of the Philippines longer than anyone can remember.

For some reason, scientists insist on deriving our Oceanic Negritos from *elsewhere*—even though human life in the Pacific region is dated to "more than 30,000 years ago."[40] "Perhaps tens of thousands of years old" are the nine feet high cement (lime and mortar) pillars in the New Caledonian Isle of Pines;[41] still, historians tell us that the first humans arrived there around 2000 BCE! How could the thousands of Oceanic peoples and languages have "evolved" in such a short span of time? When Europeans arrived in New Caledonia, the 60,000 islanders were speaking thirty-seven different languages! Historians tell us that Malaysian Negritos came from the Southeast Asia mainland on their way to Melanesia, and although some will admit that the history of the

Fig. 2.20 (above). Aeta archers, shooting from the boat at fish in the water. "The Good People," wrote one admirer, "have bodies so plyable . . . they can make them appear or disappear at pleasure."[42]

Fig. 2.21 (right). Little people of Polynesia fishing at night.

Filipino Aeta continues to baffle them, the usual solution is that they arrived through "land bridges" that once linked their country with the Asian mainland. But all these theories of migration turn their back on the possibility of a lost motherland, and the probability that the Negritos evolved in situ.

> *The Andamanese, the Semang, and the Philippine Negritos are so similar . . . that it is reasonable to suppose that they are descended from a single stock.*
>
> A. R. RADCLIFFE-BROWN, *THE ANDAMAN ISLANDERS*

Not only does the short stature of the world's Negritos betray a common origin from a disappeared source, but other traits as well—their huts, their customs, their mode of subsistence—speak strongly of Original Unity. Negritos and Negrillos both cover the grave of their dead with a stick or leaf-mat shelter; both populations interact with outsiders for the same articles: salt, iron, cloth, and grain. Other features suggest a shared ancestor: The Andamanese physical type appears in Papua, Southeast Asia, the Philippines, Australia, and Tasmania. Besides genetic affinities, there are notable linguistic relationships between these groups, while Father Paul Schebesta drew many parallels between the Aeta, Andamanese, and Semang—especially their economic way of life. Aeta, Papuans, and Semang all make fire in exactly the same way.

And there is this—fairy lore is strikingly similar in far different places: Japan's folklore of goblins, for example, closely resembles that of

Fig. 2.22. Photos of Papuan fire-making. The Tapiro employ exactly the same "split-stick" method to produce fire as the Aeta. Unlike their Papuan neighbors, the Tapiro know how to make fire. Their buildings and dress are also unlike the Papuans—"another race," thought Mr. Wollaston who visited them. Averaging four feet nine inches in height, the Tapiro, again unlike the Papuans, wisely build houses on stilts, cultivate tobacco, and speak an entirely different language.

the Irish. In fact, these beliefs are almost universal. The little people of myth yield to a strikingly common profile, underscoring a distinct race from a very early, scarcely known, period of man's history, and demonstrating a unique set of traits that includes their marvelous physical agility. Supple and well made are these people, expert archers, gymnasts, and dancers, like the fairy dancers of Europe—"so light and agile." The Philippine's Abenlens are of the "short, athletic type," and when the Aeta are dancing, their graceful limbs give them the appearance of "tiny Balinese girls"; they "are all agile and quick, like the African Pygmies," Georg Schweinfurth observed, who "ran so lightly that they barely touched the ground but rather seemed to skim along just above it, like sylvan sprites."[43]

"The Ihins have shapely legs and arms."[44] A psychic-sensitive once told me: "the Ihins were a very active and spritely people." Pygmy arms and legs, like their long-lost ancestors, are slim and nicely tapered. Acclaimed acrobats and athletes, these little men can climb trees a hundred feet high with amazing agility. They keep perfect time to their music, dancing in

Fig. 2.23 (below). Vedda archers of Ceylon. "The little people of adroit bow-and-arrow hunters" were also in Libya, as mentioned by Herodotus.

Fig. 2.24 (right). Obviously not a "dwarf," this Andaman Islander, standing at 4 feet 9, is a paragon of symmetry.

an exotic snaking line. The best dancer in a pygmy group garners enormous prestige. The Pygmies (of Central Africa) and the tiny Bushmen (of southern Africa) are strong and deft and lithe. The Encyclopedia Britannica has "many Bushmen well-proportioned"; these little people of the Kalahari are "well, sturdily, and truly made . . . finely modeled."

> *Lord, verily it has been a beautiful thing to see him move!*
> LAUREN VAN DER POST'S SISTER,
> QUOTED IN *LOST WORLD OF THE KALAHARI*

Their long-lost kinsmen of Sundaland, the Semang, are equally lithe; Paul Schebesta spoke of his informant, Keladi: "He was a typical Negrito of pleasant appearance and well-proportioned build."[45] Though halfway around the world, Tennessee little people were described in the same language in *Harper's Magazine,* 1869, concerning the "pigmy cemeteries": "the bones were strong and well set, and the whole frames were well formed." Not dwarfs (achondroplasiac), but perfectly proportioned and symmetrical. These Tennessee bones belonged, no doubt, to the Cherokee little people, the Yunwi Tsunsdi, "little fellows . . . well shaped and great wonder workers."[46] Out West, the short Mandan Indians had supple bodies; an 1860 traveler deemed them "well-made."[47] And across the sea, Ireland's grogach, with his soft body, appears to have no bones at all as he comes tumbling supply down the hills.

Our search for little people in Asia ends in Japan.

> The fleet of two ships carried to the north was called . . . in the Wagga [Panic] tongue Zha'pan, which is the same country that is to this day called Japan, signifying, Relic of the continent of Pan, for it lay to the north where the land was cleaved in two. . . . Thus was settled Japan. . . . And of all people, ye [the Japanese] shall be reckoned the oldest in the world.
>
> OAHSPE, BOOK OF APH 75:55

The ancient Jomon potters of Japan are thought to have been dwarfs (*tsuchigumo*), as four and a half feet long remains are found in association with their wares.[48] They survive today as the Ainu people, a living remnant of the long-lost Ihins (Ine var. Ainu, see also -ain names in fig. 8.12, p. 285). The "undersized" Ainu stock occupied most of Asia at one time; today only a few remain, all in northern Japan (Yezo). Different from Mongoloids, the Ainu sport luxuriant beards and wavy hair, their faces of a Caucasian cast. Their homeland, no doubt, was Pan, its western shore recently discovered beneath the waters off Okinawa.*

THE PGYMIES

Probably the most numerous of today's little people are the Negrillos, whose men average four feet eight and a half inches and women four feet six inches. They include the Mbuti, Mbenga, and BaTwa people of Central Africa, located for the most part north of the Congo River. "BaTwa" in Bantu means "small people." Tua (var. Twa), we know, means people, civilized people; Ba- then, seems to mean "little," and also (by virtue of newness) it denotes the germ of things. For example, in Egypt, *Ba* means "birth," while *Ba*ta is the name of the first man (and hero) in Egyptian myth. The *Ba*derian period gives the first evidence of dwarfs among Egyptians, whose counterpart in the New World, the Maya, hold the *Ba*lam as the original people on Earth, those who gave knowledge to mankind. The first place mentioned in the Mayan books of Chilam Balam is the district of *Ba*khalal.

Meanwhile, *ba*ra' in Hebrew means create; just as in the Philippines, *ba*do means "new" and *ba*go means "new arrival." This seems to be the original meaning of ba-: the first, the fountainhead. Among the Efe (of the African Ituri forest) the first man the supreme being created was *Ba*atsi.† The Ba- of all these names stands for inception, the wellspring;

---

*Vernon Wobschall in personal communication wrote about "a rock specimen off Yonaguni that has carvings on it that look remarkably like those found in the Panic language tablets in [Oahspe's] Book of Saphah. The rock came from one of the underwater pyramids recently discovered next to Japan."

†The first creation of people, being little people, is carried over in other ba- words, appearing in the names of antediluvians such as Barakel (mother of Jared and Dinah), and Bathenosh, wife of Lamech. I might include Batea, first Trojan woman and wife of Dardanus; Bara, son of Ishtar (aka In*nann*a); Bau, daughter of Anu and mother of Ea (Chaldean).

Fig. 2.25. Baderian figurine. Note the exaggerated shortness of the arms. These Neolithic people of Egypt, small and delicately built, made exceptionally fine pottery, never again excelled in the Nile Valley.

like Bat, title of New Hebrides culture heroes and like Battus, the founder of Cyrene, Libya. Where did Babylon, Bahrein, Basra get their names? Or Balkh, Afghanistan's "Mother of Cities"?

Ba- leads us back to the *ba*se, the beginning of things (see appendix B for more Ba- words).

Most of Africa's tribal names for Pygmies are prefixed with this Ba-, for example: BaMbenga, BaYaka, BaBenzele, Baka, Basese, BaBoGieli, Bako, BaKola, BaKuele, Baboukos, Batimbas, Batouas.* There are also little people, the Akebou, in Togo (West Africa) as well as in Mali, old French Sudan, and Abyssinia where abide the Suku tribe, the Obongo, and the Dongos, the latter four feet seven inches high (measured in the nineteenth century); explorers also measured the three and a half feet high Kenkobs and Reebas.

Somewhat lighter skinned than their Negroid neighbors, the equatorial pygmies are the earliest known inhabitants of the Congo Basin. Christened "Negrillos" (to distinguish them from non-African "Negritos" of like stature) they live their lives in the tropical rain forests.

---

*Africa's Negrillos number perhaps a half million, the Bayaka, Aka, Efe, and others occupying Rwanda, Burundi, Uganda, Zaire, Cameroon, Guinea, Gabon, Angola, Botswana, Namibia, and Zambia.

Last but not least are the diminutive "yellow" (fawn-colored) Bushmen of the Kalahari Desert—"The Great Thirstland," the harsh and unforgiving wasteland of southern Africa—their average height at four feet seven inches, though earlier observers (before the nineteenth century) put them at a shorter stature. The Bushmen call themselves Sa or San (Panic *sa* means "earth, land"). A fast-vanishing race, they are an extraordinary mix of *Homo sapiens pygmaeus,* Mongoloid, and Negroid. We will be hearing much more of the Bushmen in the chapters to come.

On Madagascar, the Kimos people of this large island east of Africa register as very small humans, as do the reclusive, cave-dwelling Mkokos to the north of Madagascar on Comoros Island. Madagascar itself was once home to the mysterious Vazimba people on the northwest coast. Known today through oral history, they are thought to be the original inhabitants of the island. Most interesting is that they were *white* pygmies, whom local lore credits with telepathic powers and the ability to become invisible.

Fig. 2.26 (left). Akka woman of the nineteenth century next to an African of average height.

Fig. 2.27 (below). Afrikaner explorer Laurens Van der Post stands with two adult Bushman, the shorter of age fifty, the other, a married man and father of two.

Fig. 2.28. Map showing verified locations of little people in the Western Hemisphere

THE LITTLE PEOPLE OF TRIBAL
NORTH AMERICA

And now—tribal North America, brimming with memories of a tiny race of human beings, which the student might reasonably pair with "extensive pigmy cemeteries in the United States."[49] Admittedly, my own survey only skims the surface, for as things indicate, a thoroughly researched study of North America's indigenous little people—at least in folklore—could fill a volume in its own right.

Let's begin in the east: Archaeologists did not hesitate to call southwest Pennsylvania's small burial vaults "one of the most baffling riddles in Pennsylvania prehistory";[50] however, America's early settlers, plain folk, were not so very baffled, simply concluding that they were the remains of a race of dwarfs. But how long ago? One of the earliest dates for people in North America—18,000 BP—comes from Pennsylvania itself: the Meadowcroft rock shelter in the western part of the state.[51] Author and archaeologist Jeffrey Goodman announced in 1981 that material recovered from that site could be as old as 20,000 years. The item in question was the fragment of a basket. Goodman's date is in line with Harold Gladwin's "pygmy groups" in the Americas, dating to as long ago as 25,000 BCE (in Texas and the Southwest); these, the earliest people in the Southwest, were also Basket Makers; they were "short and slender."[52]

Stone-lined and filled with shell beads and copper ornaments, these extensive grave-mounds ("tumuli") found in Pennsylvania are on a par with Ohio and Tennessee burials, the latter no doubt accommodating the Nunnehi or Yunwi Tsunsdi people of Cherokee fame. The Nunnehi, as memory faded to myth, became a race of spirit beings, **the immortals** and shape-changers who go about invisibly, but even Indian sources say one can hardly tell the difference between them and the mortal little people, the Yunwi Tsunsdi, who—according to the Cherokee—were the size of a child, reaching to a man's knee. Are they, then, the occupants of those tiny graves? At Coffee County, Tennessee, a pygmy burial ground of six acres covers the remains of "thousands of dwarf-like people." Also at Cochocton, Ohio, burials have been uncovered of a pygmy race only about three feet tall; likewise, at

Mammoth Cave in Kentucky were three-feet-tall mummies with red hair found in 1920.

Little people, in fact, are known to many of the southeastern tribes, such as the Muskogee (the women "remarkably short of stature"[53]), Creek, Chickasaw, Choctaw, and Seminole, the latter claiming that the **little people, who can't really be seen,** live in the holes of big trees; perhaps if you squint your eyes a bit, you'll see them running all around the twisted wood. Nevertheless, when you get very sick, they will appear at your bedside—but then only the sick can see them. A long time ago, say the Choctaw, while their people were living in Mississippi, certain small beings, sometimes called spirit-beings,* lived nearby. Known as the Kowi Anukasha or "forest dwellers," they were between two and three feet tall ("the size of a bitty child").

As for the northern tribes, the Iroquois (Seneca and Tuscarora) Little Ones, called *Geow-lud-mo-sis-eg,* are still occasionally spotted; healers and tricksters, these "Great Little People" are honored in the ritual called the Dark Dance. This ceremony, "very ancient," is based on a "pact of friendship" the Indians made with them long ago.[54] The Passamaquoddy (Maine) say the Little Ones were here before Gluskap; and sure enough, they became a so-called fairy race, the **nagumwa-suck,** who help out the Indians, invisibly. To the Mi'k Maq, they are the Pukalutumush, identified as the creators of the petroglyphs. The Ojibwa call their own little people Maimaigwaysiwuk; they may occasionally be seen paddling their stone canoes!

Out West, the Tewa Pueblos call them Towa E, literally "Little People" (Towa var. Tua, see fig. 4.1, p. 110); in Carlsbad Caverns, New Mexico, there are mummified remains of little people, examined in 1950 by author Coral E. Lorenzen (*The Shadow of the Unknown*). Among the Oklahoma Indians, there are two kinds of little people; finally, graves of a diminutive race of men are also reported near St. Louis.[55]

The Stick Indians (*Steyehah'ma*)—not such a pleasant bunch—are said to live out of sight, high in the hills of the Cascade Mountains; they

---

*In the above, we see that as ancestors of the Indians, the little people, in time, became **spirits or magical beings of another world.**

are greatly feared, like the *ikals* of Mexico (Tzeltal) and the *wendis* of British Honduras. Curiously, another "high hill," this one in Sioux country, carries a similar sinister reputation: mentioned in the journal of William Clark (of Lewis and Clark fame), on August 24, 1804, a "high hill" was reached in an immense plain. It was said to be the "residence of devils" about eighteen inches high. Remarkably large-headed, these little Stick Indians are armed with sharp arrows, and do not hesitate to kill anyone who tries to approach their hill. "So much do the Maha, Sioux, Otos, and other neighboring nations believe this . . . that no consideration is sufficient to induce them to approach the hill," wrote Clark in his journal.

However, on the following day, August 25, President Jefferson's acclaimed Corps of Discovery reached the Teton River in Kansas. There, Meriwether Lewis and William Clark happened to camp at another "hill," which was actually a mound, man-made. Here the bold explorers recorded an interesting bit of information about this earthwork: the Dakota Indians called it Mountain-of-the-Little-People or Spirit Mound. Later, Prof. Ella E. Clark, in her book *Indian Legends of the Northern Rockies,* related one man's account concerning the enigmatic Crow Medicine Wheel: "It is difficult to believe, but our forefathers claim the Little People lived there . . . the Elders say there were a small people, like eight-year-olds," living in the rocks near the Yellowstone.

Oral tradition has the Arapaho and Cheyenne describing a type of Stick Indian who stood from just twenty inches to three feet high, called the "tiny people eaters." In Wyoming, the Pedro Mountain mummy answers to local Shoshone stories of the Nimerigar, a race of miniscule folk who attacked them with tiny bows and poisoned arrows. As we've seen, the Shoshone vocabulary includes a word whose root is *nana-* and is translated by the compilers of the Shoshone Dictionary as "elf-like people."[56]

Up in British Columbia, the Haida nation recalls the First People coming out of clamshells (possibly dug-outs or arks), and they were "five little bodies." The Nisqualli of Washington tell a story of three brothers captured by a miraculously strong dwarf whose village, to which they were carried, was inhabited by a race of people as small as their captor. As their council sat to decide the brothers' fate, an immense flock of birds, resembling geese, pounced upon them and attacked them violently.

Stories of huge attack-birds are not unusual in tribal America, as one Cherokee tale, for example, has a band of little people (the TsundiGe'wi) assaulted by a flock of sandhill cranes, killing them all (to extinction). What fascinates us is that the same story is told of India's little people beset by cranes; every year they go down to the sea and eat the cranes' eggs, hoping to protect themselves against the rampaging flocks. In Africa, too, Homer (*Iliad* iii) described a race of tiny folk "whither the cranes fly when inclement winters and piercing frosts visit the northern shores . . . bearing slaughter . . . to the Pigmy men." Fierce battles between the pygmies, armed with lances, and cranes were mentioned by later writers such as Pliny the Elder (first century) who said the Catizi dwarfs "were driven away by cranes." Such scenes were later depicted on Greek vases, which made them appear as "dwarfish-looking men with large heads," although the pygmies, in reality, "conform in their relative proportions . . . not to dwarfs, but to full-sized people of other races . . . they are therefore strikingly unlike the stumpy . . . short-limbed . . . pygmies so graphically represented . . . on ancient Greek vases."[57]

Reaching northernmost America, we get one last look at little people. In the tenth century, when the Scandinavian Vikings reached northeastern America, near Rhode Island, they found there a race "totally distinct from the Red Man, and more approaching the Esquimaux, whom they designated Skrellingr [*sic*], or 'chips,' so small and misshapen were they."[58] It was "the same race as in Labrador . . . [whom] they contemptuously call Skralinger . . . and describe as numerous and short of stature."[59]

Fig. 2.29.
First contact with the
Inuit little people

MEXICO

Mexico's richly storied past brims with little people:

- Many of Quetzalcoatl's attendants were dwarfs.
- Stone dwarfs hold up the altar table in the shrine of the Temple of Morning Star at Tula.
- The Olmecs were inordinately fond of creating clay statuettes of dwarf gods called "Chaneques," **dangerous rain deities** living in the forest and as we've seen, attending waterfalls.
- At La Venta (an Olmec site), a statue in one of the altar's niches holds a dwarf on its lap, so like similar reliefs at Monte Alban, where tiny entryways to the chambers as well as "pygmy tunnels" have been noted.
- Everything about the stone remains at Niscute is dwarfed; the rooms are small, the ceilings low.
- In Yucatan, dwarfs were sacred to the sun-god. Tiny huts, long deserted, were photographed by Florida-based explorer Rolf Schell in the late 1950s along the Yucatan coast (published in his privately printed book, *A Yank in Yucatan*).
- At Cozumel, there is a little temple whose doorway measures three feet in height. Indeed, all along this coast are little houses and temples, answering to local lore of pygmies who once lived there. Ancient petroglyphs depicting tiny persons have been found throughout Yucatan, Belize, and Guatemala.

Beneath Oaxaca, at the old Zapotec capital, mysterious tunnels are far too small to be used by adults, being about twenty inches high. Mexican iconography of course is loaded with super-squat gods and demigods. In fact, a living representative was seen as recently as 1977 at one of the ruins, clothed in the typical Mayan tunic, the huipil. A caretaker at Mayapan (once the capital of the Maya, now in ruins) was the witness; the little intruder was about four feet tall with a long jet-black beard and a machete slung over his shoulder. Known as alux, these little men had been described to the first Conquistadores, and while their tiny stone

Fig. 2.30. Olmec dancers (*danzantes*) at Monte Alban carved in relief on building look like typical Negritos. Mayan temples are also covered with bas-reliefs and carvings of naked little men.

huts were long known among natives as "alux houses," archaeologists officiously dubbed them "votary shrines," with no further information on their origin. Let archaeologists write them off as votary shrines, but present-day Maya say they were the homes of favored alux.[60] To this day, these structures with short doorways can be seen in front of the main temple at many Mayan ruins.

This brings us to the acclaimed Mayan Temple of Dwarfs at Uxmal in the Yucatan, "with such small doors and chambers that they seem to have been designed for the use of pigmies . . . far too small . . . for normal human occupants."[61] Also known as Temple of the Magicians, a near-copy was discovered in the outlying islands in 1968 when explorers found three-foot-thick limestone walls underwater at Andros Island in the Bahamas. Among these ruins was recognized the same exact floor plan of the Mayan Temple at Uxmal.*

Mayan dwarfs of the first world, called Saiyam U*in*icob, are said to have built these ancient cities, but their world was destroyed in the first great Flood. It was, I believe, *the* Flood, the submersion actually of

---

*Here on Andros, legend persists of mischievous, small folk called Chickcharnies. These little people, it is said, once inhabited the remote forests of the island. Curious that the Bahamas is the other place that cases of Laron syndrome are reported.

Fig. 2.31 (left). Alux. Nearly all of Yucatan's thousands of Mayan ruins have tiny stone houses with doorways less than three feet high. Drawing courtesy of Loren Coleman.

Fig. 2.32 (below). Mexican deity from *Vienna Codex* and Peru image. Why are so many Guataman deities pictured as dwarfs? The answer, I think, has to do with the modest height of the Great Ancestor.

an island continent to the west—Pan. The temple at Uxmal, as far as James Churchward and Auguste LePlongeon could determine, "was a memorial commemorating the loss of the Lands of the West."[62] Of this land—and the three-foot-tall people who survived its submersion—we will be hearing much more in the chapters to come.

The great explorer Alexander Von Humboldt learned of a race of pygmies in Mexico's unexplored region of Chiapas near the Isthmus of Tehuantepec; later, a professor returning from this region spoke of many colonies of undersized people, having measured two such individuals at three feet six inches. Though they are getting taller, these were, no doubt, ancestors of the Lacandon, the "little men" near Lake Pelja, in the mahogany forest. By the time Count Byron de Prorok visited them in the 1930s, they measured four and a half feet, though some

Fig. 2.33. Descended of the Maya, the Lacandon were never conquered by the
Spanish, retreating instead to the most isolated areas.

much shorter. There in the jungle between Chiapas and Guatemala
they grow corn, cotton, and tobacco. I highly recommend the online
video of the Lacandon! It can be found at www.youtube.com (accessed
July 18, 2012).

Everyone knows that the indigenous people of Guatemala are very
short. In fact, some of the villages around the shore of Lake Atitlan
are occupied by Indians "small enough to be called Pygmies." At Peten
(near Nakum and Tikal), Topoxte has been described as a miniature
city, with everything built to a small scale—temples, pyramids, stair-
cases. In the jungle, too, there have been many rumors of pygmy-like
beings, extending to the hardwood jungle of British Honduras, where
"two little people" were sighted by a government timberman in 1944.
The woodsman described the pair as about three feet tall, the man
heavily bearded and the woman with extremely long hair, matching
James Churchward's account: "when I was in British Honduras I was
informed that hunters and explorers occasionally meet them back in the
dark valleys of the mountains. They are about three feet tall with . . . an
abundance of very long black hair."[63]

Fig. 2.34. Bearded and squat figure carved from volcanic stone, from Chinque, Guatemala. Drawing by Jose Bouvier.

About a century ago, investigators and observers were reporting that many natives of America's tropics "are almost dwarfs . . . women average a little over four feet."[64] Writer Bill Mack declared this indigenous type ensconced everywhere from the Yucatan to Tierra del Fuego: "The tropical rain forests of Central and South America are inhabited by a race of dwarflike people . . . in parts of Central and South America they were called Sisemite or Toyo, and the villages gave them special local names."[65]

SOUTH AMERICA

Extant from Panama to Argentina to the southernmost tip of the continent are little-known remnants of a race of little people, from the Bogenah of Panama to the Yahgan at Tierra del Fuego, many of the latter only four feet seven inches tall, living in the western part of Cape Horn. Fuegan women in the nineteenth century measured only a few inches above four feet. Chile's Alakaluf people are also short statured and thought to be among the earliest South Americans, pushed ever southward by later people.

At San Blas and the islands east of Panama are the Tupi-Tawalis, a pint-sized folk regarded as "extremely intelligent." Sedate and agricultural, their lifeways echo those of other little people we will encounter in the pages to come, hinting at the common ancestry, the Original Unity, that has so long eluded students of the past. These San Blas folk, we learn from A. H. Verrill's firsthand observations (1927), are industrious, peaceful, cleanly; the gentler sex here are "the most emancipated of emancipated women."[66] To R. O. Marsh, who also stayed with them in the 1920s, "they were dignified, friendly, hospitable and cheerful. They were intelligent and quick-witted . . . skillful seamen and artistic hand-workers. Their social organization was highly developed and stable . . . [their] culture kept unchanged from time immemorial."[67] Like the artisans we will glimpse in chapter 3 and again in chapter 4, they are adept woodcarvers and weavers of splendid cotton (the Kuna group). Most fascinating, and reminding us at once of the North American Pueblos, these little people of San Blas are in the habit of "clustering" their dwellings, their houses found densely packed together (see figs. 7.6 on p. 228 and 7.7 on p. 230 of these clusters).

The Akurias, in this region and unknown to the outer world until visited by Verrill in the early 1920s, are described as rather like little Caucasians, the women about four feet tall.[68] Their eyes are straight, noses thin and well bridged, chins well developed, foreheads broad.

Then, too, in the villages of Loja Province, Colombia, one comes across "stunted Indians." I myself have met some unforgettable little rosy-cheeked Columbians while touring the Andes many years ago. And had it not been for a recent news story, we would never have heard of another group of little white-skinned people tucked away in the mountains of Ecuador.

In a remote corner of this equatorial nation live the "Laron dwarfs," incorrectly labeled dwarfs for they are simply little people, well proportioned, though rather stout. Laron syndrome is the scientific name for the genetic differences in these people, who are also found in the Bahamas, Turkey, and Israel. Standing about four feet high, these gentle folk show no occurrence of cancer or diabetes; they are long-lived. It seems they lack a hormone (lGF1) that other humans possess. Numbering no more than three hundred souls, these Andean Laron cases are currently under study, as their hormone pattern seems to be the reason for their health and longevity.[69]

The "dwarflike" Machiguenga people in the Peruvian jungle are, significantly, the "guardians" of the Chacha ruins. Another Peruvian tribe measuring only thirty-nine inches tall was reported in a 1970 book (published by the Roman Catholic Vicariate); living along the banks of the Curanja River where Brazil, Peru, and Bolivia meet, these people are called Yushe. In Brazil itself, little people noted by earlier Jesuit missionaries, and seen sporadically in the Amazon rainforest, have been variously labeled leprechauns, pygmies, and dwarfs.

Brazil, in fact, is home to scattered Negrito tribes, Col. P. H. Fawcett having described such groups in the interior as short, dark, and hairy pit-dwellers. What Fawcett was really looking for was an ancient civilization thought to be hidden somewhere in Matto Grosso, its inhabitants dwelling in stone palaces and cultivating the arts of high antiquity. The region was full of such legends. "The Brazilian remains, which I have seen," wrote Fawcett, "show a civilisation with which nothing in any of the Americas can compare . . . they antedate anything previously known . . . their scripts astonishingly . . . ancient."[70] In fact, the living Tapuyas in eastern Brazil seem to be refugees of that civilization: "fair as the English, with white, golden, and auburn hair." From whence came this fair race? That is the intriguing question we will address and answer in chapter 5. But for now, let us move on to chapter 3 and a closer look at the highly civilized little people who inhabited Arabia 8,000 years ago.

CHAPTER 3

Legend of the Scarlet Hat

THE BLOOD-RED CAP

A simple cap, brimless and soaked with blood, goes a long way in revealing the lost record of the little people in the ancient world. More than a place of honor, theirs was a place of sanctity, giving us the holy people of deepest antiquity, the crown of humanity.

> Give me a crown, O Father, for Thy Son! A scarlet light descended . . . and God reached forth his hands and wove it into a crown . . .
>
> OAHSPE, BOOK OF AH'SHONG 54:17

It is hardly coincidental that "red moon crowns" were typically worn by the little people known as fairies, while the nixes of northern Europe wore a "red bonnet."[1] The red crown adorning Neith, oldest of beings, Great Mother and Goddess of Lower Egypt; or the red *biretta* bestowed on the cardinals of the Vatican; or the scarlet *ilatu,* "fillet" (headband) of the royal Inca; or the *shamar* of Tibet's "Red Hat" lamas—are all, every one, but faint echoes, yea, impersonations of an icon that must be chased back yet thousands of years more before unearthing the wellspring of the sacred scarlet hat.

"Haydar's Crown," dating from the fifteenth century, though the most recent of these echoes, nevertheless preserves the original and authentic theme of martyrdom—or simply self-sacrifice—injecting a rather pre-Islamic, Zarathustrian strain into the Sufi order of Persia, which in time became a dynasty of Grand Masters (sheikhs). Situated in northeastern Iran, at Shirvan, Sheikh Haydar of the Safavid Sufi order was assassinated in 1488 when his influence grew too great for the comfort of the ruling secular shah. The sheikh was beloved of his devotees, the Kizilbashes or Red Hats, better known in Farsi as Taje-e-Haydari, "Haydar's crown." These Red Hats, once in power, began the Safavid dynasty of Persia, restoring a priestly class of ruler—and Haydar's own son, now sheikh of the Sufi order, became the first Safavid shah.

Ah, Persia, so steeped in a shrouded and precious past, so much the hub of all that precedes known history. Going back thousands of years, and originating in India, the ancestors of Abraham, the great patriarch and father of the faithful, sojourned there, in Western Asia, before migrating to Arabia. The Jews, as Godfrey Higgins illuminates these lost origins, were actually "a tribe of Hindoo or Persian shepherds . . . a wandering tribe. . . . The Jewish religion was anciently the same as the Persian . . . [this fact establishing] the identity of the religions of Abraham and Zoroaster."[2] Indeed, Persians and Jews both claim Ibrahim as their founder.

And when Abraham's people formed their sacred circle of worship, the women wore sky-crescents (moon crowns) on their heads while the

Fig. 3.1. Image of Abraham shown with his spirit-familiars. Painting done in the dark by J. B. Newbrough (automatic drawing).

men wore the blood-red "Zarathustrian hat,"[3*] brimless, like the skull-caps (yarmulkes) of today's Jews or the kufi of the Arab.

OPPRESSION AND REBELLION

Behind this air of spiritual sacrifice (even martyrdom) that clung to the blood-red hat, there was a strain of real and sustained persecution. Struggle against oppression went hand-in-glove with the iconic Zarathustrian cap. A powerful icon of valor against tyranny, it made it all the way up to the French Revolution, which took *le bonnet rouge* (red bonnet) as its sweeping symbol of *Liberte!* Quite possibly, the French egalitarians borrowed their fervent motif of autonomy from Italy, where in early Roman times, the *beretto de Frigia* (red Phrygian cap) was worn, like a passport to freedom, by its emancipated slaves. In some parts of Italy to this day, if you go about with a red hat, people will say you're wearing the *beretto frigio,* and, therefore, you must be free to pass unharmed.

Fig. 3.2. A Phrygian cap adorns the Seal of the United States Senate.

In Phrygia (modern-day Turkey), the greatest of all deities—Cybele and Attis (in statue)—don the Phrygian cap, which also serves to identify the Trojan heroes of that land. Probably through Persia, the perennial scarlet hat entered Phrygia's cult of Mithra. But here Mithra was falsely elevated from a god of Dawn (Enlightenment) to the Sun itself, and from a humble god of righteousness to a Savior and god of victory. Bellicose, beloved of soldiers, his cult was marked by glittering swords, gory ceremonies, the immolation of human victims, and cruel tests of initiates. Quite

---

*The same were worn in the faithist rites of Emethechavah.

a change from the original ideal of simple self-sacrifice! But then:

> *So many religions were manufactured in Phrygia . . . [they were]*
> *great inventors of fables.*
>
> ALBERT PIKE, *MORALS AND DOGMA*

France's *bonnet rouge* reminds us also of China's red turban. In the fourteenth century, oppressed Han peasants gathered under the banner of "Red Turbans" to protest the corruptions of the Mongolian Dynasty. Known as the Red Turban Rebellion, the uprising led eventually to the Ming dynasty. The peasant group that spearheaded the revolt was a secret society.

If China's Red Turbans organized themselves in secret, so too was the Phrygian Mystery School of Mithra a secret fraternity. It is with this motif of secrecy and seclusion that we are reminded of the little people known to the Cherokee: though friendly, they did not like to be followed, keeping their houses and towns secret "with a vengeance."* There were times, though, when the Cherokee shaman (adawehi) could go into the rock caves of the Smokey Mountains and partake of secrets with the little people, learn their sacred ceremonies and accept "spirit gifts."

Secret also was the kiva sect out West, established when the Hopi chief (after the Flood) passed tablets of knowledge on to his sons for safekeeping. These brothers went separately into the world; the younger brother would recognize the older brother only because he would have the matching sacred stone tablet and would be light-complexioned—a *true* white brother (see chapter 5)—plus he would be wearing a *red cap*.[4]

Also red-capped were the European dwarfs with their "secret knowledge of magic"—even the "gods" must resort to their forges and wonderful workshops. Such was Korrig the Dwarf, a.k.a. Gwyon the Seer, with his secret knowledge of all things.

---

*The Cherokee embellished this idea in their folklore by relating that the Yunwi Tsudi so valued their privacy that they were known to put death curses on any Cherokee who revealed the location of their homes. One little Cherokee girl, looking for her lost pet pig, found the Little People in a cave; they agreed to take her home if she promised never to tell where she had been. But when a friend pressed her to tell, she disappeared in a puff of smoke!

Secrecy and persecution are themes that are inescapably linked, as we will discover further on when we touch on the well-hidden raths and souterrains of Europe's little people who were ultimately exterminated. In a sense, belief in One Great Spirit was the biggest (forbidden) secret of all: 6,000 years ago in India, because of persecutions of the "faithists" (devotees and mixed descendants of the little people, the sacred tribes), the Vedic language, song, and poetry perished—save in a small degree, such as was preserved by the remnant of faithists who had escaped through all these generations, still in secret worshipping the Great Spirit. There is a remnant in India to this day, the sect of the Divine Mother, Kali, who bestows a *brimless red hat* upon their spiritual headman. (I used to chant with them at a Tennessee ashram!)

Then, in the cycle following Brahma and the Vedes, Moses (3,500 years ago) rebuilt what had been lost since Abraham's time, reviving the Zarathustrian doctrine of Creator, One Great Spirit (so-called monotheism today), whom his people worshipped secretly under the name "Jehovih." "We swear unto thee, O Jehovih, that we will not call on the name nor worship any person or thing called God or Lord, but Thee only."[5] But in public, to avoid persecution, they called him God or Lord. Go along to get along. At that time the name Jehovih could not be spoken, save in whisper and with mouth to ear.

For the Muslims, too, this creed-in-whisper later became fixed in the doctrine of *taqiyya,* a kind of camouflage, deception, concealment—to hide from Christian oppressors or opposing Islamic cults. It was the same for the Jews: dissimulation, feigning Islam in Spain and other Muslim strongholds—living a double life—especially at times when they were faced with the choice of conversion or death. The great Jewish philosopher Maimonides in the twelfth century wrote *Guide for the Perplexed* in encoded language.

More than 3,000 years earlier, before the great Exodus from Egypt, the pharaoh had decreed that the Israelites:

- Shall not possess land or house or ox or cow or any public altar of worship or temple,
- but shall be a servant of servants, who

- shall profess his doctrines only under penalty of blood and flesh [later Hadrian's decree, after 132 CE, would again impose capital punishment for study of the Torah]; and
- if he teaches the Great Spirit openly, he shall suffer death, along with his wife and children.

The king of Egypt also enacted a law to extract the long-held secrets of the Israelite priests and sages: "And of thy arts, of measuring and working numbers, thou shalt not keep them secret longer, or thy blood be upon thee."[6] And this scenario, we shall soon see, feeds into the Masonic legend of Hirom (var. Hiram)—and his Red Hat of martyrdom.

THE TEMPLE

In Egyptian mythology, Anubis was originally a mortal with superhuman powers; later, he appears as a canine or jackal god, who mediates between the living and the departed. He acquired his title, Master of Secrets, as he came to be associated with magician cults. This stated, we can now consider the Anubi* initiates of an earlier Egypt[7] upon which Anubis' cult-of-secrets was undoubtedly modeled. As faithists in the I Am (the All One Creator), and initiates into the Rites of Anubi, these early Israelites were fast sworn to secrecy. Though any man might elect to enter the first and second degree of Anubi, only the elect, the Ihins and faithists, could receive the more advanced degrees. The fifth degree was called the Degree of Prophecy, and the place of initiation was called the College of Prophecy. Here were kept the secrets, now coveted by the pharaoh, including how to:

rule over others without their knowing it
cast spells
enter the prophetic state
estimate numbers without counting
find proportions and distances without measuring
forecast the time of things

---

*Annubia was also a ritual name among Native Americans.

find the weight of things without weighing

find the power of the capstan before it is made, and of the lever and
  screw

find the friction of things before they were moved, in order to know
  the power required

The most useful knowledge of the Earth was thus kept in secret
with the Anubi adepts. And the kings' people, even the richest and
most powerful, were beholden to them. To build a palace or a temple,
or an aqueduct or canal, or a ship or any other great undertaking, the
kings' officers were obliged to employ Israelites of the fifth degree to
superintend the work.*

The reader may by now be wondering if these were the same celebrated architects and craftsmen and engineers as built King Solomon's
Temple,† some thousand years later. Well, as far as Freemasonry is concerned, the genius of the Lodge can be traced back to the exalted and
martyred architect of Solomon's Temple—one Hiram Abiff.‡

Before plunging into the founding legend of the Masonic order,

---

*The chief architect of King Thotmes I was called *In*eni. See cognates Ihin-Ine, in
chapter 9.

†Here the link to the little people is strengthened by those three-foot-long Tennessee
coffins constructed of flat, unhewn stones: "These that build temples of hewn stone
are not my people." A similar scruple was at play in the building of King Solomon's
Temple: only blocks of undressed stone were used; no hammer or axe was to be
heard (1 Kings 6–10). The Talmud recounts that the builders were in fact forbidden
to cut the stones.

‡The name Hiram appears in old Arabic legends as Iram or Irem, who inspired the
building of a great edifice in the desert with mighty columns. The name Hiram
is also mentioned in 1 Kings 7:13–14, 46–47, where he is son of a widow and a
bronze worker from Tyre. Another biblical reference is Hiram (III), King of Tyre,
who must have gotten his name as a Phoenician from the Fonece (Semitic) adepts
around 550 BCE, mentioned in 2 Samuel 5:11 and 1 Kings 5:1–10, where he sent
building materials for the Temple. See also 1 Kings 9:26–27, for Hiram the naviga-
tor of the sea people, and 2 Chronicles 9:21–22, for the king's ships went to Tarsh-
ish with Hiram. For several centuries Phoenicians were building faraway cities and
colonies; they were artisans, metallurgists of Sidon, producers of massive stonework,
skilled craftsmen, experts in construction, carpenters, and stonemasons sent to Jerusalem to build Solomon's Temple.

which they believe to be true, let us consider the name itself. "Hirom," in Old English, is a personal name, glossed as "Exalted Brother," perhaps of the Craft. In Arabic, h-r-m means "made great"; probably *haram* (forbidden, sacred) comes from this root. Yet, in Ahamic—the sacred language of Arabinya (see fig 4.1, p. 110), Aham being the original name of Egypt—Hirom translates as . . . "red hat!" A Masonic friend of mine, Paolo Amaldi of Bologna, Italy, told me that the red hat is used in the degrees of the Scottish Rite and elsewhere, and refers to the wounds and sacrifice of the adept-initiate Hiram Abiff, principle architect of Solomon's Temple. (The surname Abiff seems to draw on the Semitic *abi,* indicating father or master craftsman.)

The tragic death of Hiram Abiff, murdered by three ambitious "ruffians" (probably a cover-up for a grander conspiracy of lower-order fellowcrafts to extort secrets), looms so large that it is commemorated in the initiation ceremonies for master Masons. Each initiate, significantly, plays the role of the victim. The drama is presented as an allegorical play during the third degree of Craft Freemasonry; the climactic (third) degree in the Blue Lodge reenacts the drama of Hiram Abiff, who is somehow at the heart of all Masonry.

Fig. 3.3. Vendome of St. Trinité. Mason taking a measurement. Dwarf builders and artificers were not confined to any single location in the protohistorical world. They may appear as the unusually gifted engineers of the Olmecs; the talented Menehune, renowned builders of homes, canoes, fishponds, irrigation canals, and so forth; the Picts (pixies) of Scotland, expert builders of the raths and souterrains; or their cousins, the Tuatha De Danaan, with their three gods of craftsmanship—the Tri De Dana. Drawing by Jose Bouvier.

Ambushed by these ruffians, who wanted to become independent master masons on their own, Hiram refused to divulge his building secrets. They killed him at high noon with a violent blow to the forehead, and the body was hastily concealed under some rubbish in the Temple, until midnight ("low twelve"), at which time the body was taken out to the brow of a hill and buried. Curiously paralleling fairy lore, it seems that many of Europe's red-capped elf people only come out at high noon and low twelve; their secret dance-circles at midnight are a permanent fixture in European folklore. Superstition says that if you put your ear to the ground at the Singing Barrows of Dorset at midday—high noon— you can hear the soft singing of the fée folk. My Masonic friend, Paolo Amaldi, told me: "in the apprentice Blue Lodges ritual, we start work (symbolically) . . . at noon and end at midnight." The Ihins by custom conducted ceremonies at high noon, as instructed by their angel-teachers.

> *Our Master Hiram Abiff retired to pay his adoration to the Most High as was his wonton custom, it being the hour of high twelve.*
>
> MASONIC RITUAL

With the Masonic Hiram, we see a compelling link to the story of the pharaoh, who extorted building secrets on pain of death from the initiated engineers (adepts of the fifth degree). Hiram—the King of Byblos (Phoenicia) around 1000 BCE—was, some say, King Solomon's father-in-law, and may have been even smarter than King Solomon the Wise. According to Josephus, who traced Phoenician (Fonece) histories, Hiram and Solomon were good friends: the two shared philosophical riddles and Solomon sometimes sent problems he could not solve to Hiram.

The Masonic candidate, of course, is sworn to an oath of secrecy; the Order has been subject to a good deal of persecution over the centuries, thanks to their dogged independence from Christendom and state religion.

THE LITTLE ARTISANS

Secret knowledge . . . persecution . . . martyrdom . . . mystery schools . . . red hats. How far back in time must we travel to capture the historical moment in which all of these elements dovetail? Perhaps we can jump-off from the biblical Hiram (in 2 Chronicles 2:13), in his role as craftsman sent from Tyre to Solomon. His mother belonged to the Naphtali tribe, people of Dan, skilled engravers. Dan, we know, was a tribe of Israel. But there are earlier links: other artificers carrying this name Dan, such as the Danaan of Ireland and the Danae of Egypt and Greece.

Engraving

On Crete, delicate carvings on tiny gems were a puzzle: no one knows their origin, or their forebears. These "masterpieces of exquisite beauty"[8] were produced by the founders of Europe's first known civilization— the Minoans. But carving on tiny gems was, at least according to the ancient sagas, the signal work of the Northern dwarfs: the beautiful goddess Freyja's famous necklace—the Brising, the most elegant, flaw-less jewelry in Asgard—was made for her by the dwarfs out of a collec-tion of tiny rare stones, strung on a chain so delicately wrought that no man could duplicate it. Indeed, dwarfs (*dan*gas) were traditionally employed in jewelry-making in Egypt.

In Turkey, north of Hiram's Tyre, at Troy (likely that Tyre and Troy are of the same *Tur*anian root as *Tur*key and E*tru*scan), exquisite carvings and inscribed earthenware vessels were found among the trea-sures of these people who—like their cousins in America, China, and elsewhere—had a great taste for art.

We can trace these little artists all the way to Africa, where the

Fig. 3.4. In Egypt, Ptah was **creator** of the world, the dwarf god of Craftsmen, who became the particular patron of metalworkers and sculptors.

tiny Bushman possesses "a remarkable delight in graphic illustration . . . astonishing gift of painting for ten thousand years at the very least"[9]—as seen on the painted rocks of Cape Colony's mountains and in the Drakensbergs, as well as Mashonaland and Manicaland in Zimbabwe. On the walls of caves, these designs are partly painted and partly engraved.

The little people were the very first engravers on Earth: the first writings after the Flood were engravings—other than those kept secret by the Ihin priests.[10] The only holy books given to mortals before the time of Zarathustra (9,000 years ago) were those "given in secret to the tribes of Ihins, of which the different nations of the earth knew nothing."[11]

To find the Ihins, the little people, in Zarathustrian times, we must go back to Abraham's (Ibrahim's) people. However, Abraham (6,000 years ago) only revived a tradition that his forebears had kept alive from the time of Zarathustra (Zardosht) himself, the first lawgiver and prophet 9,000 years ago.

THE IHINS

At that time, in the lower country of Arabinya (Arabia), there were a great people, large and copper-skinned (Ghans and Ihuans*) who had attained thirty cities, chief of which was Os'nu, the capital over all the rest. Os'nu was ruled by Che-muts, a king of great wisdom and power in his youth—but, after subjugating all the large cities of Arabinya, he became a tyrant, a man of wickedness.

Being learned in the Earth and moon and stars, Che-muts drew to his palace other men, and not a few women, of great learning, and, together, they resolved upon obtaining from the Ihins, the sacred little people, the secrets of their miracles and religion. Up to this time all the people in the world honored and respected the Ihins, for they were the forefathers and foremothers of the Ihuans.

Che-muts the tyrant said, "Because from our youth we have been taught to revere the Ihins, we have become superstitious

---

*The tall Ihuans were descendants of the Ihins—"they were called Ihuans because they were half-breeds betwixt the Druks and Ihins."[12]

regarding them. Now it is evident that they have some other means (than consulting the stars) of prophecy. It is my command, therefore, that their cities be seized, and the people put to death, offering succor only to such as reveal their secrets. With their gifts of miracles and power of prophecy, I can march successfully against Parsi'e (Persia), Jaffeth (China), and Ashem (India), and I shall become king of all the world. And ye that help me in this matter, instead of having merely cities to rule over, as ye now have, shall have kingdoms with many cities."

The learned men acceded to this, and, shortly after, the king's men fell upon the little people, pulled down their flimsy walls, putting them to flight or slaying them outright, and offering no salvation save they reveal their secrets, and give themselves up to intermarriage with the Ihuans.

Habbak was the name of the chief rab'bah (priest) of the Ihins.*

A very short, long-haired and bearded man garbed in black robe and little white cap, Habbak went to see the king and expostulate. He said unto Che-muts, "Behold, my people are older than this country. Our wisdom cometh not as other men's, but through marriage. How can we reveal? We are born veiled [with a caul]. No other people are thus born. How canst thou obtain the secrets of the womb? Besides this, we are sworn before our birth by our fathers and mothers to secrecy in our religion.

"Thou desirest us to intermarry with thy people. I foresee thy aims. Thou hopest for the gift of prophecy, which would give all power. But know thou, O king, he that desirest prophecy for such purpose can never obtain it. Prophecy cometh by the other road. If thou hadst our passwords and our signs, they would avail thee nothing, being born as thou art. I pray thee, then, to change thy decree and suffer my people to remain as they have, thousands of years!"

---

*There is a place in India, near Kashmir, called Habbak; the name is also found in ancient Sippar (Tell Habbah) as well as in Arabia and Syria, where the village uphill from Byblos is Beit *Habbak:* it is a name retained by the prestigious Habbaki family of Chemor—var. Chemuts?—a family of sheiks.

Che-muts, the king, said, "Why call ye yourselves Ihins?" Habbak said, "Because we are faithists in One Great Spirit." The king asked, "What is the secret name of the Great Spirit?" Habbak said, "I can only repeat that name under certain rules. Besides, whoever uttereth His name for earthly gain or earthly glory, uttereth in vain."

But the king only mocked him, and had him seized and taken to the lions' den, of which all kings and rich people, in those days, had one or more, as a place for casting in their disobedient servants. And when Habbak, who stood no higher than the king's shoulders, was at the lions' den, he said, "Though thou cast me in, and I be devoured,

Fig. 3.5. Cartoon of Habbak and Che-muts by Marvin E. Herring

suffer me beforehand to prophesy concerning thee and thy kingdom. Hear thou, then, my words:

"Not one thousand of my people canst thou destroy. Neither will my people raise a hand in self-defense. But thou wilt cast me into the lions' den, and I will be devoured. And this little hat, without a brim, will come out of the lions' den, and it will be a mighty power for thousands of years! It will be red with my blood, and it will be restored to my people, and it shall be called The Scarlet Hat! And in the day that it is carried in the streets of Os'nu, thou wilt be slain by thine own people!"

The king laughed, saying, "A prophecy often causeth fools to carry it out." With that, he gave the executioners the sign, and they pushed Habbak on the trap, and cast him into the den, where there were thirty lions. And they fell upon him and devoured him. And his hat was colored red with blood; and some of the people procured

Fig. 3.6. Cartoon of "The Scarlet Hat" by Marvin E. Herring

the hat and went about repeating the prophecy of Habbak. The multitude, of course, was anxious for some pretext to destroy the tyrant. So, presently, the city was in riot, and the people fell upon the king and slew him, and also slew the learned men and women who were his counselors and subsidiaries.

HABBAK

In the celestial counterpart of these stirring events, the God of Earth at that time, one Fragapatti (equivalent to India's beloved Prajapati), was sitting in the midst of his throne, when a light gathered above him, deep scarlet, with white border. And the Voice of the All Possible spake out of the light, saying, "Was I not with the Ihins since the creation of man on the Earth? And wherein they have been faithful unto me have I come in great security. Now, behold the Earth rose up against my chosen and sought to destroy them. And when they cast my faithful servant Habbak into the lions' den, yet would he not violate his oath, even though he suffered death. And I stretched forth my hand and took his hat, red with blood, out of the lions' den; and I gave power unto the hat. . . . Behold, I give you a new sign, and it shall be the Hi-rom (scarlet hat) from this time forth, signifying, Faith even unto death.

The Voice ceased, and Fragapatti turned to the red light and stretched forth his hand and took thereof, saying: Of Thy scarlet, O Jehovih! Give unto Thy servant a true Hi-rom! And he fashioned it into a cap without a brim, and laid it on the throne. Presently a swift messenger from without desired admittance before Fragapatti, announcing, "Behold, one Habbak is without, who was the wearer of Hi-rom!" And when the little angel-man Habbak entered, he went up to the throne. Fragapatti took the scarlet hat, saying, "Second only to the Creator's crown, with Hi-rom, cover I thy head in the name of

Fig. 3.7. Hirom icon. "Hirom" is the Ahamic word for red hat. In the Lodge, the master wears the red hat, and is saluted as cardinal.

the Almighty!" And he placed it on Habbak's head, and the light of it was so great that hardly any but ethereans (higher angels) could look upon it.

Then Habbak said, "By this, Thy Power, O Jehovih, will I go now and deliver unto everlasting light the king's soul, of him who slew me. And I will restore the Council also. For they will remember the scarlet hat, and it will be as an anchorage for their crazed minds to rest upon!" So Habbak saluted on the sign of high noon and departed.

OAHSPE, BOOK OF FRAGAPATTI, CHAPTER 37

A MIGHTY POWER

Given the story of Habbak, more than 8,000 years old, we have an almost unique opportunity to trace how an episode may trickle down through time to become first legend then myth. More to the point, we have at hand the evidence of a holy relic, the scarlet hat, being arrogated by those who would fain see their own name exalted and reverenced.

There is no doubt that Habbak's last prophecy ("This little hat will come out of the lion's den and will be a mighty power for thousands of years") was fulfilled! But elusive is the historical record when we try to cycle back past, say, the Egyptians or Sumerians; yet, cutting through that prehistorical fog, my colleague Vernon Wobschall, today's leading Oahspe annotator, discerns that line of continuity. He shared these thoughts with me by e-mail:

Now, because the Israelites from the time of Abraham were carrying the Light, they would have kept the hirom [red hat] in their ceremonies up to the time of Moses [who] . . . no doubt continued the tradition with the Israelites. But did the tradition continue only within [Moses'] *inner* temple, or was it also part of the outer temple as well?

The hirom was such a powerful symbol that apparently it was used in the outer temple—perhaps to build faith among the hangers-on . . . it would have been known there [in the Levant] because of the Babylonian captivity of the Jews. But is there evidence of it being there before that time? For example, did persecutions of [the sacred people] cause a scattering of tribes and a wide dispersal of the brimless hat in that cycle? Or is it because the Fonece [later called Phoenician] . . . faithists, perhaps under the Anubi rites, were the great [merchants and] traders of that cycle, and spread its presence abroad over the realms of Europe, Greece, Arabinya, and Persia?

Or, conversely, did the Phoenicians pick up the red hat in their overseas trade with Arabia, and perhaps beyond? Whichever way the legend traveled, let us have a look at how the outer temple *reworked* the legend of the scarlet hat.

THE RED HAT IN THE HOLY LAND

We have seen how the red "Phrygian cap" (already altered, and now a Santa Claus-type cap) reached across Europe by early Roman times, spreading from Abrahamic and Mosaic roots to Asia Minor (Phrygia) and thence to Italy (beretto frigio). Was it carried to Asia Minor by the Levite priests and scribes who moved across Anatolia? More than 4,000 years ago, a wave of people with "unusual amenities" and the scarlet clothing of the Levites entered Anatolia from the Bosphorus, bringing kingship and warfare—both of which the Israelites solemnly abjured. Who were these Levites? They were the outer temple of the Hebrews, the inner temple being the Oralites. Indeed, the Levites *usurped* the priesthood. "I gave . . . my ten commandments and ten invocations, to be not written but *spoken* [emphasis added] and taught from mouth to ear, to be sacred in the language given."[13]

For the inner temple was in spoken words only (hence the name "Oralites"), but the outer temple (Levite) was written—making Moses' Ten Commandments written on tablets quite unlikely, unless it was specifically intended for the outer court. The Rig Veda hymns, the earliest sacred texts of Hinduism, were kept by oral tradition, succumbing to written form only around the time of Moses. After Moses, many of the Jews began living under written laws and ceremonies (established in

Jerusalem by Ezra around 2344 BCE), worshipping the "Lord" and the "God," instead of the Creator himself. The scattered tribes of Oralites, though, still held to the One Great Spirit, keeping their service secret. And they were without sin, doing no war of evil against evil. Wherefore it was said, "The Hebrews have two laws; one which no man else knoweth; and one for them who are not eligible unto faith, being such as were called Leviticans [Levites] . . . hangers-on who had followed the Israelites out of Egypt and who for the most part had no God, little judgment and no learning."[14]

Levite priests butchered animals for sacrifice (Leviticus 27:32), a practice that all the true prophets condemned as abomination. Those who lived under the written law "were called Leviticans [Levites] . . . of imperfect flesh and spirit. But the Oralites were non-resistants, and they owned nothing, giving all things to the rab'bah for the public good. Their practice was love and harmony. . . . All the prophets and seers were born of the Oralites."[15]

When Moses was about to give up his soul, he said, "I feel a thorn pricking my side, and I know it is the Leviticans. They, not being eligible to the secret rite of Elohim (the Great Spirit), will in time to

Fig. 3.8. Moses, drawn under control by J. B. Newbrough (automatic drawing)

come possess the country and substitute their Lord God for the Great I Am."[16] Indeed, after Moses died, the Leviticans gained in numbers faster than the Oralites, worshipping Lord and God in place of Creator.

Even after millions of Israelites took kings under the false God Baal, others, still steadfast in the secret oral rites, remained true to the secret name (phonetically) and to the All Person—E-O-ih (a.k.a. Jehovih).

Now, if the Levites became animal sacrificers, the cult of Mithra made the slaughter of a bull the very heart and soul of their borrowed religion. They arrogated the holy red hat, its meaning lost: now it was not self, but a *bull* that must be sacrificed in a gory ceremony, a baptism in blood, on the presumption that all Evil may be embodied in the form of a beast—and thus vanquished! What folly! How far this concept of substitutes or even saviors strayed from the original meaning of sacrifice: "Let us perish for righteousness' sake, rather than do evil, Father Abraham."[17]

Mithraism, in its corrupted form, became wildly popular in the ancient world, traveling through the Pillars of Hercules to England and Scotland, crossing the channel to the north countries, entering the

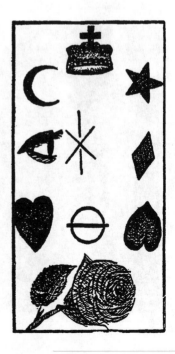

Fig. 3.9. Tablet of Hy'yi (Plate 78 from Oahspe). Before the cult of Mithra degenerated into an orgy of blood-spilling, Mithra the First (4,000 years ago) was a follower of Light. These are a few verses selected from their tablet Hy-yi (you can see the glyphs that correspond to the words **set in bold**): "My **heart** no longer looketh downward; my passions have I subdued. Yea, even the **diamond** binds me not . . . O thou **Moon**, hear my upward soul aspiring above all **corporeal** things! . . . Send forth Thy **Crown**, O creator of all moving things. O Thou Incomprehensible and full of glory! Make me oblivious to all corporeal things, and fill me with Thy going-forth forever." —Book of Saphah, Ho'ed

Danube and planting *mithrea* (lodges) throughout Germany. St. Augustine was an ardent Manichean, a sect that sprang from the ashes of Mithraism—which also made its way along the coast of northern Africa and into the Sahara. Did this North African incursion result in the hat of Fez, Morocco, the city famous for its manufacture of the brimless red "fez," called *tarboosh* by the locals? Is this where the Phoenicians, whose trade routes ran through Fez, picked up the legend of the scarlet hat?

The old Ottoman pashas wore the red tarboosh. The people of Abraham were quite settled in this region bordering Arabia—the legend of the hirom must have been transmitted to others through his people. The Arabic fez,* though, did not make its debut until the warriors of Allah usurped the martyr's cap.[18] Its bloody beginning traces back to the ninth-century massacre of "infidels" by the army of Islam, which invaded the Moroccan city now known as Fez. Tens of thousands of Christians were slaughtered there, while their attackers triumphantly dipped their hats in the river of mortal blood. Or so the story goes. How can this possibly agree with the Masonic or Shriner teaching that the Fez is a "mark of learning and scholarship"?

How far this is from harmless Habbak's hat and the principal of self-sacrifice! Mithra the false, by means of his own suffering and death, supposedly secured the salvation of his votaries. But Habbak secured no one's salvation: His death was for his faith alone!

The Sufi order, we know, has its own martyred Sheikh Haydar, his devotees known as Red Hats (Kizilbash), after "Haydar's Crown." And though their inspiration draws on authentic priestly lore of Arabinya, they too became warriors, "men of the sword," far indeed from the gentle pacifists who first gave the world the scarlet hat.

We find that the Freemasons (the Church's eternal nemesis) may justly wear the scarlet hat, if only because they, like the Ihins of old, profess no Lords or Saviors or salvation by proxy, but only faith in the Great Spirit, the Almighty Master, whom they call "The Architect." Enraged by their "blasphemy," the church fathers countered by attacking the Masonic

---

*Red and brimless, the fez, which even the American Shriners took on as their mystic headgear, is also worn in Polynesia and Peru.

tale of Hiram Abiff, calling it "mere legend" and biblical plagiarism, and dubbing their Grand Master Hiram a "pseudo-Christ," and so on.

Masonry, however, measured against these histories, is dramatically vindicated. The age-old Order maintains an oath of secrecy and passwords; holds "Jao" (like Jahu, Jehova, etc.) as the Ineffable Name; marks the grave with branches of acacia, just as the Ihins used that evergreen in their rites to signify Immortality of the soul.* The Masons pay adoration to the Master of All at the hour of high twelve, just as the sacred people saluted in the sign of high noon (and the fairy kingdom kept that hour sacred for their ceremonies). Finally, the Masons devote their mission to the helpless and distressed, just as upliftment was the great mission of the Ihin priesthood.

The Vatican's cardinals, on the other hand, may not be entitled to wear the scarlet hat. The cardinal approaches the Holy Father, kneels before him and receives his biretta; the pope places the biretta on the cardinal's head saying: "This is red, as a sign of the dignity of the office of a cardinal, signifying that you are ready to act with fortitude, even spill your blood for the increase of the Christian faith . . . and for the spread of the Holy Roman Catholic Church." But when was the last time you heard of a cardinal spilling his own blood for his faith?

Nor did the wearer of hirom ever promote a god or savior or go out for conquest and Crusades. Vernon Wobschall, again, helped me through the theological thicket of these histories by pointing out that when Christ replaced Baal, the clergy no doubt saw the advantage of the blood-red brimless hat. By early Christian times, the symbol of the red hat was well-known and respected. "One wonders," Wobschall adds, "whether the heavenly officers of [Christendom] . . . around the mid-1200s [at which time the biretta was established in the Holy Roman Empire] felt that their kingdom was deserving of the faith-till-death message of the red cap. . . . The hirom could be seen, after all, as a type of victory sign. . . . The rallying cry of Blood for Christ's sake—meaning, go to *war* for it—had finally paid off."

Thus it came to pass that taking the red hat to exalt one's office or

---

*Still sacred in Arabia and also the tree of Osiris in Egypt, acacia was the prime oracular tree in Canaan. Noah's ark was made of acacia wood, while the Essenes edged their compounds with these pretty trees. The underlying meaning, in all cases, was Eternal Life.

one's campaign or one's favorite god became fashionable in the ancient world, and no sooner did it travel to other lands (most likely through the Phoenicians) than cunning hands seized its gospel, deploying its power for other demagogic ends. Kings took over where martyrs left off, and now in Korea a cord of red silk is worn by a person if he has been touched by the king—it is considered sacred. In Peru, only the royal (and despotic) Inca enjoyed the privilege of wearing the red ilatu on their aristocratic pates, the headpiece—a fathom long—consisting of a scarlet band wrapped four times around the head. The Techuitle, an Aztec people, also bind the head with a red fillet, to signify membership in an "eminent order of merit," consisting of the bravest and most distinguished men.[19] We also might ask how Panama's San Blas Indians came to use a red dance crown that is unique in all of South America: they said it was a relic of ancient times worn only by the chief.

In Nicaragua, Hirom's hat is truly echoed: the tyrant Somoza fed rebels to the panthers in his private zoo (echoes of Chemut's lions den). And when the freedom fighter Sandino was assassinated by Somoza's thugs, it was Sandino's hat that became the most potent icon in Nicaragua.

In the late eighteenth century the Easter Island monuments were still surmounted by "redstone topknots." These cylinders of red stone were fashioned to make the headdress (*pukao*) of the famous *moai* statues, with their forbidding, intimidating countenance. Its red color is held sacred by the islanders: the color of dried blood. They say it is a sign of knowledge. But how did the Red Cap theme reach the Pacific? Phrygians and Phoenicians held supremacy at sea, and as Barry Fell, in *America B.C.,* has shown, Libyan navigators (kin to the Phrygians) crossed the Pacific. In 1973, Fell demonstrated convincing links between the Libyan and Polynesian languages, as well as Oceanic links to the Anatolian (Phrygian) sea peoples.

> Libyan influence spread far and wide especially in the Indo-Pacific region . . . some of them settling parts of the Pacific . . . the early Polynesian inscriptions are essentially Libyan . . . [and] the Anatolian elements in Polynesia . . . are consistent with a Libyan origin.
>
> BARRY FELL, *AMERICA, B.C.*

By yarrow and rue, and my red cap too,
Hie over to England.

"The Witches' Excursion"

THE SYMBOL OF THE CAUL

It is curious that a certain malevolence attaches to some members of
Europe's elfin kingdom who don the red hat (usually pointed): garden
gnomes of Europe, the notorious kallikantzaros of Greece, the Barabao
shape-shifters of Venice, the Cornish piskies (pixies). The little people
living inside the Irish rath of Enniscorthy also wear the red hat. Sprites
known as Redcaps in the British Isles are the wicked goblins, four feet
tall, who inhabit ruined castles and murder travelers who stray into their
homes. They dye their hats with their victims' blood. Today, pop culture
follows suit with juvenile games, such as the popular trading card game
"Magic," which features a card by the name of Murderous Redcap. Here
a goblin is depicted, brandishing a dripping dagger and blood-soaked hat.

Ruby and carbuncle was the crown so rich,
Which upon his head bare the little Elberich.

Caps of the northern elves are reputed to make them invisible (a
bit like Pluto's Helmet of Invisibility, forged in the Underworld of the
dwarfs). The dwarfs of Rugen glide invisibly into people's houses, their
caps rendering them imperceptible. One of the most acclaimed artifacts of the Norse dvergar (dwarfs) is their "concealing helmet," affording them instant invisibility. Portugal also has the cap of invisibility in
its folklore, and so does India, whose *yeck* is a shape-shifting demon,
his cap conferring invisibility. Acquiring one of these elfin caps made
you safe and invulnerable; the power of the little people would help
you hide, and give you courage. Perseus, son of Danae, succeeded in his
quests by aid of just such a cap. The worst thing that could befall the
underground people, the elves, is to lose their cap. The *fuddittu* (Sicilian
elf) loses all his powers if his red cap is taken away.

But this "cap" is not really a cap, rather it is a metaphor of the infant caul (or veil or "skin-cap"), associated with Ihin births and with the gift of supernatural powers. In Iceland and Norway, for example, the child born with a caul (*fylgiar*), the membrane over his head, is considered very lucky. He or she will be attended by a blessed spirit, acting as his double, warning him of danger; only those with the gift of second sight can actually see this double, which is itself called *fylgiar*.

In far-off Tibet, too, magic and sorcery are strongly associated with the Red Hat Bon monks (in contradistinction to Yellow Hat Buddhism, the more reforming school to which the Dalai Lama belongs). Helena Blavatsky, the nineteenth century's Empress of the Occult, warned of this sect of Tibetan mystics known as the Red Hats. The tulku lamas, it seems, would monopolize the red hat, the hirom, to reinforce their hereditary rights to fiefdom, wearing the scarlet crown called "Shamar" as symbol of their lofty office. At one time, theosophical students spread fear of any Tibetan who utilizes a red hat or crown. While the great master Padmasambava, known as the second Buddha, donned a red hat, as do many lamas besides, it is the Bon sorcerers in particular who are associated with black tantrism and other unsavory rites.

We can appreciate how the allegory of Buddha's "red hood" draws from the faded memory of Habbak's "veiled" people—born with the caul of insight; for in the esoteric tradition of Zen, Buddha's red hood is the key to the well-known episode where Bodhidharma spends nine years in a cave immersed in "wall contemplation" (read: uterine wall). This, Buddhist scholars tell us, is an embryological allegory. The nine years represent the nine months spent in the womb.

The initiate asks: Tell me about Bodhidharma with the caul. Answer: During the nine months spent in the maternal womb, the caul is put on—the equivalent of Bodhidharma putting on a skin cap during his "nine years before the wall." It is the donning of the caul.

Here, with substantial changes, have the Buddhists lifted a sacred motif from the holy tribes of old Arabia. For in the olden day, only the little people were (genetically) equipped to hear the Master's Voice, for they came into the world veiled, the caul or hood or "head helmet," like the thin membrane of amnion that covers the newborn mammal at birth. When a human is born with the caul, with the amniotic sac still intact, the sac balloons out, covering the baby's face as he emerges into the breathing world.

The veil, it was believed in aftertime, protects its bearer against danger; thus was it superstitiously gathered and preserved as a valuable charm against malevolent spirits. The caul, moreover, made one "special," even destined for greatness (some famous caul-babies include Liberace, Sigmund Freud, Napoleon Bonaparte, Edwin Booth). He may become a saint, as in Grimm's tale of a boy born with the caul who grows up "full of virtues," a "luck-child." (The king, of course, is jealous and orders him killed—then, of course, his plan is foiled.)

The caul has long been a cardinal sign of clairvoyance and divination, for its possessors, as Habbak expostulated, were born with the Seeing, and just as the Mayan sages say the first humans possessed the cosmic sense, their sight encompassing the universe. Lord Byron, Khalil Gibran, Marie Laveau (the voodoo queen of New Orleans), and Peter Hurkos the Seer were all born veiled, which, as tradition holds, "enables him to see spirits."[20]

More common in premature births, the caul is rather rare. As a good luck portent among the Romans, it was tantamount to being born with a silver spoon in one's mouth. Such a child, it was thought in Scotland, will be a fey—that is, a psychic—and awarded with a fairy companion (the fylgiar). With the caul-bearer's supernatural powers, he can divine the future and protect anyone from harm against the forces of evil, particularly witches. The Benandanti of medieval Italy were a pagan agrarian cult of those born with the caul, all of whom could see ghosts and true witches. At night they had the power to go out and do battle with an army of witches, but then the Inquistion got wind of them.

It was a strong belief that one would never drown if he possessed a caul (related to the caul-bearing survivors of the Flood?), which was then eagerly sought as a talisman by sailors, willing to pay almost any price when on their way to sea. Carefully preserved, the caul was worn about the neck as a sort of amulet.

I would not be surprised if the caul also merges with the lore of the *caul*dron, or magic vase, for such can usually be traced back to *Homo pygmaeus,* be it the fairy cauldron at Borough-hill in Surrey, or the Norse cauldron of Odhrerir, which held the draft of poets and—having been concocted by the dwarfs—imparted ancient wisdom and occult knowledge. Add to these the Welsh cauldron of Cerridwwen, which confers oracles and inspiration, the inexhaustible cauldron of Dagda (one of the four magical treasures the Tuatha De Danaan brought to Ireland), and the magical cup, which can divine truth, given by Ma*nannan,* not unlike the "magic vase" of Taliesen, adorned with pearls and given to the little korrigans—it contains the "wondrous water of universal knowledge"— is this not the opened mind, the enlightened mind?

Other korrigan stories of Celtic provenance recount the celebration of a great nocturnal festival each spring, whose centerpiece is a "crystal cup" emitting its own magical light; at the end of the banquet, the cup goes round, a single drop of its liquid making one "as wise as God himself." The cauldron may be a chalice or cup or jar or vase or jug . . . or even the Holy Grail. We hear of many attempts in Celtic folklore to steal the magic cauldron—all of which are foiled somehow by a Prince of the Other World. In fact, numerous ancient people produced head-shaped effigy jars (Chimu of Peru, Arkansas, Troy, Etruria, Mycenae, and others).

Stripped of all phantasmagoria, the powers that mythological characters draw from a cauldron are those of the veiled head, cup, or *kapf* belonging to the wise and gifted little people of yore.

Once, a cherished ambrosial cauldron was stolen from the fairy hills—a great treasure with magical powers: The Rillaton Cup. A Bronze Age golden treasure, now in the British Museum, it was found in a barrow (sidhe) in Cornwall, and recalls the story of a Druid who graciously handed out drinks to passing travelers, served in a golden goblet. One day a greedy hunter galloped away with the goblet; his horse, though, fell and the hunter broke his neck, the goblet still clutched in his hand. It was buried with him in Rillaton Barrow.[21]

Kind of reminds you of Habbak's warning to King Che-muts: the treasure of the little people is worthless in the hands of the worldly minded. In folktales, everywhere, especially fairy lore, there are countless yarns of this type, warning that those who prey on great prizes usually suffer a downfall, not knowing the simple key: Good Faith. Even faith unto death!

CHAPTER 4

The Paragon

The knowledge we possess about the past is only a small portion of the complete story of mankind.

ANDREW TOMAS, *WE ARE NOT THE FIRST*

DANCERS OF GOD

In chapter 3, we stepped into one moment in time, the time of Habbak and the sacred people who were almost like little gods on Earth: a paragon for the rest of humanity. History, on the other hand, paints its heroes and civilizers as tall Aryans, the contribution of the little people totally lost to the mists of time. Yet it is curious that the peoples to whom musicologists have turned to for the ultimate in song and sound are the pygmies of Gabon and Ituri, Bushmen of southwest Africa, Semang of the Malay jungle, Negritos of Malacca, Veddas of Ceylon, Andamanese, and Solomon Islanders: all little people. This is hardly a coincidence.

As long ago as 4,500 years came the first recorded mention of Africa's pygmies. An expedition to find the source of the Nile, sponsored by Pharaoh Nefrikare in the Fourth Dynasty, stumbled upon "a tiny people who sing and dance to their god" in a great forest near the Mountains of the Moon (today's Uganda). The commander sent a report to his king that such extraordinary dancing had never been seen before. Nefrikare replied, ordering his expedition leader to bring him one of these Dancers of God.

The lapse of four and a half millennia has not changed too much for the forest people, whose exceptional style of music and dance has attracted musicologists, particularly to Gabon and the Congo's Ituri rainforest. UNESCO has collected field recordings and archived them. There is pygmy music online, too, including "timeless vocals" by a chorus of women. Even the Twa men will sing their baby to sleep with a sonorous lullaby. Walking through their beloved forest, the pygmies may start dancing and make up songs as they go along. They imitate and improvise; they yodel and harmonize their "cascading melodies." These communal vocals are characterized by dense contrapuntal improvisation and complex polyphonic music, not attained by Europeans until the fourteenth century.

Music permeates the daily life of the Twa. "At all times the forest was full of the song and dance of life."[1] Twa, the very ancient name of Central Africa's pygmies, simply means people, race, or nation. (Further north are the *Tua*reg tribes of the Moroccan Sahara, a people with a mysterious written language of great antiquity: Tifinar.) Once a universal term, Twa or Tua or Tuan continues to be used by today's little people (in Malaysia, Kalahari, etc.) to signify European or Caucasian or even "White God." Among the Maru-*tua*ha tribes (Maori), Earth Mother is **Papa*tua*nuku**—*atua,* in Maori, means "a god"; the chief was also an atua. Among the Papuans, the way to address a European is *tuana,* meaning "master" or "sir."

The term is most likely Panic, for we find it in:

- Polynesia: atua = god or tutelary idol, as well as the spirit living in mortals and nature, but especially in their very sacred ancestral leader. The king who brought writing was named Hotu Ma*tua.*
- West Ceram: *tua*le = the Sun Man.
- Australia: The *Ina*-per-*twa* were the very first human beings, according to the aborigines of Arunda; atua means "man's spirit." *Twa*n yirika = the Great Spirit, while Atua Oknurcha is their Moon God.
- Celebes: home of the small *Toa*la people (women 4 feet 6 inches).

Tua found its way to the European lexicon as well: Consider the *Tua*-tha De Danaan and the Irish giants called Tuath Fidga; another Irish hero of royal lineage was *Tua*n MacCairill. *Tua*m is also remembered in County Galway. *Tua* turns up just as readily in America, too: the Towa were the little people of the Mi'k Maq tribe; and in South America as well, hinting once again at the Original Unity of man before the great diaspora of the Flood. The predynastic Incas had an alternate name for Viracocha: *Tua*-paca. Tua also happens to be an old name of the Nile River.[2] How far back does this name go?

Long, long ago, the name "Tua Git" was given to the sacred little people of China—meaning "men of spiritual light"—reminding us a bit of the Twa people, pharaoh's "Dancers of God." The word *git* by itself meant "light," as in *git'oo,* "light ahead" (Panic). It also meant, by extension, "moon"; thus *git-hi,* in Old Persian, signified "star." In Algonquin, *git* meant "sun" and *git-che* meant "lord." In Ebra (precursor of Hebrew, see fig. 4.1 below) git signified "the gentle moon," also denoting "sacred"; which quite possibly morphed into Indo-Germanic *gut,* cognate of English "good." *Git'hoi* in Chinese was "good healing."[3]

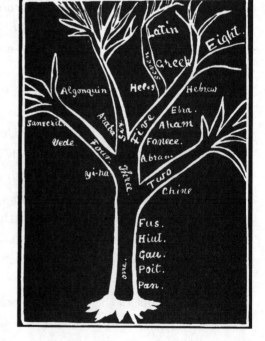

Fig. 4.1. Language Tree, from *Oahspe*

My chosen shall preserve the four days of the change of the moon as sacred days.

OAHSPE, THE LORDS' FIRST BOOK 1:66

Significantly, the Mayan calendar was originally based on the lunar year, determining their ritual calendar. Moon-oriented were the old votaries of the holy people, the Tua Git, for its cycles were the times set aside for worship. Thus do we find the **Sumerian moon god** with the dwarf appellation Nanna: he who controls time by lunar months and knows the destiny of all. Just so, the mythological Norse dvergar not only support the world, but govern the waxing and waning lunar phases.

Thou shalt labor six days, but on the seventh it is the moon's day
. . . and thou shalt go to the altar of thy Creator and dance and
sing. . . . Keep holy the four days of the moon, for they are the
Lord's days.[4]

Later, in Exodus 20:8, we are told to "remember the Sabbath day, to keep it holy."

The Hebrews reckoned by the moon, King David of Israel declaring: "Blow the trumpet in the New Moon . . . on our solemn feast day . . . for this is a law of the god of Jacob." Indeed, reckoning by the moon was one of the traits that nineteenth-century ethnologists found among Native Americans, causing them to take the "Red Man" as one of the Lost Tribes of Israel!* The observant tribes of India also kept holy the moon days, and here, *git* came to mean "song" (e.g., Bhagavad *Gita*)— for sacred singing ceremonies took place according to the phases of the moon. Similarly, among the Polynesians whom Captain Cook encountered, the four phases of the moon entailed taboo periods of time. Africa's Hottentots also perform sacred ceremonies according to the phases of the moon. But not for a minute was the moon *deified* by the holy tribes: only its phases observed in a sacred manner.

---

*By 11,000 BCE the only three tribes in the world that retained the sacred teachings of Noah's sons were the faithists of the Hebrews, the Vedics, and the Algonquins.

Fig. 4.2. Ancient glyphs incorporating Git, Light: "Let my chosen keep the four holy days of rest during each moon, for on these days do my guardian angels change the watch."[5]

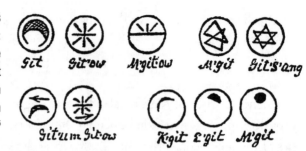

Long ago, when these rites were held, "the Ihins *clapped their hands* [emphasis added] at every step. These ceremonies were [held] at least once for every quarter of the moon."[6] The sacred tribes *never* worshipped the sun (a later fiction); they were more moon people, like today's Negritos who still keep holy the moon days and the dance steps: the Siamese Semang, for one, dance every month at the time of the full moon, the women "*clapping* their hands"—a custom started long ago by the Ihins, the very first religionists on Earth—and it is continued by their descendants, the Ainu, whose women clap their hands during ritual dance. In Europe, Brittany's tiny korrigans used to dance at the full of the moon; fairies, as a rule, come out at night to dance, sing, and make merry. On moonlit nights they would, back in the day, do their circular dances at ancient burial sites, leaving "fairy rings" on the ground.

In far-off Hawaii, the little Menehune also enjoyed dancing and singing, and like the brownies and other household sprites halfway around the word, they could be heard chanting as they skitter about at night, helping around the house.

An interesting twist: the Saisyat, the shortest of Taiwan's aboriginal tribes, must have once intermarried with *Homo pygmaeus,* judging from their Ceremony of the Pygmies, called *pas-ta'ai.* Local legend says a group of pygmies once taught the Saisyat to sing and dance, but because they (allegedly) molested the women, they were entrapped and massacred; hence, the ceremony is meant to appease those spirits, and is held on the tenth full moon. This tradition not only suggests interbreeding, but also underscores the recurrent theme of persecution and genocide of the little people.

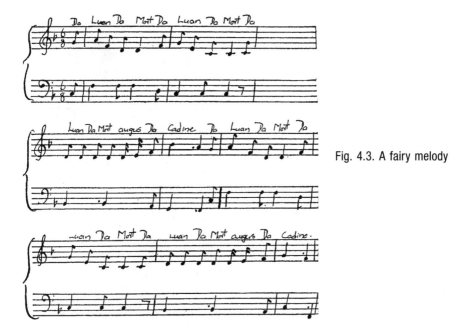

Fig. 4.3. A fairy melody

The Bushman of southern Africa holds special dances at certain states of the moon. These little people of the Kalahari follow the practice of the holy tribes, clapping their hands rhythmically during the medicine dance, singing and clapping. "For Bushmen, their music is by far their greatest art," their mood songs "rich in every note."[7] The spirits of the dead, the gauas, also attend; it lasts all night.

All these singers and choristers are renowned in each of their particular locales for their superlative music and its transcendent quality, so attuned to the spirit world. If the gentry have sweet, silvery voices, the singing of the Welsh little people, the Tylwyth Teg, is "exquisite . . . a soft strain . . . of rapturous sweetness,"[8] approximating the fine voices of the two-feet-tall korrigans of Breton, and not unlike the fairy music of the Maori, so "enchanting to the ear." In America, too, Georgia's little people, the Nunnehi (or Yunwi Tsunsdi) are great lovers of music; sometimes deep in the woods, beautiful songs can be heard.

A wayfarer in the German countryside heard the sound of distant music of uncommon, "inspiriting" tones, then saw a number of little men and women who had joined hands and were whirling around in a dance of great delight and singing thereto "in the sweetest manner possible." In

Fig. 4.4. Chaldean bas-relief at Lagash, showing a scene of worship; note the (short-statured) figure clapping hands to the ode of the singer below. The custom of clapping was retained also by the Creek Indians, the Aeta,* and the Malaysian Negritos in their spirit-linking singing sessions.

the same general region, on the Isle of Rugen, the White Dwarfs would come forth in the dead of night, when mortals sleep, and dance their joyous roundels making the sweetest and most delicate music.

The Ihins of old, we learn, spoke in delightfully musical voices, remembered no doubt in the figure of Europe's tree nymphs, the Dryads (up to three feet tall) who possessed a voice "so musical . . . like the bubbling of springs."[9] The speech of Chile's Yahgan little people is likewise musical and soft, very much like that of Africa's forest pygmy, who is known to speak in a lilting, sing-song way. This sweet voice is one of many signatures of *Homo pygmaeus,* and it is interesting that the Panic word *him* meant "sweet" (i.e., gentle like a "hymn"). Finally, the elf kingdom is renowned for "sweet singing, sweet and soft like the air." In Eastern Europe as well, the fairies are renowned for "the sweetest ditties."

---

*One of the most charming videos I have seen online is of an Aeta boy singing "You'll Always Be My Baby." Available at www.youtube.com, search on "Aeta/Ita Boy Singing" (accessed July 25, 2012).

WORK BY DAY, SING BY NIGHT

What made their manner and their music so uncommonly sweet, so heavenly, so *entrancing?* Yes, many did sing themselves into a kind of trance, as the customs of today's little people attest. There is pygmy music that is intentionally monotonous, meant to induce an altered state of consciousness. Indeed, the Panic word *chawnt* meant "monotonous singing to induce trance." Trance-dancing is at least 20,000 years old, portrayed in the celebrated shamanic cave art of the Paleolithic.[10]

The Negritos of Batek build large huts (*haya' tebew*) especially for singing sessions; sweet-smelling flowers are brought in to decorate the hut and performers. The Batek work by day and sing by night—all night—during which some participants, often the shaman, might go into trance to be one with the spirits. Among the Semang, the *cenoi* (spirit guides) can possess the shaman in trance, speak to people through him, and convey songs or instructions for curing.

Both the Semang (Malay) and Aeta (Filipino) Negritos maintain the great tradition of *recitative* song, not unlike the Peruvian *haravecs,* a class of priests who sang the national dramas; or like the Hawaiians who chant their histories and genealogical accounts, the memorized recital of their Creation poem running to 2,000 lines! Until recently, their forebears, the Tahitians, could chant all the legends of the ancestors. In the

Fig. 4.5. Lenggong ceremonial platform constructed for singing on the seventh night after a death.

South Seas, we also encounter the mysterious "singing boards" of Easter Island, the indecipherable rongorongo tablets that are believed to be, not a system of writing, but rather a memory device for hymn-singers, who use the symbols as reminders of stories and lengthy ritual chants.

In the Old World, one of the earliest traditions says that Osiris, the great civilizer of Egypt, passed on his teachings by means of hymns and songs. This was the ancient way, just as the biblical Psalms and Persian Gathas were sung to preserve the words of the prophets and the Oral Law. In America, the Pawnee and other tribes sang the creation story. So did the Hopi, whose saga records that the world just prior to ours was destroyed by a flood with waves taller than mountains: "They were enjoined to sing . . . the songs of the flood [to] establish its history to endure forever on earth."[11]

Indeed, the faithful ones who did not forsake the teachings given by the Great Spirit were the very people, the chosen people, who survived that consuming disaster. The kachinas (supernatural beings impersonated by present-day men of the kiva society) play a central role in Hopi ceremonial life; when the Hopi first emerged from the underworld (that is, the Flood) they were accompanied by the kachinas, whose songs and dances helped them establish the new Earth. Later, the Hopi replicated the kachina's masks and costumes to maintain contact with them and perform the songs and dances they had taught them so long ago.

Fig. 4.6. A picture from Hopiland, of Hopi-Tewa potter Helen Naha. I stayed at First Mesa, summer 1967, on my first field trip, studying the Tewa language.

The Hopi singer intones the drama of escaping from their flooded homeland. The rite of song, still held at Oraibi, Arizona, recounts the rising water, the frightened people, and the miraculous escape.

Among the Peruvian Indians, old songs were handed down from very ancient times telling of the flood, the darkness, and the coming of the teachers who arrived "with a great fleet of rafts," like Naymlap who led a small armada of balsamwood boats, arriving in America from the Pacific. Other South American coastal legends-in-song recall the landing of a strange people whose country had been destroyed, people from the South Seas. The ancient songs of the Tupis of Brazil relate "destruction by a violent inundation . . . a long time ago . . . only a very few escaping."[12]

The saga was classically given in twelve parts: On the Plains, the painter and humanitarian George Catlin witnessed and described the Flood Dance of the Mandan Indians, performed by twelve men around their "ark." Concerning this number twelve, John Ballou Newbrough remarked: "The Indians who followed the Ihins were worshippers of Egoquim [the Great Spirit], and they kept up the dance; even to this day [late nineteenth century] some of the tribes have preserved the whole *twelve* dances [emphasis added]." In the case of the Mandan, their twelve dancers seem to represent the original twelve dances, just as among the Seneca, twelve women sing the chorus paying homage to the "Great Little People" in their Dark Dance ritual, which remembers the "pygmies" who taught them their sacred songs.

SHARING IS THE RULE

Something else peculiar to the Tua Git, the Little People of Light, is their gentle, collective—even harmonious—way of life, usually with women on an equal footing with men, as discovered, for example, among the Andamanese in the Bay of Bengal, and the Yahgan. In Yahgan society there is equality in all things, no chiefs or rulers, women shamans as well as men. Joseph Campbell once pointed out that "the little Yahgans . . . the Pygmies of the Congo and of the Andaman Islands . . . do not [have] . . . a strong patriarchal or matriarchal emphasis;

rather, an essential equality prevails . . . [with] no special privileges or peculiar rights to command. . . . Nor do the rites involve any physical deformation."[13] And this is how James Churchward described the *first* civilization, on the continent of Mu (the submerged land): "they had a communistic form of government."[14] In the same vein, the pioneer anthropologist, A. H. Verrill, who conducted extensive field work for the Museum of the American Indian (Heye Foundation), dubbed South America's little Akuria people as "communistic": utterly without kings or emperors, tyrants or despots.

> *Their lifestyle is communal.*
>
> PHILO, ON THE ESSENES

As we have already seen, the *earliest* Hebrews (Oralites) were of the same persuasion. They owned nothing, giving everything to the rabbah (spiritual headman) for the public good; neither would they live under kings. Nor did the Tua Git of China have any king, serving the Lord only. The same sort of disposition was found in earliest America, where the sacred people "lived without kings or governors. . . . And the tribes were made into states, with chief rabbahs as representatives, and these states were united into the Algonquin government, made and maintained for the benefit of tribes that might suffer by famines."[15]

Today, of all the extant tribes in America, the Hopi, the "Little People of Peace" (as the missions named them), reflect most faithfully this ancient way. It is god-made not man-made laws that they honor. The village chief, as of old, is their *spiritual* leader. His job is to constantly exemplify and enlist the proper observance of things, and to preserve the welfare of his people. Actual force is seldom required, for public opinion among the Hopi is the most effective control. To the casual visitor, government is so lacking in form as to seem nonexistent. "But back of this disarmingly artless administration lies organization and discipline that might well be emulated outside of Hopi country."[16]

Neither do the Negritos of Malaysia have a tribal organization: there is virtually no political power in Batek society; no one can coerce another, not even husband or parent. Sharing is the rule:* the women do not fail to bring samples of their daily meal to neighbors, wrapped in leaves. There is a "low level of conflict within Batek society."[17] In the rain forest, children play boisterously but have few competitive games. And although Aeta children have foot races and vine-climbing contests, nevertheless, these Filipino little people "attained a degree of social unity and cooperation . . . never observed before."[18] The Aeta have no sense of money or land ownership.

Among Malaysian Negritos, the *penghulu* (headman) is only a spokesman for outsiders. It is not too different among the little people of the Kalahari Desert in Africa: Among the Bushmen who call themselves zhu twa si, "the harmless people" (note the universal *twa*), the headman is "virtually indistinguishable" from the people he leads. Neither is it "in their nature to fight." They simply don't allow *envy* to build up: "Their culture insists that they share with each other."[19]

To the north, among the forests of Central Africa, the Pygmies (Twa) have no form of chieftainship at all. Their "leader" actually has no authority, and is little more than a reference point for outsiders. African pygmies wander across hunting territories that are collectively "owned" by the whole group. In their egalitarian society, survival depends on the work of everyone in the group. The big hunt requires seven nets to form a wide enough circle—very much a group affair. One finds no witchcraft and no war among these little people. Negritos of Malacca and other Malay regions never make war either; murder is virtually unknown.

Far to the north of Africa, we recognize something of this collective purpose and partnership in the social compact of Ireland's little people, who worked together with "astonishing activity and perseverance."[20] Brittany's Temple of Carnac with 4,000 large stones, locals say,

---

*If Malay magicians jealously guard their secrets, their Negrito countrymen freely share with each other the cures they learn from the *hala'* (shaman or spirit guide)—and never for pay. As for economics, the Semang communal clearing for planting (*lading*) is common property of the whole group; The Pleh, a Senoi people, live in a communal house and cultivate a communal clearing to which each member has equal rights.

is the work of the Gorics, the little men no more than three feet tall, who carried these enormous masses *on their hands*. Now, we have heard some wild theories and outré legends supposedly explaining how colossal megaliths and monuments were put in place. At Tiahuanaco, for instance, Spanish visitors in colonial times were told that the stones had been lifted miraculously off the ground and carried through the air to the sound of a trumpet! A similar but equally improbable tale presumes to explain the impressive earthworks and megaliths of Ireland, built by the Danaan—those aristocrats, scientists, and poets, their architecture a marvel in mathematics and engineering. Music, it was supposed, was their principal magic; by manipulating harmonics they could lift and move massive objects: "possibly even planets!"

But this is pure moonshine. The only magic indicated is the magic—the miracle—of Unity: harmony and mutual effort! The little people of Ireland built (as did the Menehune) with *many hands working together,* making any task easier and quicker. So coordinated and spritely were these people that the stones seemed to fly through the air. To the little Danes and Pechts (Picts) are ascribed all the marvelous raths and souterrains of their region; in northeast Antrim, the Pechts, when making a fort, are said to have stood in a long line, handing the sod from one to another. No one moves a step. In building the round Tower of Abernathy, says an 1823 account, the Pechts stood in a very long row "handing the stones one to another"—in the very same way that the great pyramid of Cholula was built, according to the Aztecs: by passing the bricks "from hand to hand."[21]

THE ISLANDS OF WISDOM

In Europe the task of the Margot fairies, reputedly born of the moon (moon people), is to "educate human beings in every field"; as mentors, they have "guided primitive societies with their wise counsel"—even after they die, for they are "chosen souls."[22] In the same way, the Cornwall brownie is a distinguished mentor who teaches children patience, courage, and trust. All the little people of the British Isles, so easily confused with spirits, brownies, fairies, or **gods** were, nonetheless, flesh-

and-blood mortals, known at one time as the Gentry, the Good People. The Daoine Sidhe, say the chronicles, came from the oldest, noblest families of "perfected men." Echoing "Sidhe" are the Siddhi in India, meaning "philosopher."

All told, the earthly counterpart of the fairy is a genteel race, leading mankind in civility and knowledge; little in size but big in character. Thus does legend remember them as inhabitants of "the Islands of Wisdom." Under constant guidance from high-raised angels, the Ihins of old (12,000 years ago) were a living "sermon before the tribes of druks and cannibals that covered the earth over."[23]

Virtuous were the fée (Spanish *fe* means "faith"), many stories declaring their faithfulness; when the fée give advice, it should be followed to the letter—for they have correctly predicted years of famine, war, and plague to the Swiss, and given the science of prophecy to the Bretons. Reclusive, the Good People on the Isle of Man preferred to dwell away in the hills, owing to "their dislike of the vices of town"; they were a holy and pure race, and the households that they deigned to visit were thought to be blessed.

In Yucatan, dwarfs were sacred to the sun god, just as the Egyptians had their **dwarf gods**. The Cherokee recognized the Nunnehi as "the Immortals," while Europe's fairies were called the Ageless Ones

Fig. 4.7. Mexican god of well-being and good luck, the dwarf Macuilxochitl, not unlike Ekkeko of the Andes who, also portrayed as a little man, brings good fortune to the household. Chickcharnies and Geow-lud-mo-sis-eg are also omens of good luck, as is the dwarf god of Egypt, Bes.

(the elves, in olden tradition, "lived a thousand years"). The Tuatha De Danaan, People of Light, and heroes of the old Irish, showed all the signs of immortality, for hadn't their forebears been the first men on Earth to attain everlasting life?

In the Scottish lowlands, a lad who, without hesitation, joined in a fairy fest, "thrave like a breckan," (thrived like a weed) and became a proverb for wisdom and an oracle for knowledge ever after. In fact, the ancient Welsh bards openly *revered* a being named "korid-gwen" (akin to the korrigan and goric), who possessed universal knowledge. The Welsh fairies detested nothing so much as lies, being strict lovers of truth. The leprechauns, too, never told a lie; a paragon for all, they were the elect of the Earth.

Fig. 4.8 (left). A protecting amulet from a terracotta figurine of Assyrian date, used to repel the evil spirits.

Fig. 4.9 (right). Alabaster statue of Nebo, Assyrian and Chaldean soothsayer, prophet, and inventor of writing, his temple at Borsippa. Both figures depicted as little men.

Fig. 4.10. A green enameled statuette shows Mesopotamian Shu uplifting the sky; his priesthood bridged heaven and Earth. Shu was King of the sky, Earth, Hades, water, mountains, and winds.

There is a verse in *Irish Colloquy of the Ancients* referring to the worship of the Sidhe, the Good People in the fairy knolls. This brings us, in turn, to Egyptian and Olmec *reverence* of the dwarfs, a race regarded as directly connected to the gods; for they, the pure tribes of little people—the Ihins—were in constant communion with the angels, who had been assigned as guardians over them from the beginning. As standard-bearers of the higher realms, some little people were even depicted *holding up* the heavens: the four dwarfs Austri, Vestri, Sudri, and Nordri support the sky; when the Norse gods created the dome of heaven, they placed a dwarf at each of the four points to hold it high above the Earth. Though this is a legend of the far North, we find its exact counterpart in Mexico whose sacred book, Chilam Balam, recounts that after the downfall of the Third Sun, the four Bacabs, sons of the supreme god, were appointed to support the four corners of the Earth. These Skybearer dwarfs, an Aztecan friend tells me, were called "Sustainers of the Cane Mat, symbolizing the seat of our Mexika High Chiefs."

Though myth turned them into **deities**, they were once quite human, as in Africa, where the Jalaf people remember their Yumboes: Just two feet high, of white color, dwelling underground (inside mounds? holding up the world?), they are called—just as they are in the British Isles—the "Good People."[24] Once they vanished from the face of the Earth, their memory was revered; as were the Aziza, a fairy race of Dahomey, who teach mortals practical knowledge—as well as revelations of the gods. The name Aziza is somehow reminiscent of Vazimba: in nearby Madagascar, the Vazimba aborigines were a dwarf race of mysterious people, quite white like the Yumboes of Africa. Vazimba tombs rest on sacred ground; indeed, some of the Malagasy kings have claimed a blood kinship to the extinct Vazimba.

I foreordained not to go within darkness to battle it, but to stand outside it, and give an example of righteousness [the Ihin] for man to look upon.

OAHSPE, THE LORDS' FIFTH BOOK 4:2

The idea of an exemplar, a lost and holy race, excelling in goodness, the blue-bloods of antiquity, repeats itself in the Americas. Here, the little people became mentors to the Crow Indians: "Our forefathers claim the Little People lived there once, it was a sacred place many years ago."[25] For some tribes, memory fades to myth, and now these mentors, lost to history, are **ethereal spirits** that ensure humans behave in culturally specific, proper ways. But of old, they were *living* teachers, paragons of virtue, the sacred tribes of yore, like the "exceedingly wise" Sumerian Noah. Indeed, they were the very *sons* of Noah, who spread a Golden Age throughout the world.* The recollection of such a lost world, a terrestrial paradise, is one of the deepest and most widespread of tribal memories. The Popul Vuh of Guatemala said these "first men" knew all, could see the large and the small in the sky and Earth. In the Chilam Balam of Chumayel, it is said: "They adhered to their reason. There was no sin; in the holy faith their lives were passed. . . . At that time the course of humanity was orderly."[26]

THE HELPERS

Leaders of men were these flood survivors, the children of Noah—the sacred tribes of Shem, Ham, Jaffeth, and their offshoots. They were in India, Persia, Arabia, Egypt, Africa, China, and America. They taught the barbarians. They were men, not gods or spirits: a priestly race, the first on Earth to make a covenant with their Creator. "To Ham I allotted the foundation of the migratory tribes of earth. . . . All colors were the tribes of Ham . . . allotted to teach the barbarians."[27] Migrating always westward, the Hamites taught mining, metals, crafts, and also about the world beyond.

> The druks [barbarians] inquired, saying, "How shall a man live forever?" The Ihins answered, saying, "There is a spirit in man unseen and potent, which shall never die . . ." And many of the druks pon-

---

*Probably 23,000 to 18,000 BP, with prosperity, growth, no war, and widespread commerce in the immediate postdiluvial times—a golden age, also recalled by the Chinese.

dered on these things and their thoughts quickened their souls within them, so that they brought forth heirs unto everlasting life.[28]

It was in this manner that mankind as a whole became heir to immortality: by upliftment, through the priesthood of the Ihins, the sons of Noah.

The Jaffeth in China were also the head and front of learning, teaching all the applied arts and industries to the barbarians. James Churchward identifies this civilization as "Uighur" who brought from Mu the essentials: astronomy, mining, textiles, architecture, mathematics, metallurgy, agriculture, medicine, and writing. It was a vast civilization, eventually reaching Europe, principally through Asia Minor.

And in the New World [18,000 BP], the people of learning built great sailing boats, and they surveyed the way for canals, they found the square and the arch, they led the Ihuans (Indians) to the mines.* Without them, the Ihuan could not build his own house. . . . Patiently they taught and instructed the Ihuans in all things and industries.[29]

"Without his aid, they could not boil a pot," said the Iroquoian Hurons, of first man.[30] Crow Chief Red Plume once went on a vision quest, and on the final night was joined by "three small men and women" who became his mentors. Another member of the Crow tribe remarked that the wee people (living in the Pryor Mountains of south-central Montana) created many of the rock paintings. "I believe . . . they had a strong role in our tribal taboos and religion."[31] Some of this rock art can be seen on the walls of caves near Bighorn Wheel.

---

*Hence the reputation of the Teutonic elves (generally dwelling in recesses of the Earth), as guardians of mineral wealth and distinguished for their skill in metallurgy—"handy smiths" with great subterranean wealth. The Swiss trolls are also expert smiths, with great treasures in the dolmen in which they dwell and of which they are regarded the builders. Black dwarfs are expert especially in steel, to which they can give a degree of hardness and flexibility that no human smith can imitate: bends like rushes, hard as diamonds. In old times, arms and armor made by them were in great demand; shirts of mail manufactured by the dwarfs were as fine as cobwebs, but nothing could penetrate.

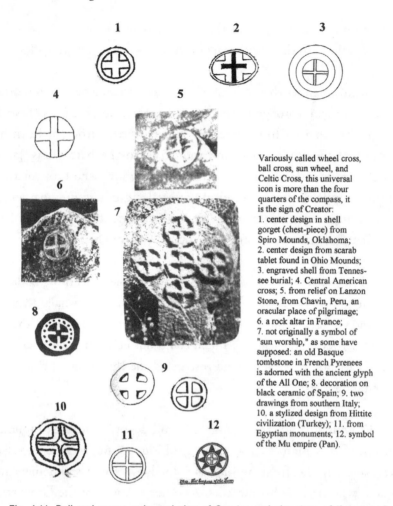

Variously called wheel cross, ball cross, sun wheel, and Celtic Cross, this universal icon is more than the four quarters of the compass, it is the sign of Creator: 1. center design in shell gorget (chest-piece) from Spiro Mounds, Oklahoma; 2. center design from scarab tablet found in Ohio Mounds; 3. engraved shell from Tennessee burial; 4. Central American cross; 5. from relief on Lanzon Stone, from Chavin, Peru, an oracular place of pilgrimage; 6. a rock altar in France; 7. not originally a symbol of "sun worship," as some have supposed: an old Basque tombstone in French Pyrenees is adorned with the ancient glyph of the All One; 8. decoration on black ceramic of Spain; 9. two drawings from southern Italy; 10. a stylized design from Hittite civilization (Turkey); 11. from Egyptian monuments; 12. symbol of the Mu empire (Pan).

Fig. 4.11. Ball-and-cross, universal sign of Creator and signature of the sacred tribes, appears in bold paints on Crow medicine shields. The more than eighty medicine wheels in North America really had to do with calendrical turning points, harvesting times, sowing, and so forth.

"You see," explained archaeologist Mike Wilson, "there are traditions of 'Little People' who . . . came to impart knowledge. The Crow talk about them."[32] Bighorn's cairns enclose cavities that only a *crouching* human could occupy. "Some feel it served . . . as a vision quest site." In Central Guatama, we see the same custom among Mayan shamans who continue to meet little people in their vision quests. They are instructors or spirit guides: Their Preceptors.

The histories embedded in Oahspe credit the sacred little people not only with the first religion, but also the first clothing, the first words, first to labor, first to sing and dance, first images on stone, wood, and clay, and the first to build cities.[33] In Cherokee tradition, the little people traveled all over the world and brought back news to Turtle Island; as a result, some Native Americans became skilled astronomers, medalists, chemists, architects, and so forth. This knowledge was possible because of "the Little-People-Who-Wore-White," say the storytellers.

When the Wyandots were assailed by strange monsters ("flying heads"), they said, "Let us send for the Little People, they may be able to help us"; they were their **gods**. And when the Indians suffered from thirst, one said, "I perish for water. I will call the Little People. They will find me water." And soon "there stood before him one of the Little People. He was a tiny man whose name was Goma." Goma showed him a spring. "Goma often visits his children. If you see a man not nearly so big as the smallest babe, watch him closely . . . his long beard is as white as snow."[34] Those beards, as we will now see, are another signature of the lost race of little people.

Fig. 4.12. Goma driving away the stone giant

THE HEALERS

The Shoshone, Cheyenne, Arapaho, Sioux, and Crow Indians cast the little magical people as healers. The Crow, as noted above, celebrated the wee people who gave not only art, wisdom, and religion, but also powerful medicine for healing. Such recollections are found also among the Choctaw where, in one tale, the little people take a Choctaw child to their home in the wilderness and train him as a doctor, transmitting their special formulas for herbal medicines. The Choctaw say that during the darkest nights you can see a strange light wandering about in the woods. "This is the Indian doctor and his little helper" looking for curative herbs. The Choctaws, so rich in little people lore, were unlike their neighbors—a nation of farmers, ever inclined to peace and industry, "distinguished for their poetry and music."[35] Indeed, it seems that the "civilized tribes" (Choctaw, Cherokee, Muscogee) are the same ones with keenest recollection of little-people mentors.

GOOD MEDICINE

We sometimes hear that the Essenes (keepers of the Dead Sea Scrolls) were the most renowned herbologists of their time; only *they* knew the healing powers of certain plants. But where did they get this wonderful knowledge? Did their medicinal secrets come down through the half-breed Ihins of southwestern Asia, those Shepherd Kings and Listians who knew all kinds of formulas and spells? Perhaps so. In old Iraq, the name of the Sumerian goddess of medicine and healing was *Ba*u; this Bau was also known as *Nini*sinna and *Nin*azu (Nin- names signaling *Homo pygmaeus,* see appendix D). Another Ba- group is the Bari (a.k.a Motilone), a short tribe in Venezuela whose command of ethnobotany was studied in the 1960s: these primitive people possess a vast knowledge of the biodiversity in Amazonia and use 80 percent of the plants around them.

The little people, distinctively full-bearded (like the Israelites),* seem to have shaped the model of shaman or *curandero* in many parts

---

*See figures with beard: 1.3, p. 10; 1.10, p. 22; 2.6, p. 44; 2.34, p. 79; 5.2, p. 146; 6.2, p. 179; and 9.5, p. 318.

of the world. Osiris, bearded, taught the Egyptian people how to cure diseases, and he also introduced the planting of wheat and barley; Bes, the bearded Egyptian dwarf god (see fig. 2.1, p. 32), would also become a **divine healer**, while Ptah, Egypt's Creator dwarf god, usually shown bearded, was god of medicine and learning as well as the reputed father of Imhotep, who was considered the first physician in history. The beard was somehow a critical mark. Later Egyptian priests would put on a false beard for sacerdotal functions; a *faux* beard was also donned by the pharaoh as symbol of authority. G. V. Childe thought Kish beards (First Dynasty, Mesopotamia) depicted on kings "may be false," that is, in imitation of the ancestor.

Fig. 4.13 (above). Pure Negrito of Zambales, showing hair on chin. The presence of beards—whether of the Menehune, Nunnehi, Pomo, and Hupa (California), White Eskimo, Ainu, Mapuche (Chile), African pygmy, Beni Hasan (Egypt), or Israelites—signal heritage from the little people.

Fig. 4.14 (left). Bearded figure on door of Kukulcan Temple in Chichén Itzá. Note short stature.

In Mesoamerica, the Mayan god of healing, Itzamana, father of the Bacabs and discoverer of the medicinal properties of plants, is depicted with a beard, so conspicuously unlike the glabrous Yucatecans, with "long jet-black beard" (see fig. 2.31, p. 77) and the little Lacandon with their "vast knowledge of native medicaments."[36]

The angels . . . talk to him [man] in his sleep, and show him what is for his own good.

OAHSPE, BOOK OF SETHANTES 10:5

We also learn that the bearded and blue-eyed Nunnehi come in dreams and show the Cherokee how to protect their corn from predator-birds, using a spell.* Among the Iroquois, these dream helpers are a healer tribe of little people. The Cherokee medicine man, it was well known, consulted the bearded little people (Yunwi, Nunnehi) for remedies and plants, herbs, and roots needed for the ailing. Sometimes the Nunnehi bring the right medicines to the sick; one tale speaks of a man cured of smallpox by the little people!

Among the short, pale, and bearded Mapuche Indians of Chile,† the medicine man (*machi*) is actually a woman with the power to see and converse with spirits. "As these machis possess a good knowledge of medicinal herbs and are expert osteopaths and chiropractors, their treatments . . . effect truly remarkable cures . . . they are often called upon by the [Latino] inhabitants of the country in times of necessity."[37]

Indeed, here at Monte Verde in Chile, archaeologists have discovered the use of plants with medicinal qualities—13,000 years ago![38]

Possessed of certain distinctly "Caucasian" features, like the Mapuche, the little people of Malaysia are more fully bearded than their

---

*White and bearded, like the Maya's Itzamana, is the semidivine teacher, **Samé**, of the Brazil Indians. He taught them agriculture and magic, rather like the Norggen of Europe (Tirol), three feet tall, with prominent beards, who tell people when to plant crops.

†The Mapuche resisted the colonial Spanish invasion, and have done so up to the present moment. On May 13, 2010, hundreds of Mapuche and their supporters staged a peaceful demonstration protesting political imprisonment of their people. Torture in custody is one of the ordeals that incarcerated Mapuche must endure.

Mongoloid neighbors. No surprise there, for in tracing the little people, pale and bearded—and quite likely the first doctors on Earth—their offspring, including their mixed descendants, have retained an ancient knowledge of curative plants.

The result is that today's Negritos, despite their very primitive surroundings, are especially skilled herbalists. They know hundreds of plant species with medicinal properties, down to the different parts of plants for different purposes. "The Negritos are acknowledged by all Malaysian races to be the foremost experts on the medicines derived from forest plants."[39] They sell (not too cheaply) their jungle roots to the Malay, who even go to the little forest people for contraceptive herbs.

The Mani Negritos of Thailand are likewise noted for their fine remedies: a certain Mani "wonder medicine" helps with birthing. Their great variety of herbal medicines are much sought-after by the Thais.[40]

"We heal the sick"—say the fairies, through medium Lucie Piazzo.[41] The link between the diminutive tribes and herbal expertise is just as notable in Europe, where the two-feet-tall korrigan can cure maladies by aid of charms, as do the wood damsels of Tyrol, who share with the peasants their knowledge of medical herbs and agricultural expertise. The Shetland trows (brownies), we also learn, are possessed of "infallible remedies"; some villagers swore by these cures. In 1696, an English lady claimed to have learned "numerous surprising cures" from six of these fairy people renowned for their magical ointments. For the Irish, the Tuatha De Danaan were teachers of medicine and smithing. The Quiet Folk (Stille Volk) of northern Europe, about two feet tall, know the healing properties of all plants and stones, and never get sick. Austria's little Wilden Fraulin, with long blond hair, teach their favorites the art of herbal healing, just as the Ice Fairies of the Alps instruct shepherds in the power of medicinal plants. These little people of Switzerland once revealed to desperate villagers the proper herbs to prevent the plague: silver thistle and pimpernel.

In Spain, the figure of Maja, the size of a ten-year-old, gives a medicinal jelly, the fruits "picked in a fairy orchard."[42] France's *tisaniere* is also a gatherer of medicinal herbs—a very wise old fairy, specializing in herb soups and old wives remedies and infusions. The French fée, according to a fourteenth-century account, would give barren women a special beverage that made them fruitful; earlier, when King Arthur was badly injured in battle, he was taken to be healed by Morgan la Fée. And as for the Eastern European Vila, he can heal ulcers and even bring the dead back to life!

Homo pygmaeus as first doctor follows suit all the way to Africa where the Bushman—never mind his extremely harsh and primitive life—"displays immense and intimate knowledge about the plants around him . . . [he is] a natural botanist, and so expert an organic chemist."[43] Growing up Afrikaner, Laurens Van der Post remembers that, when ill, his parents doctored him "with a wild herb to which the Bushmen had introduced us."[44] Medicine songs are given to the Bushmen by the Great God who sends his messengers[45] (spirits of the departed) to a sleeping person.* "And God's angels taught the chosen these things."[46]

The fairies, it is said, "know and speak all languages";[47] King Oberon (of the dwarfs), three feet tall and with a "sunny beard," can hear the angels in the sky and drive the demons back into hell. This was the gift of the Ihins who, through angelic helpers, could keep the *drujas* (dark spirits) at bay, and understand and interpret any language. "Through the Ihins can the Lord your God speak all languages, even the language of the barbarians."[48]

The Aeta have spirit guides who help the leader of sacred dances;

Fig. 4.15. Gau, a sacred instrument used to build the temples, a plumb and level combined, placed at the altar as a symbol of proof. Note that "gauge" derives from gau, which meant "fact." "And Gitchee . . . sent His angels to teach men the mystery of canal-making, to compound clay with lime and sand, to hold water, to find the gau (level) and the force of water."

---

*In connection with cave painting by the Bushmen and others (fig. 8.9, p. 279), Jeffrey Goodman devotes chapter 9 of his excellent book, *The Genesis Mystery,* to the theme that cave art is mostly about communing with spirit helpers. Among the Andamanese, a man becomes a shaman by contact with spirits—either in dream or by "dying" and coming back. Otherworldly inspiration of this kind is a sure sign of the sacred little people who were the first to practice spiritual communion, and to teach others how to receive instruction from the invisible beings: "the spirits oft appeared in sargis [embodied], teaching openly their several doctrines [in the temples]."

the shaman receives songs from his spirit-helpers, whom he sometimes takes on as his assistants. These Filipino little people are age-old purveyors of rare herbal medicines. The Batak Negritos have extensive knowledge of the use of herbs and roots, which the Christian Filipinos eagerly purchase from them.

While in trance, the Negrito shaman in Malaysia may see a patient's disease by looking into a quartz. The Malaysian Batek get remedies from the spirit world, their teachers the very angels who "helped the early humans and taught them how to live"[49]—for they showed which fruits were safe to eat, as well as which herbs to use for coughs, constipation, fever, abortion, internal pains, and so forth. The Batek healer, called *bomoh,* obtains his songs from celestial beings while in trance or in dream. Thus the ultimate source of Batek medicinal knowledge is the unseen world. A gifted shaman can send his shadow-soul to different parts of the universe, safely returning with beneficial knowledge for his people.

THE CARVERS

The original teachings held by the Hopi people include "the herbs that heal." The Hopi medicine man, like his Malay confreres, could diagnose any illness by looking (with crystals) at the body's vibratory centers. As we have seen, the Hopi Indians maintain an enduring tradition of the Flood, Chief Dan Katchongva confirming legends that his people were survivors from a previous world (age) that was destroyed. Arriving in safety, they claimed all the new land for the Great Spirit, anticipating a day of purification that the True White Brother will help bring on. Furthermore, the Great Spirit, to keep his chosen in the light (after the Diaspora), made a pair of sacred stone tablets into which he breathed all teachings, instructions, and prophecies—including the life plan for harmony and balance—and these tablets were given to each of the four races and to "the [Hopi] chief who led the faithful to their new land."[50]

This motif—stone tablets of knowledge—recurs time and again in the great traditions of diluvian man. The Hopi stand as one of the last remaining People of Peace from the prior Golden Age; in fact, the story of their teaching-tablets resonates with Josephus' account of the antediluvians inscribing all knowledge on two pillars, which, tradition held, Hermes found after the Flood. Such tablets or columns or pillars figure dramatically in the legends of the patriarchs (True White Brothers), who spoke of hallowed records inscribed in pre-flood times on sacred pillars. In the story of Lamech (son of Methuselah and father of Noah), this great patriarch impresses the knowledge of the Fathers onto two mighty pillars—just as later tradition had Moses' words of law written upon two tablets of stone. These granite and brass narratives go on to explain that the holy descendants of Seth (Adam's third son), and of Enoch, were chosen to preserve the original religion, science, and arts of peace, and to transmit them to future generations on monuments of stone, that their inventions, wisdom, and histories might not be lost. Thus they made two pillars and thereupon etched the records of the race.

Many nations recall these columns of Enoch. Lee Brown, a Cherokee, tells us that the African rendition of these stone tablets is kept at the foot of Mount Kenya, by the Kukuyu tribe. Brown mentions the astounding experience of seeing Kukuyu beadwork *identical* to that of the Plains Indians.

Along the fertile crescent, too, Gilgamesh (the Sumerian and Babylonian epic hero) engraved in stone the story of the Flood. Even in Australia, huge limestone pillars near Roper River are said to have been the work of a white race—a memorial of the Flood? At Panama, the majestic columns* of Cocle are covered with inscriptions in an unknown language, left by "intensely religious, peaceful and very industrious"[51] people with unexcelled weaving and pottery.

These potters, carvers, and engravers can be traced back to Noah—and the Hopi's ancestors—if the "Flagstaff Engraving" in Arizona, similar to European Cro-Magnon work, is any indication. "Technologically sophisticated," this engraving is said to be at least 25,000 years old.[52]

---

*Referring to a period of time some 6,000 years ago, Oahspe's First Book of God 25:5 lists the great kingdoms of Guatama, including "tens of thousands of people. And this kingdom extended from sea to sea in the Middle Kingdom (Panama). Here stood the temple of Giloff, with a thousand columns . . . And within Giloff dwelt the Osheowena, the oracle of the Creator, for two thousand years."

And god sent his angels down to man, to inspire him in the workmanship of images and engravings. . . . And the Lord spake unto the Jhin saying, go provide me a stone and . . . And the Jhins prepared a stone . . . [and] made tablets and [distributed] them to the races of men. . . . In all of these countries [after the flood] there were made images . . . and engravings . . . of the children of Noe,* and of the flood, and of the sacred tribes, Shem, Ham, and Jaffeth. By painted signs and engraved words, God foresaw that the knowledge of one generation could be handed down to the next . . . [and he] commanded man to make stone and wooden images, and engravings also, of everything upon the earth; and man so made them. . . . And these were the first writings since the Flood, other than such as were kept secret [by the priests] amongst the Jhins. [Note: This occurred 15,000 years ago.]

OAHSPE, THE LORDS' FOURTH BOOK 1:1–6, 2:18–21

And in the New World, at those miniature Tennessee burials, flints of "wonderful construction" have been recovered as well as masterfully carved shells, found in the mounds (see chapter 7). We recall, too, that the Crow Indians say it was the little people who left the rock carvings, just as the Menehune are credited with the petroglyphs carved on Hawaii's rocks. Surely all these skilled carvers share a heritage with the Maya and their beautifully painted carvings, as well as with the Aztecs and their wonderfully carved onyx, not to mention their Old World cousins: the craftsman sent to Solomon (2 Chronicles 2:23), the people of *Dan,* skilled engravers.

Fascinating, too, is the well-known similarity of Japanese and Alaskan workmanship, protohistorical, yet of "very high culture."[53] The Ainu on the Japanese Isles are world-class carvers who produce intricate interlocking designs, great puzzles of craftsmanship. We find the same interlocking chains in Alaska, where burial goods include delicately engraved articles

---

*It was 24,000 years ago, in the Arc of Noe, that the Flood, the submersion of Pan, occurred. Don't "Noah" and "Noe" have a similar ring? In fact, the Ark of the Deluge is shown on ancient medals with NOE lettered on the front of the ark. In Japan, Noe means Lord; in China, Noeji means spirit.

quite similar to the ancient artifacts of North China, and to carvings of the Ainu people as well as the natives of the Amur River in Siberia. This brings us right back to the Tua Git, Churchward's Uighurs: the northern boundary of that civilization extending into Siberia 17,000 years ago, leaving petroglyphs in the Aleutian Island and explaining high culture in Alaska long before the Neolithic.

These ancient carvers of Alaska look something like our original little people: besides being of the short "Chancelade" type, they are thought to have had fair hair and blue eyes, rather like the Han-Dropa of China—with their *engraved* ("grooved") discs at least 12,000 years old. Those "alien discs" have tiny, almost microscopic characters, written in an unknown language that took Chinese experts two decades to semidecode.

Japan, home of the Ainu, has its own recollections of a never-neverland and its ancient deity who gave happiness to the people of Okinawa from beyond the sea. Local tradition recalls that the islands of the Pacific appeared only after "the waters of a great deluge had receded."[54] The hazy outline of that early time comes into better focus with the archaeological finding that the population in Japan swelled at least 20,000 years ago—at which time all the arts improved, as seen in excellent microblade tools and the "elaborate and sophisticated" ware of the acclaimed Jomon (early Ainu) potters. With fine carvings done in relief, this style of pottery—the oldest in the entire world—has been compared not only to that of the Ipiutak (pre-Eskimo), but also to identical artifacts along the upper Amazon and Ecuadorian coast.[55]

Is it mere mindless coincidence that the most striking facsimiles of Japan's lost horizon appear at the *other* end of the Pacific Ocean where a great land once stood? Hugging the western coast of the vast and empty Pacific, places such as Peru, Ecuador, and California have proven the richest sources of early man. Can we explain that? The same time depth of 20,000 years BP (probably more) that archaeologists estimate for the flourishing of Japan also happens to turn up in connection with Peru's earliest tool-making site: 20,000 years old. Are we satisfied calling this a coincidence? The entire gestalt of "Stone Age" masters appeared almost suddenly in Peru: highly skilled masonry, bridges, canals, wonderful temples, a Great Wall (not unlike China's), stone circles, megalithic ruins, the extraordinary "Nazca lines" of southern Peru, the amazing Ica stones, and the list goes on. Plus, with Jomon-type pottery found on the coast of Ecuador—and early Ecuadorian skulls resembling the Melanesian (i.e., Oceanic type, which is also found in China at Chou-kou-tien), one can reasonably ask if *both coasts of the Pacific* were settled by refugees from Pacifica. "Words cannot express adequately the degree of similarity between early Valdivia [Ecuadorian] and contemporary Jomon pottery," remarked archaeologist Clifford Evans. "Many fragments of both are so similar . . . that they might almost have come from the same vessel."[56]

FABRICS AND FAIRY BOLTS

At Fukui cave in North Kyushu, Japan, fine pottery, the oldest in the world, appears in association with an assemblage of microblades. Here in the Far East, fine art and micro-handiwork would include the controversial discs of the Han-Dropa, those stone "records" etched with almost microscopic characters. In Europe, too, microscopic artifacts commonly called "pygmy-flints" are plentiful in Scotland: among country folk, they are unabashedly considered artifacts of the little people— "fairy bolts" or "arrows of the elves." But this is no freak occurrence. Tiny, miniature tools are in evidence at Suffolk, Lancashire, and Devon in the United Kingdom, as well as in Egypt, Palestine, Africa, Australia, the Mississippi Valley at Poverty Point, Alaska, Russia, Austria, France, Sicily, the Caspian, India, Iraq in the Shanidar caves, and Mongolia, the latter dated around 20,000 BP. Indeed, this period, the Late Capsian Age is characterized by a type of tiny flint found everywhere from South Africa to northern Europe and from Morocco to Ceylon.

Archaeologists have found a similar microlithic culture on Luzon, in the Philippines, where the Aeta little people still live. Only little hands could have done the ultrafine work required for the manufacture of these finely wrought stone tools, which include tiny knife blades with working of such delicate character that it requires a magnifying glass to detect the flaking on the edges. What hands, what eyes!

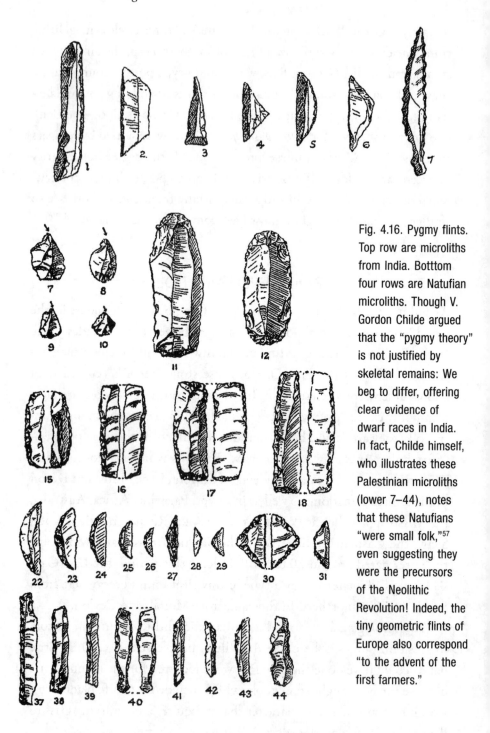

Fig. 4.16. Pygmy flints. Top row are microliths from India. Botttom four rows are Natufian microliths. Though V. Gordon Childe argued that the "pygmy theory" is not justified by skeletal remains: We beg to differ, offering clear evidence of dwarf races in India. In fact, Childe himself, who illustrates these Palestinian microliths (lower 7–44), notes that these Natufians "were small folk,"[57] even suggesting they were the precursors of the Neolithic Revolution! Indeed, the tiny geometric flints of Europe also correspond "to the advent of the first farmers."

*Whoever the people were who made them [microtools]—dwarfs or
fairies—they certainly were handicraftsmen of no mean order.*
REGINALD GATTY, "PIGMY FLINTS," *SCIENCE GOSSIP*

And what about Turkey's more than 8,000-year-old ornamental
stone beads, so finely drilled that a modern steel pin cannot penetrate them? Probably akin to these is the fine human profile incised
on Mycenaean beads of amethyst—not unlike the tiny carved gems
of the Minoans—and the incredibly tiny "granulated" gold beads of
the Manabi culture in Ecuador. Good eyes—or—special lenses? The
latter are, in fact, in evidence in Ecuador in the form of obsidian
mirrors* carved like lenses.[58] The Gentry's sight, at all events, "is so
penetrating . . . they could see through the earth."[59] Even America's
Stick Indians, a diminutive (and feared) race, could shoot their little
arrows and hit the mark at distances far greater than the ordinary
Indian. In Africa, tiny flint tools are also found in Bushman territory,
where these little people are avid honey hunters: "It was quite unbe-
lievable . . . how far those slanted, oddly Mongolian eyes could follow
the flight of a bee. Long after the European or black man lost sight of
it he would still be there marking the flight."[60]

Answering to these delicate microblades of the Mesolithic are
the incredibly fine textiles found, again, in little people enclaves. In
Helwan, Egypt (where ground lenses of ancient manufacture were also
found), archaeologists dug up a piece of cloth, the fabric so fine that
today it could be woven only in a special factory with great technical
know-how. Dwarfs seem to have been the producers: Egyptian "dwarfs"
were traditionally the "overseers of linen" and chiefs of the royal textile
works. These "dwarfs" may have descended from the ancient Ihins who,
as long as 70,000 years ago, according to The First Book of the First
Lords, "tilled the ground and brought forth flax and hemp, from which
to make cloth for covering the body."

The ten-thousand-year-old clothing (perhaps Natufian) found at

---

*Lenses from 12,000 years ago and earlier include the crystal lens dug out of the
ruins of Nineveh, as well as examples from Egypt, Iraq, and Jordan. Others have
located ancient lenses in Libya, Mexico, and central Australia.

Beida, Jordan, is also striking: these people "dressed elegantly in fabrics made from spun yarn."[61] At Turkey's Çatalhüyük, one finds obsidian mirrors and beads with holes so small only modern technology could duplicate it; the famous site also boasts some of the world's oldest remains of finely woven cloth, woolens, carpets, and delicate textiles, which date to 9,000 years ago: the "Stone Age!" This industry can be traced further east: ancient Iraqi textiles look as if "embroidered with fairy hands."[62] Further east yet: within a series of cathedral-like caves in the Subis Mountains, explorers came upon prehistorical "fabrics of such fineness and delicacy that with the best will in the world one cannot imagine savages making them."[63] Perhaps these are all spin-offs from Uighur textile industry, judged by Churchward to be 17,000 years old, or from the fabrics of Russia, "tens of thousands" of years old, manufactured into trousers, coats, and so forth.[64]

New World counterparts might include the acclaimed weavers of San Blas. Too, the Nazca area of Peru is known for its ancient master craftsmen who produced exquisite textiles:[65] the world's most beautiful fabrics, unsurpassed in technique and beauty. The finest yarns, the most delicate threads of cotton and wool, wonderfully woven and gorgeously colored, world-class examples of the embroiderer's art—cannot be imitated by any machine. Made famous by the discovery of a burial ground here in 1925, these brilliant-colored Peruvian shrouds and tapestries are minutely stitched (500 threads per inch), obviously made by virtuoso weavers, spinners, and dyers. One is tempted to compare these

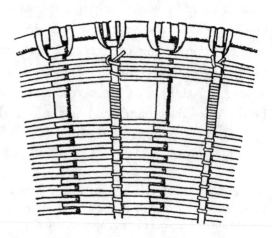

Fig. 4.17. Section of Andamanese basket, using process known as wrapped-twine work. They also make good string, nets, and sleeping mats.

to Toltec "robes of fine texture," or the exquisitely woven textiles found in the American mounds, or even Hopi textiles, so prized by other tribes. They remind us also of Filipino Negritos' "skillful weaving and plaiting." Some ethnographers are surprised by Andaman pottery and advanced plaiting techniques for baskets; yet, all of the above are facets of the same treasure-house, brought by the "gods of craftsmanship"— the Sidhe—and reminding us of the delicate linens of the fairy folk and how Scottish fairies produced "webs of the finest cloths."

The nymphs do weave their robes . . . wondrous to behold.

HOMER

CHAPTER 5

His Flesh Was White as Snow

It may be that we have not yet located the earliest Caucasoid homeland . . . it is hardly likely Europe.

CARLETON COON, *THE ORIGIN OF RACES*

WHITE SKIN, SMALL FEET, AND LONG HAIR

In 1891, J. B. Newbrough* commented on the little people—the Ihins described in Oahspe—as having been originally of two types: "one was white, and the other was yellow. The yellow is discovered." This "yellow" is probably referring to the fawn-colored pygmies of Africa and Sundaland; Newbrough's contemporary, Armand de Quatrefages, professor of Anthropology at Paris Musée d'Histoire Naturelle, had recently "discovered" the Negritos of southeast Asia. But what about the white ones?

"Their skin was as white as the swan of the wave," said the legends describing the fairies of England.[1] Let us begin by considering the coloring of the Old World "dwarf" people, which throws light on the former existence of a very small, very pale race of man, which once filled the world with skills and virtue—the paragon we explored in chapter 4. And who *were* the Caucasian-like skeletons from North America 24,000 years

---

*It was through Newbrough's hand (automatic typewriting) that Oahspe came into the world.

142

ago?[2] "Ethnologists," cautioned James Churchward, "have classed certain white races as Aryans that are not Aryans at all, but belong to a totally different line." Yet he adds, "The forefathers of the white Polynesians, of the white Mayas . . . and of all our white races were one and the same."[3]

Long before the vaunted Aryans, a white (though not "Caucasian") people dwelt in *every* land—a source of inspiration to the cavemen and other tribes wandering in darkness. There is a reason the Basque race and language, for instance, are *pre*-Aryan: The white stock from which they sprang was not "Indo-European" at all, and neither is Basque head type or blood type classifiable.

Myth and fable leave us but the faintest recollection of this archaic white race: the charming story of Cinderella, for example, has been refashioned so many times that it has lost touch with the origin of her small feet and tiny glass slippers. Yet the little people were reputed to be master cobblers of wonderful skill, and it is not until we learn of the "fine glass shoes" of Europe's dwarf people that we can connect the dots: the White Dwarfs of Rugen, cheerful and good-natured, always wore glass slippers at their nocturnal dance fests (read: Cinderella's ball). Besides being great artisans, they were "very handsome in their persons, with clear light-colored eyes and small and most beautiful hands and feet."[4] Remarkably small feet, one of the signatures of *Homo pygmaeus,* were indeed characteristic of short Neolithic man in Italy and Switzerland.[5] We also note the small hands and feet of the Bushmen and the Akka—"hands of great delicacy" (Georg Schweinfurth), as well as the "unusually small feet . . . very dainty graceful bone-structure" of New Guinea's pygmies,[6] in addition to the Hopi maidens' beautifully "molded little feet."[7] The Yahgan of Chile were a small people, also noted for their tiny hands and feet, while the Tapuya of Brazil were "fair as the English, with small feet and hands, delicate features."[8] In China, Pan-Fei, a semi-mythical royal maiden, beloved of Emperor Ho-Ti, had tiny feet, an ideal of feminine beauty. (Did this "ideal" feed into the foot-binding craze of China?)

We come upon related hidden histories in Grimm's "milk-faced" maiden named Snow White—sepulchered in a *glass* coffin—and her encounter with seven *dwarfs*. Normandy, along the same lines, has a type of fée called Dame Blanche, "White Lady"; her skin, "white as milk," appears also in Scandinavian legends of elves with "lily-white hands," and also, for that matter, in the King Arthur cycle where the fairy king's daughters have "faces white as snow . . . as white as lily in May."

If the Welsh dwarfs were called "the Little Fair People," in Ireland, the banshee is described as "a little white creature" by a woman who'd seen one. Twentieth-century sightings make us wonder if there are not a few survivors of the small—and very pale—race called "Ihin": A lad named Harry Anderson, in 1919, saw a column of twenty little men marching in single file toward him one summer night. They were shirt-less, bald, and had pale white skin.[9]

Even Greece has its little kallikantzaros, as pale as Europe's mine dwarfs; they straddle the fence, as do Europe's fairies, between **spirits** and actual mortals. One Celtic little man, seen at Cork, had a *yellow* face and white hair. Yellow man? In Mayan myth, the first men were molded from a paste of yellow and white maize. Just so, Corn Mother of the Abenaki Indians had yellow hair.

More than 50,000 years ago, according to Oahspe's First Book of the First Lords,[10] the little people called Ihins were white- and yellow-skinned, well-made, small, and slender—that is, before the great amal-gamations saw them blend with the larger, darker races. Their hair was white or yellow, long and silky. Eight thousand years ago, Queen Min-neganewashaka in North America had "yellow hair, long and hanging down."[11] Long tresses, according to Charles Darwin in *The Descent of Man,* were so greatly esteemed by the American Indian that "a chief was elected solely from the length of his hair."

India's legendary Dorani, with her lovely hair like spun gold, had locks so long "it was often unbearable." Upon this long-haired race was, no doubt, based the story of Rapunzel, with her wonderful long hair, fine as spun gold.

Of the Ihins, I provided testimony in all the divisions of the earth, with long hair belonging to the tribes that worshipped the Great Spirit.

OAHSPE, THE LORDS' FIFTH BOOK 3:5

Fig. 5.1. Mummified Jivaro Indian head, with long black hair, like that of the Venezuelan crater people as well as the Arawaks and the Quichua, with hair almost to the ground. Harold T. Wilkins mentions seeing in the wilderness white people in canoes, with long black hair, and dwarfs with hair that reached almost to their feet.[12] Since all people on Earth have Ihin blood, it is not surprising to find even the tallest or most savage tribes, like the Nittevo of Ceylon, with some of the distinctive traits of the little people: in this case, the long straight hair. North of the Nittevo, in India, the ancient Negritos were said to have hair down to their knees and heavy beards.

The Indians have long memory (and sometimes that long hair): In the Pomo (California) creation myth, the First People were beautiful and very long-haired. Indeed, the Pomo and Hupa, by their heavy beard, so unlike most Amerinds, appear to be genetically linked to those First People. The Cherokee remember the tiny Yunwi Tsundsdi as handsome, with long hair falling almost to the ground.

At one time, these long-haired ones were worldwide. In Maori tradition, there were once "very small, fair people [seen] dancing in the sand with their slight fair figures and long yellow hair."[13] Half a world away, in the British Isles, one fairy-elf was described as possessing "the finest hair in the world." "All the prehistorical Sidhe (mound people)," said Robert Graves, "had blue eyes, pale faces, and long yellow hair."[14] Sir Arthur Conan Doyle (who believed in fairies!) alludes to the characteristically long, straight hair of Ireland's wee bodies, so like the handsome Scottish fairies who are "finely proportioned, with fair complexion and long yellow hair."[15] Golden-haired imps appear regularly in King Arthur's court, while a French fable describes a dwarf three feet high with "hair yellow as fine gold."

The mermaids of Brittany are known to sing sweetly while combing their lovely golden hair; one ballad croons about their "hair, yellow as gold . . . I have seen the fair mermaid. I have also heard her singing; her songs were plaintive as the waves." They are a bit like the Russian Rusalky, also very beautiful, with pale skin, white breasts, slender bodies, soft voices, and long wavy hair. Nor is she different from the beautiful Germanic wild-woman who lives within the hills and possesses "uncommonly long and beautiful hair."

Finding this slender, long-haired beauty remembered in Scandinavia, Wales, Ireland, Scotland, North America, New Zealand, Russia, France, and Germany—do we chalk it up to mythological imagination, or a piece of the forgotten past?

"LIKE A CHILD OF THE ANGELS"

The king of the leprechauns was spoken of as "swan white." In Wales, a twelfth-century priest, as a boy, was taken underground (read: inside mounds) to the "beautiful country" of the Little Fair People—all were small but very well proportioned, and they were all fair-haired. Some etymologists believe that the word "fairy" itself comes from "fair," in the sense of pale; for they are called, by the Welsh, Tylwyth Teg, which means "the fair family." But it could also be "fair" in the sense of beauty, or even in the sense of just and virtuous.

We realize that the word "elf" itself (var. aelf, alb-, elb-) means "white." In the Mother language (Panic) *alf* meant "a new beginning,"[16] while *alef* signified "foremost." This "new beginning" takes on added

Fig. 5.2. A Swedish elf. In the northern languages the beneficent elves are called alfs or "Light Alfs" or **Spirits**, similar to the Danish Ellefolk.

meaning in connection with the virtuous—"foremost"—survivors of the Flood, who gave the world a new beginning.

This we know: alb- means "white," as in albino or albumin. Lady *Alb*ine and her sisters, say the Chronicles, arrived from Troy and settled Britain (*Alb*ion) in the time of Jahir, the third Judge of Israel. Similarly, *Alb*a Longa was the place that Aeneas, also of Troy, settled in Italy, where he became its king. So we may ask, where did these Trojans and proto-Europeans—long before the Aryan invasions—get their whiteness? Let's scroll all the way back to Noah and see how far the legends confirm the historicity of pale little people surviving the Great Flood.

The story of Noah in the apocryphal Book of Enoch recounts how the antediluvian patriarchs were reminded of their white-haired ancestors when Lamech's wife bore a son whose flesh was "white as snow" and long locks "white as wool." Radiant "like a child of the angels" (resembling the Sons of Heaven) the infant, named Noah, rose from the hand of the midwife, opened his mouth, and praised the Lord of Righteousness.

All of which proved quite disturbing to his father Lamech, who feared the wonder of this strange birth, until his grandfather Enoch explained the heavenly-earthly admixture "in the time of Jared, my father." And because Enoch walked with the angels and could read the tablets of heaven, he knew that a great Flood of Waters would come to cleanse the Earth and remove its corruptions; but this child, Noah, would be saved—along with his sons Shem, Ham, and Jaffeth.

The white locks of the earliest patriarchs were somehow important, perhaps a signature of the sacred tribes; in fact, the Persians have their own heroic legend of "White-Headed Zal,"[17] which parallels the apocryphal story of Noah. Zal was born with hair perfectly white, which alarmed his father, Sahm. Like Lamech, Sahm feared it was a demon-child, but unlike Lamech, he proceeded to expose the boy to the wild beasts on Mt. *Elb*urz (elb-, meaning "white," is just another variation of alb- and elf). Saved by the great bird Simurgh who nourished and protected the babe, Zal, a noble boy ("every day did Zal increase in wisdom and in judgment") grew up to become the parent of Rostem, the hero of the great Persian epic *Shah Nameh*.

The enlightened Chinese, on the other hand, took a white-haired infant to be a positive omen, a blessing, an auspicious sign! Just so, he appears in the wondrous birth of the prophet Lao-tze, founder of Taoism. "When he was born he had the white hair of an old man."

"SHINY BRIGHT LIKE THE SUN"

Continuing ever westward, the legend did not die. The little nixes of Germany, Iceland, and Norway (skilled dancers, with awesome prophetic powers) possess the same delicate features we have been tracing, as well as long blond hair, "almost white,"[18] while the lovely nymphs of the wild have golden or *silver* hair. Northern mythologies repeat the now-familiar description of these white-whites: "his flesh was as white as snow and his hair as white as wool," recalls one legend of Thule (Iceland, Greenland), referring to the awe-inspiring ancestor of man. "And his eyes were beautiful"; sickness and sorrow were unknown in that day, continues the storyteller. These golden-age Hyperboreans,* with extraordinary gifts of clairvoyance, whose priesthood was mostly about the Otherworld, were said to be almost *transparent,* and the women breathtakingly beautiful. England's banshees, like these Hyperboreans, have curiously transparent skin, as do the Spinners of France and their White Ladies; in Celtic lands the fairies are known as "the opalescent beings." Indeed, the White Alfs and Siths are said to be of a delicate opaline hue, while the dvergar (Norse dwarf) was pale, of an almost ghastly pallor, something like the transparent pallor of a pure Swede.

"The Goddess," wrote Robert Graves in his book *The White Goddess,* "is a lovely, slender woman . . . deathly pale . . . [with] startlingly blue eyes and long fair hair. . . . Her names and titles are innumerable . . . [she is] the Mother of All Living," and she is called Leucothea, lit. "white goddess," by the Etruscans. I believe this long lost ancestor-cum-goddess had skin almost transparent—indeed, colorless. It occurs to me that the "blue bloods" of yesteryear, like the Trojans who founded Eng-

---

*Eustathius wrote of these "northern Pygmies, who lived in the neighborhood of Thule." The Lapps, from Greenland to Lapland, are the last of these short, lank-haired people: descendants of the Magdalenian hunters of Chancelade stock, western Lapps call themselves Samen, meaning "white."

land and Italy, descended from these people of translucent skin. Every man of note and royal family, after the fall of Troy, claimed to descend from the noble line of Priam (king of Troy); even the French kings Dagobert and Charles the Bald claimed to belong to the illustrious Trojan race. After all, doesn't "blue blood" (represented in blue-skinned idols like Buddha, Krishna, and Kneph) approximate the bluish appearance of veins that show through near-transparent skin?

A. H. Verrill tells us that the mountain-dwelling Quichuas at considerable altitudes in the Andes, are "often actually purple . . . owing to their lighter skins."[19] Images of Mexico's Toltecs were painted with blue fingers as was the Mayan King Can. The beautiful-faced dwarf-god Ptah of Egypt has skin of celestial blue, as did Thoth, Ammon, and Shu, while the color of the four-foot-tall Scandinavian Mound Folk is described as "pale blue transluscent." For certain rites, the Picts, Britons, Irish, and Thracians, according to Pliny, tattooed themselves using a blue dye: "the color perhaps sanctified them to the Goddess."[20]

The thread of oral history, at all events, agrees on one point: the survivors of the Great Flood were a humble, virtuous people—and that is why they were *chosen* to survive! "Destroyed [is] the Land of our Fathers (Lemuria). . . . The first great waters came . . . [but] the good were chosen and saved," recount the Mayan priests, who say that their ancestors learned in advance of the coming of the deluge: "Go and choose the good and the wise and bring them . . . to a new land." *Mayab,* in fact, means "the Land of the Chosen Ones."[21] Likewise does the Pima creation myth involve the salvation of *chosen beings* from the Flood. The Skokomish of Mt. Rainier relate that the Great Spirit was displeased with the evil in the world, and secluded the good people before causing a universal deluge.[22] Among the Arikara Indians, it is said that the Creator caused a flood to get rid of the unruly giants, but saved the little people by "storing them in a cave."

Other North American tribes identify a man named Tapi as the Indian "Noah," called Tupa in Brazil, and Tapi in the Valley of Mexico, where he, a pious man, was told by Creator of All Things to build a boat to live in, after which the Earth was submerged. This name Tapi is intriguingly similar to Egyptian Zep Tepi, referring to the first civilizers, or to *Tapi*ro (the little people of New Guinea) and also not unlike the **supreme ancestral deity** of the Malaysian Negritos: *Tape*rn (var. Tapadn) who, like Noah, was "white as cotton." The Kintak Negritos (themselves copper-colored) say that Tapern is "fair in color . . . with white hair."[23] To the Jahai Negritos, he is "shiny bright like the sun." Most of these little people agree that the **Creator** "is as white as wool": like Tapern's older brother Kari, the Thunder God, who has long white hair. The Batek say that Jawait, another deity, has a big white beard. These folk, though brown, nevertheless have a remnant of this light coloring themselves: the iris of Malaysia's Negritos is reddish yellow in color.

Why do Kenta Negrito ladies paint their faces white? Papuans, Australian aborigines, and the Semang apply a similar chalk color*— perhaps in emulation of that ancestor.[24] Mr. Wollaston pointed out that the New Guinea people also like to dye their hair yellow using lime.

In Kenya, Pokot girls entering the puberty rite are covered with white chalk. The Mbuti also dab their bodies with white clay for certain rites, as did some tribes of the Belgian Congo and of Borneo: like Tenosique boys of Mexico doing the rain dance and the Tierra del Fuegans who daubed their faces with white paint. Here in South America, the Caribs painted white all articles to be used in ceremonies. In North America, the Creek people, at the end of their Busk (Harvest) festival, smear themselves with white clay—perhaps in commemoration of the sacred little people of yore. Indeed, Ohio moundbuilders of later times used lavish amounts of galena to paint the body white; more than twenty-five pounds of these sparkling white crystals were found among grave goods at the "Great Mica Grave" of Mound City.

It is not surprising that our Indian *Tap*i, Papuan *Tap*iro (see fig. 6.3, p. 184), and Negrito *Tap*ern have linguistic cousins in South America; namely, the pale *Tap*uya and *Tup*i tribes, who fought for centuries against Carib invaders, resulting in considerable admixture. It then became fashionable for the less sophisticated Caribs to dye their skins yellow in accordance with the prevailing skin color among the Tupi. The Tupi themselves, who regarded yellow as a sign of nobility, strove to go one better and tattooed themselves in that noble color. Numerous

---

*In Xenophon's time, one tribe on the Black Sea covered themselves with white paint or chalk or gypsum "in honor of the White Goddess."

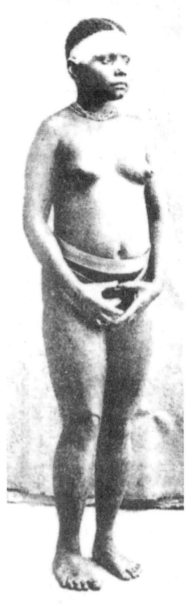

Fig. 5.3. Top: Papuan with face whitened by sago powder; the reason for this custom, said Wollaston, "we did not discover." Bottom: Andamanese man with white clay pattern on his face, supposedly expressing "the personal value of the painted individual."[25] Right: Andamanese woman with white clay on her forehead for mourning; the stuff, highly prized, is also applied to pubescent boys and on other ceremonial occasions. It is believed to have a protective and purifying value. Young Xhosa boys of South Africa are also smeared with white clay in the initiation ceremony.

other Native American tribes are fond of painting themselves with yellow ocher. The Chimu/Chavin civilization of Peru used yellow powders in their religious rituals. Yellow, of course, is the Mexican national color as well. Heaven, said the Mexicans, is full of "birds of yellow plume." Yellow is their sacred color and "was so among the most ancient peoples."[26]

WHITE INDIANS

The name "Tapi" also turns up among the *Tapi*rape Indians in the Amazon rain forest; Tupa, the *deified* ancestor in Bolivia, is the first son of Our Great Father and **Thunder God** among the Guarani Indians. Other variations of this name abound, such as Tupinamba, Tapajos, Tupac, one of the last Inca kings Topu Caui Pachacuti IV (sixty-third Inca) and Topa of the Incas, 1463–93 CE. Could this be a cognate with Egyptian *topi,* meaning "prophet," or with the sacred Tabot, the Ethiopian ark of the covenant? All of one root in the Inca language are *tapac* meaning "royal," tupa meaning "lord," and *tupac* meaning "bright, shining"—just as the Negritos say *Tap*ern is "shiny."

In the Society Islands, when Captain Cook finally found a suitable native guide, the man's honorific name was *Tupi*a, and he was chief, priest, and most intelligent of the Polynesians Cook had met. Tupia joined Cook's travels for a while. Meanwhile, Tupai kupa was also the name of a prominent Maori. Tapu, fundamentally, means "sacred" in these languages, and of course this is the origin of the loan word "taboo," which Captain Cook—as it happens—introduced into the English language. "Taboo"* (like *haram*) conveys the forbiddenness of things sacred.[27]

The *Tapu*yos people, bearded, some with white or golden hair,[28] were found by the conquistadores in very large and prosperous villages, with temples, textiles, and gems. These golden-haired *Tapu*yo "Indians" in eastern Brazil are considered refugees of a lost civilization. As we saw earlier, Col. Fawcett described them as "fair as the English." On a mission, England's intrepid Col. Percy H. Fawcett thought he could

---

*Other places in Oceania carry this name, *Tabu*aemanu, for instance, in the Georgian Islands. On Tahiti, *tupa-pau* means "burial place" (part of ancestor cult?), while moua *tabu* means "sacred mountain"; in their mythology, Hoa-*tabu*-iterai was the first mortal son of the gods, "sacred to the heavens." On Tapiteau Island are pyramids; while on the island of Raiatea, the principal temple is *Tabu-tabu*-atea. In fact, this was the name of several places of worship in the South Seas: "the word may mean wide-spread sacredness."

find this lost civilization of the Tapuyos' ancestors, a people who once dwelt in stone palaces and cultivated the high arts, including sculpture and stone carving. The part of Brazil he explored, Matto Grosso, is full of such legends, as well as intriguing ancient scripts, both ideographic and alphabetical. The Tupi race of Brazil, Col. Fawcett thought, were of Oceanic origin. Did their ancestors survive a great disaster in the Pacific?

Perhaps so: Daniel Brinton, the esteemed American folklorist and linguist, reported that "the Tupis of Brazil . . . were named after the first man, Tupa, he who alone survived the flood . . . an old man of fair complexion, *un vieillard blanc* . . ."[29] Paul Radin, who together with Brinton was one of the great early ethnographers, spoke of the Arawak tribes as "men of light color with long hair and beards."[30] Harold Gladwin adds that the Arawaks "may have been Polynesian." Before Anthropology became a cautious, timid science, many nineteenth-century Americanists agreed that "tribes of the Polynesians have, at some remote period, found their way to the continent."[31]

Now the Polynesians themselves are neither Australoid nor Negroid nor Mongoloid, but rather a combination of races possessing "a strong white element."[32] Indeed, on some Pacific islands, the race founder, Kontiki, is said to be bearded and white. Remarkably fair people abide at Baie des Francais and Mangeea as well as on other islands of the Pacific.[33]

Tracking these light-skinned progenitors from an Oceanic homeland, we might well consider the Sioux legend of Nu-Hohk-A-Nah, "First or Only Man," who, in ritual enactment, dresses in a white wolf fur; he goes through the village announcing that a great flood has inundated the world, and that he alone has escaped in his big canoe. What are all these myths and rituals telling us?

Col. Fawcett, for one, was convinced that the last relics of a forgotten civilization were ensconced in central South America. "With my living eyes I have seen these ruins"; and, if studied scientifically, "a whole ancient civilization would be revealed—the secret of the Lost Continent . . . our origins [would be] more clearly realized."[34] Are those origins to the west? The megalithic ruins seen by Fawcett are suggestive of those found at numerous islands of the Pacific such as Panape, Easter Island,

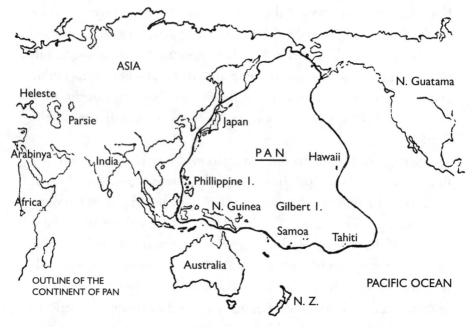

Fig. 5.4. One version of the map of Pan, this one showing what is thought to have been its triangular shape, with connection in the northeast to the northwest coast of America.

Malekula,* and the Marquesas.[35] The ancestors, in one Guari (central Peru) myth, came from "the west, across the ocean."[36] The Aztecs, too, say they are among the seven tribes of Chichimec who came from "a semimythical place to the west of Mexico."[37]

Forensic evidence from blood types indicates a strain of DNA in American Indians that shows relationship to Pacific Islanders.[38] Going against the twentieth-century "scientific" flow, Prof. J. Macmillan Brown, former Chancellor of the University of New Zealand, proposed that a lost continent in the South Pacific, inhabited by white men, lent its culture to Peruvian civilization; further, it was these Polynesians who brought the Mound culture to America. In the Andean highlands "we find tribes, which it is difficult to believe have anything in common with those of other portions of the New World," thought anthropologist A. H. Verrill. "Many of the central and South American tribes are far more . . . Polynesian than Mongolian in appearance."[39] In western

---

*The Malekulans attribute their megalithic-building tradition to five culture-bearing brothers: white men with aquiline noses.

South America, Verrill goes on, "we find words . . . identical with words of the same meaning in Oceanian dialects. In their arts, habits, and religious beliefs there is [also] great similarity . . . many astonishingly alike"; the bearded Bolivian Sirionos, with "typically Oceanian features, bear no faintest resemblance to any other known Indian tribe."[40]

Common points abound: Bolivian and Brazilian panpipes are almost identical to those of the Solomon Islands, down to pitch and tones. The great anthropologist, Alfred Kroeber, saw it as "a startling parallelism. . . . The absolute pitch of the examined instruments from Melanesia and Brazil is the same. . . .This is so close a coincidence as to seem . . . beyond the bounds of accidental convergence."[41] Melanesians and Brazilians are alike also in the habit of chewing lime mixed with a narcotic; they share the ikat style of weaving and cat's cradle, also found among the Papuans who contrive to produce the elaborate configuration of a bird. In Melanesia and Polynesia as well as Columbia and the Amazon, people built comparable palisades around their villages. Baron Erland Nordenskiold compiled about fifty items found both in South America and the Pacific islands; if it was due to actual migrations, they were of "exceedingly remote date"—very remote indeed, as the Flood occurred 24,000 years ago.

"Sword clubs" of South Sea Island origin were found in several Peruvian graves. Polynesians and Peruvians elongate their ear lobes in just the same way. Quipus, moreover, are used in both Peru and Polynesia, the knotted cords still carried in 1830 by Hawaiian tax collectors. Curious that the ancient Babylonian economic overseer was called *qipu;* quipu-type record-keeping with strings and knots were also known in China and Ryukyu Island. Did they originate in the East (i.e., the Pacific)? Bottle-gourds (a squash) of Peru are identical with those of Polynesia, along with a host of species, including amaranth, peanut, jackbean, lima bean, jicama, and sweet potato, the last having the same name (*kumar*) in both Peru and Polynesia (and in Sanskrit as well). Same style of oven, too, and fishhook, and method of stupefying fish with poison. Same rain cloak made of leaves in Columbia, Panama, and Melanesia.

Writers have also remarked the compelling parallels of Tiahuanaco (Bolivia) and Panape (Caroline Islands), the entire complex of Tiahuanaco built along the same lines as Metalanim on Panape, down to their stone-lined canals. Similarities between the statuary of Tiahuanaco and Easter Island are also striking. These connections, argued Swiss writer Erich von Daniken, "automatically force themselves upon us . . . we find stone giants belonging to the same style . . . haughty faces with their stoic expressions."[42] The Vinapu stone ruins on Easter betray a construction style identical to that found at Peru's Cuzco, Machu Picchu, and Sacsahuaman. Scholars, in all frankness, agree: the natives themselves could not have accomplished such engineering feats. An important piece of history has been lost—or suppressed. In South America and Oceania we find highly comparable pile houses, men's secret societies, slit-log drums, fish weir, slings, blowguns, swizzle sticks, grooved mallets, short clubs, battle-stilts, five-pointed stone mace, and signal gong, not to mention the arts of trepanning and tattooing.

Pierre Honore, like Macmillan Brown, thought immigrants from Polynesia must have reached America, remains of which migration he found in Brazil and Ecuador. Notable are similarities in language; in fact, it is the *oldest* Peruvian languages that show greatest similarity to the Polynesian, "so the migration must have taken place in very early times; and there can be no question of these immigrants having transmitted a higher civilization."[43] Would this explain "white men who came from the sea" (Popul Vuh) or "White Indians" in the vicinity of the Xingu River in Brazil? All along the upper tributaries of the Amazon one hears reports of white tribes *still* inhabiting cyclopean cities. Brazil Indians remember their past, especially the **semidivine teacher Samé**, who taught them agriculture and magic and had a white beard. Is Samé cognate to Sahm, father of the white-haired Zal—or to Samen—or to the *Sam*oans?

By the early twentieth century, there were reports of White Indians by "nearly every known tribe."[44] Col. Fawcett himself encountered pure whites on Acre: these Tahuamanu people were big and handsome, red haired, and blue eyed. All across Brazil Fawcett photographed White Indians in back villages. And to answer to those tall Tahuamanu are the white-bearded *dwarfs,* four feet tall—"pygmy men"—of the Amazon, near one of the dead cities, these little people "Greek in type."[45]

Builders of Brazil's Trans-Amazon Highway also came across a white-skinned, red-bearded tribe, called the Lower Assurinis; their language was different from traditional dialects of the region.

To the west, the Mapuche "Indians" of Chile are a pale and bearded people, like their countrymen the Chilotes—the latter an enterprising breed of men and women who inhabit the island of Chiloe. They are short, "red cheeked little men" with enormous energy, light skin, and black hair. There are even *blonds* in Chile among the natives of Punta Arenas and the Chono Indians, somewhat like Chile's Alakalufs and Araucanians, who are also short and stocky.

The Andes also has its "partial albinos" with blue eyes and auburn hair; buccaneers of the seventeenth century spoke of their "milk-white skins,"[46] while a 1924 report mentioned Indians along the Caribbean coast of Darien, the San Blas tribe, a noticeably superior group, not at all "savages," among them some with almost white hair.[47] Explorer R. O. Marsh was astounded when he first sighted three maidens of the Chucunaque: "Their almost bare bodies were as white as any Scandinavian's. Their long hair, falling loosely over their shoulders, was bright gold!"[48] Too, among Panama's Guaymi agriculturalists, are seen many pale and hazel-eyed people.

The Yuracaras Indians of the eastern cordillera are also "remarkably pale-colored." On the coast of Columbia, as well, White Indians are secluded in the hills (Cordillera), and in great numbers; they said this was so from ancient times. In one family, though the parents were both dark, five of their children were white, and two were dark. Among them were people with dark blotching on their white skin. Most of these children have golden hair and hazel-blue eyes. There are, in addition, the pinkish-yellow Akurias of Surinam and British Guiana, "wholly distinct from all other known tribes. They are the *smallest* [emphasis added] of all South American Indians . . . almost pygmies [and] scarcely darker than a Caucasian,"[49] according to A. H. Verrill.

In Venezuela, too, White Indians once inhabited a settlement called Atlan. There is a coastal Panamanian town of the same name, Atlan, with very light-skinned people; yet another paleish group in the Venezuelan forests are the Motilone, part of the Chibcha family, calling themselves

Fig. 5.5. Photos of San Blas Indians, taken in the 1920s

Bari. These Motilones may be related to the White Indians, *los Paria,* living near the Orinoco.

Pre-Columbian mummies from Nazca, Peru, with reddish brown* and blond hair are well-enough known. The Spanish in Pizarro's day

---

*For red-haired mummies in Canary Islands, China, Egypt, Kentucky, Peru, New Zealand, United States, and Russia see www.burlingtonnews.net/redhairedrace (accessed July 27, 2012).

saw blond Peruvians, most notably among Inca nobles and their ances-tors' mummies with "ash-blond hair." Pedro Pizarro noted: "The ruling class in the kingdom of Peru is fair-skinned. . . . Most of the great lords and ladies look white like Spaniards . . . the noblewomen are . . . beauti-ful . . . the hair of both the men and the women is blond as straw, and some of them have fairer skins than the Spaniards. . . .The Indians say that they are **descendants of the gods**."

At conquest time in Tiahuanaco (Bolivia) lived a bearded white race, settled around Lake Titicaca, in the Valley of Coquimbo, but all were exterminated by invaders.[50] Traditions state that a superior caste of white-skinned men came to the Andes long before the Inca: "In the very ancient times the Sun God, ancestor of the Incas, sent them one of his sons and one of his daughters to give them knowledge. The Incas recognized them as divine by their words and their light complexion."[51]

It has been asked: How did the Inca develop such a high civiliza-tion? *Did* they develop it? Or . . . do these blond mummies tell a tale? Can we reconstruct the Great Ancestor as belonging to a light-haired race? Garcilaso de la Vega, as a boy, was taken to see those mummies, one of them with hair "white as snow": it was the eighth ruler of the Sun; he had died young, so it was not the whiteness of old age.

In the Chachapoya region of Peru, the natives look like Europe-ans (perhaps with Norse blood), blond and light-skinned, speaking the Quechua (Inca) language at the time of conquest. Today the almost Armenoid-type Chachas, as they are called, are situated on tributar-ies of the Amazon. Every indication of high civilization is here: canals, temples, bridges, excellent stonemasonry. The Chachas represent the tail-end of the legendary white-skinned, light-haired Cloud People of Peru, residents of a lost city deep in the rainforest, the area covered with a cloudlike mist (Utcubamba province, northern Peru). The city was evidently wiped out by disease and war in the sixteenth century. One chronicler wrote of the Chachas: "They are the whitest and most hand-some of all the people that I have seen." Their citadel is tucked away in one of the most far-flung regions of the Amazon. But the Cloud People once commanded a vast kingdom across the Andes.

WHITE INDIANS

These whites, not only in South America, but in the Old World as well, were made into **gods**; yet, we have every reason to believe they were mortals, not gods. At a certain phase of unfoldment, one branch of these whites became kings and queens, models of nobility who were deified in aftertime by the hand of tradition. All these white and yellow monarchs—Queen Minnegane, Lady Albine, King Aeneas, all the Nin queens and goddesses of Sumeria (appendix D), Tawanana, Tuatha De Danaan, Tupa, Topa Inca, and so on—were flesh-and-blood mortals; some were prophets and heroes: Noah, Abraham, Zal/Rostem, Lao-tze, Samé. With great consistency, the white ancestors of the Long Ago are portrayed as teachers, benefactors, civilizers, and like the great artisans and metallurgists of the pale dwarf kingdom, they became builders and craftsmen, muses and wisdom keepers.

When this "superior caste" of colonizers came among the unlearned (the barbarians, the druks), they seemed as very gods, all-knowing, all-powerful, somehow divine. And they *were,* in a sense, "children of the gods," as the aborigines called them in Peru. Indeed, "God" ended up with a long white beard simply because his own people, his chosen, his prophets, were thus endowed. Man's supreme ancestor, mortal though he was, became, in time, **supreme ancestral deity**. And if the unlearned of South America thought their megalithic sites were "built by the gods," we can take the matter with a grain of salt: Godhood is simply a metaphor of greatness, whose true meaning is—godlike. "As the first race [asu] went down into the earth, the second man [Ihin] rose up by my angels, *becoming like unto Lords and Gods* [emphasis added]."[52]

The Mesoamericans, nonetheless, kept the dogma: among the Huichol people of Mexico, the principal deity is "Our Grandmother," a **white-haired earth goddess** (meaning: goddesslike). Harold Gladwin truly marvels "how beardless brown Mexicans could ever have imagined a bearded white figure as a god."[53] Their old chronicles tell us that Uxmal's House of the Dwarfs was erected in honor of the "White God," just as the Aztecs (Nahuas) arose from darkness by virtue of a "white god" (fair-skinned mentor and ancestor). Prof. Buschmann thought that the name "Aztec" itself came from "Iztac" meaning "white."[54]

In the 1890s, blond-white "Indians" were seen to be settled in small villages among the dense forests of Honduras and Guatemala. These white Guatemalans gave an authentic account of the Quetzals, their ancestors, a people of milk-white skins and light flaxen hair. The Guatemalans (a very short people themselves), tell of remote villages of White Indians, among which are the Lacandones, "dwarfish" and white with a tinge of brown; "maybe they, too, are survivors of a once ruling white race of South and Central America."[55]

"The first settlers in Mexico were a white race," declared James Churchward. "Through Yucatan and the inland parts of Central America a white race predominated . . . called Mayas . . . traditions stating that the first people who inhabited those countries were a white race. . . . Temple inscriptions in Yucatan say they came there from lands that lay to the west of America. Polynesia lies to the west of America."[56]

Relict whites are in the islands, too: One author met a Martinique aristocrat in Fort de France who described a village high in the northern mountains that is inhabited by albinos: little pink-eyed people white as chalk. Occasionally one sees a few on the streets of Fort de France. (Martinique was once called Manda*nino*; the word "albino" itself breaks down to alb- "white" and –ino "little.")

CULTURE-BRINGER

Long before contact with the Europeans, the medicine man of the Croatan Indians (North Carolina) communed with the spirit of "First White Man." A white race seems to have inhabited North America even before the Red Man. The Shawnee, for one, knew that white people had lived in the valley before them. Along the same lines, the Maidu (California Indian) creation myth claims that the first people whom Earth Starter made were "as white as snow"—just as there once were White Indians on Channel Island, off the coast of California (one tribe known as the Pinug*nan*). Culture-bringer of the Iroquois, Ioskeha, was also a White One. Among the Algonquins, it was universally held that their ancestors were Abenakis: literally, "our white ancestors."[57]

In 1811, very ancient burials were found at Warren County, Tennessee, the females with hair "of a yellow cast and of very fine texture."[58] This was Cherokee country. The Cherokee, we know, had found a little folk—the Nunnehi/Yunwi Tsunsdi, with "pale white skin,"—upon arriving in the southern Appalachians. They were a "weird race," though quite civilized, with blue eyes and bearded faces. Did they intermarry? William Bartram, in his time among the Cherokee in 1773, saw some females "as fair and blooming as European women."[59]

The Chocktaw also encountered pygmy beings called Kwanokasha living deep in the thick forest, their homes in caves; one young brave met three such beings all with long white hair. My friend Peter Hartgens told me he met a few remarkably tiny and pale women at Mohawk powwows. Among the Menominee, Dakota, Mandan, and Zuni Indians are some individuals with "pale-skins," auburn hair, and blue eyes.[60] The Mandan, in particular, seemed a breed apart. Indeed, the Mandans believe themselves to be the first people on Earth. Why? For one thing, they were *different*: European settlers on the northern Plains confirmed reports from the 1720s of White Indians thereabouts. In these Mandan villages one encountered people, some rather short-statured, with varying shades of complexion and hair, pleasing symmetry, and proportion of feature. Mandan noses, too, were different than most Indians, not as arched as the Sioux, nor as broad. The women, it was remarked, were notably modest in their deportment. There was a mildness and sweetness to this people.

Some Mandan infants had bright silvery hair, almost white; a twenty-five-year-old man had eyebrows perfectly white. Mandan eye color tended toward hazel. The artist George Catlin reported that "the Mandans of the Upper Missouri speak of their first ancestor as a son of the *West* [e.a.], who preserved them at the flood, and whose garb was of four milk-white wolf skins."[61] The flood legend was strong among the Mandan. They held a keen remembrance of the first land, virtually organizing their ritual life around it; its inhabitants numbered among their own holy ancestors. An image of the ark, like the Greek ark of Deucalion, was preserved from generation to generation. Called the Big Canoe, this large structure at the very center of the village stood as an object of religious veneration, central to the annual religious ceremony in which one man imperson-

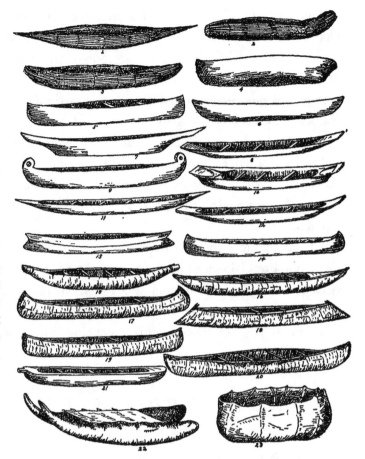

Fig. 5.6. Mandan boat (at bottom)—different from other tribes. Also different were their "beehive" huts made of earth. Their language, mythology, and customs were also unusual, as were their earthenware boiling pots, an art unknown to the other Indians.

ated Nu-mohk-muck-a-nah (the First and Only Man). Mostly naked, he is painted with *white* clay so as to resemble this ancestor. He enters the medicine lodge and goes through some mysterious ceremony—in the course of which he narrates the sad catastrophe of the Earth overflowing with water—adding that he is the only person saved from the calamity, and that he landed in his Big Canoe on a high mountain. The rite is culminated with offerings that are thrown into the river and sacrificed, just as the Hebrew, Chaldean, Sumerian, Central American, and Oahspen legends of the Flood end in a sacrifice of thanksgiving.

Moving on to the Northwest, our search through North America ends with the case for White Eskimos (and little Alaskans: see fig 2.29, p. 74). Known to whalers centuries before ethnologists lit upon them, the blond Inuit of the Canadian Arctic were conspicuously different from other

Eskimos, lacking all Mongolian features, many of them with perfectly blue eyes, red hair, and blond eyebrows. "The Innuits assert the men first made were white."[62] These old accounts seem to mesh with other evidence of proto-Alaskans, perhaps 10,000 years ago, who enjoyed an advanced culture and possessed a complexion as fair as the Cro-Magnons. Even politically correct archaeologists like Leonard Cottrell have observed that the sophisticated art of the Eskimo is a clear sign of direct descent from an "ancient form of civilization," which was, we now discover, shared with the Japanese Ainu (another Cro-Magnon branch) a sharing that extends even to their name: Inuit is simply a permutation of Ainu (pronounced "eye-new").

Another clue is the ancient word *sak*. Uni*sak* is an Eskimo village, their shoreline claimed to be the first ever made by Creator. Now this syllable, *sak,* is a marker as good as any DNA marker, leading us to the elusive white ancestor, not only in the North but at every imaginable location. So let's take a look at this interesting "linguistic fossil" of the Mother language.

FAIR-SKINNED LITTLE PEOPLE EVERYWHERE

Some kind of "Paleo-Caucasoid" people, much like the Ainu of Japan, inhabited North China (at Chou-kou-tien) 25,000 years ago, a non-Mongoloid modern type. The Ainu people live at *Sak*halin, an island just north of Japan. *Zac,* we learn, meant "white" both in India's Naga-Maya language and in Mayan. As a loan word, *zac* may vary with *sak,* particularly in languages with no *z* sound, like Spanish. In Japan, we might suppose that sak (as in *Sak*halin or O*sak*a) is reminiscent of its white aborigines, the Ainu people. South of Japan and into the Malaysian archipelago, the *Sak*ai are the most fair-skinned natives, rather yellow in hue ("light as a Chinaman"), many of Caucasian cast. Across the Indian Ocean, west of Malaysia, the *Sak*alava tribesmen of Madagascar inhabit the area once occupied by the extinct, white Vazimba little people. (Concerning Va*zim*ba, interesting that on the mainland, in *Zim*babwe, "Vad*zim*u" is the name of the revered ancestors, guardians of the land.) Also in Africa are the *Zak*aras, a tribe on the Ubanghi River.

Given the gray antiquity of this word sak/zac, it is no surprise to find it dispersed throughout the world and representing a founder race: Wi*sak*a, for example, is the benevolent culture hero of the Kickapoo, We*sak*aychak to the Cree. Among Virginia Indians, *Sag*kokok meant "the gods." The Algonquian "Sauk" tribe, we realize, was earlier transcribed as "Sac." This ancestral sak knows no geographical bounds, appearing in places of renown, particularly at sites of monumental architecture that still astounds the world.

- *Sac*sahuaman, Peru, with its cyclopean walls. By extension, sak also meant "royal" in Quechua (Sacsahuaman means "royal eagle"); only nobility were allowed to enter (as in Hawaii, where commoners were excluded from the temple cult), savoring of the elitism that infused the corrupt Sun Kingdoms of antiquity.
- Pi*sac,* Peru, the site of remarkable masonry and an ancient observatory (see fig. 7.5, p. 227).
- *Saq*qara, at Memphis, with Egypt's oldest stepped pyramid, 200 feet high.
- *Sac*hn, Babylonian sacred precinct of ziggurats; *zaq*aru, in Akkadian, meant "to build high," while E-*sag*-ila was the lofty Temple of Marduk, whose great festival of Renewal was held in the month of *Zag*muk (March–April).
- Kato *Zak*ro, a great ruin in Crete, where Dionysus was called *Zag*reus and the palace *Zak*ros; in Greece, were the *Zak*kala people of Lydia (Turkey).
- In Turkey itself is the archaeological site of *Sak*ce Goza.
- *Sk*ara Brae, Scottish village in the Orkneys with prehistoric buildings, sturdy walls standing since the Neolithic; entryways are much too small for the modern height of humans (designed for smaller people). "Scot" itself may have once been *Sac*ot, and Skara could have been *Sak*ara (elided vowel).
- *Sac*bes, "sacred roadways" of the Maya, literally "*white* ways," but also "sacred ways" (as in Latin *sac*er); these raised causeways were elevated up to fifteen feet and connected important civic sites.
- *Sak*ajut, archaeological site in Guatemalan highlands.

- *Zac*uleu, also in Guatemala, capital of the highland Mayan Mam, with a great fortress, platforms, ballcourt, and so forth.
- *Zac*uala, section of Teotihuacan with murals.
- *Zac*apu, Mexico, site of the cult of harvest.
- *Zac*atecas, Mexico, with its massive ruins and extensive ancient mine-works (echoing East Africa's Ki*sak*i with its extensive ancient irrigation system legendarily built by an alien superior race).
- *Zag*ora and *Zac*atenco, other Mexican ruins. At Palenque, Lady *Zac*-Kuk, a semidivine figure, was the Royal Mother of the Land. Among the Quiche, words for "dawn . . . light, bright, glorious . . . noble [are] all derived from *zak,* white. We read in their legends that the earliest men . . . were 'white sons.'"[63]

This coverage would not be complete without mention of: *Sac*hem, "chief," and the high priest of Bochica who was called *Zaq*ue, which also meant "king." The high civilization of this Columbian empire was called Zacs, led by the Muysca (a.k.a. Chibcha people) whose priest anointed his skin with glittering gold dust to commune with the goddess. Likewise, in Bolivia, the Guarani's sun god was called *Zag*uagua, his headdress so bright men could not look upon it. "Zaques," thought Lewis Spence, "are probably the remnants of prehistoric races of vast antiquity."[64] These zaques spin off to: *zag*e, "sanctuary," *sag,* "head," and *sag*-in, "military governor" (in Sumerian). It is also likely that Russian *zak*on, meaning "law, religion, code," is part of this constellation of words, along with *Zak*ir, an Assyrian king; *Zak*utu wife of Sennacherib; *Zag*ros Mountains; *Zag*reb, Yugoslavia, and so on.

English words such as sacred, sacrament, sacrosanct, sacrifice, sage, and even *sag*as of wisdom—all belong in this family. (In the Pacific, the meaning of *saka* takes on a **supernatural cast**, referring to all people and things—charms, ghosts, cunning persons, certain tribes—with special powers.) And let us not omit the Buddha (*Sak*yamuni), who in keeping with his *sac*red office, was of the *Sak*aya clan; also in India is *Sac*hi, the wife of Indra, Lord of Heaven (and King of Fairyland); here, again, *Sak*ka is the word for a type of white fairy or demigod, bestowing helpful gifts on the deserving Hindu.

Fig. 5.7. Portrait of the prophet Sakaya, with spirit familiars in background (Automatic drawing done in the dark by Dr. J. B. Newbrough in the 1880s.)

The people of Central Asia, particularly between the Black (Pontos) and Caspian Seas, are of light complexion, with varying color of eyes and hair, and are among the descendants of the white ancestor: some natural blonds are found in Ka*zak*stan, as well as among Afghanistan's Pashtun and Nuristani (Nur- means "light") in the northeastern inaccessible mountains, where one in three are light haired. In addition, many Tajiks and *Sar*ts, in the same general region, are light eyed, like the green-eyed Shikak tribe of Kurdish Iran. Also in Pakistan, the Kalash tribe has some blonds, as do India's Kashmiri people.

As they moved westward, these light-complected people finally appear in Turkey as our Trojan blue-bloods and pale Hittites (see fig. 7.22, p. 254), and in the North Caucasus. In this great land, crossroads of east and west, legends of little people with white hair are still told among the folk around Nemrut Dag, an old burial mound with colossal statues. Long ago, they say, before the Prophet, here in the Taurus mountain range, lived people with white hair, in whose memory some of the holy places were built. They were "smaller than normal people."

The Pontos region (north Turkey, near the Black Sea), supplies some of the richest traditions of the Great Ancestor. Acording to classical myth, from the marriage of Heaven (Ouranos) and Earth (Terra/Gaia) came Pontos; then, incestuously, Gaia and Pontos, mother and son, sired Keto, the "fair-cheeked," as well as the famous Telkhines and Lykos: all of them white-white. "And Pontos begat **Nereus . . . a trusty and gentle god** who is true and lies not . . . and does not forget the laws of righteousness." Pontos also begat daughters—the sea nymphs, "exquisite, delicate, milk-white maids."[65]

Pontus' son, Nereus, then married Doris—evidently of the pygmy race (as "Dorus" is mentioned in the classics as parenting *pygmaios*.) Both Aristotle and Philostratus speak of little people descended from Pygmeus, son of Dorus (whose tribe brought iron to Greece). The Pontos area, joining Europe and Asia, is the very cradle of our modern whites. Anatolia/Asia Minor, with her Hittites, Trojans, Lydians, Lycians, and Phrygians, gives us the Jaffetic branch* of Noah's sons, leading to the Etruscans, Greeks, Britons, and other founding populations of Europe. And *these* are the "Asianic" whites who are eventually known to us as Caucasians.

It has been said that anthropology "officially" knows of no other pygmy (i.e., undersized) groups besides Negrillo and Negrito anywhere in the world—certainly none of a white or Caucasoid racial type—and definitely none living anywhere in Europe, mainland Asia, continental Australia, Polynesia, or the Americas. Yet I have found evidence of a fair-skinned race of little people in dozens of locations, and on almost every continent. These include:

---

*The *Shem*itic branch was in India and the *Ham*itic in Africa.

- Yumboes, Africa
- Bushmen, southern Africa
- Vazimba, "white pygmies" of Madagascar
- Badarians, Egypt (fig. 2.25, p. 68)
- The Original Vedda, Ceylon
- Senoi, Malaysia
- Ainu, Japan
- Han-Dropa, China
- Abenlens, Philippines
- Tarifuroro, New Guinea
- Maori, New Zealand "Atua" people
- Tapuyos and Laron, South America*
- White Dwarfs, Brazil
- Akurias/Surinam, South America
- Martinique
- Chilotes, Chile
- Lacandon, Guatemala
- Choctaw Kwanokasha, Nunnehi, etc., North America
- Turkey
- Proto-historical Hebrews[66]
- The Picts, Scotland
- The Lapps and Chancelade Man
- White Eskimos
- Ellefolk, Scandinavia

BLONDISM

Back to our worldwide blonds: "Blondism" was common among the now extinct Tocharians of western China (probably the tail-end of Churchward's Uighurs). South of China, in Nepal, the Newars are "an anciently civilized people with light yellow skin and delicate features." The fair Lepchas of Sikkim, too, are noted for the beauty of their women. In India, the *Pand*avas are the five heroes and brothers of the *Mahabharata*, their name presumably based on Sanskrit *pand*u, "white, yellow-white,

---

*There are Laron cases also in Bahamas, Turkey, and Israel.

Fig. 5.8. Lanoh woman of Perak (Malaysia) of almost European cast

pale." South of India, the Andamanese supreme being (perhaps formerly the ancestor) is a white-skinned figure with a long beard. In addition, the Jaray of Cambodia have European features and pale skin.

James Churchward thought a white race, probably the priestly class, was dominant on Mu. If any or all of the above-listed people originated on Pan, a noticeable remnant, in situ, in the Pacific itself, was encountered at contact, such as the "white beings" at Malekula, New Hebrides, the Ambat people.[67] The Maoris of New Zealand recall a fair race called A*tua,* while on Motu Island (Banks group), the legendary hero is Kwat, a white man. Today, the Solomon Islands still have some blonds, as do parts of Melanesia and the South Pacific, such as Vanuatu and Fiji. "Indigenous blond mutations?" I doubt it. In addition, there are massive stone tombs on Rotumah, where natives are light-skinned and of particularly "inoffensive manners." Easter Island itself, when first seen by Europeans in 1722, was full of people of varying color. The natives said that several hundred years ago their ancestors were exterminated in a massacre; they were people of light skin and reddish hair. There are also whites at Suuna Rii, with reddish hair, magic, and age-old food plants; one also finds red-headed women on Tahiti and in the Malay Peninsula among the Semang and *Pan*gan.

The *Ba*gabo people of the Philippines say their **Creator-god**

Melu is white; indeed, the ancestors of these Aeta folk, according to a thirteenth-century Chinese account, had yellow eyes. There is some blondism there still among these Negritos. Small framed, curly haired, small nosed, the Aeta are thought to be the earliest inhabitants of the Philippines. Especially pale are the Abenlens, living deep in the isolated Zambales Mountains of Luzon, where they hid during the Japanese invasion. They are a strange, small people, unlike the regional Negritos— shorter still (no more than four and a half feet high), and "light . . . almost blond in complexion"; others are olive-skinned with light brown eyes. Most possess fine features and wavy, unfrizzled hair. Abenlens fair coloring may be taken as representative of the earlier type, for they are reclusive and never mixed their genes with neighbors or conquerors.

All the way Down Under, the Australian Aborigines, especially in the west-central part and central desert, show a high frequency of blond-to-brown hair, occurring in as many as 90 percent of children and quite a few women, some with outright blond hair. They are probably descended of the "Caucasian" type who inhabited Australia (Lake Mungo) 20,000 to 30,000 years ago.

We also come across light-skinned folk, the Rampasas, on the Indonesian island of Flores, as well as on New Caledonia and Fergusson Island; though primitive types (hairy, heavy brow ridges and jaws), some are light brown and blond. In New Guinea as well, "we saw men of a light, nearly yellow, colour . . . The hair of young children is often quite fair . . . [A] pygmy people, known as the Tapiro . . . [have] skin of a lighter colour than that of the neighboring Papuans, some individuals being almost yellow. The stature averages 4 ft. 9 ins."[68]

SAR

Nobody knows where the Bushmen originated.

ELIZABETH MARSHALL THOMAS,

THE HARMLESS PEOPLE

A telling tradition of the African Herreros, a Bantu tribe, says that after a great deluge, white men came and mingled among them. Local legends of white gods have long intrigued scholars of Africa; if oral history be credited, those **gods** once inhabited their country. In a twentieth-century report on Kalahari cave art in Damarland, the world's leading authority, Henry Breuil, declared that this painting was unmistakably the work of a mysterious race of white people.

Yet not so mysterious, as these proto-historical whites, the deluge survivors the Herreros so correctly recall, were worldwide; and wherever they landed they left their genes. Short, but not "dwarfed," the Bushman is well proportioned, on the model and scale of the "symmetrical" Ihins (see fig. 2.24, p. 65). Today Bushman babies are born pale pink. Full grown, the Bushmen are the lightest and shortest people in Africa, probably related to "Boskop Man," their large-brained antecedent of Upper Paleolithic times, an unusual variety of the modern Caucasoid type. Boskop men, a puzzle to paleontologists, lived in South Africa at least 10,000 years ago. Loren Eiseley found them "ultrahuman" but "fetalized," meaning, "pedomorphic" or childlike (see fig. 2.27, p. 69) where a Bushman father of two children looks like a boy himself.

The Boskop skull was childlike, the jaw delicate, the teeth small and graceful; Eiseley pictures the owner of those teeth "nibbling sedately at the Waldorf." And how he rhapsodizes these "first true men . . . these unique people," with their refined facial structure and artistic sensitivity (cave art). Though long extinct, their genes live on in their mixed descendants: the Bushmen of the Kalahari.[69] The bulbous forehead (round and prominent) of the Bushman (also evident among the Semang) is considered a Boskopoid and pedomorphic trait. The Bushman is a "child-man," mused Lauren Van der Post, wherein "the two are firmly and lovingly joined."[70] The pedomorphism of the Bushman female face will at first make you think her a girl, until you notice the wrinkled skin of her body.

It is of particular interest to the theme of this chapter that the Bushmen of Africa are called Ma*Sar*wa. This very ancient, maybe once universal, root *sar*, is yet another linguistic fossil, providing a key to unlock the lost history we have been tracking. On the basis of language alone, we can surmise that our lost race of the Mesolithic (of which the Boskop are an early branch and the Aryans the *last* offshoot), were light

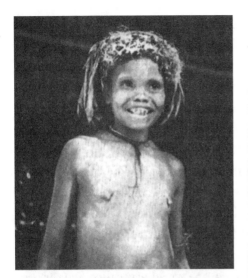

Fig. 5.9. Pedomorphic Negritos. Top left: Kensieu woman of Kedah, a group noted for their "infantile features." Pedomorphic means "retention of conditions normal in infancy."[71] Tonga Negritos also bear a "childish face," while among the Pi Tong Luang of North Thailand, the women seem "childlike in physical appearance."[72] Bottom left: Aeta woman, pretty and pedomorphic. Right: Andamanese, especially the Onges, are "facially infantile." Also called "neotony," survival of youthful traits into adulthood is known in certain animals, especially birds.

skinned. In Akkadian, the root *sar* meant "white," and among these ancient Mesopotamians, Goddess *Sar*-pan-itum was consort of Marduk who himself was A*sar*i in the Babylonian language. Sarku meant the "light race" in the Chaldean language, whose gods were An*shar* and Ki*shar*, the parents of Ea and Inlil. *Sar* varies with *shar*, which came to mean "king"; not too different from the Muslim *pasha* and *Shah*, the Persian "king." *Sharrim* meant "royal." *Zarah* was the name of an Edomite god-king, *sarpanch* is "headman" in India, and in Hebrew, kai-*sar* means "crown"; while in Etruscan, ai*sar* means "gods." The Egyptian name for god Osiris is A*sar*.

In Avestan, though, *zar* meant simply "old." "The oldest men on earth," according to a Cretan tablet, were called Mi-*sar*. And as we have seen, the tiny Bushmen, who are the oldest, whitest, and shortest people indigenous to Africa, are called Ma*sar*wa. In fact, the oldest (i.e., first) prophet and lawmaker in the world was Persia's *Zar*athustra. Theosophists say the oldest sacred language in the world was called Sen*zar* (var. San*sar*, the parent language of Sanskrit, originating on Rutas, i.e., Pan).[73]

The *z* sound, we know, varies with *s* in some languages. Was Zar ("white") the model on which the person of Zal was made? Zal is Persia's first hero who, like Noah, was born with white hair. These founders are remembered at such places as Sar-i-Pul, an ancient site in Persia; Sarepta, a Phoenician port; Sardis, Sarabit, and Sarbut in Egypt (with ancient ruins and mines); Zaraniq in Yemen; Zarqa in Jordan, Sargasso Sea, and even Sardegon, the capital of "Atlantis." Buddhists, too, hold *Sar*mana and *Sar*anganatha as alternate titles of their prophet. And with prophecy in mind, we also see *sar* shading into the meaning of "shamanic,"[74] as among the Siberian Tungus, whose shaman is reared in a certain tree called *Sar*ga, upon which ritual white cloths are hung.

In India, where many of these *sar* words originate, *Sar*nath is the stupa near the holy city of Benares, while *Sar*na is the sacred grove of Bengal and Ap*sar*as are a class of goddesses. Here in Mother India, we find the qualities of holiness, whiteness, and deepest antiquity combined in the person of *Sar*asvati, consort of Brahma himself and **goddess of learning, writing, and the arts**: in short, the personification (and *deification*) of higher mind. In Sarasvati we perceive the embodiment of that early white race of teachers, the sacred and learned tribes of yore. Famed for her transcendant nature, she is, iconographically, a beautiful woman with snow-white skin. Associated with the color yellow, her votaries wear yellow garments.

Sarasvati is pure and modest, not gaudy like other Hindu deities. In one hand she holds a book: the sacred teachings. She is a fountain of knowledge and refinement. As a river, the Harappan civilization developed along her course. As a healer, she brings right medicine. As originator of writing, she aligns with the "fully literate" (G.V. Childe) culture of Mohenjo-Daro. She is in fact the Shemite or Indic version of:

1. the little people who introduced the earliest form of writing*
2. the Norse legendary dwarf named Dvalin who invented the runes
3. the 12,000-year-old system of grooved hieroglyphics found on the Han-Dropa disks

Sarasvati is also goddess of speech. First man (asu) had no real speech.[75] Before man began to walk upright and use his lips and tongue in enunciating words, he spoke in the thorax; indeed, *upright* man is a speaking man: the column must be erect, vertical, not only to support his enlarged brain, but to permit the development of speech. It is for this reason that the talking birds (starling, raven, parrot) can utter words, for their larynx is vertical. Neither is articulate speech possible without a flexible neck (cranial base); this flexion is missing in asu man. The australopithicine (asu) palate and pharynx are unsuited for articulation.

In Hopi myth, the First People could not talk; just as the Maya Quiches say the earliest antediluvian race was without intelligence or language—for when Gucumatz and Tepeu first attempted to fashion human beings, the result was a creature that could not speak or worship their creator. Neither did H. P. Blavatsky's Third Root Race have spoken language; they lived like the druks, the ground-people, and like the grunting Bats: in holes in the ground.

---

*On writing: "And the rabbah made records in writing on stone, which they taught to their successors, and to whomsoever desired to learn of the Lord."[76] (This took place about 24,000 years ago.)

Giver of speech, India's Sarasvati deploys all the higher faculties, setting man apart from animals; teaching the barbarians. On the subcontinent, children, students, and scholars adore her. In the *Puranas,* the first continent is named the Land of the Gods, Sveta-dvipa, literally "white continent," home to Blavatsky's Third Root Race, which, she proposed, had a Yellow Father and White Mother, followed by a holy stock of divine dynasties, always recognized by their moonlike complexion.

Divine dynasties: It was the wish of kings, in the ancient day, to partake of that holy stock. Indeed, King *Sar*gon's name meant "true legitimate king" in the Assyrian language, and by extension, *saray* means "palace" in Turkish, leading also to the Kha*zar* Turkic Empire. Later forms—Cae*sar,* kai*sar,* and Russian t*sar* (c*zar*)—are no doubt traceable to this root. And the same would hold for Abraham's exquisite wife *Sar*ai, praised in the Dead Sea Scrolls: "No maiden is fairer than she! How perfect her hands!"

Last of all, the blond and green-eyed *Sar*matians, moving ever westward, became the "Caucasians" and "Aryan invaders." Witness the light-eyed *Sar*ts of northwest Asia; or *Sar*ruma (the "Childrens' God" of the Hittites at Yazilikaya). *Sar*ku is another Hittite divinity (pronounced almost the same as Spanish *zarco*—"light-eyed"); while *Sari*-kale is a Hittite shrine, at Boghazkoy, and Troy itself is called His*sar*lik. In fact, there was once a more-or-less continuous chain of white tribes throughout northern Asia, best known to us as the blond, blue-eyed Scythians—the first people to ride horses and wear trousers.

In Afghanistan are the Ha*zar*a people; Ha*zar* is also a Paleolithic cave site in Iraq, as is *Zar*zi. We remember, too, the pale kallikant*zar*os of Greece. And let us not forget *Zor'*ya, the **Slavic goddess** of dawn; or the talented *Sar*acen builders and artificers who came to Spain (bringing the "light-eyed" *zarco*, which people in the Rif are called zarkan); like unto the *Sar*sen stones in the British Isles (the 25-ton upright megaliths at Stonehenge). This great family harks back to the elusive pale-skinned civilizers, lost in the fog of prehistory, tens of thousands of years older than those latecomers called Aryans.

CHAPTER 6

The Night of Time

Is there life in the deeps as well? A race yet unknown. . . ?

SCHILLER

AN UNDERWORLD EXISTENCE

Legends from Turkey to Tennessee recall the ability of little people to "disappear"—like the British fairies called "Pillywiggins," who vanish as soon as they are glimpsed; or the northern dwarfs' *tern-kappe,* "cap of invisibility." In Turkey's Taurus Mountains, one legend has a magical maiden taken in marriage against her will. On the journey away from home, she asks the Earth to open—it does, and she disappears. The Greeks, in turn, have their dwarf race, the Kallikantzaros. Dwelling in the ground, they only come out at night. These "kallies" seem to behave a bit like Teutonic and Scandinavian dwarfs who also dwell in rocks and caves and recesses of the Earth, not unlike the Welsh little people (Tylwyth Teg) who live in an enchanted garden hidden by a door in a rock that leads to a "secret passage."

In the Tennessee mountains, the Nunnehi also abide in rock caves in "their beautiful place underground." Their dancers could sometimes be seen walking into the river and "disappearing" before the Cherokee's startled eyes. There are even Civil War stories of soldiers seeing smoke rising from some hidden settlements of the Nunnehi. One Canadian tale about the Iroquois Little Ones (Geow-lud-mo-sis-eg) "just vanishing" is quite recent: An eyewitness watched them as they crossed the road and disappeared down into a hollow area.

Even the living-and-breathing forest pygmies in Africa seem to be so well camouflaged that they can be passed without ever being noticed. Until the nineteenth century, our knowledge of the pygmies was so scant, "to the point," says Colin Turnbull, "where they were thought of as mythical creatures, semi-human, flying about in tree tops, dangling by their tails . . . subhuman monsters . . . with the power of making themselves invisible. They blend so well with the forest foliage, that you can pass right by without seeing them."[1] The Negritos of Malaysia also move about "so quietly that I could never shake off the impression that they materialized out of thin air."[2]

Thus we realize that legends of "magical beings" can be born in a variety of ways: at Monte Alban (Oaxaca, Mexico), "dwarfs" were at one time used in magic displays, involving an intricate network of stone-lined "pygmy-size" tunnels—one has to crawl to get into this warren of narrow twenty-inch-high passages. These underground causeways, with tiny steps, connecting the various temples, were used by the Mayan priests in a classic trick of disappearance and reappearance.

Mexico's most important underground complex, inspiring a wide range of legends, is found at the Loltun Caves in Yucatan. Here, corridors and chambers are arranged something like a wheel-cross (see figures of the universal circle-cross: 2.7, p. 46; 4.11, p. 126; 7.9, p. 232; and 7.20, p. 250). This fabulous complex in the Puuc Hills, famed for these sacred buildings and caverns, was used from the remotest of times. Its carvings and glyphs are "not the work of the Maya but of some older race . . . the first inhabitants,"[3] the small, hunchbacked men called "Puus" who built the caverns of Loltun and were supposedly destroyed in some catastrophe in the Long Ago. Are the Puuc Hills cognate with Pukeheh, a Southwest Indian "god" who saved his people from a Flood, or with Pukar, a city destroyed by the flood, according to the Tamil people?

Hawaii's Menehune, like so many of the world's little people, seemed to have an underworld existence that included the knack of "disappearing" into the ground. Not unlike their congeners in Mexico, the Menehune are credited with building the tiny (irrigation) tunnels on Kauai,

Fig. 6.1 (left). Who are all these squat gods of Mexico? Detail of wall painting in a Monte Alban tomb. Drawing by Jose Bouvier.

Fig. 6.2 (right). Figure of a Puu dwarf. Note peaked cap. Drawing by Jose Bouvier. Even the word "pygmy" (originally *pug*me) seems to share a common (Panic?) root with this Puu(c). The term was once almost universal: they were the "sprites" of mythology, like Luzon's "goblin or forest spirit" called *Pug*ut, or the legendary Puk of Jutland, or England's mischievous Puck, resonating with the Amerind Puck Wudj Ininee, "little man of the mountains." The little men, among the Mi'k Maq, are the Puk-alutumush. Following suit at points south are the Puc-ro river (at Darien) with its White Indians and little people, the legendary mountains of Pukato Ti from which a white teacher came to the Brazilian Kayapo Indians, bringing agriculture, and the *Puc*aras fortress in Peru where white people with beards were exterminated. Also wiped out were Japan's Koro-*puk*-guru, an underground race. Too, in far-off Australia, are the Tja-*puk*ai people (another name of the little Barrineans, fig. 2.14, p. 54); while in Egypt, the *Pu*anit are the dwarfs who settled the land of *Punt*. Drawing by Jose Bouvier.

and like their cousins in other lands, they are given to hide in crevices and high rocks to make themselves "invisible." Some say that black dwarves still exist on Kauai, around the place where carved channels of stone carry water down from the hills, eventually reaching very low, long tunnels.

One time a school superintendent and forty-five children, according to Rev. K. W. Smith (who spoke with witnesses first hand), saw a group of Menehune playing on the parish property near the school. When the wee folk spotted the schoolkids, they stopped playing and dove under the parish house, seemingly into some entrance. Folklore has it that a tunnel runs from under the parish house all the way up to their home deep in the mountains. Some Hawaiians believe the Menehune still live thereabouts.

While features of subterranean infrastructure may help explain these so-called disappearances, other tales of invisibility devolve no doubt into the unseen world of discarnate spirits—ghosts and apparitions— endowed with the ability to make themselves seen, accounting also for the shape-shifting little people of legend, spirits who can manifest as animals, insects, other people: anything.*

THE VANISHING

In New Brunswick, Canada, the intriguing Tobique tunnel (belonging to the "vanishing" Geow-lud-mo-sis-eg) is entered under a huge steplike rock ledge. The opening is an 18-inch-diameter hole; some say that the built-in step and tunnel are "creations of the Little People"; it has never been thoroughly researched.

For reasons that we will very soon explore, some of the little ones of long ago tunneled through the earth of the Underworld.† The Bayan-Kara-Ula interlinking caves in the Himalayas, explored by Beijing archaeologists in the twentieth century, were found to be artificially carved; they are more like a system of tunnels and underground store-rooms, boasting walls that are well squared and glazed. Within were found skeletons of strange people four feet four inches tall.

Not surprisingly, the wee people of Celtic lore also have their underworld hideaways and disappearing act. When the Celts arrived in

---

*Italy's classical Lars, answering in most ways to the Gothic dwarfs, were not people at all but actually Etrurian spirits, of dead lords (lars), who act as protectors. Teutonic elves, also protectors, are held to be the third rank of angelic beings.

†Living "under the earth" can mean several things: pit-dwellers, ground-people; those living *inside* the mounds; the Indian pygmies of classical times who "lived under the earth"; or the mine dwarfs of Europe.

Ireland, they saw the "wee bodies" disappear in a mysterious way, and without stopping to investigate, imagined they had become invisible. Good story for the campfire. Related British tales have elves who simply "vanish into the earth." But if the elves and fairies of the British Isles could vanish into the Earth, it was less an act of magic than a case of spritely agility combined with artful engineering.

Underground dwellings in Orkney and East Scotland are attributed to the little Picts; just as the mysterious tunnels at County Down were thought to be the work of the Tuatha De Danaan. Legend says that after being vanquished by the Milesians, these conquered people of Danaan were allotted the portion of land underground, the sidhe mounds and raths (cellarlike buildings). But as they retreated more and more into the woodlands, these "fairy nations" became increasingly secluded, and successive races more superstitious of them. Elfland or Land of Fairy was finally driven completely underground: hiding. (The name of the Scandinavian elves, *huldu,* means "the hidden people.") The Celts, as we learn, eventually killed off most of the little people, whose remnant then fled underground, surfacing only at certain times.

Large numbers of these artificial mounds and souterrains, many with several chambers, stud the landscape of Antrim and Down. Rather than "disappear," the wee bodies simply passed into their souterrain— whether grotto, sidhe, rath, barrow, cavern, or rock shelter. At Stranocum, Newberry, one subterranean gallery is only three feet six inches high, indicating a race of small inhabitants. One of many local stories has it that a "fairy woman" begged a nearby cottager not to throw her waste water out front, as it falls down her chimney. Another householder, returning late at night "from a gossiping," was met by a pretty little boy who said, "Coupe yere dish-water farther frae yere door-step, it pits out our fire." She complied with this reasonable request, and prospered ever after.

The elaborate passage grave at Newgrange in eastern Ireland was brought to mind in 1981 when the Murray Farm Tunnel Chamber in Holmes County, Ohio, was discovered. The Ohio complex was identical in various features to Ireland's narrow passage graves. A normal-size person has to creep through the opening, which is no taller than two feet. Some 6,000 years old or more, the Ohio tunnel chamber was cut from solid rock and is nearly sixty feet long, just like its counterpart in Ireland. Discovered while an oil company was preparing the site for drilling, the Ohio chambers, of "mysterious purpose," have headroom of only four feet. Not only were experts reminded of Ireland's famed underworld, but the *orientation* of the Ohio chamber was found to be identical with that of the ancient ruins at Uxmal, Yucatan; the streets and plazas of which are for the most part oriented 9 degrees east of true north. And there at Uxmal is found the Pyramid of the Magicians (a.k.a. House of the *Dwarf*); in fact, tradition holds that a dwarf erected that one hundred twenty feet high pyramid in a single night! (The Puuc capital of little people was here at Uxmal.)

UNDER THE GLOW OF THE MOON

This Uxmal legend goes on to describe a "dwarf boy" who once struck such fear into the people and the ruler that he was ordered to be executed. The ruler, however, promised to free him if he performed three impossible tasks—one of which was to build a giant pyramid in a *single night*. This he did, legend says, and became the new ruler. Now this "single night" business is queer but by no means unique: Bolivia's Tiahuanaco, if their legend be credited, was also built overnight. "After a long night, there dawned, standing upright to the eyes of our forefathers, the great ruins you now see."[4] Were these builders* also little people?† Pre-Incan ruins, *underground,* have distinctively low ceilings and passageways.

These questions brings us right back to the clever little Menehune and their mountain tunnels; for these Kauai people, of enduring memory in Hawaii, could also accomplish great tasks at night. Master builders, the Menehune preferred to work under the glow of the moon; in a single night, say the storytellers, they planted a taro patch, irrigated it, and surrounded it with solid stone walls and stands of sugar cane and banana trees. According to one Kauai legend, the related Mu folk (tiny

---

*Consider the tiny Masonic builder in Fig. 3.3., other little master builders[5] (farfadets), and the Dan builders.
†Other legends say it was built by impious giants.

forest people in the wet uplands and deep valleys), sleep by day; they can't go into sunshine, for they live in caves and have large sensitive eyes. Besides, they prefer to avoid people, conducting their work and business at night, always making sure to finish the job by cockcrow—if not completed by then, they abandon the work.

Yet this unlikely scenario is no different in western Europe, where the little people work the graveyard shift and inhabit underground dwellings. Known as *bwca* in Wales, these brownies, like the pisgie of Cornwall, are helpful beings who do chores for a favorite family at night when everyone is fast asleep. If seen, they appear as small men with shaggy hair, about three feet high, dressed in ragged brown clothes.

The little people of Tennessee were night owls too, and like Kauai's Mu folk, were blinded by sunlight, and would only hunt and fish after dark. They were quite civilized, but their eyes were large* and terribly sensitive to light. We will probe this "sensitivity" later. But for now, let us follow those large eyes.

THE MOON-EYED ONES

The Tapiro pygmies of New Guinea have eyes larger and noticeably rounder than their Papuan neighbors.

In Malaysia, too, the Kedah Negritos possess a rotund contour of the *norma occipitalis,* meaning: they have round-set eyes. Large and round eyes (a pedomorphic feature, see fig. 5.9, p. 173) occur in other early races, cropping up in such far-flung locales as Hawaii, Tennessee, Bolivia, Philippines, Greece (Mycenae), Turkey, India, Tibet, equatorial Africa, Java, Central America, Sumeria, Venezuela, the Andes, and France (with its statue of a **Gaulish god** with huge eyes). We are more than curious to discover if these "moon-eyed" folk share a common pedigree, as the artificial caves built by these little people at widely separated locations have already excited our interest in a possible shared ancestry. The little chickcharney of the Bahamas also built *in* the earth—and had huge eyes.

---

*Linking them to the early moundbuilders who Caleb Atwater said had very large eyes.

Fig. 6.3. Types of Tapiro Negritos, 1912. The headman would not let the visitors see their women.

　　Are these moon-eyes related to the distinctly large and *rounded* eye orbits found on Neanderthal skulls? These Paleolithic cavemen had particularly large eyes, as did "most early men, and they are round,"[6] exemplified by the *Australopithecus* specimen (asu man) found in Chad, Africa. Perhaps this aboriginal type helps explain the tendency of the African pygmy's eyes to "protrude, as if from . . . goiter"—a condition that corresponds strikingly to the "bulging eyes" of Java's hobbit man and to the tiny Lacandon people of Mexico, with their "bulging almond eyes," like the goggle-eyed figures in the Acambaro collection. The eyes are prominent also among the little Andamanese, south of India, Quatrefages noting that they are well to the sides and separated by a very

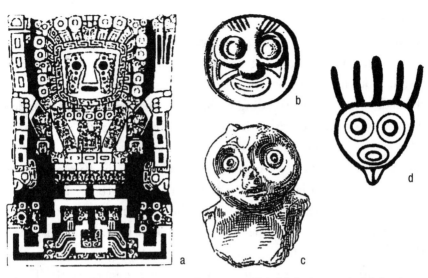

Fig 6.4. Images with round eyes: (a) a Tiahuanaco idol; (b) Cretan mask; (c) Creek Indian (Georgia) burnt clay image; (d) Northwest coast petroglyph. Compare these to cognate saucer-eyed images from ancient Sumeria (fig. 9.5, p. 318).

noticeable space, reminding us of India's "goggle-eyed" goddesses, and even of Etruscan (Italy) figures with enormous eyes.

These pop-eyed folk point us to the oldest races on Earth, and so do eyes set wide apart: Pygmies' eyes, besides bulging, are often set wide apart, resembling those of the Bushmen and the tiny Palauan specimens who, like hobbit, had small faces, large teeth, and a "wide gap between their eyes"—very much like the feral, completely wild, orang pendek of Sumatra. Africa's Zinjanthropus, an australopithecine approximately of the asu type had his eye sockets set far apart.

This morphology reminds us of W. Scott-Elliot's reconstructed Lemurians, whose eyes were set so far apart they could see sideways without turning. Add to this group the Ainu of Hokkaido who, for all their "Caucasian" features, also have those primeval eyes: set far apart. And with those ancient eyes (set in "modern" faces) also belonging to the little Etruscans (a civilized race of astronomers) and to an Ainu namesake at 'Ain Ghazal (temple builders of the Levant with "big staring eyes"), we can better understand South America's round-eyed Tiahuanaco idols, representing an advanced civilization of the archaic era, so similar to the master race at Cocle, Panama, several of its statues with beards and eyes set far apart. Cocle is considered the oldest culture in the New World: "exceedingly ancient."

Early in the twentieth century, the *Philippine Journal of Science* wrote about living persons on Luzon who resembled Paleolithic Neanderthals: massive jaw, receding chin, heavy brow ridges, and rounded eye orbits, combined with fairly small stature (five feet), "all approximate to . . . the antediluvian man of Europe," descendants of the latter exemplified by our (proto-Italian) Etruscans who retained those "wide-set" eyes (bulging, too, at least on some of their terracottas). From what stock did they hail? These bulging and wide-set eyes are a distinguishing mark of the archaic humans who came about when the robust cavemen dominating the Old World began to blend with the incoming survivors of Pan: a shorter, more gracile people. Those big-eyed Etruscans seem to have migrated from Asia Minor, and yes, we find Hittite (Turkey) figurines with eyes "oddly prominent." At Troy, on the western coast of Turkey, the Palladium is dedicated to an owl-headed goddess, the great-great grandmother of Pallas-Athene; yet this is the same face seen in Peru and Bolivia . . . same shape, same size, and with curious owls' heads arranged in just the same way. Troy's discoverer, Heinrich Schliemann, thought the connecting link was *Atlantis,* but most of these "owl" eyes actually have closer ties to the *Pacific:* appearing in New Guinea, Malaysia, Hawaii, Java, Sumatra, Andamans, Palau, and the Philippines.

The ancestors of the Filipino little people had *round* yellow eyes— the description resonating with the "jaguar"-eyed yellow people living in a Venezuelan crater—this South American "Agarta" (Underworld) at the bottom of two craters seen by a pilot in 1964. In fact, these extinct volcanoes were found to be connected by an underground passage. Does this Underworld of subterranean chambers sound familiar? Local tribes in Venezuela speak of strange people sometimes seen in the woods. "Their skin is the color of yellowed ivory and they have big eyes like a jaguar's, and long hair of different colors."[7]

But this far-flung family resemblance does not stop here: As Venezuela gives way to the mountains in the south, the thread resumes again with the "moon-eyed albinos" of the Andes (reported by Harold

T. Wilkins). In Peru, an ancient auburn-haired people were depicted as "owl-eyed": one representation of which we may view in the round-eyed figure (described as "owlish") among the Nazca earth-drawings of southern Peru. These mysterious Nazca lines and figures have been attributed to a people who built a sunken temple (again, underground), featuring an idol possessing large, round eyes, who is rather like Tlaloc, the Mexican rain god, portrayed as "goggle-eyed" (at Teotichuancan), resembling, too, the round-eyed Toltec colossi (stone warriors) at Tula, Mexico.

"UNEASY AMALGAMS"

These large round eyes tell us something about the mixture of the high and low in the Long Ago, about the great little people "fraternizing" with the round-eyed hulking ground-people, resulting at times in magnificent progeny with most of the "good genes" of both parents. James Churchward's large-eyed Muvians (Lemurians, i.e., people of Pan), like the civilizers of the pre-Incan Andes and of the Central American Maya, were tall, white,* round-eyed masters-of-all-things—the idolized genius who stares back at us from the tombs of antiquity, such as the sculpture of Makemake (the **round-eyed Creator**), found in a burial cave on Easter Island—whose legendary "Bird Men" are also sculpted with big, staring eyes.

Concerning these "ops" ideograms at Tiahuanaco (i.e., round-eyed idols): the Jesuits placed a secret manuscript in the Vatican Library, translations from an Incan sage of the seventeenth century, which indicated that Tiahuanaco was at one time entirely underground; that it housed an astonishing civilization going back to "earliest times." Arthur Posnansky dated Tiahuanaco's subterranean temples and "goggle-eyed" beings, correctly I think, to 16,000 BCE.† Tiahuanaco, legend holds, "was built before the sun shone." Her monoliths are so big and

---

*Tallness from the large ground-people and whiteness from the Ihins, the little people.

†Likewise, the same family of beings, sculpted at Mexico's Teotihuacan, represent "the earliest divinities" of Mesoamerica.

cumbersome yet so well cut that they seem to be the work of super-beings or, as legend says—"built by the gods."

Concomitant with these godlike men—and predating all known history—was a series of unwise cohabitations and unlawful mixings, which Loren Eiseley calls "uneasy amalgams," sometimes resulting in hideous and abnormal races—mongrels and giants alike—*both* sharing the progenitor's tell-tale large and round eyes. At the gigantic end of the spectrum were the builders of Cholula's enormous pyramid (Mexico), gigantic men of "deformed stature," matched in the Old World by the Cyclops and Titans. Cyclopean Tiryns (in Southern Greece) was leg-endarily built by "round-eyed giants" summoned from Lycia. Cyclops, of course, means "round-eyed" (cycl- means "circle" and -ops means "eyes"), each Cyclop sporting one huge eye in the middle of his forehead.

In most traditions, though, the one-eyed was but a symbol stand-ing for something wild and unreasonable, sinful and inhuman, like the "one-eyed" Arimaspians of Scythia, ever lusting after hoards of gold, with an eye only for material gain. The one-eye (of self-glory) served, really, as an ancient metaphor alluding to those godless men who raised monuments to *self.* Madame Blavatsky identified these as the fourth Root Race, the moon-colored people who built huge self-worshipping cities and statues at such places as Easter Island and Mexico (Olmec), both of which places left sculptures of moon-eyed figures. Titanic kings were these sons of Cain, according to Hebrew legend, and they "endeav-ored to immortalize [their] name by means of monuments."[8]

GODS, MEN, AND MONSTERS

These Titans, in classical myth—Cottos, Gyas, Briareos, Cyclops—were the offspring of Father Heaven and Mother Earth, a brood that began with monsters, though they improved as they went on. Related legends speak of gods creating imperfect creatures, botching the job, and here the several bibles agree: Genesis says "all flesh had corrupted his way upon the earth." Oahspe says "and of monstrosities betwixt man and beast there were many."[9] "They bring forth in deformity on the earth."[10] Before the Flood, mortals were descending so low in breed and blood

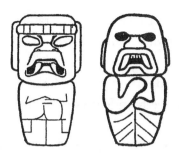

Fig. 6.5. Olmec "misshapen gods" are represented in their art and religion by these "jaguar-men" and other monstrosities.

Fig. 6.6. The stooped Yaks burrowed in the ground like beasts of the field, and went sometimes on all fours. Yaks are depicted in catacomb frescoes of Peru, appearing as a queer manimal with bent back and long thin arms.

that "idiocy and disease were the general fate of the tribes of men."[11] For when the Ihins mingled with the giants and druks, their offspring were afflicted with catarrh, ulcers, lung and *joint* diseases (hence, deformed).*

And it is the same in the Babylonian creation epic, where we find Earth peopled by gods, men, and *monsters;* thus was it said that the Chaldean Goddess produced a crop of monsters. Pan-the-satyr, for the early Greeks, was the most hideous and debased form of those miscegenations. "They resembled centaurs and apes," avers one Hebrew legend, and as the early chronicles in Oahspe tell it, the oafish and grotesque Yaks were produced when the druks (a.k.a. Cain, a.k.a. *Homo erectus*) dwelt with the animal-like asuans (*Australopithecus*).

I am afraid that what science calls "mutations" (or Loren Eiseley calls "genetically strange variants") are nothing more than the result of unwise mating. Of all the sons of Noah, Ham mixed the most (and the most unwisely): his offspring resulting in furry tribes with long curly red hair. Such beings with hairy bodies, deformed bones, snarling fanged mouths,

---

*Like the deformed Puuc (see fig. 6.2, p. 179) or the "small and misshapen" Skralinger, such misshapen men in the Americas have been confirmed archaeologically: Owen Lovejoy, for one, excavated skeletons with "strange physical deformities . . . [and] many unusual bones."[12]

and claws, are not "symbols" of anything or mythic fantasy; rather, they are remembrances of the monstrosities that were not corrected until Apollo's time, 18,000 years ago.[13] North America's Stick Indian, as one example, is said to be small, vicious, and cunning, a semiman who is very skinny, with long arms and sharp teeth and claws on their hands and feet.

Claws? Sharp canines? On humans? Well, yes, such prominent canines are still noticeable among some Melanesians and Australians. Before Apollo's mission of beautifying the races, "men and women [had] hands with claw nails, fierce and warlike, and hair in tufts . . . [their] eyes drawn down like a lion's, and mouth wide and falling open."[14]

Thus does Brittany folklore speak of "hairy fairies," with hands terminating in talons; like Ceylon's Nitttevo, they are pygmy-size. The three- to four-foot-tall Nittevo, extant until the eighteenth century, had clawed hands (curved nails). An extremely fierce people, they were perfectly human in shape and form, though covered with thick reddish hair. They ate whatever they could catch with their long claws—talonlike, long and powerful. The Bushmen of Africa also have clawed nails, along with other unusual, archaic traits: steatopygia, labia majora, knob-nipples, not to mention those primeval wide-set eyes.

Fairly monstrous are Central Europe's trolls, usually represented as short and stumpy with shaggy hair, dark wrinkled faces, and deep-set eyes (though very bright). Their voice is cracked and hollow; their hands have claws like a cat.

HOW DIMINUTIVE WERE THEY?

The Han-Dropa tribe of Tibet, of unknown breed, were supposedly so ugly that their Chinese neighbors tried to exterminate them. Puny and fragile, four feet tall, they possess disproportionately large heads. Their eyes are large with pale blue irises. A similar whispery race was known to live in North America, south of the Cherokee, a tribe of little people called Tsundige'wi, with very queer-shaped bodies, no taller than a

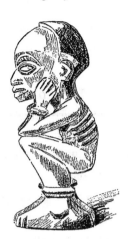

Fig. 6.7. Benin sculpture,
large-headed dwarf like
the Han-Dropa and Nimerigar

man's knee, living in nests scooped in the sand. The little fellows were so weak and puny said the Cherokee that they could not fight at all, and were in constant terror from the wild geese and other birds that came to make war upon them.

Sure, there have been schemers and scammers over the centuries who have tried to pawn off phony mummies of weird little men and other oddities to eager buyers. Even in the fourteenth century, Marco Polo complained of fake pygmy mummies, sold by natives of Sumatra: "'Tis all a lie and cheat," he wrote, explaining how these "little men" were manufactured on the island out of monkeys with faces just like a man's. More recently, Loren Eiseley met a bluff fellow, a rancher, at a bone hunter's camp out West.[15] The fellow tried to sell him a two-feet-tall cave mummy of "a pygmy or a dwarf," its arms neatly folded (like the Tennessee skeletons). "Two hundred bucks," demanded the rancher. No thanks, Eiseley declined the pleasure of owning the blackened, leathery corpse. All right, replied the rancher; he would take his prize to the carnival. "There's money in that little man," he sniffed. A fake? Who knows. Hoaxes, though, cannot account for *all* such specimens, some of which directly resulted from the mismatching of human races in the Paleolithic. Oddly, most of the littlest ones seem to come from America (Guatama), of which we learn: the Guatama Ihins "in course of time *became diminutive* [emphasis added]." They stopped marrying and "the Lord took them up to heaven"[16] (i.e., extinction).

How diminutive were they?

Human fossils only fourteen inches high have been found in California.

The Wyoming Shoshone and Cheyenne speak of a supersmall race of people known as the Nimerigar whose shortest members stand twenty inches high. Lewis and Clark, while on the Plains, heard tell of these little human "devils" with large heads. One has to reckon with even more recent accounts of sightings. One such, reported not long ago from Bend, Oregon (and posted online at the Paranormal Phenomenon Forum), involves the appearance, along a quiet creek, of two little people no more than eighteen inches tall, wearing skin garments. From the circumstances, it was surmised that "the little men weren't happy about the logging [there] and destruction of the forest." A certain verisimilitude is lent to the episode by age-old local legends of Stick Indians in this region, along with similar reports of miniature men in the Cascades and Vancouver Island.

But the most celebrated (and best studied) of America's mini-men is the Pedro Mountain Mummy—a Nimerigar?—found near Casper, Wyoming, by a pair of gold miners blasting through a gulch in 1932.* Fourteen inches tall, this creature was no taxidermist's scam, but a very well-preserved individual, perfectly formed, and upon X-ray, found to possess an authentic skeleton. A full-grown adult, this Pedro Mountain man had been buried in a seated position, cross-legged, his hands calmly resting in his lap.

The region, we know, is replete with legends of small people; in fact, of two very different kinds: (a) the wicked Nimerigar (Stick Indians), and (b) the Teachers of Light, known to the Medicine Wheel Crow. But just when I was about to say that most of these superpygmies are found in the New World, I came across an October 24, 2005, story out of Tehran, Iran, which reported the mummified corpse of a twenty-five-centimeter dwarf near Shahdad city of Kerman province.† This only recharged local

---

*See his picture at www.legendsofamerica.com/wy-littlepeople.html (accessed July 28, 2012).

†There were also, near lake Zerrah, Iran, Negrito tribes who are thought to have formed the black guard of the ancient kings of Susiana.[17]

rumors of an ancient dwarf-city in Kerman, which is in the same area as Behistun Rock (see "dwarfs" fig. 6.9, p. 198). Experts believe the critter, like the Pedro Mountain little man, was mummified under natural processes. One more thing: Police in Kerman arrested two smugglers planning to sell the mummy for about three million U.S. dollars to a German buyer.

But we have digressed. . . . One loose end concerning our large-eyed predecessors is their extreme sensitivity to light.

BLINDED BY SUNLIGHT

Col. Fawcett's Brazilian Bats sleep all day in their hollows and hunt by night; with great keenness of vision, like the Bushmen, they nonetheless cannot endure the rays of the sun. In this class are the large-eyed hardy night-workers, like the Tiahuanaco builders, who, in turn, have their congeners in the Smoky Mountains where the Yunwi Tsunsdi help householders with their work at night; their cousins, the "moon-eyed" Nunnehi, lived underground and were "blinded by sunlight," emerging only after sundown. The earliest record says these moon-eyed little people could not even *see* in the daytime. So, too, do the pale Dvergar (the word "dwarf" comes from it) of Norse epics live underground and avoid any sunlight, which is supposedly lethal to them and to the Finnish trolls as well.

> *Day's dazzling light annoys*
> *Us, darkness only joys;*
> *We therefore love to dwell*
> *Deep underneath earth's shell.*
> A TROLL DITTY FROM THE ISLE OF RUGEN

Nocturnal primates, as a rule, have larger eyeballs than their diurnal counterparts.

Owls possess eyesight especially adapted for nighttime hunting, their retina packed with rod cells, the vision receptors that are sensitive to low light levels. Remember the owl-eyed images in Troy and

Peru and the people who built Tiahuanaco in a single night? Or, more realistically, "in the night of mankind," as sixteenth-century Incas called it; for the world, say the legends, at one time was dark and had no sun. Those ancient Peruvians reputedly "saw best in moonlight."[18]

And it came to pass that great darkness covered the earth . . . and clouds came over the face of the earth; the moon shone not, and the sun was only as a red coal of fire; and the stars stood in the firmament as well in the day as at night [referring to a period ca. 70,000 BP].

OAHSPE, FIRST BOOK OF THE FIRST LORDS 4:12–16

In the beginning, according to much of South American myth, it was "always nighttime." Around Lake Titicaca (Tiahuanaco), the sun was thought to have hidden himself (giving them their "moon-eyed" gods).[19] Similarly, in Mayan myth, the world was sunless at first, Mexican legend recalling a time when the world was left in darkness. It was the god *Nanahuatl* who brought the world out of darkness (*Codex Chimalpopoca*). Scholars think this myth is poetically symbolic of night giving way to day, but why grasp for *symbols* when myth can uncloak the palpable Night of Time?

In Wyandot legend, an underground city was created after the destructions of Flood and Fire and North Wind; the little people, say the Indians, still live in that Lower World, only surfacing at night. Wyandot myth, moreover, speaks knowingly of spells of darkness.

Once, when the jealous Sun was killing people with her heat,* the Little Men changed a Cherokee into a rattlesnake to kill the treacherous Sun. But instead, the snake killed Sun's daughter, leading to a period of darkness when the Sun stayed indoors. The Choctaw of Oklahoma also

---

*Peruvian legend follows the first people out of the cave Pacari, the Lodging of the Dawn, while Tamputocco is named as the cave of origin of the Incas. Various legends of Peru (in common with most American myths of Emergence) have their ancestors emerging to the Upper World from caves and rocks in the underworld. In Mexico, it is from the seven caves (Chicomoztoc). For the Plains Sioux, it was Wind Cave in South Dakota.

have a legend of Earth plunged in darkness for a long time; their Place of Emergence* was *Nan*ih Waiyah. A California Indian myth (Wintu) states, "There was a kind of dim light all the time."[20]

Legends of dim times may also correspond to the nebulous period some 13,000 years ago, when "the lands of the earth were covered with darkness . . . a veil [came] over the face of the sun, and it shone not in brightness for many years."[21] More recently, perhaps 3,500 years ago, an "ajian forest" (atmospheric densities) lasting for 400 years brought darkness upon the Earth and led to the end of the little moundbuilders: there was "darkness around about the earth on every side . . . a state of darkness for four hundred years, and the sun shone not."[22] Another 400-year period of dim light, in the Near East, was discovered by examining ice cores which indicated "particularly low temperatures . . . between 6400 and 6000 BC."[23] Corresponding effigies with "big staring eyes" were found in this region (Jordan Valley).

A. Hyatt Verrill saw White Indians among the San Blas people;[24] they are spoken of as "moon children," the belief being that they are the offspring of Moon God and Indian Mother, and are thus of a partially celestial origin. They can see better after dark than in the daytime, like the *Indios bravos* of Brazil's Matto Grosso, cannibals and head-hunters, who "see better in the dark than a prowling feline."[25]

Not confined to the New World, recollections of these night owls are echoed in Greece where the Kallikantzaros live below, surfacing only at night; in Hawaii as well, sunlight was "fatal" to the little Menehune and their cousins, the large-eyed Mu people who lived in caves and slept by day.

---

*There were times, for example, about 9,000 years ago when *a'ji* (densities, skyfalls) fell to Earth, and the belt of meteors gave up showers of heat; "the sun became as a red ball of fire and remained so for one hundred and sixty-six years." Molten heat falling to Earth is remembered on the Upper Maranon of Brazil, where legend recalls that hot steaming water poured down on the Earth, burning and scalding everything. Natives of Haiti told colonizers that men once lived in caves, driven there by the parching rays of the sun. The Andamanese, in turn, say their ancestors were once annoyed by the *continuous* heat of the sun; while the Melanesian saga of creation speaks of no night at all; the whole day was light.

PERSECUTED AND HIDDEN AWAY

The Menehune, like so many little people around the world, legendarily go to work at night, merrily helping with chores around the house; yet, we wonder: Were they, in fact, captive workers? Were Europe's mine dwarfs actually *conscripted* to toil in the mines? And what about their mischievous pranks, especially their clever ways of concealing themselves? Is this some garbled version of hiding from oppressors? Blackbirders? Slavers? The Tahitians who migrated to Kauai (the Menehune were there before them) forced their predecessors into servitude, driving the rest back into the canyons and valleys. (A secondary meaning of "menehune" in the Tahitian language is "slave.")

Embedded in all these myths of underground life is a hidden vein of flight from persecution and genocide; in Oahspe we learn that before the Flood the Ihins of the Old World were eliminated to a man: "my chosen had become exterminated [by tall Ihuan warriors] on all the divisions of the earth save Pan."[26]

Thou killest my prophets.

OAHSPE, BOOK OF GOD'S WORD 1:9

Apollo slain by Python, Osiris slain by Typhon, Bacchus slain by Titans may all be myths representing the slaughter of the Old World's priests and sacred tribes, the little people, more than 24,000 years ago. Genesis 6 recalls these depraved, murderous, giants, as does the Book of Enoch, the latter declaring that they, the giants, were at their worst in the time of Jared (antediluvian). Meanwhile, German lore states that the giants degenerated ("altogether wicked and faithless") to the point that they "would too much oppress the dwarfs."[27]

Before the flood, in four great divisions of the earth, Vohu (Africa), Jud (Asia), Thouri (Americas), and Dis (Europe), they did not leave one alive of the Ihin race. In Whaga [Pan] there was a remnant, and they were scattered far and near, in separate places *hiding away* [emphasis added] from their evil pursuers [the large

Fig. 6.8. Map of the names of the continents before the sinking of Pan/Whaga.[29]

|huans]. . . . My chosen were persecuted and hidden away in the valleys and mountains, even on the tops of mountains [where we still find their mixed descendants today].[28]

OAHSPE, THE LORDS' FIRST BOOK 1:25, 32

Much later, in the Old World, the tribes who had amalgamated with the sacred people were persecuted when their mark of circumcision was banned by tyrants. The purpose of circumcision was to make the holy tribes recognizably distinct from all others, so they might "preserve the seed." "My chosen go away by themselves and build their cities, for I raised up separate from the world's people, the Ihins."[30] The chosen people lived apart (and married endogamously), as symbolized in the person of Enoch:[31] while all these abominations defiled the earth, the pious Enoch lived in a secret place. None among men knew his abode. Genesis seems to agree on this point, giving us to know that the patriarchs lived apart, in isolation from the rest of the world.

But persecution and exploitation of the small people was worldwide. A Mayan story of creation recounts: when it was decreed that man should be formed, the gods "made a number of manikins" of wood (*manikin* means "little man" in the Dutch language), after which "everything both great and small abused the manikins."[32] In like manner, the Teutonic dvergar were bound in servitude to King Svafrlami; some historians believe that the Gotho-German dwarfs were subdued

Fig. 6.9 (above). Old Persian Behistun Rock dated to 516 BCE is King Darius's monument to himself, carved in the cliff face. In front of him are nine captured rebel chiefs, little men: in the very same area as the rumored "dwarf village."

Fig. 6.10 (left). Sculpted on a Peruvian temple wall, a Chavin captive warrior is shown cut through below the waist.

before the tenth century by a more powerful people, their remnant fleeing to the mountains, concealing themselves in caverns.

Conquest slabs, moreover, depict nude little captives as found in different lands including Mexico, Egypt, and India. Carvings in Iraq on the palace of King Ashurbanipal show war captives of short stature (ca. 650 BCE). The king's servants are also depicted as little people on Assyrian reliefs (693 BCE), as well as on fourth-century BCE Persepolis reliefs at Behistun.

The prophet Isaah was sawn in half 2,500 years ago. Manasseth, son of Hezekiah, had established idol worship and by law abolished the worship of the Almighty; he caused the prophet Isaah to be sawn in twain because he worshipped the One Creator. The horrid practice was repeated in later times, with the sufferings of the Sikhs at the hands of Muslims: paintings recall spread-eagled Sikhs being sawn in half for refusing to embrace Islam. The memory of this brutal method was even projected onto the beginning of things: in Assyrian creation, the goddess Tiamat was cut in half, "her maw was split," one half made the heaven, the other made the Earth.

Persecutions of the little people were everywhere: In America, the warring Creeks journeyed from the south to drive them from their homeland, according to Cherokee history. The Creeks made sure to press on during a full moon that blinded these nocturnal people. The low stone wall at Fort Mountain (now a State Park in North Carolina) is a remnant of that war, which the moon-eyed people fought against the Creek, at the end of which they fled north and took up their subterranean habit in the mountains.* One might mention, too, that despite all the Cherokee's fond folklore of their own little people, the earliest account I have found says: "These wretches [the little people] they [the Cherokee] expelled."[33] William Bartram, the great botanist and explorer, directly quotes the Cherokee who say they came from the west and exterminated the former inhabitants, the little white people, driving them from the country.

Out West, the Yakama word for Stick Indians is *steyehah'mah,* meaning "spirit hiding" (under cover of woods).

Hawaii's Menehune, too, gradually went into hiding. Once a half million strong, only sixty-five of them remained in the town of Wainiha (Kauai), according to an early-nineteenth-century census. One (apologist) Kauai legend holds that the Menehune themselves decided to withdraw, seeing they were intermarrying too much with Polynesians, their race lost. They then "disappeared," retreating to remote inaccessible places in the mountains. But they, too, were driven out.

In the same vein, the Ainu people originally occupied all of the islands of the Japanese archipelago; then, at the beginning of the Neolithic, groups of Mongolian descent (the future Japanese) pushed out onto the islands, killing off the little white Ainu as they went. Almost

---

*The subterranean theme, combined with persecutions, carries through to Hopi history, mentioned in the next chapter, where they escape their oppressors through *tunnels* built for them by the kachinas; just as "escape tunnels" underlie many Mayan sites.

completely exterminated, too ("hunted like wild pigs"[34]), were many Negrito populations of Sundaland who, like the Ainu, became refugees from Mongolian, and later Indian, invasions.

Father Paul Schebesta spoke of the "inhuman treatment of the Aeta by the Christian Filipinos,"[35] they, too, were driven to inaccessible refuge areas in the mountains. In Schebesta's compassionate account, we learn that some Negritos became domestic slaves to the dominant culture;* Muslim Malays regularly took Negrito children for slaves in the nineteenth century. Here in Malaysia, the tribal name Semang is a pejorative term that came to mean "debt slave." The Semang Negritos live in an "incomprehensible state of fear that their children might be kidnapped. That is probably the chief reason that they flee and hide before every stranger . . . based on sad experience of former times."[36]

In the Celebes, the tiny Toala "people of the woods" (women only four feet six inches tall) are frequently enslaved by the Bugi. This was going on as well in the Andaman Islands; W. H. Flower, in 1888, tried to explain their ferocious and inhospitable behavior: "This hostility to foreigners . . . found much justification in the cruel experiences they suffered . . . especially kidnapping for slavery . . . [by] the Chinese and Malay traders."[37] The Orang Asli, in the interior of the Malay peninsula, were often captured and enslaved by the Malays, as were the Pangan, a forest people now inhabiting the most isolated areas. Today, the Malay do not even allow the little forest people to enter their house, their attitude one of amused contempt: "they are nothing but animals." In the old days, Malays hunted them down, enslaving those they considered desirable, and killing the others.[38]

Negritos on the Asian mainland are also "in a condition more or less of degradation . . . resulting from the oppression with which they have been treated by their invading conquerors,"[39] the Siamese, for example, among whom Negrito slave women were formerly kept. It is well known, too, that in Ceylon, at the end of eighteenth century, the Veddas rounded up the last of the Nittevo, drove them into a cave, and set a brush fire at the entrance, suffocating them all! And the extinguishing of the last of

---

*Oh, there were some Negrito groups the slavers didn't bother with in the Philippines, for, as captives, the Aeta would simply sicken and die.

these little pugnacious people who had, in fact, been taken as serfs was accomplished by the Sinhalese Lambakanna Dynasty.

Other Negritos (of Malaysia and the Andamans) were rounded up and brought all the way to China, in which country the little Han-Dropa tribe was also chased down and killed, hunted by "men with the quick horses": Mongols? The Chinese term for Negritos is "Kun-lun," which is also the name of a mountain in northwest China (see fig. 2.11, p. 51). Kept by the rich as household slaves since the eighth century, they were considered by the Chinese "their legitimate prey." Ancient history? There was a news story, as late as 1933, of the Han-Dropa still being held as slaves by the Chinese.

And in Europe, a very old manuscript from Scotland (Hebrides) reported that men from Argyll in the year 1 CE drove the pigmies from Cunndal, a cave near Luchraban, to the Pygmies Isle. A few perspicacious historians view the medieval "fairies" as identical with the small races of Lapps, Picts, and Iberians who populated Britain and Scandinavia in the Neolithic and Bronze ages, and were pushed out by the Celts and Germans—the Celts eventually killing off the "wee people," while the remainder fled underground. No, their souterrains were not for burial or ritual purposes, as has been suggested (by descendants of their oppressors); they were *hiding places*. Concerning Scotland's "weems," Sir John Lubbock owned that "when concealment was an object, the dwellings were entirely subterranean."[40]

It is the same sad story with the Vazimba little folk of Madagascar, driven out by the Huva people who had come from Asia and conquered the highlands. In Africa itself, the Akka pygmies of Gabon* were exterminated by the M-Pongos, while those who remained were enslaved (around 1868). Africa's little folk, the original inhabitants of the rainforest, time out of mind, have now become the most marginalized and oppressed people in the world. Even today, many pygmies in the Congo

---

*Today, as we speak, the governments of Gabon, Cameroon, and Congo are rapidly evicting pygmies from their forest habitat so they can cash in on quick profits from the sale of hardwood, with groups like the Hutus and Interahamwe determined to exterminate the pygmy altogether, to take over their forest resources. It is actually the same situation in Sri Lanka where the little forest-dwelling Veddas are threatened by timber barons.

live as slaves to Bantu masters. It has been customary in the Congo for wealthy people and traditional leaders (*mwami*) to capture and enslave the defenseless pygmy, now known as *badja* and recognized as property of his master. Indeed, the Bantu consider it a "time-honored tradition." In Uganda, slave labor at the mines is still in force, echoed in the Kalahari, where diamond exploration has thousands of Bushmen forcibly removed from their homeland, reports of torture coming from this region. Here in southern Africa, farmers in the remote veld still take Bushmen as slaves. In the early years of European occupation, the little Bushmen, driven to the great wasteland of the Kalahari Desert, were subject to a regularly planned and wholesale destruction on the borders of Cape Colony.

> For two hundred years and more, all along the steadily expanding European frontier, he [Bushman] was shot on sight and hunted down with horse, dogs and guns with as great ardour as the lion and other carnivorous animals of the veld. . . . One of the many tragic sights of the closing phase of his history . . . was the reappearance, at odd moments . . . of some wrinkled old Bushman come from afar to harvest the honey . . . only to be shot down in his efforts by some Griqua or European invader . . . [who had pushed his people] steadily inland, took over the vital waters handed on to the Bushman by his long line of ancestors, killed off the game which had sustained him unfailingly . . . plundered his honey . . . systematically eliminated . . . the necessities of bare survival . . . [And yet] they found it strange that he should be angry and embittered and in his turn should resist, kill and plunder. . . . Calvinistic storms of abuse and misrepresentation [are] raised against the Bushman . . . reproach used as a smoke screen to hide the naked humanity of the little hunter from the hearts of those about to crush him with their own inhumanity.[41]

THE "HEATHEN" RACE

Do these circumstances contribute somehow to the almost universal stories of malevolent dwarfs and evil pygmies? Have the little people been demonized by the hand of the oppressor? In many, many places we hear of wild and wicked little men, and indeed some of these are degenerate races. In Madagascar, for example, near the erstwhile home of the noble Vazimba, wild men, small of stature (called *kalonoro*), inhabit the woods. There, around the Marojejy Mountains, deep in the forest, live this frightening and bizarre (*hafahafa*) people, with long flowing beards and glowing eyes. From whence came these awful little men? We learn from Hindu scriptures "there was born into the world evil offspring" prior to the Flood.

There is no shortage of folktales recounting the deeds of sinister little people. A raft of misfortunes and dark supernatural happenings are attributed to Europe's fairy, goblin, pixie, elf, and gnome; the brown dwarf oppresses as nightmare, bites as fleas, scratches and tears, and leads you astray into bogs and marshes. Many is the story of the ill-luck that shadowed a person for *mistreating* the little people. Ah, there's a clue: weren't at least some of these "evil dwarfs" simply retaliating for abuse and persecution? After all, the Serbian little people (*vilas*) bother none but those who intrude on their roundels. Neither do southern Germany's Wichtlein cause people any harm except when they are abused and cursed by them. Others will only fight when cornered or in self-defense, usually involving attempts on their lands. In these Teutonic and Scandinavian legends, dwarfs, dwelling as they do in rocks and caves, are the powerful guardians of mineral wealth; not friendly to man, they can be vindictive—or at best mischievous—like the elves who are inclined to plunder the peasants' cornfields (as do African pygmies on Negro plantations, and Aeta Negritos who raid Filipino plantations for food).

To Lauren Van der Post, the Bushman is "a criminal, perhaps, because, starving, he has stolen one of the many sheep now owned by men who had stolen all his land."[42] Responding to charges made against the Bushman, which label him "cruel, treacherous, vindictive, [an] incorrigible thief," Van der Post countered: "There is no doubt that, in the moment of his final bitterness, deprived of his country, surrounded, doomed . . . the Bushman did do many terrible things to confirm the accusations made against him."[43]

Mission-work among the Bushmen, we might note, has been singularly unsuccessful. Neither was the Twa Pygmy ever converted: Colin

Turnbull recalls an incident when the local missionary asked Kenge what he thought of the Christian God. Kenge (Turnbull's favorite Twa informant) said with his usual frankness, "It is the biggest falsehood I know."[44] Neither could the Hopi, "Little People of Peace," be converted: The Franciscans, since 1629, tried to convert the obdurate Hopi, setting up three missions that only led to trouble and unrest. The people resented Spanish interference with their native rites, and were, moreover, enslaved and forced to drag from great distances heavy logs for the building of the mission church. Cruel punishments were meted out to the resisting Hopi: the hair shirt, as well as burning with hot turpentine after beatings, all of which made them ripe for rebellion, which did come.[45]

When the little people of the Philippines (Aeta) refused to be converted, the Spanish called them *infieles* (pagans). In the case of the Russian Rusalky, known, among other things, to *tickle* their unfortunate victims to death, their enemies are lured into the water; those who bathe at night *without a cross* around their necks are easily drowned by the Rusalky, who—though now spirits—were originally girls who themselves once drowned or committed suicide or were buried without a church funeral.

Yes, part of the picture—this cast of malevolence—springs from the wee folks' refusal to accept the new religion; even in ancient Greece, the queen of the Pygmaioi refused to honor the state gods, in this case, the goddess Hera (for which heresy, she was cruelly punished). Then, in Christian times, the Irish fairies rebuffed the teaching of St. Patrick and St. Columbkill; according to the far-seeing research of David MacRitchie, the little people of Ireland went into hiding around the sixth century, as religious war was waged against the Picts. But since the interlopers felt some guilt and fear concerning these conquered souls, "numerous rumors were born concerning the ghosts of the Picts, still roaming through the land. And this in turn led to the elves and fairies." MacRitchie perceives a similar origin to the "ghosts" of Flemish folklore: the tiny but strong Fenlanders, evidently Negritos, who inhabited the country before the Celts, "lived for a long time hidden, for fear of the new people . . . [and] they became changed in the imagination of the dreamy Germans into mysterious beings, a kind of ghosts or gods."[46]

Hairful little lasses and stumpy little fellows! These are scattered today! Scattered today over the wide world! . . .[They] were full of music and dancing and traditions. The clerics have extinguished these. May ill befall them! And what have the clerics put in their place? Beliefs about creeds, and disputations about denominations and churches!

ANGUS MACLEOD, 1877, FROM
BRIGGS, *THE VANISHING PEOPLE*

Propaganda abounds. Among the Devon peasantry, it was fancied that pixies were the souls of infants who died before being baptized; sometimes a changeling afflicts a home because the baby wasn't baptized early enough.

Parents, to prevent the korrigan from stealing their children,* would place the youngster under the protection of the Virgin by putting a rosary about its neck. The original korrigans, it seems, were great princesses, but having refused Christianity, they were struck by the curse of God, which in turn, animated them with a violent hatred of religion and the clergy. The sidhes in the same vein, loathe holy water; while the Norse trolls of the woodlands hanker after Christian blood.

In European tradition, only the sound of church bells frees a man from the net of the trolls, putting them to flight. It is the same in the Slavic world where the ludki (little people) were effectively driven away by the sound of church bells. They, too, were counted as pagans:

---

*On kidnapping: Among the articles of tribute allegedly exacted by the wee-bodies (the legendary race of Irish Neimhidh) were two-thirds of one's children. Mothers would pin their children to their sides to prevent their abduction by the pixies. There are many such tales of supernatural kidnappings. Could the culprit be wild men? *Homo erectus*–type gangs out on raids? The hairy, wild, and archaic Ebu Gogo on Flores reputedly stole food and children from "humans." We realize, though, that often enough, the *opposite* was the case: kidnapping *of* little people among the Andamanese, Semang, and so forth. And in Africa, the Bushmen were in great demand as slaves, "all along the frontier the more desperate and adventurous characters among my countrymen [Afrikaner] added to their living by kidnapping Bushman children and selling them to the land- and labour-hungry farmers. . . . [A]n early traveler speaks casually of seeing "wagons full of children returning from a raid across the frontier."

in Serbia, Hungary, and Poland. In fact, it is said that the ringing of church bells is what drove the trolls and other mountain people permanently out of Germany and Scandinavia. A neat metaphor, or should we say a euphemism, for expulsion and persecution.

In each of these cases (including the bathers who neglect to wear a cross or a rosary), the "legend" is little more than an admonition against spurning Christian ritual, pointing to the perils of defying the church. It is all simple-minded propaganda. Example: Anyone who can say the paternoster backwards will not be bothered by evil elves![47]

What can we conclude about these evil little people? We are reminded of the old saw that the gods of the *former* era are made into the *demons* of the succeeding one. "Not infrequently a change of religious faith has invested with dark and malignant attributes beings once the objects of love, confidence and veneration."[48] As theological ammunition, Old Europe held the fairies as a portion of the fallen angels who will not have it so easy after the "final judgment." Is this some sort of twisted rationale for the abuse of "heathen" races?

Many of the builders of the souterrains, suggest the old chronicles, were enslaved or pressed into servitude. Legend, moreover, holds the brownies as "servant of humankind" as a means of expiating the weight of "Adam's curse." The Pechts (Picts), employed as serfs, carried the heavy slabs, in one tale, for the giant Finn McCoul's cave; and like the Swiss "Servan," they and the little grogachs are known to thresh corn or do other menial chores for the farmers. But was it compensated? Irish artificial caves with several chambers were the hiding place of this Finn McCoul when another giant came to fight him. Finn was the chief of the Pechts—or rather their master—and they worked as slaves to him and the Fians: grinding rye, and so forth. These tales are little more than reminiscences of a conquered race of small stature.

All sorts of pagan witchcraft have been ascribed to these "heathens." Sudden death of children in Eastern Europe was blamed on the little men, the Domovoy. So now the peasantry has someone to blame for illness, frightful dreams, accidents, unpromising offspring ("changelings"), madness, misplaced articles, and theft. Even stroke—"elf-stroke"—can be caused by the touch of a sprite, while some even blamed the Irish fairy for the terrible potato blight. And with the supposed changelings (awful babies switched with one's own offspring), people got to blame someone else for their problem.

Such changelings have more to do with spirit obsession: one's own dark spirits. Indeed, much of the mischief blamed on sprites originates with disembodied, earthbound (EB) entities: usually their own dead relatives! Most notably have poltergeists been confused a thousand times with goblins and little people. Other disruptions are blamed on the Menehune: When the Menehune approve of a project, they work all night—but when they disapprove, they disrupt the work with equipment breakdowns and other unfortunate happenings. Or so the stories go. But these are all typical tactics of excarnate mortals, spirits in turmoil, the unhappy, parasitic dead. Thus were the Menehune mistakenly regarded as mischievous beings, very much like the Yorkshire "boggarts," who will "capsize bowls of porringers" at table or smash crockery and earthenware or blow out candles or "pixie-lead" people astray: all classic poltergeist manifestations, issuing from the nefarious dead (or should we say undead?).

The Nis or Puk of Jutland, who usually abides under the roof, sometimes amuses himself by playing tricks on the servants, tickling them in their sleep or pulling off their bedclothes; he is also known as Nick Knocker or Pulter-Claas (after the racket he makes; *pulter* means "noise"). And this is our poltergeist. Trickster, in Native American lore, is much the same, renowned for pulling pranks on people, often in the middle of the night; thumping on the side of your camp, braiding horse manes, or tying up clothes on the line. All this mayhem—pinching, crowding, "bad luck," and so forth—supposedly done invisibly by the so-called little people or "fairies" is no doubt accomplished by our own formidable familiar spirits, the subject belonging to the science of Psi—and not to the history of the little people, really.

The little people, in many locations, are fading fast. The last remnant of the Bushmen sit around their night fires and sing an old song: The day we die, a soft breeze will wipe out our footprints in the sand.

When the wind dies down, who will tell in the timelessness that once we walked this way—in the dawn of time?

For the reader who would like to find out more about current abuses of the African pygmy, here are some news items and leading advocates.

"Thing—Thing: Globe-Trotting by Tricycle," NYTimes.com (accessed September 19, 2012). This pertains to deep Forest and Pygmy Fund.

Wikipedia.org Human_rights_in_the_Republic_of_the_Congo (accessed September 19, 2012).

Lovell, "Congo Pygmies Appeal to World Bank over Logging," available at www.reuters.com (accessed September 19, 2012).

"Advocates Draw on Communities to Free Enslaved Pygmies in Eastern Congo," available at www.advocacynet.org/resource/1136 (accessed September 19, 2012).

"Pygmies are Victims in Congo Atrocities," available at www .survivalinternational.org/news/94 (accessed September 19, 2012).

"Rwandan Pygmies Facing Squalor and Exclusion," available at nimbrung.net/world-brreaking-news/Rwandan-pygmies-facing-squalor-and-exclusion (accessed July 29, 2012).

Minority Rights Group International, www.minorityrights.org (accessed September 19, 2012).

Rainforest Foundation, www.rainforestfoundation.org (accessed September 19, 2012).

World Peasants Indigenous Organization (WPIO), www.wpionet .org (accessed September 19, 2012).

Pygmy Fund, www.pygmyfund.org. Founded by Jean-Pierre Hallet in 1974 (accessed September 19, 2012).

Juliet Hutchings, blog, film, UN Indigenous Peoples Forum. Visit blog at http://advocacynet.org/blogs/index.php?blog=108 (accessed September 19, 2012).

CHAPTER 7

Mounds of Mounds

They were the sacred little people, yellow and white, living apart on the mounds.

OAHSPE, FIRST BOOK OF GOD

The tiny fairies . . . were mound-dwellers.

KATHARINE BRIGGS, *THE VANISHING PEOPLE*

THE WEE ONES

When the starving people of Ireland migrated to the United States during the potato famines of the 1840s and saw our "Indian Mounds" scattered across the land, they just assumed these formations were the work of the wee bodies. Though demeaned and despised, these dirt-poor Irish laborers actually identified the American moundbuilders more accurately than formidable intellects of the time like Henry Rowe Schoolcraft, and later Alex Hrdlicka, who summarily dismissed the Lost Race theory, insisting that the mounds had been built by the Native Americans themselves. It was to become one of the hottest academic debates of the nineteenth century (and by no means settled today).

The Irish peasantry held a deep and abiding tradition of fairy mounds, the green sidhe (raths and souterrains), built by the little Picts and Danes and Tuatha De Danaan. To the Hibernian and Caledonian eye, the American mounds were a carbon copy of the countless "hollow hills" dotting the Irish and Scottish landscape. "The strong resemblance," argued one American investigator, Caleb Atwater, "between the works in Scotland and ours, I think no man will deny."[1]

But deny they did, and still do . . .

One Americanist wrote, knowingly, "the mound builders were *distinct from any of the other North American tribes* [emphasis added]. . . . Their pearl-encrusted garments, their finely woven textiles . . . prove that the mound builders were . . . far in advance of the Indian tribes."[2]

Distinctly un-Indian were such mound artifacts as: inscribed tablets, hieroglyphic writing, telescopic tubes, astronomical calendars, glass beads, batik weaving, advanced agriculture, metallurgy, architecture, temple pyramids, as well as the science of surveying, which involves the mathematical ability to measure angles.

But there are all kinds of mounds, old and new. The Indians in Florida, for example, were still building them (up to forty feet high) when De Soto and De Leon got there in the sixteenth century; these newer mounds, though, were *sepulchers*—not the original type, which lacked any trace of inhumation. The Indians simply *used* them later, for burials, just as in Mesoamerica nations built pyramid temples on top of the *old mounds*. Some of the latter-day tribes sought to imitate the ancient builders, as did the Choctaw, but the Chocktaw's mounds were, again, built for burial. The earliest mounds were for the living—not the dead—nor for the ritual entombment of god-kings or any elite whatsoever nor for aggrandizement of any kind.*

The Creek Indians reported, accurately, that the *oldest* mounds were the work of the ancients many ages prior to their arrival. In fact, most Indians said the moundbuilders were a different race. Some tribes, in the nineteenth century, declared the moundbuilders had been people who "came from another world and dwelt on earth for a long season, to teach them of the Great Spirit and of the Summer Land in the sky."[3] They were the holy people of Gitchee-manito.

---

*The Elk nation, for example, erected a new mound for great events, such as national festivals or the historic amalgamation of separate nations or dynastic changes. In Peru, mounds were built to hold the houses of chiefs and their families, to place the residence of the ruler in a commanding position, thereby elevating the cacique above his subjects. Mounds were turned into royal tombs in China.

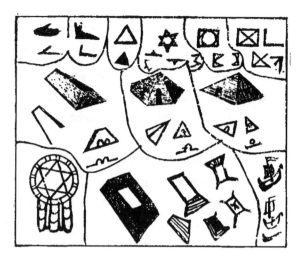

Fig. 7.1. Oahspe's Plate. 83: "Bible of the Mound-builders." Note the *umane* altars at center, bottom. Fashioned to this day by the Sioux Indians, the umane is so *wakan,* so sacred, that it may not be touched or stood over or even looked at by certain persons.

Gitchee, the Creator! The World Maker! Manito—spoke in the souls of things:

Speak, O earth! Have eyes, O earth! Have ears, O earth! Behold Me, Your Maker!

And man rose up and said—Here am I, O Gitchee! The Creator looked, and lo and behold, the Ihins stood before Him, the little people, white and yellow.

OAHSPE, MOUNDBUILDERS, FIRST BIBLE OF NORTH AMERICA[+]

In the middle of the nineteenth century, when vast burial grounds of tiny people were discovered in Tennessee, with splendid copper artifacts and freshwater pearls and other fine ornaments, so distinct from the known Native American assemblage, writers began to speculate about the origin of these unaccountable "little men," wondering if they were indeed beings from some other world. But the learned societies scoffed, ridiculing the Tennessee finds: "Vestiges of human forms of unnatural dimensions were *supposed* [emphasis added] to have been discovered," sniffed the *American Antiquarian Society* in 1856.

Yet the Cherokee knew them well, they were the little people, the Nunnehi (or Yunwi Tsunsdi), the moon-eyed people who had left a series of small mounds and stacked rocks arranged from one end of the region to the other.

MOUNDBUILDERS WORLDWIDE!

The contest afoot, European scholars were determined to find Old World origins for this sophisticated culture in "savage" America, remarking the similarity of the American mounds to the "high places" of the Israelites; a few even thought they found the Ten Commandments in the mounds.

But at the end of the day, no common genetic markers were found in the blood of Amerinds and Jews.* Other writers floated evidence linking the American mounds to the Hindu *tells* of Mohenjo Daro, as well as to the Danes, Phoenicians, Babylonians, Chinese, Atlanteans, Welsh, Vikings, Romans, Malaysians, Irish, and Numidians! In fact, there *were* ancient mounds in many parts of the Old World: mound fields of Bahrain, Turkey, Egypt, Jordan, countless round mounds in Iran and in Iraq the "leveled mountains" or "artificial hills" of the Sumerians, to name but a few.† The "startling prominences" on the plain between the Tigris and Euphrates were flat-topped with steep sides; they studded the landscape everywhere. British diplomat Austen Henry Layard, traveling out to the desert from his government post in Mosul, marveled at "a line of lofty Assyrian mounds . . . one of the first settlements of the human race."⁵

Rabbinical writings, meanwhile, spoke of a legendary "mountain" called Alconuz, which contained the tomb of Adam in a vault, Adam's own pure descendants dwelling at the higher levels, the heights, while the offspring of Cain remained at the foot of the mountain. But, say these records, in the course of generations, the two communities mingled, the higher caste corrupted by the lower: a fine allegory of the moundbuilders, as we come to understand them as a separate people, a holy people, who nonetheless mixed, in time, with the other races of men.

There are also "unexplained" mounds in the Motherland itself: at Melanesia and New Caledonia, where dwell some rather light-brown and even blond natives, and at Samoa, where the Pulemalei Mound (among other flat-topped, forty feet high "star mounds") contains *no burials*. There is hardly a place on Earth *without* mounds; we find them

---

*Their common cultural root was by the other road: the continent of Pan.

†Some of the mounds and *tells,* of course, are simply ruins of old cities—but not all.

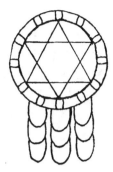

Fig. 7.2. Above: Mukagawin. And "the prophet shall have a Mukagawin, the true sign of poverty. . . . For whom I have made to live in poverty in this world, I will exalt in heaven. I have made only the poor to be My prophets."[6] Not only was this "Star of David" found among the American mounds, but like the Hebrews, these early Americans had first fruit ceremonies, circumcision, rites of purification, similar holy days and commandments. Right: Look-alike cosmogonic diagram of the land of Mu, 35,000 years old.

in Central Europe and many parts of Russia and Scandinavia. There are the tumuli of Africa, the kurgans of Siberia (about eight feet high), the Greek and Turkish *tepes* (which contain *sanctuaries,* not burials).

To trace this word *tepe* (var. *taba*) is to go on a worldwide hunt. In *both* the Old and New Worlds, it translates as "high place," "hill," or "monastery" (sanctuary), usually a mountain enclave. *Wei-Tepu,* in Amazonia, is Sun-Mountain. *Taba* (which gave us "table") may be at the root of other holy places in the New World, such as *Taba*sco, the most important ritual site of the Olmecs. Here in Mexico, in the Quichua (see below) vocabulary, *tepeu* stands as an appellation of divinity, translating as "lord" or "ruler" (of those sacred heights). In fact, **Tepe-u** is one name of Creator in the Popul Vuh.* The word *tepec* in Nahuatl (Mexican) and in the Turkic language designates "hill,"† which is to say, the mounds upon which those holy sanctuaries were built. Among the (Malay) Batek, cognate *tebew* is the large hut specially built for sacred singing. And in

---

*Reflected in many Mexican place-names such as *Tehuantepec, Chapultepec, Tepexi, Ixtepete,* and so forth.

†*Chapultepec,* for example, is "Grasshopper Hill."

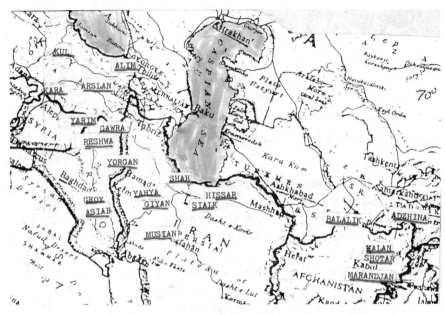

Fig. 7.3. Tepe map showing a selection of monasteries all prefixed by "Tepe" in the southern sweep of the Caspian

Africa, ancestor rituals continue to be held on hills in Zimbabwe, the heights considered the most sacred part of the precinct.

The *tepes,* reclusive spots of safety and worship, may relate to India's *tapas* (var. *tepes*), which in Sanskrit denotes "austerities," the sacred disciplines that ultimately infused the wider world with the ascetic ideal, the Law of Conduct and piety. *Tapas* entails self-control, the inner heat mastered through yogic exercises, akin to Tibet's *thab,* meaning "method" (toward enlightenment).

> Where [in Guatama] is the place and boundary of the little people whom I delivered in the time of the flood?. . . From the mountain rivers (Amazon) to . . . Mexico and Nicaragua . . .
>
> OAHSPE, THE LORDS' THIRD BOOK 1:5

Discovered in the nineteenth century were eighteen-feet-high man-made mounds and highly artistic urns and ornaments inside mound-dwellings of the lower Amazon.[7] There are "puzzling ruins," too, in the mesa country where Argentina, Bolivia, and Chile meet, structures with a "distinct resemblance" to those of the American Southwest; agricultural desert dwellers, these South Americans built pit houses and "clustered compounds," resembling the Pueblos also in their basketry, pottery type, copper bells, and stone artifacts. "These items," archaeologist Betty J. Meggers was convinced, "are not just similar. They are virtually identical."[8] Even the language of these artificers has "been traced from Nicaragua to Vancouver's Island. . . . The [North American] Shoshone language has many and marked affinities with that of the Aztecs [and they] . . . partake in some measure of the same blood as the Aztec."[9]

The mounds and pyramids in Honduras, Bolivia, Peru, and Patagonia entail one other common denominator: an unknown race of builders. Artificially modified "mountains" on the Marcahuasi Plateau of Peru continue to puzzle students of prehistory; sixteen-feet-high mounds with flat tops cover the landscape of Caral, Peru. The builders at Tiahuanaco, Bolivia, also shaped artificial hills, absolutely level on top; while in Venezuela, William Pidgeon found similar truncated mounds, resembling those of the southern United States—these, he imagined, were "the habitations of a great people."[10]

Moundbuilding was worldwide! But what was the link? The idea of a common origin seemed irresistible; but what was it? Was it hidden, *below the water*? Obvious though it is, only the most adventurous writers are willing to entertain a common source. The Original Unity of mankind is a topic that has come to be shunned, if not tabooed, by the intellectual establishment. Hence, the "experts" remain gripped by the "mystery," though the answer is hiding in plain sight.

The Maya built their homes mostly on mounds, called *kus*. Manmade mounds cover Tikal, extending for miles into the jungle; artificial hills dot the Yucatan. At San Lorenzo, Mexico (old Olmec grounds), the entire plateau is an artifact on a gigantic scale, one such mound—a half mile wide—standing at 150 feet! All of which came as a shock to staid archaeology: "We have no idea who built them,"[11] states Michael Coe, which cheats the reader of a considerable body of knowledge that persuasively links Central Americans to both their northern *and* southern cousins.* Resembling the teocallis of Mexico, America's temple mounds are "probably of a similar origin,"[12] thought Sir John Lubbock.

Even Arizona's Hopi Indians trace their forebears to migrants from Mexico, where, at Tula, as one tradition holds, the people split up, some heading north to Arizona. "The Hopi are remotely related in language to the ancient Aztec Indians in Mexico."[13] Pueblo ceremonials resemble the rites of Mexico's Huichol Indians, while the ball court and ball game of Arizona's Hohokan people are intriguingly similar to that of the Maya. There is also the efficient agriculture and fine pottery of the Hopi that set them off from the nomadic tribes of America's Archaic Period. Neither does the (southwest) Zuni tongue have any affinity with North American languages but much vocabulary in common with Mexican tongues.†

Why, we may ask, does adobe "cluster" housing (see figs. 7.6, p. 228) at Casas Grande, Mexico, so closely match the architecture of the Hopi and Zuni? Architecture easily links north and south in other ways as well: obviously Mesoamerican in style are the earthen ceremonial plazas and burial mounds of the Alabama Creeks also known as Muskogee, a tribe with notable little people genes. The largest mound in North America, Cahokia in Illinois, is designed along the same lines as those at Mexico's Teotihuacan, Monte Alban, and Cholula. Some of the great mounds at Hopewell, Ohio, have been directly linked to Mexico: A civil engineer, long involved in these earthworks, one James A. Marshall, saw the Hopewell structures as bearing the same stamp as those at Teotihuacan, both using the same unit of measure (187 feet). Such "geometers," he reasoned, must have made the trip from Mexico to Ohio. Indeed, the Ohio-born scholar, J. B. Newbrough, saw the Americas "inhabited first in Central America, Mexico, [then] Texas, and the Western Missisippi."[14]

The key, the hub, had to be Central America, for all indicators mark it as "one of the first colonies established from the Motherland" (the inun-

---

*See North American people who look so Mexican: figs. 1.1 on p. 8 and fig. 7.12 on p. 238.

†Words like *zi* ("hair") and *ahka* ("take") in Zuni are identical in the Otomi (Mexican) language; while Zuni *pu'a* ("break") and *tachchu* ("father") are Aztecan words. In fact, the Keresan language family of the Pueblos is Hokan-Siouan, which phylum extends to Mexico and Nicaragua.

dated Pacific lands); "the particular spot where they landed was Mexico."[15] The capital city of the Quetzals was established thereabouts: in Guatemala ("Guatama" is a very old name of the Americas, one of the five landing places after the Flood; hence "Guatema-la"). These Quetzals, of milk-white skin, were the first foreign settlers in Mesoamerica. Guatemala is the nation of the *Quiche*-Maya people, and in South America, its cognate *Quechua* is the language spoken by their long-lost cousins, the Incas.*

Linguists have linked the highly civilized Mexican Tarascans to the North American Zuni as well as to Peru's Quechua. Peter Kolosimo, in *Timeless Earth,* observed, "The ancestors of the present-day natives of Peru and Argentina came from the north. These were men of a white race. Even today there are a few survivors of the pure descendants of these peoples and they are pure white, namely, the Uros of Lake Titicaca, who live in the same place where the famous civilization of Tiahuanaco once flourished."[16] G. C. Vaillant formerly of the American Museum of Natural History found common ceramic styles, tracing them all to a pre-Mayan source in Guatemala, which was the center of migration; they eventually reached north to the Mississippi Valley and as far south as Peru. In fact, the Chimu of Peru say they came from the north: their customs and their crania, their pictograms and spiral staircase of the caracole style, are like the Maya's, who also "exported" the god Guatan (Whirlwind) to the ancient Peruvians.[17]

> The fleet named Guatama was carried to the eastward, and the country whither it landed was also called Guatama. The Lord said: From this place shall my chosen spread out north and south . . .
>
> OAHSPE, THE LORDS' FIRST BOOK 1:53

This is the reason the *oldest* cultures are in the interior: for the migrations followed a north-south axis, not exploring the coasts till much later.

> *From this center [Mexico] their arts spread north and south.*
>
> HAROLD T. WILKIN,
> *MYSTERIES OF ANCIENT SOUTH AMERICA*

---

*Which language in turn is linguistically similar to Japanese and Basque as well as some languages of the islands in the Pacific, especially Maori.

True civilizations were first developed in Central America . . .
rather than in the areas to the north or south . . . [it] was the cradle.

A. H. VERRILL,

OLD CIVILIZATIONS OF THE NEW WORLD

Sir John Lubbock found "the earthworks most abundant in the central parts of the United States . . . decreasing in the north as we approach the Atlantic . . . and west of the Rocky Mountains." Interesting that "in the *central* [emphasis added] parts of North America, the Indian tribes generally believed in a Great Spirit," while Lubbock and others found no real religion among the Indians of Canada "or any kind of worship among the Comanche or Dacotahs."[18] Also spread over the more central portion of the continent are brachycephalic people (round headed) of Ihin heritage. This "central brachycephalic area" is mapped in Prof. Roland Dixon's *The Racial History of Man* (plate 34).

Finally, in the Americas, food plants also were diffused north and south, according to Jared Diamond's *The Third Chimpanzee*. Maize culture alone gives us "food for thought," suggesting the very same pattern of Dispersal, both north and south from Guatema-la; for the oldest cultivated corn in the Americas is located in southern Mexico and in the highlands of Guatemala. Beans and squash also seem to have originated in Mesoamerica and spread both north and south.[19]

In the next section we will see how agriculture itself may be a good deal older than the Old World's vaunted Neolithic Revolution; for in the Americas it was the race founders who brought corn, a boon spoken of in many native traditons: First Man brought maize. In Mexico, after the Flood, it became the task of the gods and goddesses to supply the new race with sustenance, whereon they set about searching for a suitable food for humans; at the end of which saga, it is the **Aztec sky deity Nanahuatzin*** who helps bring corn seeds to man. In one Zuni tale, it is Corn Maiden who accompanied the First People to the surface of the Earth.

---

*Nan is, in fact, the word for bread in western Asia, and, as we have seen, also a word for "short."

If some of the original inhabitants of America were of trans-Pacific origin [Pan], then Central America would have been the most promising locality.

A. H. VERRILL,

OLD CIVILIZATIONS OF THE NEW WORLD

The cradle of the Aztec race, says the mythology of the Quiches, was a pleasant land: *Pan*-paxil-pacayala, where "the waters divide in falling, or between the waters parceled out and mucky."[20] That name *Pan* (representing the Motherland to the west of Mexico, i.e., in the Pacific) again appears in legendary Teotlal*pan,* the "Land of the Gods," boasting agriculture and obsidian mines. In this land was a store of white corn and yellow corn, which the sacred animals carried to make the flesh of man. Even in North America, the Chippewas say maize was brought by the sacred *Quiches,* the first men who were molded from it!

Kisha Manito is the name of Creator among the Menomini Indians of North America. In fact, Quiche (also spelled Kiche) is pronounced the same as Sumerian *Kish,* which was, according to their King List, the first capital after the Flood,* that overwhelming Deluge described in detail in the Mayan Popul Vuh and Codex Chimalpopoca.

The Mayan people of Chiapas (touching Guatemala) claim to be the first arrivals in the New World, their great leader named Nima-*kiche.* From whence? The Aztec goddess of maize and patroness of agriculture had her "home in the *west* [emphasis added]."[21] One of the first Quiche colonies was on the river named *Pan*uco, while the city of Panuco itself, on the Gulf and boasting superb temples, is where the Toltecs say they landed—their language radically different from that of the Aztecs; they were "an ancient race, of mild manners and considerable polish . . . [with] uncommon skill . . . [enjoying] prolonged peace

---

*Going back to flood times and the diaspora (from a common homeland), naturally we find linguistic similarities in very different parts of the world. There is a Kich tribe also along the Nile. Kish, a major Sumerian city, has an important groups of tells (mounds) at Ur, where the cult of Kish and Temple of the Mother of the World once flourished. Iconography (as well as extant groups) show these Mesopotamian people as the *same racial type* found among the Quiche of Central and South America: long, high-bridged nose (like our "eagle-nosed" Cro-Magnon), large head, bearded chin, large round eyes.

. . . fostering growth in the fine arts."[22] Indeed, we find, as expected for the *landing-place* from the lost land, most Pan names *are located in the center of Guatama,* that is, Mexico and Guatemala.

- To*pan,* the Aztec World Above (vs. Mictlan, the World Below)
- Yodo*pan,* ancient name for the people of Mexico
- Waneo*pan*ganosah, "the middle kingdom" in Central America[23]
- Hon'ya*pan,* oldest name of Central America[24]
- *Pan*ajachel, on Lake Atitlan in Guatemala
- Sta. Izabel Ixta*pan,* the earliest known culture in Mexico, a mammoth-and-artifact site, dated to 18,000 years ago
- San Felipe Hueyotli*pan* and Zaha*pan* river, in Puebla's Valsequillo region with the picture of a 20,000-year-old mammoth carved on its own bone; in Puebla also is Caula*pan,* with a 22,000-year-old stone scraper
- Kich*pan*ha, Mayan site with first signs of writing (note "Quiche" plus "Pan" in the name)
- Tlalla*pan,* the land Quetzalcoatl came from
- Te*pan*titla, palatial residence famous for its murals, near the Pyramid of the Sun; Xolal*pan* and Teo*pan*caxco, elite districts in the central sector of Teotihuacan
- Maya*pan:* both names enter extensively into the Yucatecan lexicon; together, "Maya" plus "Pan" creates "Mayapan," name of the ancient capital
- Tepex*pan,* near Mexico City, one of the oldest known (12,000 BP) cultures in Mexico, yet with a morphologically modern skeleton (note Tepe- in the name)[25]
- Teo*pan*tecuanitlan, Olmec archaeological site recently discovered
- Ahuacha*pan* Pass, which opens Chalchuapa (Salvador) to the Pacific, earliest Olmec populations here
- Pijiijia*pan,* Olmec site with massive sculptures
- Chia*pan*ec region, east of the Isthmus
- Mataca*pan,* in the Tuxtlas Mountains
- Tlaco*pan,* Aztec city and Nahua tribe
- Och*pan*itzli, Aztec harvest festival

- Meztlia*pan*, Aztec island (meztli means "moon," *apan* means "lake")
- Teo*pan*zolco, Aztec ceremonial center at Cuernavaca
- Tlane*pan*tla, a sacred Mexican site
- archaeological sites: Iztapala*pan*, Tlayaca*pan*, Tzom*pan*titlan, Tenene*pan*co, Urua*pan*
- Tec*pan*ec Empire (Nahua tribes), in Basin of Mexico
- Pal*pan*, hill above Tollan ruins
- Tux*pan*, in the Gulf coast area
- Coma*pan*, fortress/cemetery, and Tuza*pan*, fortress, both in Veracruz
- Ajal*pan* in Tehuacan Valley
- El Totonaca*pan*, land of the Totonacs (here showing -pan as "land")
- Pa*pan*tla, in province of Cempoala, with pyramids, as in Tusa*pan*
- Atiza*pan*, site in valley of Mexico
- *Pan*taleon, on the Pacific coast of Guatemala*

See other "Pan" names in appendix C.

Our moundbuilders, significantly enough, seem to have first appeared along the west coast of Chiapas. They were "white people of great intelligence and skill," opined Josiah Priest in *American Antiquities and Discoveries in the West*, 1833. It has become increasingly clear

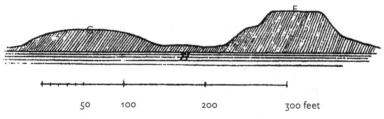

50   100   200   300 feet

Fig. 7.4. A Georgia mound, thirty-seven feet high

---

*Pan names for other features of the landscape: Mo*pan* River in Mayan lowlands, Lake Zum*pan*go in the Basin, Xamil*pan* River in Puebla, Rio Grande de Acto*pan* (river through Cempoala), Papaloa*pan* River (site under excavation), Paja*pan* volcano in Vera Cruz, Belmo*pan*, capital of Belize, Co*pan* (Guatemala-Honduras border, important Mayan city, one of oldest and most beautiful, with deep overgrown jungle, exquisite sculpted stele, "elegant designs," pyramids, dead city, huge temple complex). Honduras and Nicaragua: people known as the *Pan*samak Sumus: their name for the Elder Brother who created the world is Pa*pan*. Nicaragua also has the city of Pancasan.

that we will never solve the "problem of the Moundbuilders" if we persist, blindly, in the "Red Man" theory. A regional chronicler here in my own part of Northeast Georgia wrote:

> Scientists say that the Indians must have been the mound builders. . . . However, we were taught that the Mound Builders were a prehistoric race that lived here before the Indians. In my childhood I used to hear of a legend, told by the Indians to the first white settlers—namely, that a race of people lived in the valleys of the Tennessee River before them called the "Little Men," and that they were the mound builders.[26]

The early American mounds were no more built by the Indians than the Mayan pyramids were engineered by unlearned *poblanos*. These stately prominences along the landscape were as foreign to them as the craters on the moon; they regarded the mounds "with comingled ignorance and wonder."[27] Nevertheless, the moundbuilders were *indeed their forefathers,* though indirectly through intermarriage and amalgamation.

> *Me know nothing about them. They were here before the red man.*
> A Missouri Indian, when asked about
> ancient graveyards (William Corliss, *Ancient Man*)

The original moundbuilders were the peculiarly sacred tribes, founders of the great priesthoods of Mesolithic America. They engaged in no warfare, built no palaces or monuments or formidable statues of themselves: all of which came later, in the Sun Kingdoms, and speak clearly of elitism and political despotism. The first moundbuilders knew no pomp and glory, no luxury or ostentation; neither were their mounds burial places for the distinguished dead, for kings personifying gods—unlike the later Scythian, Lydian, and Greek kings and their mound-tombs. Temple and ceremonial complex, after all, inevitably savor of a privileged class for whom the structures eventually became glorified tombs or memorials.

The moundbuilders go back tens of thousands of years, and the mounds were their *homes,* not their graves! Sure, today most Mississippi Valley mounds are sepulchral, "immense tumuli"; and "the same usage obtained . . . throughout Central America . . . [the burials] of some distinguished chieftain . . . deposited in the temples."[28] But of more recent date are these burials, which along with fortifications and weapons are found *only at later levels,* on top of the underlying strata.

Here is a clue to that earlier horizon: agriculture and terracing—the terraced mounds are older than the bluffed.

THE FIRST FARMERS

Agriculture and the Little People
The vast mound works of ancient North America, as Sir John Lubbock saw it, "indicate a population both large and stationary . . . which must have derived its support, in a great measure, from agriculture."[29] Connecting the dots: the small-statured civilizers whom we visited in chapter 4 brought—in their bundle of wonderful things—agriculture and "seeds of the earth," like the dwarf "Megwoments," Food Giver of Yurok myth. Is it coincidental that the first bringer of food is a dwarf? I don't think so. For it has not escaped our notice that Europe's brownies and fairies are also distinctly proficient at food cultivation, forever threshing corn and performing farm tasks "overnight." In America, too, the Cherokee little people come by of a night, and in the morning the householder finds the corn gathered or the field cleared, as if a whole force of men had been at work. Over in Ireland, it is the same; at Ballycastle, a man lays out bundles of corn at night for the grogachs to thresh. Ulster brownies, too, thresh corn for farmers, while Shetland brownies grind grain for them.

Then there are the fabulous gardens of the Ellefolk, the little mentors who tell farmers when the time is right for planting. Rusalky, the dusky elves of Russia, bring good luck to crops; the grain grows better wherever they have held their dance circles. The Rusalky also control the rain and wind, increasing (or destroying) a year's crop. In fact, according to *The Secret Commonwealth,*[30] the little people "had their own agriculture" even before men inhabited most of the Earth, indicating a time long before the Flood, when cities and agriculture filled the Earth—but all was destroyed by war: "the earth was tilled" to feed the cities as long ago as 42,000 BP,[31] which was the first civilization of little people on Earth. "They tilled the soil . . . [but all was] dissipated by the dread hand of war . . . their cities are destroyed."[32]

Agriculture in the Americas has been traced to no more than 8,000 years ago, but that doesn't mean it wasn't here earlier. If 8000 BP is the oldest date for New World agriculture, that is as far down as they've dug; lower fossil beds remain largely unexplored for they are "way too old" (or so it is thought) for remains of men's industries. Such depths have been reached mostly *accidentally*, serendipitously: one of the oldest Pleistocene skulls was found by workmen excavating a dry dock in Buenos Aires harbor; Europe's Heidelberg Man was discovered at a depth of eighty feet while working a commercial sand pit; Neanderthal was first discovered by workers quarrying for limestone.

Two hundred feet below Mexico City (by drill core extraction), pollen grains of cultivated corn were tens of thousands of years old; meanwhile, grinding tools unearthed in California are shelved at 70,000 BP.[33]

In the Old World, agriculture made its way to Eastern Europe around 8,000 years ago. But from where? One must always turn east to answer such questions. Domesticated rye, for example, is confirmed in Syria 10,000 years ago; while horticulture was "already well established . . . mastered" in Turkey (Anatolia) at least 13,000 years ago,[34] and they appear to have had "prior experience in agriculture . . . [which was] perfected elsewhere."[35] There were farmers in Palestine 14,000 years ago.[36] Wheat and barley were domesticated in the Nile Valley 18,000 years ago[37] probably by the ancestors of the little people who were reported by the classical writer Hecataeus: these *pugmalos* (pygmies) of the Nile were an age-old agricultural people, as were the *pygmaioi* of Libya: "Apollo told us when to plant, and when to reap,"[38] which puts the date at 18,000 BP.

These dates may be (evasively) called "proto-Neolithic," but, hey, they are downright *Meso*lithic. Consider, too, Churchward's date of 17,000 BP for agriculture among the North Asian Uighurs. Indeed, the Fertile Crescent's touted "Neolithic Revolution" (around 9000 BP) blithely ignores agriculture practiced in Melanesia 11,000 years ago (yams, sago)[39] and in *Thailand* 13,000 years ago. *Terraced* fields in Southeast Asia and Indonesia are probably that old, while the proto-Malay folk at Kota Tampan (ancestors of the Lenggong little people) 11,000 years ago practiced

farming and manufactured porcelain containers: only settled agriculturalists were likely to develop such ceramic arts and industries.[40] Improved
ceramic arts are a recognized index of civilization, with true pottery
industries betraying agricultural societies.

In the Americas it is always the little people who seem to "bring agriculture," especially after the Emergence (read: Flood times). In fact, it is
right in the area of those tiny graves in Tennessee and Kentucky that
archaeology has located some of the earliest American cultigens: squash,
sunflower, and so forth. All the oldest mounds, moreover, are located
in alluvial regions, affording "ample scope of agricultural pursuits . . .
this rich alluvial soil was once the seat of a numerous and permanent
population . . . [who] supported themselves by the cultivation of maize."[41]

The fifth great king was P-, king of the city of L-, on the High
Heogula Ophat [Tennessee], with thirty tributary cities of tens of
thousands of inhabitants. Here was situated the school and college
of great learning . . .

OAHSPE, FIRST BOOK OF GOD 25:6

In Mexico, the all-nourishing god of maize and lord of harvest is
named Gha*nan* while his South American counterpart is Maire Mo*nan,*
who was **Creator's successor** and taught the *Tupi*namba the arts of
agriculture, much like First Man of the Tupis (Brazil), who taught them
agriculture. Here we find convincing evidence of agriculture *before* the
Flood; that is, before 24,000 BP, for the pre-Inca creation myth has
Pachacamac planting the first corn, yucca, vegetables, and fruit *before*
creating the present race. In other words, these agriculturalists belong
to the Second Age, which "ended in cataclysmic deluge."[42] Archaeologist
George O'Neill thought the Peruvian Chachas "a vast civilization that
built cities and contoured agricultural terracing, which undoubtedly
maintained a very large population."[43]

In Taiwan, Saisyat oral history recounts how a group of pygmies
once taught them how to farm. In fact, numerous prehistoric Polynesian people were adept farmers. The key is the vanished little people:
in Hawaii, *terraced* farming was a trademark of the little Menehune;[44]

that's how their movements are traced—once driven off the large islands, they withdrew to the islets of Nihoa and Necker, as evidenced by the path of their distinctive terraces.*

Terracing may well be the key to these pre-Neolithic horticulturalists and civilizers. Across the empty (emptied) Pacific Ocean, beans and peppers were grown in the Andes at least 11,000 years ago.† There are terraced hillsides at Tiahuanaco, and maize terraces at Ollantay (Peru) and at Pisac. Advanced techniques in terracing and weaving and metallurgy are to be found at Peruvian sites such as Viru Valley (the "Gallinago civilization"). At Machu Picchu, houses and gardens were arranged in long terraces. Covering the slopes at these exalted heights, crops were skillfully grown at surprisingly high altitude; these sites contain miles of walled tiers of agricultural terraces.

Irrigation techniques in Mexico, Peru, Egypt, and Mesopotamia are almost identical, hinting at a common source. (Most of those populations practiced terracing, weaving, fine art, cire perdue, metallurgy, etc.) Is it accidental that we find these advancements at places identified as enclaves of the little people?†

The Maya, with *extant* little people, introduced an advanced system of irrigation and drainage, enabling them to grow continuing crops to feed millions. At Monte Alban near Oaxaca, Mexico, the ancient city, flanked on all sides by terraced steps, lies atop an artificially leveled "mountain." There are 2,000 terraces here and many others at such sites as Cacaxtla (where archaeologists marvel at extraordinary prehistorical murals). Agricultural terracing in Mexico's Puebla Valley dates from very early times indeed, while radar and aerial imaging confirms the same in Belize, Quintana Roo, and the Maya Mountains.‡

---

*No one knows who built the outstanding terraces ("elaborate affairs") on Palau, whole hills sculpted to resemble step pyramids. But recent finds suggest they were little people.
†It is thought that Middle Stone Age microliths were fitted on to a *sickle* for harvesting work.[45] We find these "pygmy flints" at the same spots settled by our protohistorical farmers: north Europe, Scotland, Russia, Egypt, Palestine, Southeast Asia, China, Japan, and the Philippines.
‡East of Taiwan, in the Philippines, the Aeta Negritos practice *terraced* rice cultivation; so do the peasants of Madagascar (where little people once dominated) in the hilly country, as well as the people of Southeast Asia—and beyond.

Fig. 7.5. Top: Rice terraces in the Philippines. Agricultural terracing is likely to prove an index of large prehistorical populations. Bottom: Pisac terraces, Peru.

In North America, the Pueblos, unlike other desert tribes, are preeminently agricultural, known for their clever irrigation systems, time out of mind. The Hopi say their ancestors domesticated corn in the *First World*. Not only did the Hopis bring—from Mexico to the Southwest desert—their civilizing horticultural arts, but they distinguish themselves above all as People of Peace: the most civilized "art" of all. We will not find their ancestors, the Lost Race of the First World, among any warrior tribes, though we will find their *protectors* among those strong fighting men. We will not find the Lost Race among any people of war, among royalty or grandiose dynasties. Nor will we find the Lost Race among those who sacrificed humans or even poor dumb creatures. And we will not find the Lost Race among sun worshippers; we will not find the Great Ones, the Old Ones, among those who succeeded them and built colossal monuments and temples of hewn stones, covering them with polished copper. But, "These are My chosen that live in mounds. . . . In those days [more than 23,000 years ago] the Ihins . . . tilled the ground and brought forth grains and seeds good to eat . . . And

Fig. 7.6. Top: Hopi Old Oraibi village in the 1920s, kivas in foreground. To the first Spanish explorers, the neighboring Zuni village looked "as if it had been crumpled all up together." Bottom: A postcard I brought home from Hopiland, in 1967, of Walpi Indian village.

their food was of every herb and root, and grain and seed, and fruit that cometh of the earth. . . . They toiled by day, bringing within their cities the fruit of their labor."[46]

I left the ruins of my cities, which had no gates of entrance, and houses without doors of entrance, that ye might have testimony of this race of [holy people].

OAHSPE, THE LORDS' FIFTH BOOK

DESCENDANTS OF THE MOUND BUILDERS

Early theorists correctly postulated that the Pueblos and their forebears, the Cliff-dwellers, with their many-storied adobe towns, were descended of the original moundbuilders, a peaceful and industrious people, as are, famously, the Hopi and Zuni. Never on the offensive but apparently defensive, the Pueblos arranged their village in such a way that doorless houses are stacked one over the other in protective clusters, each tier being set back of the one below, so that the roof of a house below forms the dooryard of the one above it: with as many as six or more tiers! Entrance was through a skylight or hatchway in the roof, reached by ladders, which were pulled up at night or when dangerous animals or an enemy appeared, "thus transforming the village into a fairly impregnable fortress."[47] After the Flood, "In the lands where I will take My people, let them build mounds and walled* cities with ladders to enter, after the manner of the ancients. *In all the divisions of the earth* [emphasis added], alike and like shall they build walls . . . that beasts and serpents may not enter."[48]

They were in Greece, too: cluster houses and enclosure walls* (known as "sacred enclosures") at *Zago*ra in the eighth century BCE, as

---

*Zuni *walled* towns were unusual in typical Native American practice, but we do find them also at Paint Creek, Ohio, and in Georgia, near Macon, the walls encircling sixty acres of "Brown's Mount"; and in Mexico's Teotihuacan Valley, at the Zacatenco village called Cuanalan, where "houses from this early period have been found in apparent *clusters inside walls* [emphasis added]."[49] Tulum (Mayan) is also a walled city, of sixteen acres: "the doorways look as though they had been planned and built for miniature beings. . . . The buildings resembled dollhouses clustered to form a town."[50]

Fig. 7.7. Top: Abandoned Libyan village at Tripolitania. Drawing by Jose Bouvier. Indeed, Barry Fell found affinities between Zuni and ancient Libyan languages. And as the Libyans are said to have led to the Berbers and Tuaregs, we find the same clusters in Morocco. Bottom: Moroccan adobe (*attobi*) Berber village, almost identical to the Pueblos of the American Southwest.

well as on Cyprus and in Scotland—"the Picts . . . Pigmies in stature . . . did marvels in building walled towns."[51] Even the primitive little people of southern Africa built in a like manner, the Bushman constructing "round walls of stone on top of the hills near his permanent waters. The walls were made . . . without opening or roof of any kind. At night he would merely climb over the wall."[52] Covering "all the divisions of the earth," we find Pueblo-style "clusters" also in the north of Africa, Turkey, and the Near East.

Both Philostratus the Elder and Herodotus, the "father of history," wrote of extremely short people in Libya, where *Bat*tus founded Cyrene. Now it is interesting that Libya's Maxye people claimed to descend from the men of Troy in western Turkey; and, yes, Libya's own cluster houses look a great deal like Turkish (Hittite) ones. Çatalhüyük's continuous perimeter wall (no entrance) actually consists of abutting buildings that

Fig. 7.8. Turkish "clustered" town without streets, at Çatalhüyük, flat roof and ladder the only means of access. They too had outside defense walls. Drawing by Jose Bouvier.

"cling together." One entered through the roof by a wooden ladder. For the archaeologist to pass through one interior room to the next, he "must crawl through a small doorway."[53] And judging from their wheel-cross (see fig. 2.7 on p. 46 and fig. 7.9 on p. 232), they shared an ancient heritage with the Pueblos, moundbuilders, Trojans, and many others.

Also inhabiting cluster houses were the predecessors of the Sumerians (savoring of Turkish and Trojan origins)—as seen in the ruins at Choga Manis—where houses are all abutted one against the other. We find the same in South America among the San Blas; there are similar clustered compounds in Argentina as well.

For the sacred tribes—wherever they lived—were sworn against war and killing, and could defend themselves only by making their homes inaccessible to potential invaders and predatory animals. Being people of peace, the Hopi Indians built high mounds and ladders to enter their dwelling through roof holes (rolling back the *nuta,* the straw-thatch opening). They also provided a roof hole in the *kivas* (semi-underground spirit-chambers), where the smoke hole did double duty as roof hatch.[54]

In the Mandan origin myth, ascent and descent from the *inner Earth* home was by means of a "grapevine"—was this a rope ladder? ("Inner Earth" may simply reflect their living in the "hollow hills," i.e., *in* the mounds, as in Turkey, where structures were sunk into the hilltop, creating "cellars in the Earth.")

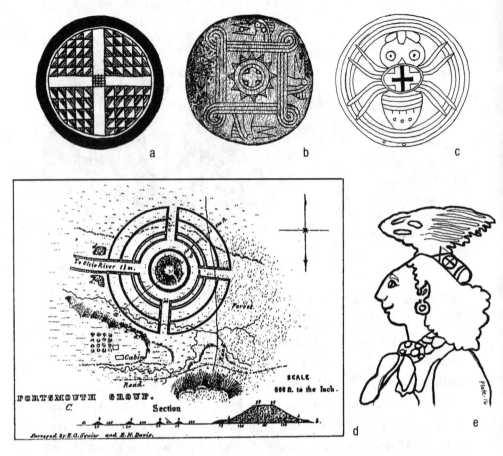

Fig 7.9. Variations of the wheel cross (ball-and-cross) icon. (a) "Cluster-people" of Libya painted ball-and-cross icon on pottery bowls. (b) Ball-and-cross seen at center of shell gorget. (c) Ball-and-cross on scarab. (d) Round Ohio mounds with four equidistant openings also form this icon from above view. (e) Flathead Algonquin Indian in the time of Hiawatha; note the ball-and-cross sign on her headdress. The ball-and-cross icon is also found in the ruins of Troy. These protohistorical Trojans were a devout people (see 5,000-year-old Tablet—Pl. 80* in fig. 2.7, p. 46).

> In all the divisions of the Earth . . . My angels shall teach you how to build ladders and how to use them. And . . . at night ye shall take the ladder in after you . . . And man provided the cities with ladders and he provided the mounds with ladders also.
>
> OAHSPE, FIRST BOOK OF THE FIRST LORDS 3:7

---

*Plate 80 tablet of KII served as ceremonial guide in Troy, Persia, Greece, and Arabia.

"All the divisions of the earth": It's back to Scotland we are, with its Pictish mounds so closely resembling those of America, along with the same cluster motif—as in the Shetlands, where the earliest archaeological levels sport strange windowless stone buildings, like a huddle of Eskimo igloos, as well as "roundhouses" that left an open space in the roof. At Skara Brae in the Orkneys, north of the mainland, stands a remarkable Neolithic site of stone houses, connected by very narrow slab-roofed lanes, *only four feet high*. Doorways here are about three feet high ("a mere hatch"). The whole village, apparently of small-statured occupants, had a low sort of mound built up around it, making it a quasi-underground affair. Of "unknown origin," this village plan was all fitted together into one *compacted mass of houses* and passages. Each house had a large central smoke-hole in the roof.

The "weem" dwellings of Scotland were places of concealment. In the Arthurian legends, the fairy who reared Lancelot dwelt on the summit of a hill, so secret that no one could find it. "The so-called Picts' houses . . . so common in the north of Scotland [were] sunk beneath the surface . . . On digging into the green mound . . . a series of large chambers [open up] . . . converging towards the centre, where an opening appears to have been left for light and ventilation."* (See fig. 7.19, p. 249.)

Yes, the mounds (and "clusters" and outer walls and roof-holes) were built in many parts of the world—Old and New—each adapting the protective design in its own way. And there is no reason we cannot include in this general category the dwellings of the white and brown dwarfs in the Nine Hills of Rugen, which are all small mounds, as well as the structures of the Norwegian Mound Folk, elves of great skill, the master smiths and shape-shifters of the Eddas.

The most conspicuous Old World analogue of the Hopi cluster

---

*In parts of Africa, the defensive aspect of the roof hole is known to this day; a quick exit through the roof is employed by the rebel troops defending the villages of Darfur. The roofs of their Land Cruisers are cut out "so men could pile in and out instantly," recounts Daoud Hari, in *The Translator*. This modern strategy, though, reflects a deeper tradition in Africa, for in the ruins of Zimbabwe, there are high oval towers, like those at Machu Picchu, with no windows or openings, save one at the top, "as though they could fly in and out of the roof." There are similar traditions in Sudan, Zambia, and among the Mulumga people.

Fig 7.10. Hittites portrayed as very short people. Left: A Hattini depiction of a Hittite king-priest. Right: A Hittite plate in the Swiss Truniger Collection.

village, complete with roof-hole and ladder, is in Old Turkey—Anatolia, the region from which Herodotus' little Libyans said they hailed. A terraced town, with canal and irrigation works, the Hittite settlement of Çatalhüyük is perhaps the oldest known city in the world, with "densely clustered houses" as well as the world's earliest mural and landscape paintings, the oldest finely woven cloth (using biconical spindles), fired pottery, and cuneiform writing.* These early Hittites, among the last of the sacred communities, enjoyed an enviably harmonious society,† much like the Pueblos, with all the earmarks of civilization, including democratic councils and female equality. Here animal sacrifice was substituted for human. All of which signal the legacy of the faithful tribes, a distinctly "separate" people. Indeed, the Hittites practiced the levirate "to preserve the seed" of their own holy race.

---

*As long ago as 7400 BP (with deeper levels still unexcavated), this old Hittite town, Çatalhüyük, was filled with comfortable brick-and-timber houses solidly packed together into a single mass of architecture, without any streets or alleys. The famous site contains the oldest known examples of metallurgy in the Near East. Sorry, no stonework in this "Stone Age" town. No streets either, only bunched up houses, like Hopi clusters, these mud-brick homes standing wall-to-wall. People entered their home by ladder, for above the hearth was the roof, pierced by a smoke vent which also served as the only "window."

†Although they were the trusted friend of the peaceful Abraham, according to the book of Genesis, later the Hittites did become warriors; they reached the height of power and aggressiveness around 1300 BCE.

And there were *mounds* all across their territory: the Turkish plains. The Hittites were close allies of their neighbors, the Trojans, and together comprised the "royalty" and blue-bloods of the ancient world. They built their towns on the plan of the sacred tribes—layered dwellings—like the Pueblos. And they were short of stature, descendants of the Good Little People.

UNDERGROUND CITIES

We know that the little folk of Cherokee memory were, like their cousins in the Old World, reclusive in their mounds. The little Nunnehi/Yunwi Tsunsdi lived throughout these southern ranges and were especially associated with the town of Franklin, North Carolina, which was built on the site of the Cherokee city of Nikwasi, where one can visit the noted "Indian Mound," which once supported the Cherokee sacred council house. The Cherokee did not construct the Indian mounds, however; they had merely found them in place upon migrating to the region. The little people had built a large townhouse *under* (read: *inside*) the Nikwasi mound, and it was claimed that a perpetual flame burned within it.

Fig. 7.11. Author's son and his wife at Tallulah Falls (Ugun'yi) in North Georgia; its inhabitants were a species of little men and women. The Cherokee avoided the spot. Tourist brochures say: "bring your binoculars and watch the tiny little people crossing the suspension bridge."

The early settlers in America came upon thousands of mounds of varying heights throughout the Mississippi and Ohio valleys and waterways;[55] some had been whole cities, protected by earthen walls, such as Mound City at Poverty Point, Louisiana. H. H. Brackenridge ("On the population and tumuli of the aborigines of North America," *Transactions of the American Philological Society,* 1818) estimated that the mounds along the lower Mississippi had "a population as numerous as . . . the Nile or the Euphrates . . . Cities similar to those of ancient Mexico, of several hundred thousand souls, have existed in this country."

Hmmm, archaeologists say the first cities came about around 4500 BP, but a lost horizon lies buried deep in the unexplored Earth. For a long time after the Flood, there was no war, and there were thousands of cities everywhere by 21,000 BP.* Even *before* the Flood, "The Lord called them [Ihins] together, saying: Come dwell together in cities. . . . And the Ihins . . . built mounds of wood and earth . . . hundreds and thousands of cities and mounds built they."[56]

Indeed, in the Third Age (of Hopi history) there was a mighty civilization, full of big cities—but war and other evils destroyed it, and a Flood was loosed on the world. Archaeology has found traces of this fallen civilization, particularly in the extensive trade networks of the Mississippi Valley mound culture—and in South America as well, with "long-distance travel between the tropical forests and the Pacific coast."[57]

By 18,000 BP, there were four million of the Ihins spread throughout Tennessee, Kentucky, Ohio, Kansas, Lake Michigan, and Lake Superior. "And the[y] built canals from Lake Superior to Texas. And ten thousand canoes crossed them carrying copper and silver from the north regions to the south."[58]

---

*Natchez Mound, thirty-five feet high, covered seven acres; in Natchez country (in the valley of the Big Black River), all the Indians (Creek, Chickasaw, Choctaw, Seminole, etc.) located their earliest ancestry near an artificial eminence, twenty feet high. It was called *Nan*ihwaya (the name of a mound near Philadelphia, Mississippi, where the Choctaw found the Kanakawasa, the little people), Nan- recalling a "dwarf" race.

*. . . from Bolivia to Lake Superior, we find everywhere the traces of
a long-enduring Copper Age.*

IGNATIUS DONNELLY,
ATLANTIS: THE ANTEDILUVIAN WORLD

The Chippewa/Ojibwa Indians along the shores of Lake Superior
have a tradition recalling the origin and manufacture of copper imple-
ments; and here are found articles of pure copper, the first metal tools in
America, as well as the remains of ancient mines. Vast copper works along
Lake Superior and its islands run down to depths of sixty feet, while glass,
iron, and copper artifacts are found inside the mounds of this region. All
of which suggests a great maritime and commercial people who traded
copper, tin, and bronze and silver—during the "Stone" Age.

A FAR-FLUNG EMPIRE

Two of our great American presidents were avid archaeologists and
moundhunters—Thomas Jefferson and William H. Harrison—Jefferson
excavating a local mound in 1784, as described in his "Notes on Virginia."
Today, many American mounds have been obliterated to make room for
golf courses, roads, and other development. More than a hundred years
ago, the acclaimed Adena moundbuilders were discovered in Ross County,
Ohio, some of its sculptures depicting a "dwarf race" (see fig. 7.12, p. 238)

A ceremonial earthwork— like Etowah, Georgia—the Ross County
mound is *mortuary,* with chiefly burials fashioned of log tombs. The
local Indians would tell Anglos that such mounds were dedicated to
great leaders, containing the relics of kings, prophets, and chiefs of
signal renown. But this sort of grandiosity does not jibe with the *first*
moundbuilders. One student of the problem, William Pidgeon, came
to see that the *stone* mound was indeed Indian work, built in imitation of the more ancient *earthen* ones. In fact, most of the mounds
we see today were built by the successors of the original moundbuilders; the latter simply lived on (and in) the mounds, always flat-topped,
of course ("platform mounds"), always "featureless." Conversely, the
conical mounds (not level atop) are newer, more recent. Large mounds

Fig. 7.12 (left). Dwarf effigy of pipestone, found on the Adena estate in Ohio. Did this ceremonial pipe honor the ancestor? Drawing by Jose Bouvier.

Fig. 7.13 (right). Figure of kneeling dwarf from Temple Mound, Tennessee. Drawing by Jose Bouvier.

with commodious spiral paths leading to the top, such as the Temple Mounds in the south, are also more recent—none more than one or two thousand years old—whereas the original mounds (*deliberately* steep and inaccessible) go back probably more than 20,000 years.

> Hoajab's capital city was F. with thirty-three tributary cities, of tens of thousands of inhabitants, on the plains of He'gow [Ohio]. . . . [O]n the plains of Messogowanchoola [North Ohio and Indiana] were . . . forty and seven cities of tens of thousands of inhabitants . . . and they crossed the plains in many directions.
>
> OAHSPE, FIRST BOOK OF GOD

Ten thousand mounds in the Ohio Valley alone speak of a far-flung empire and extensive trade routes with Ohio as its hub. And with more than twenty millenia of moundbuilding, remains give up several different racial types: the Adena people are short-headed, their successors, the Hopewells, long headed. But the *first* moundbuilders were small people. Skeletons deposited in coffins not more than four feet in length were found near Cochocton, Ohio, in an ancient cemetery situated on elevated ground: "They are very numerous and must have been tenants of a considerable city . . . the inmates are all of this pigmy race."[59]

When the first ancestors of the Navajo emerged, monsters roamed the lands.

DAVID M. JONES, *MYTHOLOGY OF THE AMERICAN NATIONS*

... They slept on mounds at night, that they might not be molested by beasts of prey and by serpents.

OAHSPE, THE LORDS' FIRST BOOK 2:14

NEITHER FLESH NOR FISH

F. W. Putnam of the Peabody Museum placed man's antiquity in the Ohio Valley to the time when he was the "contemporary of the mastodon and the mammoth"[60]* (both are types of extinct elephants).

So now we ask: What *really* induced these people to raise such enormous heaps of Earth? Let us answer this by considering a very old (but spot-on) tradition among the peasantry of the German states; namely, that God created the Giants to slay the wild beasts and great dragons, that the Dwarfs might thereby be more secure. But in a few years the Giants, as this old legend recounts, would come to oppress the Dwarfs, for they, the giants, became "altogether wicked and faithless."[61] The Teutonic legend is remarkably analogous to the early chronicles of the little people as found in Oahspe's Book of Aph: "My chosen on Earth ... are a harmless and defenseless people. Therefore, I have wisely created the barbarian; for he shall destroy all evil beasts and serpents; and the forests shall fall down before him" (this phrase referring to the extinction of megafauna). Thus did the large-bodied Ihuans become the official guardians of the Ihins, the sacred people: "Since it is not lawful for the Ihins to kill beast, nor bird, nor serpent, behold, their cities ... are invaded by all manner of evil beasts. ... The Ihuans shall slay all such. ... And they shall guard around about the cities and mounds, where abide my chosen."[62]

The Seneca Indians have a rite for the "Great Little People," one aspect of which recalls this old scenario, for it mentions the "animals

---

*"The legends of China and India and America all give the same name, Hogawatha, for the mastodon."[63]

that the Little People fear" and how they were protected against them.[64] Their giant protectors—"taller and stronger than any other people in the world"—were the ancestors of the American Indian: "Call them Ihuan for they shall protect my chosen. . . . They shall drive away all manslaying beasts, and I will make mighty nations out of the seed of the Ihuans. And the Lord commanded the Ihuans saying: Protect ye the Ihins, the little people, white and yellow . . . the sacred people. . . . And it was so."[65]

It was in this time (Age of Apollo, 18,000 years ago) that a new commandment was given to man, which was to go forth and subdue the Earth, "to slay every beast of prey and every serpent that cometh before him."[66] As the Carolina Indians told it, the good spirits came to them and told them to "overpower the beasts of the wilderness, that they may be assistant and beneficial to men,"[67] (i.e., they were not hunted down for the pot). All this is portrayed quite faithfully in prehistoric drawings and motifs representing the (later idolized) hero subduing beasts. In Egypt, a stela of Horus has this man-god overcoming evil animals and reptiles. In China, legendary giants could tear apart a living rhinoceros; in India, Harappan seals and figurines depict the Lord of the Beasts, a forerunner of Shiva, destroying wild and dangerous animals. Mesopotamia has the mighty hunter Nimrod strangling a young lion. Here, the **Sumerian earth god Enki** subdues the monster Kur, while Shamash fights Zu. The Babylonian hero Gilgamesh, prototype of St. George, bravely fights bulls and lions. Greece, too, had her heroes like Perseus and Heracles slaying dragons and man-eating birds; while Thor of the North grappled with beasts and boars, and the Teutonic Siegfried battles the dragon.

Fig. 7.14. Shamash fights Zu.

In America, Kutoyis, the Blackfoot culture hero, slays giant animals and monsters; Gluskap (Penobscot) kills a giant moose and a monster frog. The Apache culture hero takes on outsized antelopes and monster eagles; "In the early days," says Jicarilla Apache myth, "animals and birds of monstrous size preyed upon the people."[68] Were they teratorns, or like the giant owl figures remembered in numerous Amerind tales? Pleistocene beavers (*castorides*), in Mi'k Maq and Wabanaki legend, were as big as bears, and *eremotherium* (giant sloth) were twenty feet tall. The Algonquin Manibozho conquers many animals, even the prince of serpents, while another

Fig. 7.15. Right: Illustration of Wyandot first Great Council of large animals. Below: Romanticized image of huge panther bringing a baby girl to the village.

hero, Michabo, destroys the reptile king. Snakes, in the time of the Anda-man islanders' ancestors, would catch people and eat them. They were as big as a tree; even large birds, say the Andamanese, could capture people. No, these are not allegories or "symbols" of anything. Such leviathan and behemoth, I daresay, draw on the very real threat of the prehistoric world: the seriously outsized beasts of the Paleolithic.

It is not mere conjecture that early man coexisted with fearsome megafauna; for such records survive to this day not only in oral history and scripture but also in petroglyphs and actual remains (see appendix F). Recollections of enormous animals come from a variety of Amerind tribes: Penobscot, Naskapi, Delaware, Wyandot, Iroquois, Osage, and so on. In their folklore, the brave Indians typically try to stop the ram-page of some great beast.

America's first moundbuilders built their high places neither as aggrandized burial grounds or ceremonial sites, but simply as sanctuar-ies against the very creatures they were forbidden to kill, for the Earth was swarming with poisonous reptiles and enormous man-eating beasts of prey. In America, millions of Ihins lived in the midst of these creatures. "My righteous shall live in mounds of earth and stone and wood, where the Ugha (serpent and tiger and all other evil-devouring beasts) can not come upon them. . . . And the sacred little people lived . . . on the mounds, killing nothing created alive; living in peace and communing with their Creator."[69] For they had been commanded: "Thou shalt not kill man, nor beast nor bird nor creeping thing, for they are the Lords' . . . And if thy habitation be in the wilderness, thou shalt build mounds of wood and earth to sleep on at night, that serpents and beasts may not molest thee."[70]

We see a facsimile of that ancient commandment of nonviolence in the Hopi legend of the Long, Long Ago. In the previous world, the peo-ple were taught by the Creator the supreme law of the living: Thou shalt not kill! When the Hopi were suddenly attacked from all sides in the sacred lands of Lemulia [*sic*] (a.k.a Mu or Pan),* their kachinas came to their aid with the speed of the wind and built a tunnel through which they were able to flee behind enemy lines without shedding blood.

---

*Genesis 1:29 and 9:2–3 imply that before the Flood people were vegetarians.

Fig. 7.16. Port-Pan Algonquin, plate 81 in Oahspe. In America, to qualify for the priesthood established by the Ihins, the initiate must answer these questions:

Hast thou slain any living creature?

Nay, Ong-a-pa, but housed in a mound high-built and steep, I have slept my nights away in peace, slaying naught. . . . Hid are we all away from the devouring hiss'sa (serpent) and baugh and mieuh (lions and tigers).[71]

How was it with thy forefathers and foremothers?

In [emphasis added] the mounds and on the mounds, O Onga . . . my ancestors killed not any living creature Egoquim had created. [72]

Thou art wise, and now . . . do I crown thee brother of the Hoanga [prophets]?

Peace be with thee, Amen!

(The Hoanga Priesthood was still practiced by the Osage Indians in the nineteenth century. This is part of their lost record.)

And the Jhins prospered and spread abroad over the face of the earth; hundreds of thousands of cities and mounds built they, and they rejoiced in the glory of all created things. Neither killed they man nor beast nor fish nor bird nor creeping thing that breathed the breath of life.

OAHSPE, FIRST BOOK OF THE FIRST LORDS 3:8

The record, sometimes quaintly, recollects the little people's abstinence from flesh food: Welsh fairies, for one, ate neither flesh nor fish, but lived on milk and saffron, the Tylwyth Teg subsisting on goat's milk. The Irish leprechauns and English brownies preferred milk above other offerings. The fairy women of Europe (called Good Ladies) ate bread, almonds, grapes, honey, pure water, and honeysuckle; while India's fairy people ate ambrosia and clarified butter, which resonates with the Shepherd Kings of Persia, whose land was filled with wild goats:* but not being flesh-eaters, they made butter, which was the first butter in the world.[73] We catch a glimpse of their descendants among the Semitic tribes of the Sinai who, six thousand years ago, lived "chiefly upon the milk of their great flocks of goats,"[74] the Kurdish Beritan pastoralists of Turkey, embracing traditional ways, subsist on milk, yogurt, and other products of the sheep.

The vegetarian tradition lived on among Europe's sprites, the little Red Caps, who are known to churn butter with alacrity for their favorite households; while the Elves of Sardinia enjoy goat cheese as their favorite repast. According to Herodotus,[75] the little Libyans were farmers and vegetarians.

The Israelites, too, came from a vegetarian past.[76] Judean priests were slain outright by the Levites under Hilikiah, when they, the Levites, seized the priesthood. The Judeans had refused to attend an animal sacrifice, which scruple can be traced back perhaps 7,000 years to their noble ancestors in western Asia, those (butter-making) Shepherd Kings and "Ten Lost Tribes." These paragons were emulated in later cults such as the Mysteries of Bacchus (imported to Greece from the

---

*One Bushman group will not eat goats' flesh, though food is often scarce and this animal is commonest in their district.

Fig. 7.17. Statue of Amten, found in his tomb. This Libyan noble (note his height) was a governor and member of the privileged class and, significantly, Director of the King's flax (i.e., foremost authority on the growing of grains and vegetables).

East) wherein initiates were sworn against bloody sacrifices and lived on a diet of fruits and vegetables and other "inanimate things."

The mound-builders . . . were probably the most ancient, highly cultured race in North America.

A. H. VERRILL,
OLD CIVILIZATIONS OF THE NEW WORLD

A LOST RACE

Thoughts on the lost race: The Tukano Indians of Columbia's rain forest hold Vai-mahse, a dwarf, to be their **tribal spirit** to whom certain hills (mounts) are sacred. In the same vein, the Etowah Mounds here in Georgia were taboo (read: sacred) to the Indians, who avoided it, regarding "as sacred the ground of this mound."[77] In the eighteenth century, a hill-eminence on the Red River near the Caddoes was the site of pilgrimage for all the Indian tribes who came, even from a great distance, to pay devout homage. Indeed, the Caddoes, Choctaw, Creek, and Chickasaw *reverenced* the mounds, for they had been the sanctuary of their holy teachers Long Ago, holding "the old sacred things." Just so, the Creek perform a rite of solemn consecration to the mounds at their great Green Corn

Festival, which honors the First Men, who stood as mentors and priests among the copper-colored kingdoms. Even Major J. W. Powell, staunch opponent of the Lost Race theory, could not deny the moundbuilders had a "highly developed religion." Yet they were not interested in glory.

> They dress not in gaudy colors nor ornament themselves with copper and silver and gold. They are the people of learning. They survey the way for the canals; they find the square and the arch; they lead the Ihuans [Indians] to the mines . . . These are a great people.[78]

A French trapper of colonial times who spoke the Indian tongue heard about these Long-Ago people who built the mounds and canals. "They were teachers, but very, very tiny," he was told. J. V. Yates and J. W. Moulton, early nineteenth-century scholars, thought these "buried nations were unsurpassed in magnitude. . . . Ohio [is] nothing but one vast cemetery of the beings of past ages." These two researchers collected Indians legends of the moundbuilders, concluding they were "prehistoric white men."[79]

Remember the tiny skeletons and "diminutive sarcophagi" in Ohio, Tennessee, and Kentucky? The city of Lexington, Kentucky, thought historian George W. Ranck, was built on the metropolis of a *lost race* who flourished centuries before the Indian. Yates, Moulton, and Ranck are in a small minority; it never occurred to most historians that these strange burials in America's Midwest had anything to do with the "mysterious moundbuilders." And in some ways, the intellectual tyranny (and myopia) of academia rule to this day; the archaeological community having scotched "the central myth" of a vanished race. Case Closed! The Lost Race theory has been firmly put to rest! The original moundbuilders having gone extinct (3,000 years ago—out of sight, out of mind) and now their fine artifacts are credited to either the Indians or stray Europeans who stumbled into the valley of the Mississippi. But not everyone was gulled by the orthodoxy.

> *Let the mighty mounds*
> *That overlook the rivers, or that rise*

In the dim forest crowded with old oaks,
Answer: A race, that long has passed away
Built them—a disciplined and populous race. . . .
And the mound-builders vanished from the earth.
WILLIAM CULLEN BRYANT, "THE PRAIRIES"

Favoring the lost race theory in the 1820s was one Caleb Atwater, postmaster at Circleville, Ohio. Atwater examined many skeletons in the mounds, concluding they never belonged to a people of the known indigenous type. The Indians, he observed, "are a tall people; the [early mound builders] were short . . . rarely over five feet high." Atwater's work also led him to a fundamental understanding of the Original Unity of mankind. All human cultures, he cognized, may have radiated from a single point. They came to Asia, they came to Africa, they came to Russia, they came to America, they came to Egypt (see fig. 8.1, p. 261), and their "similarity of works almost all over the world indicates that [they] sprang from one common origin." Indeed, it was their very presence that insured the progress of humanity "in the first ages, after the Dispersion, rising wherever the posterity of Noah came."[80]

SONS OF NOAH

Be it a mound in America, a tumulus in Scandinavia, a barrow in England, a sidhe in Ireland, a tepe in Greece, a tell in western Asia or a kurgan in the North, these structures "had universally the same origin."[81] William Pidgeon, in his *Traditions of Deecoodah and Antiquarian Researches,* 1852, concluded that Noah and his sons must have built mounds on every continent. (Deecoodah was his Winnebago informant). Their descendants also built strange "beehive" structures . . . known as "the well-covered house," cloaked and constructed specifically to make communion with the spirit world possible.

The Lord provided . . . oracle houses, in which he could speak face to face with mortals, through his angels . . . persuading them to industries and imitating the ways of the Ihins, teaching them about the stars.

OAHSPE, THE LORDS' FIFTH BOOK 6:3–5

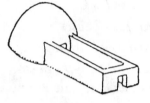

Fig. 7.18. Arpachiyah tholos (singular)

Today around Aleppo in northern Syria, one can see beehive-shaped houses somewhat of the kind that once covered the ancient Near East. Called *tholoi* (plural), the best known of these ancient domes have been dug up at Arpachiyah,* near Nineveh (referred to in Genesis 11:12).

These unusual round buildings in Western Asia are windowless: hence "well-covered." Mud-brick structures, they were approached through rectangular corridors or anterooms (*dromos*), giving them a "keyhole" shape (in bird's-eye view), a shape found both in the Old and New World, as depicted in figure 7.19.

Significantly, weapons of war were absent at Arpachiyah and at nearby Tell Halaf, this conspicuous absence of arrow and spear heads indicating an "advanced and peaceful people," according to Mary Settegast in *When Zarathustra Spoke*. Archaeologists, finding these Iraqi tholoi completely empty, tell us that their origin and significance cannot be explained; some are still guessing they were granaries or storehouses.

When the anthropologist arrives, the gods depart.

OLD SAYING IN THE BUSH

"The function of these buildings is unknown."[82] While archaeologists and other featherless bipeds simply cannot comprehend the well-covered house, we recognize them as the oracle houses of our distant forebears, the little people and their mixed offspring, the faithful tribes of yore.

The key to this unique architecture is the exclusion of light. Utter darkness. These stark windowless domes, whether made of earth, stone, or wood, are really no anomaly, for we find them all across the globe, usually in the wake of the little people.

---

*Arpachshad was a direct ancestor of Abraham; this lineage, telescoped, was from Noah to Shem to Arpachshad to Eber to Nahor to Abraham.

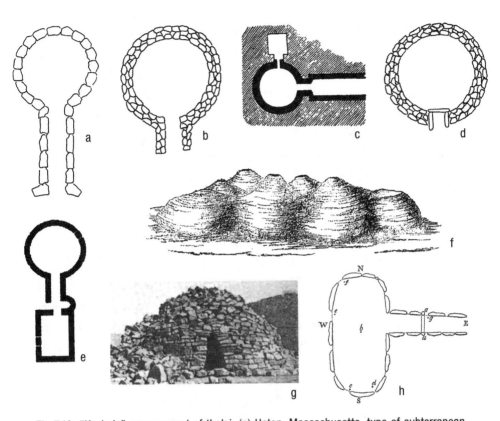

Fig 7.19. "Keyhole" arrangement of tholoi. (a) Upton, Massachusetts, type of subterranean tholos with corridor leading to the round sacred chamber. Twelve miles south of Worcester, the Upton entryway, of megalithic stones, is fourteen feet long. The entrance is *only four feet high*. Were they colonial rootcellars, as archaeologists say? No, say others, pointing out that these structures are very similar to the beehive domes of Scotland, "best suited for a race of people not more than three feet tall."[83] This arrangement was also found among America's southeastern tribes, where the entrance to the Cherokee council house or rotunda was at the end of a six-feet-long hallway. The keyhole-plan *yacatas* in Michoacan, Mexico, are also of this type. (b) Cretan tholos with dromos (Libyan influence). (c) Ground plan of Treasury of Atreus. (d) Cyrene, Libya beehive tomb; these Libyan tholoi much resemble New England beehive chambers. (e) Plan of secluded chambers at Pygmies Isle, Scotland, one chamber circular, the other oblong; thought to be used by anchorites, such beehive houses are common at Irish and Scottish megalithic sites—and also at "America's Stonehenge" in New Hampshire. (f) Group of beehive houses in the Orkneys, Scotland; there are 2,000 "tumuli" in the Orkneys. (g) Beehive tomb in Oman, entrance only three feet high, third millenium BCE. (h) Plan of chamber in a Danish Bronze Age tumulus; Sir John Lubbock found evidence that these mounds had been used previously as houses; perhaps before that, they were spirit chambers.

Ancient Celtic temples had no windows; in Ireland, next to Newgrange's "fairy mounds," we find tholoi, which Robert Graves understood to be the *oracular* shrines of the Dagda (Tuatha De Danaan). Newgrange, thirty miles north of Dublin, on the River Boyne—formerly Boinne—is built on a forty-five-feet-high mound. The largest and greatest of Ireland's sidhes, it is flat-topped, the ground plan forming the shape of a Celtic cross, the most distinctive signature of the lost race (see "wheel cross" images in figs. 2.7, p. 46; 4.11, p. 126; 7.9, p. 232). The site, unsurprisingly, is devoted to the "Son of the Good God," the complex said to belong to the fairy folk, (i.e., the distinguished Tuatha De Danaan, tribes of the goddess Danu).

Tholoi (not such a mystery, after all) were also built in Spain, Portugal, Malta, Babylonia (Uruk III), Croatia, Zimbabwe, North and South America, Turkey, Persia, Laos, and Bulgaria. Virtually worldwide, these beehive "tombs" are also found in China, Italy (Etruscan), Crete (Minoan), as well as at Mycenae (on mainland Greece). The Egyptian versions were oven-shaped tombs with vaulted roofs.

Fig. 7.20. The encircled cross. Celtic Cross (left). The encircled cross or "sun-wheel" also appears in bold paints on the Crow medicine shield (right) and on a New Guinea Shield (at Bogajim) (right). Sign of the Creator, the wheel-cross was used by the Flathead Indians, in the Glastonbury scripts, in Sumerian and Persian pictographs, in Mexico, the Gobi Desert, Troy, Scandinavia, on rock carvings in Egypt, China, and the Near East, at New Granada (Columbia), Hopiland, Oklahoma, New Mexico, France, Wales, and even on UFOs! The circle represents Love, the cross represents Light.

Did you notice that—just like the mounds—the tholoi were later turned into bombastic tombs? Tholos-like structures in Africa, though, convey the original purpose, for they are called *masobo,* translated "ghost house," indicating communion with spirits: "by inspiration, the Lords established spirit chambers . . . where the prophets sat to learn the decrees of the Lord."

Like the featureless tholoi at Arpachiyah, the windowless domes that Col. P. H. Fawcett found in Brazil were completely empty, their interior free from the grime associated with any cooking or illuminating agency, which tells us they were not mundane dwellings at all:* they had a specific, consecrated purpose; namely, to link up with the Immortals. And because of their generous size (up to thirty-two feet in diameter and even larger in Iraq), such structures present themselves as gathering places, communal sanctums.

In fact, most of the formal domelike buildings of the ancient day were dedicated to otherworldly matters, being temples, mosques, tombs, observatories, ceremonial chambers, spirit huts, or council rooms—like Lebanon's Domes of the Prophets or Sumeria's iconic Sacred Hut (dedicated to In*an*na), or the *iwans* of Persia or the vaulted roof at Ctesiphon (once the Persian capital) or Egypt's *serdab.* Several millennia ago in Egypt, to attain the degrees of Anubi, "rites and ceremonies were in dark chambers, and the angels of heaven . . . took part therein . . . [teaching] mortals by the voice, the mysteries of spirit communion." Completely unlit, these ancient temples of darkness[†] were without any openings or windows: "The ancient prophet caused the worshipers to sit in the dark."[84]

---

*Likewise, altar-containing mounds on the Ohio River were "destitute of remains."
†One may ask—why were the spirit chambers of the ancients kept so scrupulously dark? The practice, we realize, remains in force *to this day* among indigenous Americans. The Mayan adept is trained in darkness, immersion in the dark a theme of Mayan shamanism, meant to sharpen the initiate's senses and enable him to read auras. The ceremonial structure of the Great Plains is the dome-shaped earth-lodge. Among the Iroquois, the Seneca *Dark* Dance in honor of the Great Little People, invites these tiny ancestors into the circle, and they come in and sing in their own language, their songs filling up the dark room "as if something had opened out that was larger than those who released it, and that had some kind of independent existence" (Wilson, *Apologies,* 208).

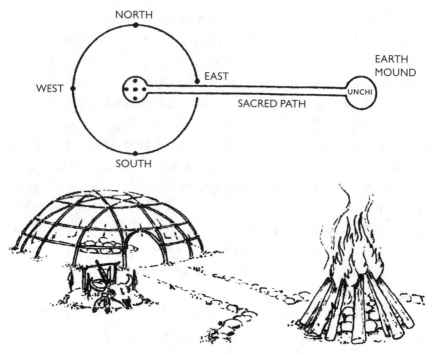

Fig. 7.21. Native sweat lodge in keyhole configuration. Some medicine wheels are also of this shape.

It is the same with the Lakota Indians when they perform the *yuwipi* ceremony: "Yuwipi has to be performed in complete darkness . . . not a speck of light can enter . . . [then] the singing and drumming starts . . . the spirits enter . . . [and] are in harmony . . . they'll sing and talk with us," recounts Mary Brave Bird.[85] While yuwipi is a "finding-out" ritual, *inipi* is the Lakota purification rite, the sweat lodge, the configuration of which bears the "keyhole" shape of the tholoi, with its armlike path extending outward from the hut.

A close relative of this family is the round, subterranean kiva of the Pueblos, the Southwest version of tholos, round and dark and sacred; some kivas even have the familiar keyhole-shape, like those discovered at Mesa Verde.

In Western Asia, the holy tribes, the principal seers and sages of their day, were called Shepherd kings (a.k.a. the Royal Shepherds): "Nowhere in all the world did man prosper so greatly in [natural] philosophy as he did in Parsie [Persia] . . . and most of all among the shepherd kings. . . . [Their] oracle structures were made without windows, so the angels could come and teach their holy doctrines."[86] Thus could early Christian writers affirm that "prophecy came not by the will of man, but holy men spoke as they were influenced by the Holy Spirit."[87]

Should the archaeologist be confounded when he finds no weapons of war or utilitarian articles within these holy shrines? (In the early American mounds, too, "weapons are but rarely found."[88]) Will agnostic professors ever twig to the sturdy signs of a faith that once covered the Earth? All along the sweep of the Caspian, from Turkmenistan to Anatolia, beehive structures dotting the landscape count among the unmistakable signatures of the Old Ones, the Teachers of Wisdom.

In my judgment, the Catal Huyuk materials suggest a westerly variant of the assemblage known in the upper Tigris-Euphrates region as the Halafian.

ROBERT BRAIDWOOD, *PREHISTORIC MEN*

Noah, they say, beached on Mount Ararat, which is near Çatalhüyük. Now Abraham was Noah's descendant through Shem through *Arpaschad:* Were his people the peaceful Halafians? The *Arpach*iyah site (Iraq) contains fine examples of Halafian art (see fig. 8.10, p. 283). The distinctive amulets and figurines of these people—particularly articles carved from obsidian—are yet another sign of the wise and gentle Shepherd Kings who "lived in peace, wandering about, making trinkets, which they oft exchanged with the inhabitants of cities."[89] One of the earliest-known permanent settlements of these nonagressive artisans appears along the mound-covered Anatolian plains, where their successors, the Hittites, produced high-quality trinkets with a delicate finish, obsidian mirrors, and ornamental stone beads so finely drilled that a modern steel pin cannot penetrate them. The Hittites themselves, we hasten to add, built tholoi sanctums 8,000 years ago, such as found at Hattusa (with its distinctive "cluster" housing); Çatalhüyük, also "clustered," had sixty-three windowless communal cult buildings and only a hundred and three dwellings, indicating a center of worship. These people had a deep and expressive ritual life, their shrine rooms beautifully

Fig. 7.22. Image of a noticeably short Hittite couple carved on their coffin lid. Drawing by Jose Bouvier.

ornamented. It was a surprisingly large town for the so-called Stone Age, perhaps six thousand people.

As we recall, the Hittites were short, stocky, and bearded, with long hair, tunics, and curled-tip shoes. They preferred diplomacy to force of arms, and they were intensely religious. Are not these ancient Anatolians an offshoot of the devout tribes of little people who made their way west across Asia? Assyria's Tepe Gawra (see fig. 7.3, p. 214), not far from Arpachiyah and old Nineveh,[90] combines the signatures of the Old Ones: adobe buildings (not reed huts); its lowest level ("late

Halaf") has the circular, domed tholoi, fifteen feet in diameter.[91] These large settlements of the Halafian type are distinctively lacking in streets ("clustered"), their living quarters crammed into a beehive complex of rooms—many windowless—with an opening in the roof, to permit entrance by ladders.

Clusters and ladders . . . tholoi and mounds . . . the arts of peace and the circle twice cut. . . . these are the signs—the assemblage, the constellation—that comprise mute testimony of the holy people of Long Ago. Asia Minor (Turkey, Anatolia), thought James Churchward, was inhabited by "civilized peoples, tens of thousands of years before history began to be recorded. . . . Remains at Troy [on the west coast of Turkey] will help us identify the[m]. . . . Far back in the prehistoric past in Asia Minor . . . were highly . . . enlightened people."

Did Higher Intelligence (the angelic host with whom these people communed inside their tholoi) teach these pre-Hittites their sophisticated industries and technologies? Old Turkey, after all, had the first wheel, first wheat, first coins, finest pottery, jewelry and textiles, comfortable homes, polygonal masonry. Among their ruins were found advanced metalwork (copper cylinders) not supposed to be in the Neolithic "Stone Age," as well as examples of superb craftsmanship in wood, obsidian, smelting, not to mention articles produced with "lathe-like" perfection.

At other sites with tholos-like structures, again we find sophisti-cated artifacts, such as platinum objects dug up in the dead cities of South America; this metal melts only at 1,800 degrees Celsius. How were such high temperatures achieved by these early people? Let us con-sider the answer given by the Byzantine Emperors who long kept the secret of "Greek fire," and when asked about it, "they blandly replied that an angel had revealed the formula to the first Constantine."

Indeed, the Navajos declare they received their sacred house plan from their tutelary spirits. Thus is their round *hogan* "constructed to encourage harmony, just as the spiritual beings first instructed," recounts Charlie Cambridge, the only Navajo with credentials in both anthropology and archaeology. Cambridge adds, "The circular hogan possesses spiritual power," as legend claims the first hogan was "con-nected to heaven."

Fig. 7.23. Hogan in Monument Valley. Today, even if the Navajo family has a newer home, they still maintain the traditional hogan for ceremonies and to "keep themselves in balance."

One might suspect that the Spanish word *hogar* (meaning "home") shares the same ancient root from which hogan is taken: *hoogadoah,** which was indeed the "well-covered house" prescribed for rites and ceremonies of the moundbuilders, in which space the angels could come and teach.[92]

> For the light of My angels to come and abide with My people, ye shall provide the hoogadoah, the well-covered house, and it shall have but one door, and pieces shall be put therein, so that when My chosen are within, all shall be dark, that My angels may teach them.
>
> OAHSPE, BOOK OF SAPHAH

No tribe has monopoly on this school of direct inspiration, which runs from Alaska to Mexico, wherein "to summon a spirit to answer inquiries . . . a circular or conical lodge . . . [was] covered with skins or mats [allowing only] a small aperture. . . . Once [the seer] was in, he carefully closed the hole. . . . At length the priest announces that the spirit is present."[93]

The angel-teachers might answer questions, as Mary Brave Bird once explained, "The yuwipi man translates what the spirits have told

---

*In North Africa (Sahara) is the Hoggar region, "home" of the Tuareg, whose culture may derive from the "clustered" Libyans; here there is a mountain sacred to the Libyans, covered with Tifinar (inscriptions and beautiful rock art), as reported by Count Prorok who calls this a "terraced civilization,"[94] with walled cities—in the Stone Age!

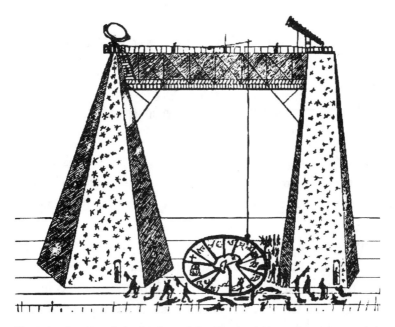

Fig. 7.24. Star Temple in the time of the Shepherd kings. Astronomers of those days knew nearly as much of the heavens as we do today. The Persians, Chinese, and Indians—9,000 years ago—were far advanced in learning, which is proven by the stars and planets they named and mapped.

him."* The spirits might intervene for the welfare of the people as a whole, for example, to save them from drought[95] or to assist in curing ceremonies or in any number of crises. They also came as teachers of spiritual methods,† as well as of scientific/cosmic knowledge. For, in Egypt, The Lord said unto man: "Build thou a chamber within the temple of the stars. And man so built . . . [and] God gave to man the

---

*The well-known sand paintings of the Navajos may have been oracular in genesis, something like the sand writing referred to in the Book of Osiris, which brings us back 12,000 years. Compare to Ezra Bible, Chronicles 21:12, a case of automatic writing from Elijah. The Book of Osiris says of the Star Chamber: "the seer sat therein, with a table before him, on which sand was sprinkled. And the Lord wrote in the sand . . . the laws of heaven and Earth."

†Methods: Over a few millennia, we see a westerly spread of these culture elements that seem to correspond to the movement of Monasticism from east to west (see fig. 7.3, p. 214), from Samarkand to Anatolia, reaching Egypt as early as the fifth millennium BCE, according to Sir Flinders Petrie, and culminating in the Essenes.

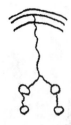

Fig. 7.25. Ojibwa Mide sign for spirit "trickling down the sacred remedy" from heaven. In other chapters, we have found the Ojibwa/Chippewa bond to the little people to be intact; a fact that is underscored by their connection to the Motherland and their own "Noah": Minabozho.

names of the stars and their seasons. . . . And the seer gave it to the king, and the king proclaimed the words thereof. And God gave man sacred days . . . for ceremonies; according to the times of the moon and stars gave he them" (Book of Osiris).

In the Egyptian rites of Anubi, only when the initiate advanced to the higher degrees,* was he "taught the arrangement of the heavens; the places of the sun and stars and moon."[96] Modern man has long puzzled over how the Chinese, Indian, Persian, Babylonian, and Hebrew astronomers knew the size, speed, and orbit of the planets.† Legend and archaeology dovetail here, pointing to the well-covered house as the inner sanctum of revelation where the secrets of the gods were handed down to their mortal protégés: the little people and company.

---

*After learning the secrets of falling water, the application of lotions to the skin that would make poundings and rappings, the secret names of the Great Spirit, the dominions of the presiding gods, the appropriate anthems and salutations.

†Note also that the Hopis in their kivas learned time based on Venus. See the work of Ron Anjard.

CHAPTER 8

Tall Tales and Short Subjects

THE CLOSED MIND

"I am sorry," said H.-P. Blavatsky-X (excarnate), on a "visit" to Carl Wickland's seance circle, "to say that . . . you live in a time when things are breaking up. . . . All theories will go down and philosophy [the study of Truth] will rise."[1]

Are not their doctrines trembling on their foundations?

OAHSPE, BOOK OF OURANOTHEN

In our search for the little people, we have had to parse fact from factoid, truth from tall tales and—not least of all—from bogus theories. The tallest tale of all is the descent of man—a sapient, godlike, being, with a miraculous brain—from animals and nature's random mutations. We have long been led by pseudoscientific explanations of our origins, amid the obstructionist climate of the professional establishment, with its vested interest in not rocking the academic boat.

AOL (analytic overlay) is a very fine CIA research term, referring to the bias we may deploy in *interpreting* data; in a word, if evidence doesn't fit our ideas, we find ways to get rid of it. Such data, in the academic patch, has been labeled "anomalous," "out of place," "aberrant," "erratic," a "curiosity," simply a mistake, or—a permanent mystery:

"Probably we will never know. . . ." The carbon dating of fossils, a colleague of mine explained, comes under AOL: they just throw it out if the date looks "wrong." Early dates (ca. 48,000 BP) for man in the New World—scientifically determined and proposed by the acclaimed Louis Leakey, no less—were rejected simply because "They're too old."[2] If evidence conflicts with the current "model," or worse, suggests a completely new *non grata* model, that evidence is usually labeled "complex" and left for further (funded) research to solve. All this points to the intellectual version of (political) damage control. Watch out for these words: anomalous, complex, mystery—the vocabulary of denial, agenda, the idée fixe—the closed mind.

AOL is nothing new. The first *Homo erectus* remains ever found (by Eugene Dubois, in 1891) were dismissed as a deformed ape. The stooping Yak (an offshoot of erectus, see fig. 6.6, p. 189), unearthed in the mid-twentieth century at La Chapelle, France, was identified as an arthritic Neanderthal. The first Neanderthal itself, discovered in the mid-nineteenth century, near Dusseldorf, was, with its "apelike" skull and deformed limbs, thought by some to be a Mongolian cavalryman with rickets. This heavy-browed creature met with academic scorn and was breezily dismissed by a variety of experts who dubbed him: an ancient Dutchman, a wild cannibal, a hydrocephalic idiot, an 1814 Cossack, a deranged hermit, and so on.

BLEACHED BLONDS?

When R. O. Marsh was about to leave Darien (Panama), with extraordinary revelations about the White Indians in that region, the media invented "news" of his expedition (which took place in the 1920s). One (unqualified) individual was interviewed and declared that "the whole thing was a fake and the White Indians mere albinos."[3] Other critics accused Marsh of smuggling white people into the San Blas country.

It has become an idée fixe that the white race is strictly Aryan or Caucasian or Indo-European. For example, the hapless Ainu of Japan, a very archaic people, are made to represent an "ancient migration" from Europe: simply because of their (taxonomically) troublesome light color

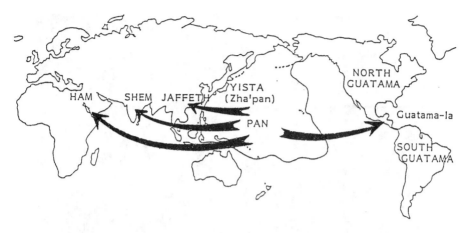

Fig. 8.1. Schematic of the flood diaspora, showing the names
and direction of the fleets out of Pan

and "Caucasian" features. But they came, I daresay, from the opposite
direction. Consider Noah and his pure white sons; as all logic dictates,
they had to come from *somewhere* before landing on "Mt. Ararat" (in
the Caucasus), right? The Noahs of the world, escaping a catastrophic
flood, made landfall, in fact, in almost every country *except* Europe:
India, China, Japan, Africa, and the Americas.

As we will soon discover, these little and white flood survivors are
reckoned in each of those landing-places as the *oldest* people in the
world, legend often remembering them as yellow-haired. In Africa,
the "yellow" Bushmen are the oldest of tribes; while the aborigines of
Flores, the Rampasas, as well as those of New Caledonia* and Fergusson Island, are paler than their neighbors: though mixed in type (some
hairy, with heavy brow and jaw), yet others are coffee-brown and even
blond-haired. The heavy-jaw and "pelted" skin, of course, are genetic
traits. But the blond hair? Carleton Coon, a leading anthropologist of
the past mid-century, isolates this blondism and credits it to "bleaching
in salt water"—because it's not what we expected! AOL.

Even the equatorial Twa (pygmies) are somewhat lighter skinned than
the surrounding Africans; since their campsites, it is reasoned, are located

---

*Are those pale New Caledonians descendants of the unknown race who left hun-
dreds of tumuli and mysterious cement pillars on the island?

Fig. 8.2. The Filipino *Ba*tak Negritos; possibly related are the Sumatra *Ba*ttas, shorter and paler than the Malays, presumably because of their "distance from the sea."

in the forest, the sun does not always find them, thus "explaining" their lighter skin tone. A whole school of thinking accounts for lighter-colored Negrito populations by invoking "de-pigmented skin" in cloudy or forested regions. But then, switching gear, the evolutionists will turn around and find a "selective advantage" to blond hair, "because it reflects *sunlight*," which, of course, contradicts their own "cloudy region" argument.

When a light-skinned tribe was found in the depths of New Guinea in 1937, anthropologists conjured "roving seafarers" who must have stumbled on this (landlocked!) region, inhabited by 50,000 people.[4] A mere handful of Europeans, with equally impressive procreative abilities, were likewise credited with the blondism typical of the Mandan Indians on the Great Plains. In this case, our virile "roving seafarers" were thought to be Scandinavian explorers of the fourteenth century. And when this theory failed to wash, the next step was to impugn the silvery locks of the Mandans as merely a tendency to early graying—even though the occurrence of white hair was *most common among infants and children!* So when *that* argument went south, the "aberration" was pinned on meaningless sound bytes such as "individual variability in pigmentation," or "aboriginal peculiarities." And if that sounded too vague, the scientific term *kwashiorkor* (a protein-deficiency disease that induces reddish hair color) was trotted out. Peruvian (as well as Egyptian and Chinese) mummies with auburn and ash blond hair, it was concluded, were due to "pigment degradation" that lightens hair over time.

Most popular is the theory that Leif Eriksson and other Norsemen deposited their white genes among the Incas; or that White Indians seen in the back villages of Brazil could be traced to migrations of the lighter Toltecs to South America, or perhaps to Eric the Red (leader of the Europeans who launched expeditions to the Americas long before the Vikings). In this general line of thinking, the moon-eyed, fair-skinned people (of the Cherokee) must have descended from Wales' Prince Madoc ab Owain Gwynedd who crossed the Atlantic around 1170 and colonized some areas: hence "Welsh Indians." Nevertheless, it is also thought that this journey was later "developed" as a piece of propaganda to bolster the British claim to the New World (especially against the claims of the Spaniards).

And what about Oceania's fair natives? From whence the "white strain in the Polynesians?" asked Harold Gladwin, reviewing the theories, most of which consider it of "Europoid" or "Caspian" origin or perhaps the genetic contribution of Indic sea-farers or voyagers from Mesopotamia, Persia, or Baluchistan; "These straws are all blowing eastward."[5] Oh aye? *How far east?* This important question we will tackle toward the end of this chapter.

White Eskimos, seen in a 1656 expedition on the shores of Davis Straits, may easily have been the mixed descendants of Norse colonists, theorists reasoned. Alternately, one might invoke "modifications" or, simply, for "some accidental reason" blond individuals were born to parents of pure Eskimo blood. Or "new alleles" for hair and eye color arose independently through *mutation,* with some kind of "selection pressure" favoring light color. But just because you're using scientific terms doesn't mean you're being scientific. If Europeans contributed their genes, this race mixing among the Eskimos should be most conspicuous in the *east* where the whalers had their headquarters, fading away as one goes west. The opposite is the case.

SCIENTIFIC ORPHANS

Like our tawny, blond-streaked abos, the poor little people are scientific orphans. According to archaeologist Richard Adams,[6] the name of Uxmal's Temple of the *Dwarfs* represents "the flamboyant and inappropriate names often given to archaeological monuments in a misguided effort to interest tourists." But Mexican prehistory and iconography verily teem with dwarfs.

The nonexistence of little people has been argued in so many ways, some quite contrived: We have already seen how prehistoric buildings with low entryways were not for a moment considered a sign of short folks, but rather a means of forcing invaders to kneel down, making them more vulnerable. *Yeah, right.* Alternately, the whole business is merely "symbolic"; the entrance to passage graves, for instance, is low "in representation of the entrance to the womb"; or, one "crawls in ceremony of rebirth."[7] But is it right to invoke symbolism when a straightforward explanation can be given?

At Skara Brae in the Orkneys, a small Neolithic village sports doorways only three feet high. These were thought (thanks to AOL) to confound potential intruders or to offer maximum protection from the elements. But *also* on Orkney are three-foot-high stone chambers (at Maeshowe), home, no doubt, to the little Picts. Nevertheless, the same verdict has been reached here, as also at Cornwall, where Iron Age underground shelters have "small entrances [that] would have been easily defended." And when miniature flint tools were found in the moorland of East Lancashire, they were identified as *ritual* objects of some sort. Please explain then why, if they were merely symbolic objects, they were found alongside equally small examples of *conventional tools*.

To deny the evidence of a lost race of little people (for neither science nor religion has a way of fitting the Old Ones into their version of anthropogenesis)—just call it erratic, aberrant, indeterminate, a mystery, anomalous. This is how Loren Eiseley made short work of the shriveled little mummy-man he was offered at the bone camp out West;

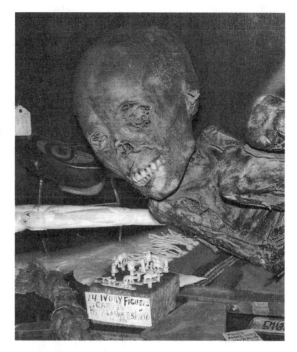

Fig. 8.3. A genuine adult mummy on display at a Seattle waterfront curio shop; she is 32 inches long and said to be 3,400 years old.

the specimen, he told his readers, was nothing more than "an anomalous mummified stillbirth with an undeveloped brain"[8]—even though Amerind oral history abounds with legends of pint-sized humans—everything from the miserable Stick Indians to the Great Little People.

Which brings us to yet another tactic used to impeach the offending data on *Homo pygmaeus*—the cry of Hoax, the knee-jerk response that has long held various mummy specimens at bay. The San Pedro mummy, though, was certified genuine by the Anthropology Department of Harvard University, and backed by Shoshone and Crow legends of miniature people. It was not a hoax, as also determined by American Museum of Natural History experts: it was an old person—not a child, not a stillbirth. Not anomalous. Nonetheless, the University of Wyoming declared it a diseased child,* and in 1980 another anthropologist studied the X-rays, concluding the withered body was that of an infant

---

*Scientists also took refuge from the paradigm-shaking hobbit on Flores by ascribing her littleness to a growth deficiency, perhaps Laron "syndrome" or microcephalic osteodysplastis or myxoedematous cretinism or pituitary abnormality; but both cretinism and pituitary dysfunction were ruled out by experts.

who suffered from anencephaly, a congenital abnormality that would account for the adult proportions of the bones! The little San Pedro man had been displayed in sideshows for years, before being purchased by a businessman; sometime after his death, it disappeared.

And what was the fate of those spectacular finds in southwestern Pennsylvania where whole cemeteries of pygmy-size stone vaults were found? Despite the very large number of graves, experts announced they were those of children. Huh? (Ordinary settlers in the region, though, had simply taken them as "a race of dwarfs.") Skeletons of tiny human adults cannot always be passed off as infantile (thanks to worn-down teeth and other "tells"). In which case, the next "out" is to label them as some other species, perhaps a small bear or gorilla. The seventeenth-century English anatomist, Edward Tyson, obtaining small African skeletons, concluded that the "pygmie" was definitely not human. He was right! The specimen he examined happened to be that of a chimpanzee.

In China, the Bayan Kara Ula human skeletons were at first judged to be a species of mountain gorilla: It was Chi Pu Tei (in 1940) who suggested that the remains of these little people (Han-Dropa ancestors) belonged to an extinct species of mountain ape. But did the apes also leave those cave drawings—pictograms of the constellations—and fabulous etched disks? And do apes bury each other? Ignored, too, was the lingering "mystery" of a Chinese dwarf village near the Bayan caves (no one taller than three feet ten inches). The mystery was "solved," though, in 1997 when experts

Fig. 8.4. The world's tallest and smallest man, both from the same region of Inner Mongolia, are shown together, shaking hands. The little guy is 2 feet 4 inches high.

determined that the dwarfism in that village was caused by excessive mercury levels in their drinking water. Nevertheless *other* experts pointed out that the levels of mercury indicated would be *lethal* and no one would have survived. Besides, mercury cannot change human DNA.

Never successfully trapped, the elusive Orang Pendek, a hobbit and feral type of human, was at one time identified as a species of sun-bear (supposedly based on a track). The bones of a cognate wild man, Nittevo of Ceylon, have likewise been identified as those of an extinct bear known as *rahu valaha,* since both groups—man and bear—had the same habits: the Nittevo lived in caves, monkey-chattered like the twittering of the sloth bears, and went in groups like the she-bear and her cubs. The tiny Nittevo as "an unsolved problem" came to mind recently with the splashy discovery of Java's three-foot-tall hobbit, "an intriguing problem in evolutionary biology." To explain his shortness, scientists declared hobbit's ancestors had been stranded on the island (Flores) and got small in order to survive. The little people who *still* live on the island, the Rampasas, according to one expert, went through a "temporary food shortage that made them small."(!)

They call this phenomenon the "Island Effect." In other words, when species form enclaves in refuge areas and inaccessible islands, they (obeying the "law" of natural selection), may get smaller and smaller as environmental conditions favor a less demanding body size. With limited food supply on islands, survival would depend on "minimizing daily energy requirements." These hobbits then were evidently subject to isolation and dwarfing, proving the marvelous ability to "adapt." Hobbit, in this scheme, evolved from a normal size, shrinking suitably to the scale of an unpromising environment.

And this is AOL. For stature is not stunted by lack of nourishment. Bushman "dwarfing," for one, can have nothing to do with food economy, simply because they previously had all the game they could eat and were *always* small people. In India "nutritional stress," indicated at a burial in Damdana, was discovered on skeletons of "substantial stature*
. . . [and] does not appear to have inhibited growth."[9]

---

*Darwin quotes the research of a colleague attempting to "ascertain the influences which act on stature . . . they did not relate to climate, the elevation of the land . . . nor even to the abundance of . . . the comforts of life."[10]

White scientists, notes M. Stewart (in www.stewartsynopsis), have claimed Negritos resemble downsized Australian Aborigines. But, he points out, the Negrito is too *old* to classify this way; he "represents an ancient, if not *the most ancient* [emphasis added], component in the prehistoric peopling of Asia."* Similarly, Jared Diamond, in *Guns, Germs, and Steel,* proposed that the Negritos may actually be *ancestors* of the aborigines and Papuans. This is quite a bit closer to the truth than its opposite—the "shrinkage" theory—which argues that the Papuan small people owe their size to "an adaptation for saving energy in constant steep climbing with burdens" (thank you, William Howells, *Getting Here*). Small stature, as such theories argue, is an "adaptation" to life in the tropical forest; animals simply getting small, in adjusting to closed habitats. Besides, (as the argument runs), it is easier for a small man to move about the jungle, climb trees for fruit, and so forth. Africa's pygmies, it has even been proposed, simply got small from "walking in dense forests"! Isn't it odd, though, that one of our most respected archaeologists informs us that *tall* (and slender) is the "appropriate [type] for those who live in tropical environments," while short (and stocky) fits "glacial conditions."[11]

Yet another way to stonewall these aberrant pygmies is to invoke inbreeding. Where, for example, did Mexican dwarfs come from? Experts now pin it on a genetic mutation, magnified as a result of inbreeding. And if that doesn't fly, insular Negritos may illustrate "dwarfing as a solution to the problem of crowding" on islands;[12] people living in the Big Apple, by these lights, should pretty soon be about three feet tall.

Pygmies, in the current academic paradigm, are just "shrunken Negroes" who have undergone "acts of dwarfing," even though there are only a few traits *genetically* linking Twa to black Africans. Wondrously, it is never for a moment considered that pygmies could have had that size originally! It must be "size reduction," which plants and

---

*Other factors (or factoids) to explain away poor little *Homo pygmaeus* include adaptation to heat and humidity, reduced amount of IGF (insulin-like growth factor) during adolescence, low levels of ultraviolet light in the rainforest, insufficient vitamin D placing limits on calcium uptake for bone growth.

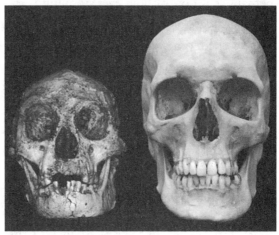

Fig 8.5. Hobbit skull photographed by scientist Peter Brown. Note the small ("grapefruit" size) skull of *Homo floresiensis*.

other animals have exhibited on islands. Island dwarfing? Then how come hobbit's home town of Flores has rats the size of pigs and lizards the size of dragons?

> *No one has been able to explain tall or short stature . . . on the ground of adaptation, climate, altitude, or even food supply.*
>
> EARNEST HOOTON, *UP FROM THE APE*

Not everyone plays the Adaptation Game: Referring to Papuan pygmies, Mr. Wollaston said, "their low stature is not due to poor conditions."[13] Robert Martin, curator at the Field Museum in Chicago, further dampened the "shrinkage" theory by pointing out that the grapefruit size of (Flores') hobbit's brain is *intrinsic:* "Brains do not shrink proportionally to bodies . . . that's why the heads of small dogs . . . are proportionally large for their bodies."[14]

PREPOSTEROUS THEORIES

More sorry arguments are whipped out to rebut the wonderfully rich iconographic evidence of little people: Egypt's dwarf god Bes, we are asked to believe, is the figure of a miscarried fetus (!), since he is, among other things, god of children and women in labor. Pure moonshine, but judging from the lengths to which scholars will go to *explain away* the little people, you'd think they had some vested interest in doing so. And perhaps they do. Without ever stopping to think that little people might be a legitimate race *sui generis* (and far too archaic to be a shrunken version of their *descendants!*), academic personalities continue, doggedly, to pursue outré theories to account for the "stunting" of Negritos. Well, I guess we'd have to rewrite the book of Evolution, as well as its main contender, the Holy Bible, if we had to factor in the role of *Homo pygmaeus* in the genesis of mankind. It's just easier to write them off.

Which is what Andrea Migliano and her team did with the little folk of the Philippines, the Batak (fig. 8.2, p. 262) and Aeta (fig. 2.20, p. 63). Migliano, of Clare College, Cambridge, England, finds fault (rightly) with the standard "explanations" of Negrito and Negrillo short stature—but in their place gives us the most preposterous theory of all.[15] The degree of sophistry, of intellectual jugglery, that has entered into Academe never ceases to amaze me.

Migliano starts out well enough by refuting the misguided theory that racial shortness is due to environmental factors such as malnutrition, if only because some of the world's *tallest* people suffer from similar deprivations. But then Migliano selects *early death* (high mortality and brief life span: many do not survive past age forty) as the culprit. Because of their short life expectancies, she postulates, pygmies compensate by "shifting the reproductive period forward" (having babies younger), which means they must reach maturity faster. Therefore, they stop growing at age twelve. The "energy" that should be put to growth, now gets spent on reproduction at an earlier age! (The Mincopie Negritos, however, do not reach maturity until age fifteen.[16])

Nicely couched in evolutionary terms, Migliano's facts are fitted into natural selection and the "evolutionary pressure" that has shifted the reproductive years back. Pygmies, therefore, are proof of how our species continues to adapt and evolve. "I am sure we are still adapting to our environment." Actually the pygmies are doing the *opposite* of adapting; they are dying off. And they have high mortality because they are ravaged by malnutrition and (otherwise easily preventable) diseases like measles and chickenpox. A losing battle against all the ills of poverty is certainly the reason for their short life span—but not for their *height*! There are many other tribes of normal height that have high mortality and malnutrition.

Only a few years after the hobbit story broke, another little man gave up his bones to a team of paleo-anthropologists: this time on Micronesia's Palau. Here in the Pacific where the last wave of little people *originated*, the skeletal remains of tiny humans are perfectly understandable. Or should be. Nevertheless, here, as everywhere else, official "explainers" need to show how these people "*acquired* [emphasis added] reduced stature for some reason."[17] Starting in 2006, limestone caves on the rock island of Palau began to yield prehistoric remains of a people whose women weighed an estimated 64 pounds, and males, 95 pounds. Small and fairly chinless like Flores man (hobbit), but larger brained, the little people of Palau (twenty-five adults recovered) "have caused much head-scratching." Nevertheless, the verdict remains unchanged: the short stature ("shrinking") is explained, alternately, by "extensive inbreeding," "island dwarfing," isolation, adaptation ("pressure for small body size"), disease ("malnourished cretins"), and so on ad nauseam.

Amazingly, Nature.com pronounced the Palau finds as those of *children;* while the discoverers themselves, led by Lee Berger, an anthropologist at the University of Witwatersrand in South Africa, never for a second considered ancestral heritage, an original gene pool, as the reason for their littleness. Here, as elsewhere, I place more confidence in dear old nineteenth-century thinking than in today's "sophisticated," computer-driven, and model-oriented theories.

> *The prevailing size of a race is a really deep-seated, inherited characteristic, and depends but little on outward conditions, as abundance of food, climate, etc.*
>
> W. H. FLOWER, "THE PYGMY RACES OF MEN"

RACIAL MIXING

Lee Berger and his team were "perplexed" by Palau man's supposedly surprising mixture of traits, some of which scientists thought were almost prehuman. *Perplexed?* Perplexed by their own theories? There is nothing at all perplexing about the *blend* of traits, at least once we get past the fossilized thinking—pun intended—of today's evolutionists. While our little people of Palau do indeed have a hard time fitting into the smooth evolutionary picture, they go right along with the rest of mankind in demonstrating a *mixed* gene pool. A wonderful, unpredictable hodge-podge of traits. Call it what you like—cross-breeding, interbreeding, hybridization, miscegenation, amalgamation—*such racial mixing has been going on since Day One.*

In Mayan anthropogenesis, the survivors of *each* World Age remained to be represented in this, the Fourth Sun, giving us a farrago of the inhabitants of the previous worlds. How true! And there is not a shred of "evolution" in it. It has been assumed that Neanderthal man or *Homo erectus evolved* into Upper Paleolithic *Homo sapiens* and Caucasians (Cro-Magnon); but fossils from China, as noted in *Scientific American* (Jan. 1999), show no "evolving" at all, only a *blending* of stocks, a continuum or fusion between earlier hominids and the more modern Chinese type. In a word, there are no "intermediate" species, just lots of blends; and no evolution—only interbreeding. The dark and the light, the tall and the short, the small- and big-brained, the robust and gracile, the wild and tame, the bearded and glabrous have—from the beginning—been thrown together, quickly scrambling the genetic pool and producing hybrids of every possible cast.

Nor does it take long for the offspring to establish themselves.[18] When the tiny Bushmen of the Kalahari intermarry with black Africans, they quickly attain a "normal" height. Measured in the nineteenth century, Bushmen living in Bechuanaland reached nearly average height after a generation or two of intermarriage: five feet four inches was common, some even reaching six feet. Should the resulting blend—of *any* two races, for that matter—be "perplexing?" Certainly not, just as any offspring in the entire world is bound to combine his parents' genes.

We need to take these mixtures more seriously, before tossing them in the "anomaly" bin or squeezing them into improbable evolutionary sequences. One skeleton of *Homo erectus* at East Africa's Lake Turkana ("a mosaic of erectus and sapiens features") was clearly modern "from the neck down," whereas the skull was markedly primitive. Now this indicated, to Brian Fagan, a prominent authority, that "different parts of the human body evolved at different rates."[19] *Evolved?* I don't think so, for these primitive traits have always been in the human gene pool and, as Chinese anthropologists claim, continue to appear in *modern populations.*[20]

Hybrids: intermixing, not evolution. Sometimes it comes to light in the natives' own record. Hawaiian oral history, for example, speaks of the mixing of their own people with the little indigenous Menehune; Kauai legend has the Menehunes and Polynesians not only coexisting peacefully but intermarrying often.

Even some of the most primitive people have mated with more advanced tribes in South America: A. H. Verrill notes "the living Indians of these districts [Nicoya, Chiriqui, Terriba] are the result of mixtures of the cultured races and the more savage tribes"[21]; while Col. Fawcett in Brazil thought the Morcegos (Bats) and their kindred the "most bestial and degenerate savages in existence." Yet some of them intermarried with the more noble Tupis and Caribs, and from this amalgamation sprang the Botocudos and Aymaras: tribes with considerably mixed genes. This region also had milk-white Indians, their skin covered with short down, who saw best in moonlight. Those moon-eyed types whom we visited in chapter 6 are of extraordinarily composite heritage. In this part of the world, "red, white, and black races comingled."[22]

Across the world, in Sundaland, given the mingling of Negritos with both Malaysian and Papuan populations, there is every shade of combination—clinal populations. This easy mixing, if we go back far enough, will prove to be the origin of every creature in the hominid family. And they are nothing but the offspring of exogamous unions!

A veritable chaos of races was spawned in the disobedient Paleolithic, intimating "that the Cro-Magnons were derived from a mixture . . . of strains . . . [and] undoubtedly carried off Neanderthal women

Fig 8.6. Filipino Zambals. Taken in 1904, the photo shows the relative heights of an American, a mixed blood, and a pure Zambal Negrito.

as mates."[23] The vaunted Cro-Magnon man—Charleton Heston in his prime, Europe's splendid six-foot-tall robust specimen of the modern type—was quite a "mixer"; and this is how the Neanderthal ended up with such a large brain, Shanidar Neanderthal's cranial capacity well over 1,600 cc, outstripping our own; today's average is no more than 1,400 cc.

Along the same lines, a child's skeleton found in Portugal in 1998 showed a striking blend of "modern" and Neanderthal features, thousands of years *after* Neanderthal supposedly went extinct! Indeed, some "Neanderthal" features, like out-sized nose and "occipital bun," survive to this day in modern Europeans as well as among China's clinal populations. That Portuguese skeleton had a perfectly modern chin and teeth, though his thick bones, short legs and hefty jaw were classic Neanderthal—*reversing,* yes reversing, the so-called "differential evolution" of body parts conjured by Fagan for the Turkana specimen; for, Turkana man shows the *opposite* combo: modern body, but *primitive*

Fig. 8.7. Five mixed-blood Negritos of Zambal. Negroid (African) and Mongoloid (Asian) blood is so hopelessly mixed among so-called Negritos (the world's swarthy little people, many with an Oriental cast) that it seems a fool's errand trying to "classify" them. The Andaman Negrito sports the woolly hair of the Negro, the glabrous body of the Mongoloid, and craniometric affinities more in keeping with Egyptians and Europeans than with any sub-Saharans; other Andaman traits resemble the Australian-Melanesian type. Geneticists waste their time, really, trying to determine whom the Andamanese most closely resemble! In a word, we are all simply—hybrids—part of the Great Plan.

skull! And so, with the Portuguese find, archaeologists grudgingly conceded "significant interbreeding."

The mixing that produced obvious Neanderthal-Sapiens hybrids still shows up a bit in the morphology of such people as the Ona Indians of Tierra del Fuego, a tribe often cited for their markedly primitive appearance, particularly the low and sloping cranial vault, which is also seen in Australian and Tiwi aborigines, some with remarkably heavy brows.

Many Negritos (rather unlike their namesake) have a high forehead, "long narrow nose of button type," and lips of only moderate thickness. For the Malaysian Negritos, there is "a great deal of fusion along boundary lines."[24] The Malay themselves are a marvelous blend of racial types,

Fig. 8.8. Left: Vedda with wavy hair. Right: Andamanese of mixed type.

indigenous stock generously layered with Hindu, Persian, and Chinese genes. Even among the woolly-haired Negritos, 20 percent of the population has straight hair, many with a reddish tinge, showing a true admixture of bloodlines. The dainty Veddas of Ceylon are a wonderful composite of modern and archaic types, with their flat feet, straight or wavy hair, small skulls, and long arms.

So stereotyping, or any typologizing that ignores or downplays crossbreeding just will not do, if we want to make sense of our racial history. Consider the marvelously mixed Ainu of Japan: white (not yellow) skinned, hairy (not glabrous), much smaller than Caucasians, with wavy (not straight) hair. Every shred of evidence that has been adduced to credit "intermediate" evolutionary types comes, frankly, from the interbreeding of the world's peoples—and that includes the earliest races. "Mixed marriage" gives us the records of the race more faithfully than any other factor under the sun and in the broad and checkered history of man. Early and incessant mixings of the races of men preclude any need for "evolution." Steady hybridization is the simple key to history's racial "mysteries." The peopling of our world is about mingling, marriage customs, prohibitions—and especially their violations. Not evolution.

REMNANTS OF A RACE

The localities in which the Negrito people are found in their greatest purity in inaccessible islands . . . or in the mountainous ranges of the interior . . . point to the fact that they were the earliest inhabitants.

W. H. FLOWER, "THE PYGMY RACES OF MEN"

In seeing these Negritos almost always confined to the mountains of the interior . . . it is difficult not to consider them as having been the first occupants.

ARMAND DE QUATREFAGES, *THE PYGMIES*

The small people of Melanesia represent an older stratum of population than their tall neighbors.

A. F. R. WOLLASTON, *PYGMIES AND PAPUANS*

The Wyandot Indians of Ohio said that the little people were old enough to remember the Flood; the Choctaw say the same: that even before the Emergence, there lived on Earth "before us the Little People." This theme extends all the way to Eastern Europe where the Serbians and Poles remember the ludki, the little people who "lived before humans." In Western Europe's folk belief, the fées (between two and four feet in height) are held to be the oldest beings on the planet, here even before the mountains were formed; and for this reason they were called The Old Ones.*

Probably the word "ell," a measurement, came from these sources. An "ell" (elbow, forearm) was the length of a man's arm; even the word pygmy has a similar derivation, coming from the Greek, meaning "fist," and serving as a measure of length, namely the distance from the elbow to the knuckles (i.e., about thirteen inches).

> *We were born just after the earth was made.*
>
> WELSH ELF

If we could probe the most hidden pockets of the world, the earliest, oldest type of man would there be manifest. The white pygmy-like Vazimba (now extinct) are portrayed by the Malagasy as the *original* inhabitants of the island. In nearby Africa, the Yao of Mozambique have a tale of the Beginning where the first people ever seen were "a little man and woman."[25] In Africa's northern parts, Herodotus's "little

---

*"Old age" in Icelandic is *elli,* rather like the Welsh word for dwarf: *ellyll.*

people" of the Libyan hinterland were later lost to history as they were driven out by hordes of stronger races; yet it was believed they had been the aboriginals of the Mediterranean world, and even "the proto-type of the little man in European folklore."[26]

Consider the distribution of the little people even today: In New Guinea and Southeast Asia, the people seem to get *shorter and lighter* as you penetrate the uplands. What does this tell us? "In New Guinea, stature goes down with altitude. . . . Some of the highland tribesmen are small enough to be called Pygmies."[27] It was the same in Ceylon: "as one leaves the coastal plain and climbs the central mountainous core . . . they [natives] grow shorter . . . and somewhat lighter in skin color."[28] One of the reasons we know, or hear, so little about the world's tiny folk is their isolation. The ancient community of pygmies in the Orkneys was isolated, almost entirely on its own. South India's Negritos, remnants of the earliest stratum of population, live in the more inaccessible mountains, crowded back into refuge areas. All across Polynesia, too, the Negrito dwells in the interior and in the mountain vastness, Hawaii's Menehune secluded in the forest uplands, while the "pygmoids" of New Hebrides and other parts of the western Pacific inhabit the mountainous interior. In America, the pygmies known to the Seneca Indians also lived in the rocky heights; while the Nunnehi were ensconced in the most inaccessible reaches of the Nantahala range (North Carolina). The little Lacandons live in the most unreachable Mayan jungles; the Orang Asli ("original people"), in the most isolated islands of Malaysia; the Han Dropa sequestered in one of the least known ranges of the Himalayas; while the T'rung are hidden away in the remote mountains.

> *The pygmies fled to the ends of the earth . . .*
> HAROLD GLADWIN, *MEN OUT OF ASIA*

Among such isolated groups we are bound to find *earlier* versions of man, more like the ancestor. As an example, the remote Filipino Abenlens have lighter skin than the Aetas, shorter stature, wavy hair,

Fig. 8.9. Mt. Tapiro, seen from the tucked-away village of the Pygmies. "All these people . . . are remnants of a once widely distributed race," concluded A. F. R. Wollaston.

a different language, and the same "graceful limbs" attributed to the Ihins of old. It is also a fact that, moving eastward across the tableland of New Guinea, one finds the lighter-skinned people merge into the darker Papuans. At one time these lighter folk, the Papuan Tarifuroro, "inhabited the whole of this tableland and were driven back westwards by the more virile Papuans."[29]

Armand De Quatrefage, the nineteenth-century's eminent Professor of Anthropology at the Museum d'Histoire Naturelle of Paris, and others, believed the Negrito race, as a whole, once inhabited a vast domain of Indo-oceanic Asia, extending from New Guinea all the way

Fig. 8.10. A Tapiro pygmy: "What kind of lunatics were we to come to New Guinea?" declared the intrepid Wollaston;[30] the year (2012) of this writing marks the centennial of that treacherous expedition.

west to the Persian Gulf, and from the Malay archipelago to Japan.* In other words, Negritos appear to have been once dispersed throughout southern Asia. India's Negritos are considered the oldest strata of inhabitants. Much of the Java, Thai, and Sumatra fossil remains are those of pint-sized Negritos.

The stature of early man is often near the upper limits of pygmy stature.

HARRY SHAPIRO, *PICK FROM THE PAST*

---

*To archaeologist Leonard Cottrell, the Ainu (though now confined to northern-most Japan) seem once to have covered a considerably larger area of the Far East. Physiological evidence links them to the Kha of the Annamite chain as well as to the archaic white stock of Australia, giving them the earliest possible history in Asia and Oceania. It is believed, moreover, that the Austro-Asiatic language family was once spread over the whole of the southern Indo-Chinese mainland.

Negritos ranged over the whole island of Luzon at one time.[31] These Aetas are known to be the oldest residents of the Philippine Islands. Prof. J. Kollman of Basle thought they (as well as all the Negrito and Negrillo populations) are the oldest form of human beings "and that *from them* the taller races have been evolved [emphasis added]," rather than vice versa.

We suspect that many of the African tribes and places whose names begin with Ba- were once little people territory, ba- concealing the meaning of "how things began." "It seems reasonable to assume that the BaMbuti were the original inhabitants of the great tropical rain forest," thought Georg Schweinfurth, who "rediscovered" the Akka pygmies of equatorial Africa in 1870, and who cast both Bushmen and Pygmy as remnants of the "aboriginal population of the continent."[32] W. H. Flower, contemporary of Schweinfurth, thought the same: they are "the remains of a population which occupied the land before the incoming of the present dominant races." The Bushmen are the "pure remnant of the . . . First People . . . his oddly slanted eyes filled with the first light of man."[33] Their distinctive artifact, the graaf (digging stick with its perforated stone), found all the way up to Kilimanjaro and beyond, indicates the extent of their former home. They were driven south by Bantu tribes as well as by European and black southern African encroachments. Archaeology confirms the presence of Bushmen throughout much of Africa at an earlier time. Philostratus noted little people among the tribes of Ethiopia; and to this day, mixed Bushmen types are found as far north as the Sahara.

The link between the cave art of France/Spain and the Kalahari is strengthened by skeletal finds: around 12,000 years ago, the rock paintings of the Magdalenian period, made famous by France's Lascaux and Monte*span* caves (as well as the grotto at *Ain;* see fig. 8.12, p. 285), proved to be the work of Cro-Magnons of *reduced stature,* "now considerably diminished [to] five feet one inch . . . no longer six feet and six feet four." These small men are a branch of the Chancelade type, "Eskimolike . . . not more than four feet seven inches" (akin to the small skeletons near Bonn with their "beautiful carved workmanship" on bone).[34] The Eskimo culture itself, according to Prof. T. C. Lethbridge, was arrested

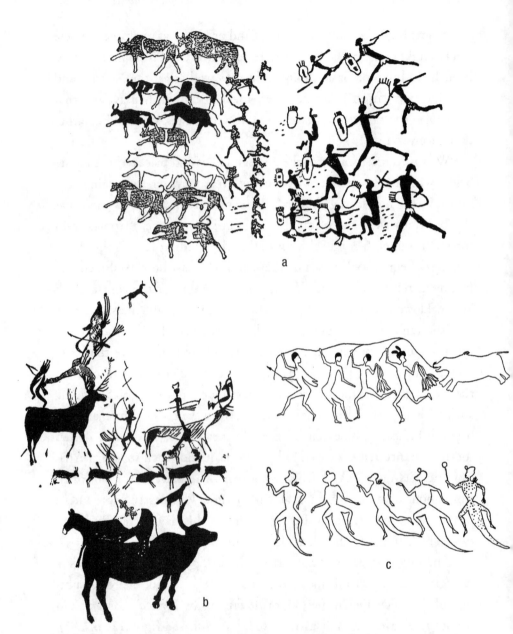

Fig. 8.11. (a) Three Bushman cave drawings; note the difference in size and color of Bushmen and black southern Africans. (b) Rock-shelter painting in Spain. The outstanding cave paintings and engravings of the Bushmen have been compared to those of Europe: "the Magdalenian drawings in the caves of [Spain] and the Pyrenees [are] suggestive of those in (c) South Africa."[35] They show "remarkable resemblances of subject matter and manner."[36] V. Gordon Childe said, "Striking agreements have indeed been detected between paintings in Spain and the Central Sahara and even South Africa."[37]

in Alaska some 10,000 years ago. Before then, the Cro-Magnon influence was dominant. Europe's Chancelade man, a mixed type, is the apparent product of tall Cro-Magnon's copious amalgamations with little indigenous races. Cro-Magnon "for at least 25,000 years [was] pretty consistently mixing with Negroids and Mongoloids," according to Carleton Coon . . . and some of them were little people.

It should be no surprise, then, when we come upon rock art in the Sahara that depicts the co-existence of adult humans ranging in size from small to gigantic. Giants and dwarfs *shared* the archaic horizon; the tallest and the shortest races in Europe are respectively the Norwegians and the Lapps, yet they live in the same region. In Africa, too, the diminutive Bushmen and the tallest race of the country, the black southern Africans, are close neighbors. Ethiopia, too, was once a land of giants and dwarfs.

In this Cro-Magnon-like cave art* of the Bushman, Laurens Van der Post sees an "astonishing gift of painting," its scale running from the Cape of Good Hope for about 1,500 miles north into Rhodesia, and then another 1,500 miles to the Atlantic coast. "Vast as that area is, it is not the whole of his painter's story, but it is enough to indicate the size of his practice . . . [for he is] not only the first man of Africa but the oldest form of human life left in the world."[38]

> *There is every reason to believe that these Bushmen represent the earliest race of which we have, or are ever likely to have, any knowledge.*
>
> W. H. FLOWER, "THE PYGMY RACES OF MEN"

But "earliest" doesn't necessarily mean most primitive. It is a striking fact that the earliest Egyptian, Sumerian, Chaldean, Hittite, and

---

*We have seen samples of similar cave art among: the Crow Indians; Bayan Kara Ula, Melanesian, Malaysians; Negritos/Lenggong, Lanoh cave paintings of Tambun at Gua Badak of Perak origin, dated to at least 11,000 years ago. Noting the shamanistic trance depicted at Lascaux, a clairvoyant once told me that she saw these people of the Magdalenian performing automatic drawing in the dark caves—a place of spirit communion.

ancient American eras appear in certain ways to be the *most* advanced. Egyptian "workmanship was higher in the earlier periods."[39] At Sakkara, Imhotep built a step pyramid "with a mastery that Egyptian architects were never quite able to equal afterward . . . the more recent edifices [of Egypt] tend to be poor copies of their ancient models."[40]

> *The older Egypt was, the more it was cultured.*
>
> PAUL SCHLEIMANN

Recorded time ("the dawn of history"), in many cases, presents itself as the *tail end* of a lost horizon of greatness.

> In times past, the same countries were inhabited by a higher race (Egypt, Africa, South America, and so forth).
>
> OAHSPE, BOOK OF THOR 4:8

At Teotihuacan: "The archaic clay sculpture showed a realism never afterwards achieved in Mexico," just as the realism of Olmec art was "hardly ever achieved in later time."[41] In the northern highlands of Peru, the ruins of Chavin de Huantar attest to an ancient ceremonial center with terraces, mounds, well-constructed stone buildings (the earliest to date in Peru), ventilating shafts, dry masonry, courts and plazas—all of which bespeak a civilization far higher than archaeologists had reason to believe existed in South America at so early a date. Peru's famed Nazca lines, it has been observed, were produced in two phases; the skill and technology of "the earlier of the two phases was the more advanced."[42] "Not infrequently," wrote A. H. Verrill of ancient Peru, "the later cultures were inferior to those of earlier date."[43]

At the American mounds, artistic standards were apparently higher in prehistoric times, the older mounds more imposing. And in Iraq, Arpachiyah's *lowest* level produced the best art, the most exquisite pottery of the ancient world—"masterpieces . . . it almost seems as if the first fruits of Anatolian art were more manifold and distinctive than the products of its later development."[44]

Fig. 8.12. From Arpachiyah and Tell Halaf, exquisite ceramics, circa 6500 BP. These Halafians (of "unknown origin") were very skilled in small-scale craftsmanship. Tell Halaf is near the village of Ras-el-'Ain.*

---

*Part of the Ine- family of names, this Ain, as found also in nearby 'Ain Ghazal (a temple city), incorporates the idea of "oldest" or "most sacred," and probably denotes the same in other parts of the Near East, as it appears in Ain-esh-Shems (sacred Coptic spring), Ain Shems (ancient Palestinian name of Beth-Shemesh), 'Ain Mallaha (Palestinian Natufian village) with Mesolithic microliths, 'Ain es-Sultan (near Jericho); 'Ain Mauhaad, Ain Hanech and 'Ain Guettara (North Africa); Ain Jalot, and Ainos (Thrace). In its purest form, it appears as Ainu, but we find it (euhemistically) transformed by the time it reaches Europe, changed now to Beings of the Otherworld: Emain (island of Faerie, the Irish Elysium), kithain (Sidhe of dreamlife), Aine (fada queen of Limerick), Etain, a Celtic fairy wife, Aino (bride of Vainamoinen in the Finnish epics). Even the Great Creator is G'ain-ji (southwest New Guinea). Once a universal term, Ain appears also in Mexico: Dainzu (great ancient site of Oaxaca), Jaina (Campeche, with ancient dental surgeons).

At Easter Island, where the little people are remembered, there are three levels, the oldest the most advanced. So let's see what the lost horizon of "Pacifica" can tell us about the *real* missing link: the land of Pan.

PANOLOGY

Pan (rather than "Mu" or "Rutas" or "Pacifica" or "Lemuria") is the name I use for the submerged lands of Oceania. Pan-tiya, according to the Tamil of India, was a land swept away by the Flood, just as among the Karens of Burma, Pandanman designates the time before the confounding of languages.

> Behold, I will carry them to all the divisions of the earth, and people it anew with the seed of my chosen.
>
> OAHSPE, THE LORDS' FIRST BOOK 1:45

Generations of writers, noting the striking analogy between Malay, Malagasy, American, and Polynesian languages and customs, have surmised, almost wistfully, "that they were originally one people."[45]

The submersion of Pan—a saga pieced together from scores of traditions—looms as the greatest human disaster of all time, occurring some 24,000 years ago.[46] I do not view it as a coincidence that Valsequillo's (Mexico) artifacts of the modern type are given this date: 24,000 BP. Or that Tiahuanaco has been dated to 23,600 BP.[47] Or that man and mammoth, at Tlapocoya, come together in the "New" World at that date.[48] Or that artifacts made of bone yield that date in the Yukon and Alaska.[49] Or that the first Caucasian-like fossils in North America are of the same age.[50]

In China as well this timeframe is given for the first "Paleo-Caucasoids." Meanwhile, in both Europe and Africa, the earliest dated rock art is 27,000 to 19,000 years old ("22,000 BP or earlier," as Steven Mithen dates the shamanistic cave art of the Bushmen). The earliest "Venus" figurines in Russia are also dated to 24,000 BP; this distribution of Venuses is so extensive in the Old World as to suggest "a large population movement [in] the final . . . period of the Ice Age."[51]

Yes! But should we assume this "movement" *originated* in the Old World? "Could there," Harold Gladwin wisely asks, "be some other explanation?"[52] Since both the Bible and science locate the Great Flood in little Mesopotamia, it is politically incorrect to find it in the Pacific, of all places; but perhaps the deluge of Genesis *does* refer to some local inundation in the Fertile Crescent. But not *Noah's* flood—the Greater Deluge. And speaking of the Fertile Crescent: "We still know practically nothing about their [Sumerian] origins."[53]

Sumeria (Iraq) could not possibly be the "germinal" unit of all of the high civilizations of antiquity—as Joseph Campbell, and the scientific establishment in general seem to think. Campbell states that the Mesopotamian Gilgamesh Epic (of the Flood) "leads us back to the very cradle of the human race."[54] And where might that cradle have rocked?

Was the Old World as a whole *seeded* from elsewhere?

When the Motherland [Mu, Pan] started out to people the earth . . . [it was] eastern Asia . . . where she planted her first colonies . . . we may look for the earliest records of man: not in Europe, Egypt, or Babylonia. They were the tail-enders.

JAMES CHURCHWARD, *THE CHILDREN OF MU*

The best-informed (or least-biased) historians have concluded that "Java and . . . all of southeast Asia is a serious rival" to Africa as the "cradle of mankind."[55] If moderns came out of Africa or the Levant and spread throughout the world, why should such civilized industries as rice cultivation be evident in China or India *before* it got to Africa?[56] Michael Cremo has presented arguments for modern men out of Pakistan, Russia, Siberia;[57] take your pick.

But we are still in the primordial weeds, for the out-of-Asia theory doesn't work any better than out-of-Africa. Genetic studies find that the great migrations of the Paleolithic moved out of Sundaland, going north and west, to populate Asia and beyond, instead of the other way around. In addition, DNA analysis of the Onge (Andaman Islanders) reveals a special change in the Y chromosome, casting the Onge as *ancestral* to the populations of Asia (again, rather than the other way around). Theorists are always trying to move the ancients from the mainland to the islands. Why? Because it is necessary to do so in order to prove the out-of-Africa (or even out-of-Asia) model.

> *Who went which way?*
>
> VINE DELORIA, *RED EARTH, WHITE LIES*

So what land did my earlier-than-Asians come from? The word for "land" is *pan* in the Auca Indian language of Chile, as well as in Mexico (as for example in Teotlal*pan*, "Land of the Gods"); while *Pananu te tai* in Polynesian means "Sea flows to the land." One Tahitian memory holds that "all the islands were formerly united in one *fenua nui* (large continent), which the gods in anger destroyed, scattering in the ocean the fragments of which Tahiti is one of the largest."[58]

In 1627, Francis Bacon described just such an erstwhile land in the Pacific, drawing no doubt on Egyptian, Indian, Teutonic, Greek, Mayan, Native American, and many other cultures besides, all of which have living traditions that name the survivors of a Great Flood of Waters as their own ancestors. Now isn't it absurd to identify that universally remembered Flood as some local inundation in the Fertile Crescent? Neither should we ignore the fact that civilization, according to most traditions, was brought *from the sea* by the **gods**—or amphibious demigods—but more to the point, by a *chosen* (godlike) people.

Those people, in all such cases, came across the water, from elsewhere. And that "elsewhere" is sometimes called Mu. Mexico's *Troano Codex* actually names "Mu" as the sunken continent to the west, calling it the "Land of Clay Hills, Mu in the ocean." Concerning those clay hills: among the Andamanese, og is the word for common clay. "And the wide plains of Og, with her thousand cities . . . shall sink to rise no more."[59] *Og* in Hebrew means "gigantic": at one time in the Levant, Og was the great god of Ocean, and he walked by the side of the ark during the Flood, the water only up to his knees (according to rabbinic tradition). In Sanskrit, og-haja meant "deluge-born." The names of certain relict groups may also be relevant: Agogwe and G*og*o; while Ogir is the Norse god of the sea and death.

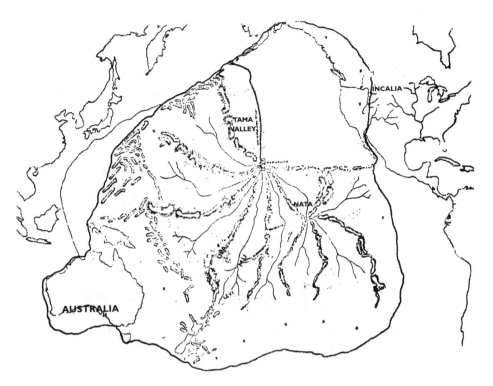

Fig. 8.13. Map of Pan showing a valley (at center) named Mu.

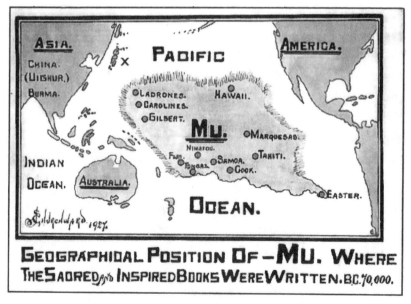

Fig. 8.14. Churchward's map of Mu, the Motherland of Man. Mu means "mother" in Chinese, while Mula and Mulai were the progenitors of the central India Korku people.

For the Irish, Tir Nan *Og* is the legendary lost land across the sea, and *Og*ham is the Irish (Celtic) tree-language (alphabet), which is evidently related to *Og*mios, their lion-skinned god, whom the Irish credit with the invention of alphabet. Og-min is the Bon Tibetan name of their culture's founder who came among them from a lost continent. Finally there is *Og*-yges, founder of Thebes, who was the Greek king at the time of the Flood.

The Mu folk of Kauai, related to the Menehune, are the little legendary forest people of Hawaii's wet uplands and deep valleys; bearing the same name is the ancient city of Mu'a on Tonga (Polynesia) as well as Pacific rim villages such as Mukawa (Ainu) and Murupi (New Guinea). That name Mu was carried to the Near East and beyond.

Name	Meaning	Location
Mu'allakah	Noah's ark said to be built here	village in Syria; Mureybut, in Syria, is said to have the oldest (11,000 year old) houses in the world.
Mu	settlement	Crete (muj = "home" in Czech)
Muza	ancient port	Arabia
Muta	mountains	Libya
Biah-mu; Mukna	temple ruins	Egypt
Muqattam Hills		Cairo
Nah-mu	name of yellow race	ancient Egypt
Mukeyyer	old name of Ur	ancient Babylonia
Lukh-mu	first god	Chaldea
Mu-lil	ruler of Earth and Hades	Chaldea
Memuneh	headman	Hebrew
Mu-karib	priest-kings of Sabea	Arabia; (many honorable/ religious names prefixed with mu: muezzin, muktar, etc.)
Mulon	title of chief	Malekula
Mu Kung	king of Gods	China
His Wang Mu	a goddess	China
Tien-Mu	a fabled land across the Pacific	China
muato	king	Congo Basin

Name	Meaning	Location
Mulungu	a god	Tanzania
Mulumga	people	Africa
Muillah	place	Morocco
Mutua	pygmy group	Uganda
Mugo	place	Angola
Muyinga	place	Rwanda
Muriah	volcano	Java
Mulu	river	Borneo
Murot	a people	Borneo
Murunde	tribal name	Australia

MU IN THE NEW WORLD

Name	Meaning	Location
Mut	Father of All Things	Tiahuanaco, Bolivia
Muyna	town near Cuzco	Peru; also Chi-mu Empire
Muyok	lost city of Chachapoyas	Peru, region full of ruins
Muyu	a pampa	Peru
Muribeca	place with lost cities of gold	Brazil
Muaco	16,000-year-old artifacts	Venezuela[60]
Muysca	culture with flood legends, white gods	Columbia
Muna	Mayan site near Uxmal	Mexico
Muluc	one of the four Bacabs	Mexico
Mutul	a Lord	Yucatan, Mexico
Chac-Mul	rain god (Chac-Mool)	Mexico
mulua	"water"	Lowland Maya
muyal	"rain clouds"	Maya
mu	"water"	Pima* and Arabic
Mu	submerged land/ Chumash Indians	near Channel Islands, CA
Hav-Mu-suv	superior civilization, say Paiutes	California

*Pima creation myth recounts premonitory warnings of an impending flood.

In the magnificent art of Cro-Magnon's caves is one inexplicable object, a seagoing vessel: the ark? Also, at Cerro de las Mesas (in the Olmec region of Mexico), we encounter a jade carving of a dug-out with paddles and the figure of a weeping *dwarf.* The Olmec provide an additional clue: their predecessors seem to have lived first on the *Pacific* coast.[61] This jumping-off place in the west is the area that produced the best and most prolific cacao, and the earliest* dated monuments.[62] All Mexican culture traces back to the Olmecs.

As for our enigmatic Cro-Magnon man: "No one knows where the Cro-Magnon came from."[63] But consider this: Ainu skulls (in Japan) are of the Cro-Magnon type; in a way, the Ainu are living fossils of one of the first modern races, their home Japan, not Africa. The common origin we search for is *east of JaPan*—the land of Pan—the source of the mysterious commonality of cultures. Interesting that Malaysia's little Bateks have a creation story that sees mankind as *unitary* in the beginning, a single fount for all mankind. "The dwarfishness [of the world's little people] . . . suggests that all of these far-flung groups may be linked in a common ancestry. . . . What is really remarkable is that they have retained so many traits in common."[64]

These same characters [alphabet][†] found in the ruins of Monte Alban in Mexico and in Egypt . . . give the names and portraits of the mighty builders of the pyramids of Mexico, Central America, and Egypt. They were all erected by the same race—the survivors of Pan.[65]

EDGAR LUCIEN LARKIN, DIRECTOR OF
MT. LOWE OBSERVATORY, 1900–1924

Yet academic fiat continues to people the continents from somewhere in the Old World—with Africa or South Asia selected as the favorite cradle. Egyptologists, for example, look to Asia for the origin of the Egyptian kingdoms.

---

*The oldest writing in the New World, an Olmec tablet, was recently found on the Gulf Coast of Mexico.

†India's alphabet has also been traced to Rutas (i.e., Pan).

With the Old World (in this case, Asia) given as the Garden of Eden, we are asked to believe "that there had been . . . migrations to Australia from . . . Southeast Asia."[66] In this view, the little people of Australia, as J. B. Birdsell argued, were remnants of a chain of migrations by ancient Negritos across South Asia to the southerly islands. On the same gospel train, Joseph Campbell saw the peopling of Melanesia as a "late diffusion,"[67] perhaps from China; finally, the ancestors of the Polynesians themselves are thought to have come *from Asia* around 1500 BCE. And when it comes to placing the *fair-skinned* people of Polynesia, they must have "hailed from some land beyond its boundaries . . . sailed into the Pacific from somewhere . . . [perhaps] through . . . Singapore."[68]

But conventional wisdom sometimes gets things backwards. Vice-versa. Standing the gospel on its head, I have to agree with Col. Churchward "that the central parts of India were first colonized by a white race . . . who came to India via Burma. . . . Their motherland was one moon's journey towards the rising sun, east of Burma. Polynesia lies to the east of Burma."[69]

If scholars attributed Egyptian civilization to the Sumerians, Sumerian civilization itself could be traced further east, to central Asia, based particularly on pottery and burial customs. The fact is that scholars have had to trace civilization ever eastward from the Mediterranean to the Caucasus to the Gobi to India and finally Southeast Asia. The origin of maize, for example, "is still obscure and may indeed have involved a Southeast Asian contribution."[70] But just one more little *push,* just one step east of Asia, *and we're in the water*—Pan! And migrations? The spread of the little people "suggests that southeastern Asia may have been the original center from which the type dispersed."[71] But one more little step east and we're in the drink: the watery grave of a great and forgotten civilization.

Pan said: My steadfast lieth in the East. I founded the words of China and India, Fonecia and Ebra; They are all my offspring.

OAHSPE, BOOK OF SAPHAH, PAN 2.1

In America, the Chickasaw Indians say they arrived from the West, where "many people came out of the ground" (i.e., "Emergence" after Flood). And in Mesoamerica, at Uxmal, a ruined temple bears inscriptions commemorating "Lands of the west whence we came."[72] The Mayan sacred text, *The Annals of Cakchiquels,* holds in memory "the other side of the sea."

Could it be mere coincidence that *Pan*ama in the south and *Pan*uco in the north (of Mesoamerica) define the boundaries of Mayan civilization? "Maya" itself comes from a Panic name, as we learn from a passage recounting the last moments of the continent of Mu/Pan: "And the rich valleys of *Mai* [emphasis added] with her thousand cities, shall be rent with the madness of men and women fleeing before the waters of the ocean."[73] Volcanoes and islands, in aftertime, took this name: Maion (Philippines), Guaca*mayo*, Nune*maya* (Pacific), Mt. Kat*mai* (volcano in Alaska) and so forth. And places: Mayaguez (Puerto Rico), Pacas-mayo, Peru (seat of the high Mochica civilization).

The name Mai, remembered and sanctified, became a commemorative term, an honorific. Thus does Maia mean "chief," "elder," "sir" among the Andamanese Negritos, where it is also the title of the ancestors. Made into a god in New Zealand, that ancestor is Ronga-mai. Among the Hindus, Maia is Divine Wisdom and Asura*maya* was a kind of Methuselah and author of the world's most ancient astronomical work, the Surya-Siddhanta; in the *Ramayana,* the first people to settle India from a lost continent were the Mayas. An almost universal name, it is found in North Guatama (Mayo Indians of the Southwest, Maidu Indians of California) and South Guatama (Mayapi, an equatorial tribe, and Mayoruna, the tribe known for their telepathic "Amazon beaming"). In Spanish, mayor means "great." The name ranges throughout Mexico, India, China, and Africa: Maidum in Egypt (with pyramids), Gal Maia in the Sahara, Tenda Maie (a pygmy region), the Mai Mai people of the Congo, and the Maithoachiana of Kikuyu country in Kenya, a race of dwarfs traditionally remembered as earth-gnomes skilled in the arts of metallurgy. The Pyg*mai*oi of ancient India, black, bearded, and long-haired, also belong in this group. In classical Rome, it was Maia, mother of god Mercury and goddess of Earth; Adonis's mother was Maira and

Buddha's mother was Maya. Maika is "mother" in Bulgarian and among the early Greeks, Maia was the very wife of the God Pan! At Maikop, near the Black Sea, is an inscribed stone with a legend of a sea voyage. A rare glimpse of the actual people who survived that "voyage" is seen in the name of the Little People of Ojibway memory: *Mai-mai*-gwaysiwuk.

Pan itself means "all" in Latin as well as in the Algonquian Abenaki language.*

Elsewhere it took on the meaning of "land" or "earth," as in Mexico's Tzom-pan-co, "place of a skull"; in yet other places it was adopted in the tribal name: *Pan*gan is the Semang name of a Negrito tribe (in Kelantan, Malacca), the most primitive in the jungle, and perhaps the *oldest*. In Sundaland, we find little people (Negritos) at Pantai, Pantar, and so on. In the same region, *Pan*oh is the Negrito shaman's spirit hut, rather like the Hebrew word for temple: panet. It is not unusual to find Pan things associated with "the spirits" (i.e., ancestors—or even the millions who went under—hence, the words *pan*ic, *pan*demonium). In Korea, pan-su is spirit-expeller, and among the black Caribs, pan-tu is ghost. In time, the word entered the ceremonies, such as the *Pan*es and the Choe-*pan,* the original names of Native American rites.[74] Among the Acagchemen (a California tribe), their annual festival was called *Pan*es—a renewal rite. In the Old World, the *Pan*-nychic rites featured the Mysteries of Demeter, while Panathenaia was an ancient Greek festival. Fadas (house spirits) in France were once classed together with Sylvans and Pans. And what about Peter *Pan:* fairies and Never Never land!

America's tiny and archaic "Stick Indians" are called "the *Pan*akhlamaichhlama . . . the little people who live in the mountains." The little people anciently living near the Red Sea were called Panchiens, while a utopia in the Arabia Sea, according to the early Greek writer Euemeros, was called Panchaia, its capital city Panara. But even where the little people have been entirely forgotten, the pan syllable is often still incorporated in the words for *first things*—the fountainhead—in silent testimony of a lost world.

---

*Pan (meaning "all") occurs in such words as pandemic, panacea, pantheism, pantheon, panoply (all arms), panegyric (speech before all), panorama, panjandrum, pandect (complete code of laws).

- The Sumu people of Central America say that two brothers created the world, the *older* one named Pa*pan*.
- Olel*pan*ti was the home of First Man among the Olelbis (California Indians).
- Po*panopano* is the Hawaiian word for the first egg-laying animals.
- The first quinoa in the New World is found at *Pan*aulauca cave site in Peru, at least 12,000 years old.
- Legend says pandanus was the first food available in Polynesia and Malaysia. (Pan means bread in Spanish.) *Pana* means elder (first) brother among the Malaysian Lanoh (Negrito). *Pan* is prefixed to a name to indicate "elder" among the Zambales Aeta. A curious parallel is "Pan," the Czech version of "Mr." (mister).
- The supreme god at Sulawesi (Indonesia) is Pang Mats, "Old Lord."
- The Chinese called the Creator *Pan*ku, the same as First Man, a being covered by leaves like a plant; while Ci*pan*gu is the Chinese name of a legendary Pacific land.

On the Chinese/Tibetan border, the Han Dropa caves were painted with drawings of a rising sun (to the east, i.e., the Ocean): Was it a memorial? The Han Dropa king, even in the twentieth century, was named Huey*pan*-La. Where did the Neolithic Chinese site, *Pan*-o-tsun, get its name? Or the Chinese town of Panyu?

In all of these countries there were made images . . . of the children of Noe, and of the flood, and of the sacred tribes, Shem, Ham and Jaffeth.

OAHSPE, THE LORDS' FOURTH BOOK 2:20

The Chinese are the people of Jaffeth (Jaffung). But people everywhere—all the Sons of Noe—retained the pan name (though most notably in Central America).

Preserve ye the names of . . . ceremonies, and especially the names of land and water.

OAHPSE, THE LORDS' FIRST BOOK 1:57

The Pacific Ocean itself was once called *Pan*thalassa, the great ocean of the Earth, while the One-continent of old was named Pangea. In America, Socia*pan* was the sea in Texas,[75] Hoola-hoola-*pan* was the first name of Lake Superior.* In South America are: *Pan*ama; *Pan*che (pyramid in Colombia), also the Columbian city *Pan*tano; the *Pan*os little people of Bolivia, who cultivated the art of picture writing: one missionary saw "a venerable man . . . with a great book open before him . . . reading [about] the wanderings of their forefathers . . . [the book] covered with figures and signs in marvelous symmetry and order."[76]

Because the sons of Noe (Noah) brought understanding and the civilizing arts with them to the "five landing places," the highest honor was afforded these men of Pan, as seen in the exalted terms in Peru.

- *Pan*tiacolla, *Pan*ticalla, and *Pan*aka, the latter designating royal lineage, inner circle; land-holding kin-groups were called *pan*acas; the actual name of all the Inca kings was Panaca (e.g., from the first Panaca Chima to the twelfth Panaca Huaycac).
- *pan*ache, royal plumes (headwear)
- the largest pyramid at Tiahuanaco is called the Aca*pan*a (Temple), set on a fifty-six-feet high mound, commemorating the beginning of all things. Za*pan*a is the legendary ruler of Tititcaca.
- Yu*pan*qui, Fifth Incan King, considered direct descendant of the ancestor of Emergence, Manco Capac.
- Si*pan,* Moche culture on northern Peruvian coast, a major ceremonial center with great (burial) mounds, artistic masterpieces and elite burials, in Lambayeque valley (see fig. 9.1, p. 299) where Naymlap arrived, leader of "the primordial sea people."[77]

In the Nahua language, pani means "equality to that which is above," while Sa*pan*i is a legendary Toltec chief. To*pan* means heaven (Aztec), dwelling place of the **gods and goddesses**; while Tlacahue*pan*

---

*We can add to North American *pan*s: the Apache Li*pan*s (an Athabascan tribe); the Wam*pan*oag (Iroquois Indians, with many tales of the little people) and Wa*pan*ucket (Massachusetts), Hapemb*pan*pan and King Teutsangtusicgammooghsa*pan*pan (Ohio); Wa*pan*aki, the name of a confederation of tribes that included Nanticoke and Mohican.

is a Nahua deity, and Tlauizcal*pan* tecutli is Lord of the Light of Dawn (represented as having a white body). Also in Mexico, *pan*tli means "pyramid," teo*pan* means "temple court," tec*pan* means "chief's house.

No less conspicuous on the other side of the Ocean are pan names for exalted ones (see appendix C for other Pan names):

- Polish *Pan*s/eighteenth century, the upper crust/elite, the landed nobility.
- *Pan*thus, Trojan priest of Apollo; *Pan*kus, Hittite council of nobles.
- *P'an*-Fei, semi-mythical royal maiden of China, loved by Emperor Ho-Ti.
- *Pan Pan*, prehistoric kingdom of Malaysia.
- *Pan*ese, royal family of Sumer; *Pan*dimandalam/India, holy district; *Pan*du and his five sons, who are the *Pan*davas of Hindu record in the Mahabharata heroic epic; also their Upanishads and the *Pan*dya kingdom of first millennium BCE, at the southern tip of India (Madurai region).
- *Pan*dora, the first woman created by Zeus; *Pan*drasus, king of Greece after the Trojan War; *Pan*dion, head of the House of Atreus; and *Pan*tikapaion, capital of the Greek Bosporan kingdom.
- *Pan*go means god in Loango/Central Africa

*Pan*tegani are a species of blessed little people in the Alps, protectors; while the La*pan*ach, in Gaelic folktales, are "little, thick-set men." What is the common denominator of all these pan memorials-in-language? Just as the *Pan*yos tribe on Rio Ucayli (Peru) were the "original people" traceable to "the lost white race of Hy-Brazil," just so do all these linguistic fossils immortalize the oldest lineage to grace their land. They came, time out of mind, from an unknown continent, and something in their nature (intelligence) made them exalted in the eyes of indigenous peoples. Something made them great. Little as they were, they could stretch out their hands and touch heaven.

CHAPTER 9

Men and Manimals

"IHIN"

The survivors of the Flood left their imprint on language first and foremost, through their very name: Ihin. Though it seems strange and unfamiliar, we hear that there were once a billion of these sacred little people on Earth. And there are many traces of their name.

At the western end of the empty Pacific, when John Richardson, an Oahspen friend, was in Japan and mentioned the name "Ihin" to a Shinto priest, he, the priest, recognized it instantly, saying they are the same people mentioned in their history books about Japan; he pronounced it Ine, as in "wine." Which, indeed, sounds like Ainu (pronounced "eye-new"), who are the short, original white people of Japan. In their own language, Ainu simply means "human being," but specifically of the "modern" (versus primitive) type; for the Ainu—through Cro-Magnon—was imbued with so much Ihin blood. There are, in this connection, various Cro-Magnon sites called 'Ain (See fig. 8.11, p. 282), such as Ain, France, where the Grotto of Les Hoteaux gave up small adult skeletons. There is more than mere linguistic link to another

Fig. 9.1. *Hin'*kwa designates es (the unseen part) within *corpor,* (i.e., spirit within body, or more broadly something within something). The Ihins were the first on Earth to possess soul power, an inner connection to the cosmos, the thing within a thing.

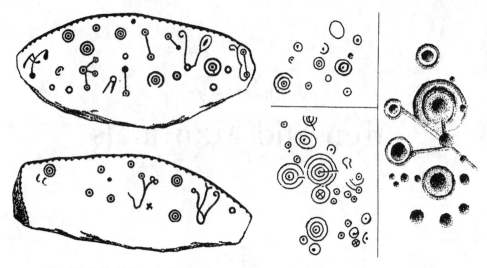

Fig. 9.2. Left: Hin'kwa is frequently seen in petroglyphs, such as these two from Forsyth County, Georgia. Right: Irish cup-and-ring marks. Still "undeciphered," though believed to be a shamanic symbol, this sign is virtually universal, inscribed in rocks and standing stones in Scotland, England, Wales, Brittany, France, Portugal, Spain, Italy, Greece, Palestine, Algeria, Switzerland, Mexico, Panama, China, Mongolia, and India.

cognate, *Inu*it (Eskimo), for the intricate carvings of the Ainus and Alaskans have been carefully compared and deemed almost identical.*

The trail leads in many directions. Hin, Ine, Ina, Ini, Ainu, Inuit are all variants of the original Ihin. In Alaska, Inuit is the plural form of inuk or inung, meaning simply "man"—but recognized also as a *spiritual being;* the close term *innua* is the Eskimo word for "benevolent spirits of nature." Drawing on the same root, the Athabaskan word for man is d*inn*i; the Algonquins say *inin*i; the Illinois Indians, il*lini;* the Iroquois, *eni*ha; the Maya, *in*ic.[1] The Lacandon name for themselves is hach w*inik,* "true people"; while in the Philippines, *Ina*gta meant "people," and was the original name of the Aeta Negritos. Among Chile's small Yahgans, man is *inn*alum, while *in*au is a special life-giving being among the Gilyak.

All these words for man tend also to mean first true man, designating incunabula, the earliest things, the *dawn of mankind* and of human

---

*Both races, short and pale, also share the unusual physiological peculiarity of a pearllike excrescence in their molar teeth formation, found, significantly, also among the short and yellow Bushmen of Africa and the little Lapps.

knowledge, usually redolent with the odor of the sacred. An Old World example would be Innu, the first city of Egypt, which, legendarily, handed down all wisdom; their great queen Isis was the daughter of King *Ina*chus (founder of the Pelasgian race). The theme of beginnings is inextricably bound to the race of little people: for the Maya, the First World was inhabited by the Saiyam U*in*icob, a race of dwarfs; in another Amerind tradition, the only survivor of the Flood was Puck Wudj *In*inee, "little man of the mountains, no bigger than an insect."[2]

The bare radical *in-* (elided "ihin") appears even in modern languages to confer the diminutive (dim*inu*tive) meaning, "small" or "smaller,"* as in German kle*ine* "small." The Norse catalog of dwarfs follows through with plentiful *in* names, like Reginn (tutor of the Teutonic hero Sigurd), Eysteinn, Fundinn, Nainn, Dainn, Dvalinn, Gloinn, and Blainn. The same diminutive suffix occurs on the Finnish names of all three sons of the Kalevala's epic hero: *Vain*amoinen, Ilmar*in*en, Lemmin-Ka*in*en.

Ireland's founding races of little people are likewise replete with Ine (Ain) names: Laigh*linne*, *Ain*ninn, Iarbh*ain*el (the Prophet), Sl*ain*ge (a king), Tailt*inn*, and the Pictish tribe Sog*ain*. We wonder if place names also apply: Rak-h*ine*, Myanmar, Be*nin*, the former name of Nigeria, Bim*ini*, Bik*ini* (in the Marshall Islands), Hahe*ine* and Huahe*ine* in the Society Islands, Bin*ini* (one of the Lucayo Islands), Kutk*ina* cave site in Tasmania, as well as Ballaw*ine* Cave in Australia with signature art, compared to Cro-Magnon's at Lascaux.[†]

In Chile (Auca), gu*ine* means "master"; and H*ain*, among the Ona

---

*Examples in English include—figure: figurine; tambor: tambourine; neutron: neutrino (particle smaller than a neutron). Spanish—monte (woodlands): montina (small wood); Himalayan—Naga: (serpent spirit); nagini (female serpent spirit); Sherpa: Sherpina. Russian—tsar: tsarina. Italian—linguini (means "little tongues"); Tuscany's little man, in folklore, is Cec*ino*, and the Etruscan region lies beneath the Apenn*ine*s and Palat*ine* (Hill); Aur*ini* were the aboriginal inhabitants of Italy, according to Pliny.

†Examples could be multiplied—Trin*il* (Java), Ujjay*ini* (India), Penn*ine* Hills, Caere*ini*o (mythological Welsh locale), Inzigna*nin* (a country spoken of by the South Carolina Indians where the ancestors knew of a people as tall as the length of a man's arm). Tarqu*inii* (Etruscan town), Rim*ini* and Vols*inii* (also in Italy), Santor*ini* (north of Crete), the O*in*oe pygmies of Nikodamos; the Timor*ini* pygmies of New Guinea; the Ba*in*ing Negritos of New Britain; Ninua (Iraq), and so on.

Fig. 9.3. Diminutive figure of a Ben*in* man
shooting a bow, on a bronze plate, West Africa.

(Chile) was the men's secret society. In archaic Mesoamerica, *ini*tyu was
the residence of the elite. The chiefly lineage of the San Blas Indians
also bears such names, (e.g., Chief Ina Pagina). Also carrying the -in
honorific were tribal chieftains on Raiatea (Polynesia) called tarama-
n*ini,* while lords of lands in Hawaii were haku *ain*a. (See appendix D
for further permutations of Ihin.)

Amerind groups and languages abound in this old word for man,
human being, or little men: Anishinabe,* N*ian*tic, Nicola, Niitsipussin,
Nimiipuu, Nipmuc, Nisenan, Nisga'a, Wih*in*asht (a Shoshone language), Tsu*ini,* T*inne*h, Ass*ini*boine, Winnebago, Menom*ini,* Mistas-
s*ini* (Cree), Tsu*ini,* Tinneh, Minnetarees, Ass*ini*boine, Innu (eastern
Algonquin), Madanin (Carib), Inama (Venezuela), Punin (Ecuador),
Assur*inis* (Brazil). I found a few more at www.native-languages.org/
languages.htm (accessed August 9, 2012): Maina, Shinnecock, Quin-

---

*Another variation of the original Ihin/Ine/Nin is: Ni-, as in Nidavellir, "land of the
dwarfs." Again in worldwide distribution, scattered here and there, the representation of things small or dwarflike is packaged in ni- words. The Spanish language
gives us niño ("child"), nieto ("grandchild"), nimio ("small, negligible"); while English itself might have built on the ancient root in words such as *in*cubus (originally a
herd sprite), nigh, niggle, tiny, thin, nihil ("trifle"), nip, nit, cretin (cret- "grow" plus
-in "small"), and others.

nipiac, Yaquina, Gwichin, Taino, Tanaina, Tenino, Tsattine, Tsuutina, Tualatin, Hwech'in, Illini, Inesenyo, Ingalik, Innoko, A'ananin, Ayisiy- iniwok, Babine, Carquin, Chilcotin, Chipewyin, Choinimni, Denaina, Denesuline, Dine, and Etchimin.

THE UNIVERSAL NAME

This same *ain,* in Hebrew, appears as *ayin* (pronounced "eye-in"), mean- ing "humble, looked down on" (literally "low," "short," "little"). One linguistically interesting Hebrew legend, found in the apocryphal Book of Enoch, concerns the Holy Watchers, a **class of angels** inhabiting the sixth heaven who mated with the daughters of men; they were called nun resh *'ayin,* or *Irin* (variant *oir,* as in Daniel 4:9 and 4:13). This Irin sounds like a Mediterranean variant of Ihin, corresponding to Ir-in Sumerian, which means "guardian" (Watcher). In the Aegean, Ayia *Irini* is the ancient name of a Bronze Age settlement in the Cyclades; today called Kea, this place was the home of poets, philosophers, and physi- cians, clearly indicating the elect, a seat of intelligence, as seen again in Huz-*irina,* the Assyrian center of learning (Sultan Tepe), with "a proper library."

Although the Ihins were certainly mortals, the hand of myth, as we have so often seen in these pages, *deified* them, sending them off to heaven, translating them to Olympus, perhaps to establish a celestial paragon for mankind. ("Fertility goddess," for example, was no goddess, but a mortal woman, revered for her holiness, as we will soon see.) The same deification is probably the case in the Sumerian Epic of Gilgamesh (fifth tablet) where the **goddess** is called Ir*ninis;* cousin, I believe, to the angelic Hebrew *Irin,* and possibly also to Eris, a nymph in the Greek pantheon. Even in the far-off Sandwich Islands and Tahiti, *eri* means "noble man," while *uri* means "white"* in the Hottentot language, i-, e-, and u- switching out, depending on dialect or language, just as the ancient city of Erech sometimes appears as Uruk.

---

*If *uri* means "white" in Hottentot, the Uros at South America's Lake Titicaca are pure white, said to be *descendants* of a race of people who came from the north.

Erin, queen of the Tuatha De Danaan, lived on an unapproachable "holy mountain" that repulses all comers, sounding very much like the Ihin moundbuilders in their lofty forbidden abode. This Irish "goddess" or queen and her unapproachable mountain looks like a dressed-up version of the earthly (not celestial) sacred tribes *living apart* on the mounds and shunning all intercourse with the worldly: "The Ihins lived secluded and separate from all other people."[3]

Intriguingly analogous to Irin and Irninis is Ericina, the Sicilian "Venus," as well as the Hittite sun goddess Arinna, her Slavic (Russian and Rumanian) counterpart, Arina, who in turn appears in Spain and Greece as Irina (meaning "Peace"); this name equivalent to English Irene. The source of Irene may be Ireland itself: In the Annals of the Four Masters, *Annala Rioghachta Eireann,* the land (ancient Hibernia) was commonly called Erin or *Eire*—after the Er*ainn* who were none other than the Firbolg little people living on their unapproachable mountain (read: high mounds).

One more ancient "Irin" pops up, this time across the Atlantic, among the Tupis of Brazil: A man named *Irin* Mage, it seems, was the sole survivor of a "violent inundation,"[4] finally linking Noah to the "Irins" and ultimately to the Ihins themselves, who alone survived the Flood on Pan.

What then is the *vera historia* behind this universal name? How did the Ihin/Irin actually come into the world? What makes that name the incunabula of all things sacred and heroic?

> *Of earth and starry heaven, child am I.*
>
> ORPHIC RITE

As we have already heard a bit about the celestial parent called Sky Father, likewise do we find in the Cuthae legend of Creation that men were born of both Earth and Divine Fire. There are many other accounts of human and divine sexual unions, such as the Sumerian one, where God Enlil becomes incensed at the weakening of the divine strain through intermarriage with "Adamic" (earthly) females. In legends of the Americas, too (Caribs, Iroquois, Quichua, *Inu*it, Athabascan, etc.), man is the product of a Primal Creative Power and "never literally derived from an inferior species."[5] In a word, he is (one-part) Child of the Stars; just as the fairy children of Europe (the little people) were produced by the marriage of "fallen angels" with mortals.[6] In the very same way does the Oahspe account describe the consorting of angels and asuans (adams), producing the Ihins. Rabbinic sages, on the same note, say the Daughters of Men (asuan, adamic) were Cainite women; and when the angels descended to Earth and "mingled" with them, "they lost their transcendent qualities and were invested with sublunary bodies, so that a union with the daughters of men became possible." And so it was.

There alighted upon the new earth millions of angels . . . [to] deliver first man (asu) from darkness. For he shall rise in spirit to inherit the etherean worlds [Everlasting Life]. Now was the earth in the latter days of se'mu* . . . in which time angels from other worlds were able to take on corporeal form.

OAHSPE, BOOK OF JEHOVIH 6:15

We hear something of this dramatic event in *The Book of Jubilees:* "the angels of the Lord descended upon earth—those who are named Watchers—that they should instruct the children of men . . . [for] uprightness upon the earth."

As Jim Dennon, the late Oahspe scholar, once explained it, "Via a starship we would now call a UFO, etherean angel volunteers were brought to earth, to teach the Asuans to walk upright. . . . Angels materialized with mortal bodies, and they mated with Asu. . . . This resulted in a new human race, called Ihins."[7]

One of Kirk Endicott's Batek informants told him that the very first Batek was created from black soil, then came a pair of beings from white soil, who became "tua," that is, the first "Caucasian" type. But "the Batek were created first . . . and were thus the original humans,"[8] whose genesis

---

*We realize that se'mu was the time when species took form, for "the earth was ripe unto giving birth to man. . . . In that day angels could clothe themselves with corporeal forms, out of the elements of the earth and by majesty of their own wills, and in innocence they mingled with the people Asu."[9]

is identical to the one that identifies Asu (the color of Earth) as the very first race of man, followed by the second race, the pale, almost transparent Ihins: "And there was born of the first race (Asu) a new race called man"[10] (i.e., Ihin). This transaction was, as one archaeologist surmised, "a quantum leap inspired from some outside source."[11]

> And they were called Ihins, because they were begotten of both heaven and earth. I sent angels to . . . rouse him [asu man] up to his capabilities. . . . And my angels drew, from his side, substance, and thus took on corporeal forms.
>
> OAHSPE, BOOK OF INSPIRATION 6:23[12]

> *Now a new race descends from the celestial realms.*
>
> VIRGIL, *FOURTH ECLOGUE*

In Levantine tradition it was the "Elohim" who came to Earth and participated in its generation, interbreeding with humans; in the New Testament these beings are described as "angels, having left their first estate in heaven" (Jude 1:6). Similarly, in the Midrash, it is Fallen Angels from the etherean realms who are behind our anthropogenesis; but, quips one esotericist, "If Moses were to send his creation story to any publisher today, he would soon get it back."[13]

What happened after the genesis of the Ihins? "And the lord commanded the angels to give up their forms, and to be no more seen as mortal. And it was done."[14] Thus does Hebrew doctrine relate that the Shek*inah* was induced to leave the Earth and ascend to heaven, amid the blare and flourish of angelic trumpets. This is not too different from the Sumerian tradition, which has God Enlil despairing of his inept human creation, and deciding to blot it out; whereon he ordered all the pure gods then living on Earth to abandon their human families and leave the planet at once.

> *The angels gave up their mortal bodies shortly after the Ihins were born.*
>
> JIM DENNON, "REMOVING OAHSPE'S ENIGMAS"

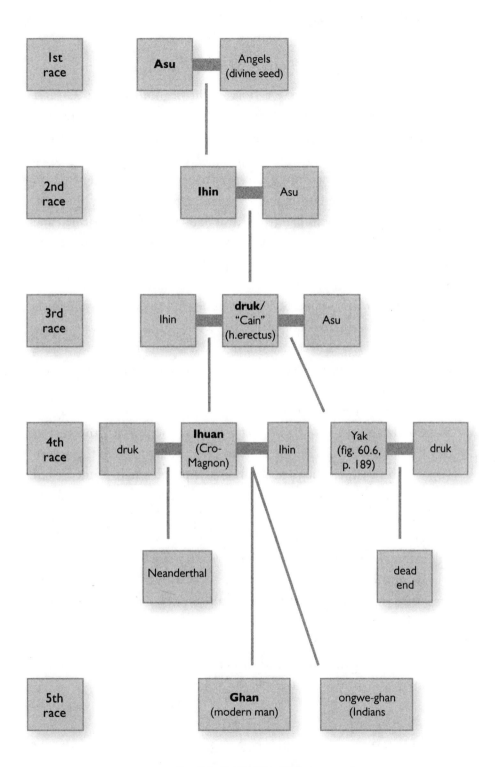

Fig. 9.4. Family Tree of Man

DESCENDANTS OF CAIN

The Chukchee (Siberia) have a story of the beginning, when Creator made First Man—an animal-like, hairy, and four-legged creature with very long and strong arms, and great big teeth and claws; he ate everything raw and could catch any animal he hunted. Fearing this man would destroy all living things, Creator decided to slow him down a bit, make him less dangerous by *shortening his arms* and making him walk upright. Indeed, earliest man (first fossil hominid), was long-armed and powerful, and he tended to knuckle-walk, his long arms helping him scuttle along on all fours, as the morphology of his remains in Africa and Asia attest. These creatures (*Australopithecus, Ardipithecus*) were manlike on the one hand, but so rough-hewn as to cause taxonomists to frown, hesitating to class him with actual humans. "Near-men" or Plesianthropus is a term coined in England as a compromise, portraying the borderline status of these "manimals," the very first race of human beings—asu man.

In Buriat anthropogenesis, this first man was made of red clay; he was woolly and *without a soul,* just as asu is described as "the nearest blank of all the living . . . devoid of sense,"[15] resonating with the Mayan Popul Vuh in which the first Creation saw people made of mud, "but they were unable to walk, talk, or breed." Devoid of sense, devoid of soul, he was without the spark of the divine, "like a tree, dwelling in darkness," in the very same way that Chaldean first man "lived without rule, after the manner of beasts." Yes, *like* a beast but *not* a beast, for a beast (unlike man) has instinct fully supplied: "Man alone . . . shall grow forever. To the beast, I gave an already created sense, to man, I allotted angels."[16]

> Man was started at the foot of the ladder, but unlike all other creatures, he was given the power to rise.
>
> JAMES CHURCHWARD

But the Ihins strayed and mixed with asu man: we saw a sample of such crossbreeding in the beginning of this book—*Homo floresiensis,* the tiny Java island hobbits, early hybrids, who came into the world when Ihins blended with the autochthonous race. In Hindu scripture it is written—"the first race asu tempted the white people"[17]—who then broke the commandment of endogamy (in-marriage), which had enjoined: "Neither shall ye permit the Ihins to dwell with Asu, lest his seed go down in darkness."[18] But the little people wandered out of the Garden of Paradise and

> began to dwell with the Asuans, and there was born into the world a new race, the third race of man, called druk [a.k.a. Cain a.k.a. *Homo erectus*], and they had not the light of the father in them, neither could they be inspired with heavenly things.[19]

Thus were the druks the first people to go to war—hence Cain's "mark of blood"—in the Old Testament.

The chosen had been commanded to marry among themselves, and to withdraw from other peoples—this scenario, in a latterday context, is repeated in Genesis 28:1. "You shall not take a wife from the daughters of Canaan [i.e., descendants of Cain]."[20]

Nevertheless, "the ground people [druk/Cain]* came in the winter as beggars to the Ihins. And behold the chosen were tempted . . . and it came to pass that a new race was born and they were called Ihuans after the manner of the ancient warriors that destroyed the chosen before the flood."[21]

"The people of Israel," complained the Old Testament, "have not separated themselves from the people of the lands, with respect to abominations of the Canaanites . . . so that the holy seed is mixed with the people of those lands" (Ezra 9:1–2).

Although out-marriage was prohibited, back of it all was divine purpose—to immortalize the human race![22] For the Ihins "were the

---

*Those of the lesser light were called Cain (druk), because their trust was more in corporeal than in spiritual things . . . And those with the higher light were called Faithists [led by Ihins], because they perceived that Wisdom shaped all things and ruled to the ultimate glory of the All One.

seed of everlasting life on the earth, and the foundation for raising up prophets and seers unto other peoples."* Here's how Vernon Wobschall (editor of Oahspe Standard Edition) explains it: "All these exchanges ensured that there would be sufficient Ihins available in the places they were needed, because they were vital to the development of humankind. . . . After the Faithists of Pan [the Ihins] landed in . . . Africa, India, and China, the [resulting racial mixtures] were used to replenish those who had become extinct [and exterminated]; for Ihins were yet needed for the maturing of man."

This view, then, is almost the *reverse* of the Platonic one, which held that "gradually the blood of the gods, which flowed in their [ancestors'] veins, was diluted with the mortal admixture, and they became degenerate." While Plato stressed the *loss* of holiness incurred by the mixing of the sacred and profane, these faithist histories, to the contrary, remind us that all this interbreeding served a higher purpose; it was a *gain,* not a loss: "Jehovih said, I condemn thee not because ye have become joint procreators . . . for ye have done [a] service unto Me . . . [as] ye have caused the earth to become peopled with such as are capable of immortality."[23]

God has made of one blood all nations of the earth.

ApostlePaul

Two roads have | made, ○ man, one leadeth to everlasting light; and the other to everlasting darkness.

OAHSPE, BOOK OF APH

"The struggle . . . to be eternal," wrote Masonic author Albert Pike, "between the Divine will and the natural will in the souls of men, commenced immediately after the creation. Cain slew his brother Abel,[†] and went forth . . . with an impious race, forgetters and defiers of the true

---

*Different traditions of how man attained everlasting life: Mayan Hero Twins descended to the underworld, beat the Lords of Death, and became immortal!
†Abel was "able" to understand spiritual things, and capable of hearing the Voice. But Cain slew Abel, meaning: the lower tribes wiped out the Ihins before the Flood.

God . . . and all nations preserved the remembrance of that division of the human family into the righteous and impious."[24]

The depraved and godless are descended from Cain.
Louis Ginzburg, *Legends of the Jews*

FORBIDDEN MATINGS

The Ihin-Asu match was only the *first* of many, many forbidden matings. It may be that some of these extraordinary resulting hybrids are not entirely extinct, like the acclaimed Sasquatch of the Northwest or Yeti of the Himalayas. Cryptozoology is an active and valid field, probing critters like the Almas of Central Asia or their cousins in the Caucasus, the white-haired Kaptar, Azerbaijan's wild man.

The man-beast of Tanzania (East Africa) is called Agogwe, a russet-furred manimal, who authorities speculate might be a survival of Austrolopithecus or perhaps *Homo erectus,* not unlike related types in Zaire, Sudan, and Senegal. When the "little men" called Agogwe—seen by many credible witnesses and also an intrinsic part of tribal lore—came to the attention of Academia, they were considered some sort of "missing link." But the only thing "missing" is a frank understanding of *interbreeding,* plain and simple: sexual union in the Long Ago—most often verboten—between the dark and light, the tall and short, the wild and the tame races. The hairy Ainu of Japan, Caucasoid and "modern" though they may be, retain asuan traits (hairy); they themselves claim their furriness came from their ancestor, the Bear!

Earlier on we examined first man, asu (with long arms and hairy body), as well as trogs like the apeish Bat people and other relict populations. We also had a taste of the monsters that this Earth has spawned, *not* creatures of mythic imagination, but real oddities, along with absolutely wild men, *Homo ferus,* all dead-ends on the human Family Tree. But a few did survive.

A. F. R. Wollaston describes a relict people he encountered in New Guinea, small, short-legged, broad-faced, short-skulled, very hairy, wide-nosed; this description on a par perhaps with the Bogenah, in the heart of Panama's Guaymi country: very short, extremely primitive, much like the early hominids with their strong, bowed legs, long arms, large hands and feet, low and receding foreheads, flat and bridgeless noses. "They are lacking in intelligence . . . almost childish in their behavior."[25] Similars include Ecuador's *shiru* (four and a half feet tall and fur-covered) and the little *dwendis* of Belize, no taller than four feet, well proportioned but hairy with long arms and yellowish faces.

The 1889 *Proceedings of the Royal Geographical Society* reported on a wild man, perfectly nude, captured in Madagascar while asleep in the branch of a tree. He resisted capture violently, a powerfully built man, his body thickly covered with long black hair. Possessed of a strange gait, he traveled very fast, sometimes on all fours. After a few weeks in captivity, he began to learn some words; it seems he had a father and brother in the forest, and when the authorities went to capture them, they "jumped from tree to tree like monkeys" (see asu in tree fig. 1.8, p. 19). The poor captured man died five months later.

Then, in Sumatra:

> . . . *it was not a man. It was not an orang-utan.*
>
> MR. OOSTINGH, WHO SIGHTED AN ORANG
> PENDEK IN THE SUMATRA FOREST[26]

Hundreds of witnesses have seen this actually gentle creature called "orang pendek": he does not inspire fear among the natives. Such alleged "missing links" are known not only in Sumatra but in southern Asia, Oceania, as well as in other islands of Indonesia and Malaysia—always in the most remote rain forests. Such are the Ebu Gogo on Flores and the Batutut (a.k.a. Nguoi Rung) of Burma, four feet high with long hair, a type also seen in Vietnam and Laos. What does science say about these extant near-men? Why, they must be a new genus of primate or a new species of orangutan or gibbon. Or perhaps a remnant of *Homo erectus* (early man)? Today's natives of New Caledonia show significant *Homo erectus* traits, especially in teeth, brow ridge, and sloping forehead. A related creature is known in Yunnan province, China: four feet high, hairy, with a human body.

Is Ceylon's Nittevo a cousin of Sumatra's orang pendek? Not everyone is convinced that the Nittevo (now extinct) were "people." Were they ape-men? Manimals? *Homo erectus?* Sure, they walked erect, had short arms, and "no tails." Tree- and cave-dwelling, and completely naked, their speech was like "the twittering of birds." And they were fierce. According the the Veddas, who exterminated them, the Nittevo living at Lenama were a cruel and savage race.

But not all of the world's relict types are little brown manimals roaming the rainforest: One Kentucky family saw a seven-foot-tall manlike creature with white hair making off with their roosters; he was probably of the same stock as the Ozarks "giant of the hills," a wild man seen many times. Seven feet tall, he is of the white race, his body covered with long thick hair.[27] Other seven-foot-tall hairy manimals have been sighted in China—in Hubei, Sichuan, and Shaanxi provinces.

> *We see hundreds of species in our modern world who are in fact survivors of previous Earth epochs.*
> VINE DELORIA, *RED EARTH, WHITE LIES*

White-skinned and black-haired is the "ape man" of Africa's Gold Coast, reputedly fourteen feet tall.[28] "Africa," thought Loren Eiseley, "like other great land areas, has its uneasy amalgams."[29]

THE GIANTS

From whence came these giants? The "fraternization" that brought tall people into the world, according to India's account of Hirto, was actually a trick on the part of the Creator of Evil, who "went to the druk [*Homo erectus*] women, speaking to them in a dark corner, and said: 'Ye have the root of Babao* to make delirious, fetch it to the white people . . . and they will eat and get drunk. And when the young men

---

*There is, we realize, great babao-tree country in southern Africa, Madagascar, and the Malaysian islands, where the Negritos in fact are renowned experts in aphrodisiac botanicals, selling them for top dollar to the Malaysians.

are drunk, go ye to them'"[30]—which is the equivalent of the Hebrew legend recalling the depraved daughters of Cain who had charms and enchantments—women of a lower order, the "Daughters of Men" of holy scripture, supposedly seduced by the "Sons of God."

The Hirto account goes on: The druks went in where the little people were drunk, saying:

> Lest the white and yellow people fall upon us, and our seed perish on the earth, make us of flesh and kind, bone and bone, blood and blood. [Whereon] Hirto, the Lord God, said. . . . "As to the newborn people, they shall become the *mightiest* of all people in the whole word, because they came out of both darkness and light. The darkness in them shall battle all darkness; the light that is in them shall then master over their own darkness."[31]

In the Book of Enoch this event is likewise referred to as the mixing of darkness and light: "The giants from the Holy Watchers is their origin." Thus came the giant (*gibbor*) from the Watchers, through unlawful mixing, which is the equivalent of saying the Ihuans came from the Ihins.

Nevertheless, I look upon the biblical Sons of God (angels) and Daughters of Men (mortals) myth as a strange reversal of the (gender) facts. For, in these matches, it was more often the *female* Ihins—not the males—who contributed the "divine blood." One could, perhaps more accurately, label the scenario: Daughters of God/ Sons of Men! But patriarchal doctrine could not brook the female line as the superior one, and hence cooked the books.

Before the second millennium BCE, women more than men were reverenced; as exemplified by the Minoans, for one, whose main deities were goddesses. Religion, in that early horizon, was centered on a goddess-type female, "with male figures . . . reduced to a secondary role."[32] In early Celtic society, for example, the cult of Mother Goddess was central. Prior female dominance is also evident in the myths of South American tribes. In these prehistorical matrilineal societies, Creation comes about through a *Female* Spirit (as opposed to the standard *Sky Father* of later horizons). The Seneca, for one, relate that life started with Sky Mother; for the Cherokee, it was Star Woman, while in similar native myths, the first person ever is the Woman-who-fell-from-the-sky. In fact, the ancient Egyptian word for "Sky" was feminine, and the word for "Earth" was masculine. In Europe, too, the Margot fairies were born of the *Earth* god Keb and *Sky* goddess Nouit.

The Sky Father/Earth Mother gospel, it seems, arose later, in patriarchal times, in synch with pseudohistories of "divine kings," developed and deployed to reinforce ancient theocracies. "They became as gods," say records of the Hamitic kings; kingship was "lowered from heaven," declared the ancient Mesopotamians; and in this manner (under "these pretensions," as Gaston Maspero put it)[33] evolved those deified god-kings of Ethiopia and the Nile, a conceit that remained in force from Sennacherib to the Caesars. In the Americas, too, the names of Toltec rulers are identical with those of Aztec deities. For in all the Sun Kingdoms, the rulers made themselves, if not the equal of gods, sons of the gods, or descended in direct lineage from the Sun.

But all such claimants were impostors, idolaters, imperialists, warriors, or sacrificers, their "divine right" a sham affording them inordinate wealth and power. We have seen the deification pattern countless times throughout these chapters. Not only were the humble little people **deified out of memory**, but divinity was later arrogated by rulers of city-states as a means to consolidate their realm—religion used to lay a foundation for demagoguery. Thus was state mythology born. The "official" Inca legend, for instance, held that the Sun had three sons—Viracocha, Pachacamac, and Manco Capac—and the dominion of man was given to the latter, while the others were in charge of the cosmos. "This political arrangement placed all the power, temporal and spiritual, in the hands of the reputed descendants of Manco Capac—the Incas."[34]

Most conspicuously did the ancients, especially of the Judeo-Christian tradition, confuse the original angelic seed with *much later events* (i.e., the mixing of the races). Thus does the Enochian record hold that the "angels sinned with mortal women, producing giants" (mighty men), while in the related Legend of Alconuz, these high-born rebel angels (Ihins on mounds) occupy the summit, with the progeny of Cain (the wandering druks) living below. It was there that the so-called Sons of God (the angels) intermingled with the so-called Daughters of Men. But Enoch got it wrong. And so did Genesis 6:4—"And it came to pass when men began to multiply on the face of the earth, and daughters were born unto them, that the Sons of God saw the Daughters of Men that they were fair; and they took them wives of all which they chose . . . and they bare children to them . . . [who] became mighty men, men of renown. And God saw that the wickedness of man was great in the earth."

Later in Genesis, Yahweh became angered by the increasingly frequent mixed marriages between these so-called Sons of Elohim and the Daughters of Men. The "Holy Watchers" is but a faint and faulty memory of the Ihin people themselves: *these were the "Elohim"*—the godlike ones. The divine seed, in the beginning, had brought *Ihins* into the world, not *giants;* it was only later, when the Ihins mingled with the ground people that giants came into the world.

In the Bible, Numbers 13:33 identifies these giants with Nephilim, the sons of Anak, perhaps akin to the Sumerian Annunaki giants who are depicted as only *half human.* Anakim, in the Old Testament, is another name for the tall Canaanites. A strong towering people (Deuteronomy 2:10–11), these were simply the offspring of the crossbreeding between Ihuan and druk—and *not* "by reason of the fallen angels," as these distorted histories tell us (Baruch 3:26).

ALLEGORY OF THE ANGELS

Language doesn't lie: we have seen a hundred bits and pieces of the Ine/Ain (Ihin) pedigree, renowned for its divine powers, their name embedded in so many words and titles (appendix D), which recall a lineage possessing a kind of primeval spiritual force.*

I would like to add Europe's beautiful and immortal Ond*ine* (water spirit) to this category of superphysical ancestors; and though she is remembered as an ethereal nymph of the sea, I hesitate to label her (as is

---

*These include: Daoine Beaga, Scottish fairy people; Aine, Limerick fada queen; Innua, Eskimo spirits of nature; the Hopi kachina; the god Hinuno of the Paiute; Hina, Tahitian First Woman, wife of Creator; Maindi, Basque fairy kingdom; Hennin, a class of European fairies; Telkhines, magical ancestors; Irin, a class of angels.

generally done) an "elemental." Instead, I see Ondine as an *allegory* of the angels who are sometimes called Elohim, those who seeded dumb humanity with their divine blood. In this connection, it is most interesting that German folklore relates: though Ondine is immortal, if she falls in love with an earthly man and bears his child, she loses her own immortality. This is something like the account, given by Rabbi Jacob ben Jacob ha-Kohen, concerning those angels who, once removed from their heavenly abode, were unable to return. When they fell from heaven, they donned the power of this ether just above us (Earth's atmosphere) and they took on the bodies of men. Then the upper power weakened.

What actual history, what piece of the untold past, lies behind the tale of Ondine and these angels who fell from heaven? Traditions of the Old World often speak of fairy brides like Ondine or the Peri-wives (with their "dazzling beauty"). The korrigans, say the Bretons, seduce handsome young men to "regenerate their accursed race." What interests us here is that the Ondines are strictly *female*. Why should that be? In most fairy lore, in fact, you don't hear too much of fairy *men's* dalliance with mortal women. You usually hear of mortal man and his "snow white" fairy bride. Why is this? By the same token, we hear much less of female giants than male ones. Why?

To reduce it to the commonplace, it seems that these old stories represent the union of large men and little women.

Before the Flood "it came to pass . . . that the brown people [large druk/Cain] burnt with desires, and they laid hold of the Ihin *women* [emphasis added] when they went into the fields, and forced them, and thus brought forth . . . the Ihuan race, the copper-colored, strong and bright and quick."[35] What do you imagine these little women looked like, pregnant with the seed of these strong and stout men?

The scenario of little mothers and big fathers carries some genetic weight. A noticeable difference in size between the males and females of a species has a scientific name: "sexual dimorphism," reflecting these hybrid races of old.

Among the Pygmies "there is considerable sexual dimorphism, the women being as a rule much smaller than the men. Negro men [i.e., normal size Africans] have taken Pygmy wives," reports Colin Turnbull,

Fig. 9.5. Sexual dimorphism.[36] Left: Sumerian cult statues of the Lord of Fertility and the Mother-goddess (at Tell Asman).[37]

Below: Egypt. Pharaoh in his harem (left) and Monthotpu (right), founder of the oldest Theban empire, with one of his wives, standing behind him.

in *The Forest People;* as of old, large men are drawn to little women, but *"the Pygmy men have not married Negro women* [e.a.]." The same circumstance holds among the Bushmen: "The Koranna [an African tribe] . . . lusted greatly after Bushmen women . . . most indigenous Africans were excited by their golden colour."[38] Sexual dimorphism goes back to the beginning: it is evident in asu and druk populations, as discovered in northwest African skeletons as well as among Upper Paleolithic Europeans.[39] These European remains—all the way east to Czechoslovakia—show women much smaller than men, as among the Chancelade type, where we have found a 12,000-year-old hybrid of Ihin (small) and Cro-Magnon (large), judging from remains at France's 'Ain caves and other Paleolithic sites with telltale rock art. In Sri Lanka, too, among the Nittevo, the females were much shorter than the males. And in America, an ancient population of La Jolla shows a marked divergence in stature between males and females, as may be observed also among the (Alabama) Muscogee, whose men were once very tall, while most of the women were well under five feet.[40]

There was an irresistible loveliness about these little "fair" women, "the handsomest of all created creations."[41] Universally admired, the beauty of the little people clings to the arcane record.

People of Mu	"exceedingly handsome"[42]
Brazil's Tapuyos	"delicate features of great beauty" (Col. Fawcett)
Mandan Indians	"quite handsome"
Plains moundbuilders	"very very tiny, though handsome"
Hopi maidens	"exquisitely molded hands and little feet"[43]
Tuatha De Danaan	renowned for their beauty
Korrigan of Brittany	perfectly proportioned, "their beauty is great"
Devonshire pixies	"handsome in their form"
White Dwarfs of Rugen	beautiful beyond conception
Norwegian elf women	exceptionally beautiful
Balder, Norse god	shining and beautiful
Hyperborean women	"breathtaking"
Scand Alf-women	"a handsome human form"

Serbian little women	"fairest of all creatures"
Thai Pi Tong Luang	"a handsome people"[44]
Aeta Negritos	slim, well-proportioned, quite pretty

And this beautiful little woman was reverenced, for her race embodied the "divine" portion of humanity; she was the White Goddess (Robert Graves), "Mother of All Living." And lo, she became none other than the acclaimed **fertility goddess**, the naked "Venus" whose figurines have been excavated everywhere from Austria to Baluchistan and the Atlantic to Siberia. This "Neolithic Goddess"—or rather Mesolithic (France's Venus of Laussel dated to 30,000 BP)— was definitely *Homo sapiens,* though the *men* at these old French sites were Neanderthaloid, suggesting, once again, the mating, the crossbreeding of the hulking caveman with the small, graceful, cultured female.

The Venuses, thought Joseph Campbell, were "the first objects of worship of the species of *Homo sapiens* . . . represent[ing] the ancestral point of origin of the whole people, and they are always female."[45] But **Great Mother *Goddess*?** No, she is—as Campbell points out—an *ancestral* figure. Not a deity, but foremother of the great Cro-Magnon. She is the same as the nan- ancestress we have traced: V. Gordon Childe calls her In*nan*na, "the fertility goddess." The people of Thailand remember the spirit-woman, *Nang*faa, perfect and tiny and fabulously beautiful; like unto Lhian*nan,* the most beautiful of all the Sidhe. Based on the same little nan- ancestress are all these faux "goddesses": Nanshe, Nanna, Nanayat, Inanna, Ashnan, Nanibgal, and so on (see appendix A).

And "fertility fetish?" No, fecundity per se is not the key to this so-called fertility goddess. The most that could be said is that the observant tribes kept the oldest commandments that included respecting the mother in her time of gestation. But what lies behind this "goddess" are the "gracile" specimens of the fossil record, and that means she was small, possessing a *streamlined pelvis.* The hip structure of *Australopithecus* (like asu) is different from the modern one, having a longer femoral neck (affecting the size of birth canal) and better center of gravity. The muscles are more efficiently leveraged, creating a stronger pelvis. The modern one is more geared to perfect bipedalism. The Neanderthal pelvis is also wider than the modern one, their "larger skulls needing a larger birth canal."[46] Of course, most of these Venus figurines are pregnant, appearing small, but with large breasts, exaggerated vulva, corpulent buttocks, and rotund abdomen.

Why are her feminine features so conspicuously amplified? Were they "used in fertility rites to aid in the propagation of the band and to invoke good health for mothers and infants?"[47] No, I don't think so. We should look instead at the very real problems in childbearing that these Venuses so graphically portray.

In pain you shall bring forth children.

GENESIS 3:16

Some fairy tales, in fact, portray the hard reality of this sexual dimorphism: Fairy mothers, recounts Katharine Briggs, had "difficult births."[48] In one story, a fairy-bride betrothed to a mortal worries that she will die in childbirth from the size of her bairn. Another tale, "Midwife to the Gentry," relates the familiar theme of "the Gentry [leprechauns] having

Fig. 9.6. Venus of Willendorf: a little woman enceinte with large-bodied offspring

difficulty reproducing and require . . . mortal midwives."[49] In an assortment of legends, especially Amerindian ones, the mother of the culture hero dies in childbirth. Quetzalcoatl's mother dies in childbirth. The mother of the first Inca, Manco Capac, died giving birth to him, which may be linked to the giants who, legendarily, overran Peru, and took their women to wife, ruining them, for "they were too big for them, and the women were ruptured and died."[50] In European lore, the mother of Brutus also dies in childbirth, as does the sister of Wotan.

These mothers were *little* women, the ancestral mothers including Inanna, Ininni (Mother of Tammuz), Hina (First Woman), Nin (queen-goddess), Aine (fada queen). In Mesopotamia, one Nippur tablet describes Ninmah as "a woman who cannot give birth";[51] just as the holy maiden Ninlil protests, "My vagina is too small,"[52] when propositioned by the **god** (that is, the conquerer) Enlil.

Yet, more than once the sacred little people did break their vows and began *intermarrying* with the tall and robust tribes of men. But in the beginning, as long as the Gentry lived apart (i.e., endogamously) childbirth was uncomplicated: the Sumerian record comments on "the ease with which the goddess [Ihin mother] gives birth";[53] just as in *Nin*hursag's (Mother Earth's) time, children were born to their mother "without the slightest pain* or travail."[54] Pingping, the world's smallest man (see fig. 8.4, p. 266) was, says his father, the size of an adult's palm at birth (see appendix E (Min/Men).

Did the early "goddess" cult center around the quest for Ihin wives, the real blue bloods of the ancient world? We are reminded of Arabia's King Chemuts ordering *intermarriage* of the little Ihins with his own (Ihuan) people. At that time (some 8,000 years ago), supposed ties to the divine realm were established by the Sun Kingdoms—in Mexico,

---

*Martha Jones in *The Lost Data on the Chariots of the Elohim* (page 59) proposes an alternative interpretation that may also be valid: smaller Cainite women revered Cro-Magnon man/Ihuan with cranial capacity up to 1715 cc and bore their offspring—with larger brain and head (see fig. 6.7, p. 191); their own pelvis was small, resulting in painful birth. Large heads were also seen in the "devils" (little people) known to the Sioux, and large-headed little alux of the Maya; and in the large crania of Bayan-K-U skeletons and Ireland's little grogach.

Peru, Rome, Greece, Mesopotamia, Ethiopia—to sanctify the ruling caste. The melding of god and potentate in state mythology gave divine sanction to ambitious kings. To ratify their status, the kings of Rome (warriors), conducted sacred marriage rites. Likewise did the Aztec Montezuma attain supreme authority via the religious route, deifying himself and ordering the execution of all those court officials who "knew too much to accept his divinity."[55]

And in Sumeria, divine kingship went hand-in-glove with elitism, increasing social stratification, and temple-controlled land. Virtually every king of Sumer boasted being the beloved husband of Inanna: "The Queen is Inanna, the naked goddess."[56] Thus was arranged the ritual marriage of Inanna to the ruling monarch at Nippur, the holy city of Sumer.[57]

> *Chosen for the vulva of Inanna am I.*
>
> KING SHULGI, FOUNDER OF THE
> THIRD DYNASTY OF UR[58]

Shulgi's divine spouse was the fertility goddess Inanna, the Venus star. Yes, Sumerologists tell us that Inanna is the *Venus* of the Sumerians, later to become Ishtar of the Babylonians. Queen of Heaven, Venus/ Inanna, daughter of *Ning*al "selects" the King of Sumer for godship of the land. One brings flax to this goddess, and by the bond of sacred marriage with her (the festival held in the spring, at first planting), the Sumerian ruler can then guarantee "rich harvests." Archaeologists, in calling this a "fertility cult," actually buy into euhemerism and the old deception that the king's "marriage" to the goddess insures nature's renewal and a bountiful harvest. But it was, mostly, politics as usual.

WHICH CAME FIRST?

With some of these acclaimed "Venuses" dated to 25,000 or 30,000 BP, we can begin to piece together the hoary lineage of the Old Ones who brought civilization not only to the Neolithic (circa 9,000 BP), but to the *Paleolithic*. Neither can we continue to date the *earliest* scientists and astronomers to Egyptian or Babylonian times, what with ancient observatories like Gobekli Tepe (which was also a ritual center, a sanctuary), now dated to 12,000 BP. This star chamber in old Turkey, with finely carved reliefs on massive columns, is *aligned north-south* (like the much later Great Pyramid of Egypt), betraying a precise knowledge of geodesy 7,000 years *earlier* than the presumed beginning of exact science.

This ancient land of Turkey, once called Asia Minor, which we have turned to so many times for light on the Old Ones, was perhaps the last outpost of the old masters. Invisibly, then, does this kingdom supply "historical" culture with the first metallurgists and astronomers, wheat domestication, town life, the wheel, coinage, tholoi chambers, and constitutional monarchy, not to mention the racial founders of Europe: "Noah," Pontus, Minos, Lady Albine, Aeneas, Brutus, and so forth.

Just as old as Turkey's Gobekli Tepe ("too old" to fit the current model) are impressive temple ruins at Cocle, Panama, found lying under volcanic ash.[59] The awesome site sports a series of stone images and, like Gobekli,

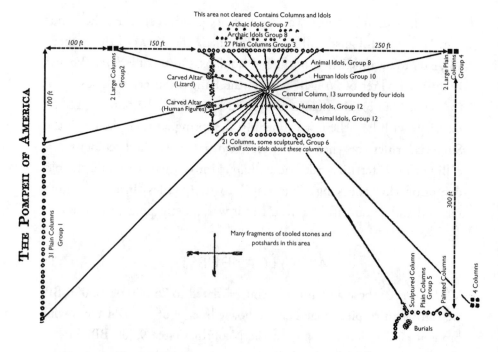

Fig. 9.7. Ground plan of Panama's Cocle Temple site

huge engraved columns in rows running, again, north-south. Its main temple is "a great cathedral."[60] Also like Gobekli, its noncanonical age—12,000 BP—matches that of one of Mexico's oldest cultures, Tepex*pan,* where a mine detector unearthed the remains of a perfectly modern type of female who "could lose herself in present-day Mexico City crowds without comment."[61] The *Codex Vaticanus,* moreover, dated the Mayan calendar system as old as 20,000 BP; while the "great white race" of Brazilian astronomers has been shelved on that same horizon: a "highly civilized" culture.

The year 20,000 BP of course is the Mesolithic, yet it supplies us with:

1. morphologically modern skulls in California[62]
2. Arthur Posnansky's date (18,000 BP) for Tiahuanaco
3. Manetho's timeframe, reckoning that Egyptian *proto*history lasted more than 11,000 years (and Martianus Capella's reckoning that Egypt's astronomers kept secret their knowledge for 40,000 years)
4. Japan's Jomon pottery
5. America's Basketmakers, as well as other ancient workshops going back perhaps 40,000 years[63]

And if James Churchward was right, India's Danavas civilized the Deccan 20,000 BP (see fig. 2.4, p. 38), while the applied arts and industries of North Asia (Uighur horizon) were at their height 17,000 years ago; this vast empire of the Mesolithic reaching Europe some 9,000 years later.

> *The early Welsh and Irish historians are generally regarded as liars because their ancient records are dated to uncomfortably early times and do not square either with conventional Biblical dates or with the obstinate theory that until Roman times the inhabitants of all the British Isles were howling savages.*
>
> ROBERT GRAVES, *THE WHITE GODDESS*

Neither does the true descent of man square with "biblical dates and obstinate theories." Neither Darwin's origin of species nor Christian creation 6,000 years ago (!) tells the real story of man. If a superior brand of humans (*H. sapiens*) grew out of an inferior one (say, Neanderthal man), then why do we find the two types *contemporary,* in Spain, for example, 30,000 years ago? Or *mixing,* as discovered in China (whose modern looking Maba skull could be 75,000 years old).[64] According to Louis Leaky, *H. erectus* and *H. sapiens* were roughly contemporary, especially in China. We find the same general pattern in Portugal,* too, which produced a kind of Cro-Magnon/Neanderthal hybrid. Recent digs in Romania (in 2003) and Czechoslovakia (2007), as well, came up with more hybrids: these cave skeletons surprised everyone, being the earliest examples of *Homo sapiens* in Europe, yet sporting distinctive Neanderthal features (great noses and molars, occipital buns, etc.): features that suggest "intermixing between modern humans and Neanderthals."[65] Meanwhile, Croatia's Neanderthals at Vindija cave, with tools of sophisticated workmanship, appear a bit more delicate and modern than they should, which paleontologist Jacov Radovcic and others reasonably interpret as the result of interbreeding between Neanderthals and moderns. Even Louis Leaky, toward the end of his long career, asked if crossbreeding could not, in fact, account for numerous *Homo sapiens/Homo erectus* composites.[66]

"The mixing of Modern Man and Neanderthal . . . is consistent with DNA research."[67] Indeed, they all co-existed: *Austalopithecus afarensis, Homo habilis, Homo erectus, Homo neanderthalensis* and *Homo sapiens!*[68] Isn't it time to reevaluate "the outmoded sequence in which Neanderthal man precedes and evolves into Cro-magnon man?"[69] And how shall we deal with the fact that "the very earliest [American] Indian skulls looked like present-day Caucasians with an Indian cast."[70] Skulls of the Cro-Magnon type at Flagstaff, Arizona, seem to be 60,000 years old.[71] The *earliest* North Americans, in Washington state, with

---

*Appearing in a horizon considered too late for Neanderthal (who was supposed to be extinct by then), this skeleton, discovered in 1998, was a small and stocky modern (at least in chin and teeth), but with lots of Neanderthal features, including the heavy jaw and short, thick bones; even staid archaeology had to concede—there must have been "significant interbreeding."

their Caucasian features, were "quite unrelated" to later tribal peoples;[72] this was Kennewick Man, his skull resembling the Ainu and Polynesian type. In Borneo, too, *Homo sapiens* dates to 40,000 BP (and they were little people); Jeffrey Goodman finds this type also in Ethiopia and Swaziland—long *before* the more primitive Neanderthals appeared.[73]

We are always finding surprisingly modern bones where they should not be. . . . Human evolution . . . may exist more firmly in the minds of academics than in any location on Earth.

VINE DELORIA JR., *RED EARTH, WHITE LIES*

Linear (or even branching) evolution, starting in 1988 with the Mt. Carmel finds, began a slow nose dive to oblivion; these old caves in Palestine showed *Homo sapiens* and *Homo neanderthalensis co-existing* 45,000 BP and crossbreeding with "every variety of intergradation."[74] Other skeletal remains in Israel (Tabun, Skhul, and Qafzeh caves) betray a marvelous fusion of Neanderthal traits (such as the prodigious brow ridge) and modern ones (high forehead, well-sculpted chin). Reluctantly did physical anthropologists classify these specimens as early moderns, lamely admitting that "populations of Neandertals and of modern *Homo sapiens* co-existed for a very long time in the Near East."[75]

Human beings of modern type and more primitive creatures have been co-existing since time immemorial.

MICHAEL CREMO, *FORBIDDEN ARCHAEOLOGY*

But which came first? A comparable scenario in Australia may hold the answer: archaeologists couldn't quite figure out why the Mungo Lake skeletons (20,000–30,000 BP) showed more modern ("gracile") features than today's Aborigines; or, for that matter, why they *pre-dated* the Kow Swamp burials (10,000 BP, in Victoria) a "more robust and rugged" type of fossil humans.[76] Well, at Prince Regent River in Australia, there are strange paintings of European types; behind them is a snake, which is the aborigines' symbol of the most remote past: Dreamtime. We should also factor in Australia's huge limestone pillars near

Roper River, said to have been the work of members of a white race—who are depicted as bearded Caucasians in rock art near Alice Springs. Archaic whites in Australia are linked to the Ainu—who are the *oldest* people of Australasia, their skulls resembling Cro-Magnon ones. But—then there was *retro*breeding: "he dwelt with beasts, falling lower than all the rest.[77]* In times past the same countries were inhabited by a higher race."[78]

So, again, which came first? Jeffrey Goodman, referring to skeletons found in Borneo, South Africa, Australia, and the Americas, fixes early dates for *Homo sapiens'* debut, showing he was "alive and well long before the Neanderthals even came into being."[79] Certainly, in chapter 5 we found "Caucasians" as a *preexisting* race in many parts of the world.[†] In Peru, the "shy, furtive and gentle" white people with beards "are the oldest race now alive."[80]

Even *Homo erectus,* a much earlier, ruder creature than Neanderthal, is found with "*sapiens*-like traits" in Africa and Asia, as well as in Europe where "a mosaic of *erectus* and *sapiens* features" abounds.[81] Why did *Homo habilis* (precursor of *H. erectus*) have a *thinner* (more gracile) skull than Neanderthal? These, and much more, are all "impossible reversals."[82]

Hiding in plain sight is the all-too-human factor of intermarriage, what Christopher Hardaker calls the Nookie Factor. So let's cut to the chase: "We could have babies together."[83] The Nookie Factor actually stands Darwinism on its head: whereas evolution has species-lines

---

*War destroyed both antediluvian and postdiluvian civilizations of the higher type, followed by both retrogression and retrobreeding. Thus are we faced with cycles, not real evolution; the curve of civilization is a waxing and waning thing. The masterpieces of Mesolithic art, for example, were never matched in the Neolithic.

†In chapter 5, we found white dwarfs to be the Olde Ones, the first people: *Homo pygmaeus.* The Old Ones (*Huehue*) in Mexico are shown with modern features and beards; indeed, the Mayan First Man was molded from white and yellow maize, just as North America's Mandan and Pomo Indians speak of their white, bearded forebears. Many tribes recall a white race before their time (corroborated by 24,000 BP "modern" specimens in California); while in South America, the white Tapuyos were refugees from a *former* civilization. In chapter 5 we also found white-haired antediluvians and Hyperboreans, as well as whites in China 25,000 BP.

branching and *separating* at some time in the past, the cross-breeding model says the opposite, that in fact the different stocks *came together,* cohabited, to form new races. And we are all hybrids. Fossils taken as representing "stages" of evolution represent nothing more than the unstoppable intermixing of Paleolithic races. The peopling of the world is about the mingling and merging of disparate types. No evolution there, just the continual confection of half-breeds, quarter-breeds, and so on, an exchange of genes since Day One.

The Fudge Factor is also at play here. With evolution, the darling of modern science, all this new evidence of crossbreeding must somehow be made to play a minor role. Despite "extremely high levels of inter-breeding between humans and Neanderthals" it is still maintained that "modern humans and Neanderthals shared a common ancestor" (and merely interbred "after their separation").[84]

Evolution is a problem. It is Western man's origin myth. Darwin-think, as I see it, is on its last legs—the search for a missing link has been a resounding failure and for a good reason: there *is no missing link.*

Man for his part, tends to be more cyclic than evolutionary; his history on this planet is rise and fall, rise and fall. But this trajectory, overall, is progressive.

> Neither have I given progress to a stone, a tree, nor to any animal, but to man only have I given progress.
>
> OAHSPE, BOOK OF FRAGAPATTI 11:18

Instead of *physical* evolution, we are in the throes of cultural and moral evolution as well as racial amalgamation, moving toward the des-tined harmony and Oneness of the Human Race. The present uptick in amalgamation of the races is the signal that heralds the dawn of univer-sal man. Apart from technological advancements and creature comforts, mankind's true evolution is a spiritual one, entailing the realization of who he is and where he came from.

> *Distinct and different from all other animals . . . he has a force*
> *or soul. . . . This great gift has been bestowed on no other form*

of life . . . [for] man is a separate and distinct creation, possessing a divine force. It is impossible that he can have come out of, or evolved from some animal not having that force.

JAMES CHURCHWARD,

THE LOST CONTINENT OF MU

A funny thing happened on the way to finishing this book. The story of the little people opened a door. My colleagues, reviewing early drafts, wanted to know more about the origin of races, how human beings came about—not through "adaptation," really, but through *combinations* of breeds. These circumstances have forced my hand, and so I must now write about Man, the Hybrid. Until then, so long. I hope this treasury of the sacred little people has been as enlightening to read as it was to research and write.

Word Derivations and Their Geographic Relationships and Historic Themes

Nan, the Universal Ancestor

Name	Meaning	Location	Comment
FERTILE CRESCENT			
Tawanana	title of queen (tua + nan)	Hittite	See fig. 7.10, p. 234
Zannanza	a prince	Hittite	
Nanayat	goddess of love	Babylonia	
Etemenanki	a temple	Babylonia	
Nanna	moon god	Akkadian	patron deity of Ur
Nanna	"mother"	Akkadian	
Nana	Mother of Attis	Phrygia	
Inanna	goddess of all lands	Sumerian	protectress
Nanshe	goddess of moral conduct and "interpreter of dreams"	Lagash	guards truth and justice
Ashnan	grain goddess (barley)	Sumerian	"The Wise"
Enannatum	grandson of Ur-Nanshe, founding dynast of . . .	Sumerian Lagash	
Gestinanna	sister of god Dumuzi	Sumerian	

Name	Meaning	Location	Comment
Nanibgal	epithet of Nidaba	Sumerian	goddess of writing
Wadi Faynan	archaeological site	Jordan	Neanderthal artifacts
Nantu	first child of Creator/Kumpara	Jivaro Indian, South America	
Nana-buluku	Creator	Fon (West Africa)	
Anansi	shaman-spider hero originally the creator of the world	West Africa	
Izanangui	nature god	Japan	
Ananda	cousin of the Buddha	India	
nano	"mother"	Foré, New Guinea	
Nanek	"ancestor"	Malaysia	
Semenanjung	31,000-year-old skulls	Malaysia	Lenggong tribe
dzanan	soul or spirit	Arabic	

BRITISH ISLES

Name	Meaning	Location	Comment
Conan	Tuatha De Danaan hero	Ireland	
St. Ronan	hero and king of Leinster	Ireland	
Leanan sidh	spirit of life, guides holy families	Isle of Man	
Tir-nan-noge	legendary lost city	Ireland	"fairy trees" here
Dunan	little fort/mound	Scotland	
Manannan	magical trickster	Ireland	made fairy hills invisible
Lord Nana	king of dwarfs	Britanny	white-skinned
Nanna	blue-eyed bride of Balder	Norse	in the Scalds

Name	Meaning	Location	Comment
NEW WORLD			
A*nan*	a deity	Arawak Indians, South America	
*Nan*cen-pinco	a king	Inca	
Nana, var. *Nene*	"Noah's" wife	Mexico	in Flood legend
Teteoin-*nan*	mother of the gods	Mexico	
Atlato-*nan*	earth and water goddess	Aztec	
nan	"mother"	Aztec	
Ixcui-*nan*	goddess of childbirth	Aztec	
*Nan*ahuatzin	a deity	Mexico	
Teocui*nani*	a sacred mountain	Mexico	
*Nani*hehecatl	lord of the four winds	Mexico	
*Nan*ahuatl	a god before the Sun	Mexico	lit: "Divine"
Te*nan*co	a Toltec center	Mexico	
Teo*nan*acatl	sacred mushroom	Aztec	lit.: "god's flesh"
Teote*nan*go	an archaeological site	Mexico	
Xu*nan*tunich	Mayan ruins	Belize	
Zi*nan*catec	Indian tribe	Central America	
NORTH AMERICA			
*Nan*abozho	ancestor, born of first human	Amerind	survivor of Flood
et*nan*es	dwarf race	Amerind	
Nana	elf-like being	Shoshone	
*Nan*ih Wayah	place of Emergence	Choctaw	little people guides
*Nan*ehi	var.: Nunnehi, little people	Cherokee	
Inzig*nan*im	little people	South Carolina, indigenes	
A*nan*tooeah	native name of Seneca Indians		

Ba, Denoting Smallness in the World's Languages

Name	Meaning	Location
baby	infant	English*
bairn	infant, child	Ireland
batu	be born	Indonesia
ba	daughter	Andaman (In *Bain* is their ancestor)
bani	sons	Ethiopia
bache	boy	Persia
bajo	short, low	Spanish
bassetto	shrimp, short	Italian
Bafur	early dwarf race	Germanic
Balder	god of Innocence	Norse
Bacabs and Hun *Batz*	dwarf deities	Mayan
bakru	race of little people created by evil magicians	South America
bagud-zinishinabee	little wild people	Ojibwa
Aba-twa	fairy race, shy and peaceful; only infants can see them	Africa

*Plus *base*, *bantam*, *bagatelle*, *bantling*, *banal* and so forth.

Name	Meaning	Location
banshee	sprite of foreboding	Irish/Gaelic
Badb	sprite	British Isles
badal	sprite	Islamic
Barabao	3-inch-tall sprite; slips through keyhole	Venice
Bagan, Bannick	household/farm sprites	Poland
bajang	spirit of stillborn children	Malaysia

BA RACES AND PLACES OF LITTLE PEOPLE

Name	Meaning	Location
Baschain, Bairrche	founding septs	Ireland
Lobaircin	earliest folk, puckish type	British Isles
Battas	Negritos	Sumatra
Batutut	an orang pendek type	Borneo
Bandra-Loks	Negritos	Indus Valley
Baratang Island		in the Andamans, which were originally the Andabans
Batak, Bagoba	Negritos	Philippines*
Batek	Negritos	Malaysia
Baining	Negritos	New Britain
Barrineans	Negritos	Australia
Bari	Motilones	Venezuela
Basque	see chapter 2	Pyrenees
Bahamas	little people, dwarf temple	see chapters 2 and 6

---

*Many places and people in the Philippines, mostly Negrito locales, are ba-named: *Bataan, Bagac, Bani, Baluga, Bais, Baguio, Babuyan, Bayatas, Iba, Balanga, Baler Bay, Banaue.*

Pan Names in the Pacific Ocean and Beyond

- At *Pan*ape, the monarch (saudeleur) of *Pan*apeol made his home on *Pan*kadira Islet
- Sai*pan,* the largest island of the North Mariana Island chain in the western Pacific
- Ra*pan*ui, original name of Easter Island
- *Pan*akiwuk Island, Southwest Pacific
- Filipino Negrito places: *Pan*ay, Pam*pan*ga, *Pan*glao, *Pan*gasinan, *Pan*yibutan
- Malaysia: *Pan*gyans (Malacca), *Pan*yan, Kota Tam*pan* (earliest known human site in Malaysia)
- Balikpa*pan,* Indonesia
- Japan (Zha-pan)
- *Pan*ama Pattu (in Ceylon), *Pan*ua tribe in India (Bengal), *Pan*daram and Mala*pan*daran people in South India, *Pan*s, a weaving tribe of South India (Negrito territory)
- *Pan*ticapes, a river in ancient Scythia
- *Pan*ayarvi, Russia
- *Pan*nonia district (Hungary)
- *Pan*aro, mouth of the Po River in Italy
- Taha*pan*es, Greece (biblical name of Daphnae)
- Spain (Es-*Pan*), Montes*pan* (French Cro-Magnon cave paintings); Maka*pan* caves and Kathu *Pan,* both in South Africa

Permutations of *Ihin*

The reader is asked to note the recurrence of certain themes represented in these Ine/Hin/Nin names: the Flood, the little people, sprites, the beginning of things, the leaders of men (sanctified).

Name	Meaning	Location	Comment
Dao *ine* Shi'	"Men of Peace"	Gaelic	heroes, fairies and gods
Dao*ine* Beaga	"The Little People"	Scotland	
Ui Ma*ine*	short people of Connacht	Ireland	the Firbolgs
Gre*ine*	sun goddess	Celtic	
Press*ina*	fountain fairy	Albania	
Temac*ine*	a Berber people of	Algeria	
Mih*in*tale	city of pilgrimage	Ceylon	shrines, sanctuary
Sec*hin*	early ceremonial center	Peru	note JuNIN province there
E*ninnu*	Ningursu's temple	Lagash	
T*in*ia	name of Zeus among . . .	Etruscans	
-*in*	lit: "temple"	Japan	(The Light Elves of Holland)
Om*ine*	mountains with sanctuaries	Japan	live in the AlvINNen Hills; and in Ireland, -inn means cromlech, (binn = "cave" in Gaelic)

Name	Meaning	Location	Comment
Ur*in*in, *N*i*n*aji, *N*ippon	places in . . .	Japan	
*N*ihongi	Chronicles of Japan		
Rusa*hin*a	ancient name of Toprak Kale	Armenia	kingdom of Urartu
Gued*in*na	a Sumerian territory in	northern Lagash	
Rang*in*ui	Sky Father	Maori, NZ	progenitor
Wandj*in*a	spirit of weather and seasons	Australian aborigine	
*Hin*amoa	Ruler of the Sea	Polynesia	since time began
*Hin*epoupou	Ruler of the Sea	Maori	
Hua*hin*e	place in	Society Islands with distinct Flood legend	their king is Mahine
Wa*in*iha	stronghold of Menehune	Hawaii	
Ka*hin*arii	place in	Hawaii	
*In*dra	god who bestowed Immortality	INdia/HINdu	Everlasting Life
*Hin*ayana	School of Buddhism		self-denying aspect
*Hin*dana	province in	Assyria	
Wal*hin*d	Farsi kingdom with "City of Man" (Peshawar)	Persia and Afghanistan	
T*hin*is	home of First Dynasty kings	Egypt	
E*nin*k	important Hittite city	Turkey	
Hen*nin*	a class of fairies	Europe	
*N*i*n*iki	word for "ghost"	Mimika Papuans	also means "ancestor"
Ma*in*di	hada (fairy kingdom)	Basque	
*N*i*n*tas	nature hadas	Iberia	
Ond*in*es	sea nymphs	Europe	

Name	Meaning	Location	Comment
Tel*khines*	first children of Ge and Pontos magical beings	Rhodes	mythic ancestors of mankind
nak*inein*	semi-human shape-shifters	Estonian	long hair, dangerous
Car*ikine*	an elf brought by sailors from	Phoenicia to Brittany	
Garr*inis*	island with megalithic art	off Brittany	
Lady Alb*ine*	founder from Troy	to England	
*Ini*sdoon	place where fairies enchant the souls of poets	Ireland	
Bo*inne* River	See Newgrange		
Gu*inе*chen	supreme god	Chile's Auca	"Master of Men"
Watu*ine*wa	Yahgan God of Life	Tierra del Fuego	
Na*ine*ma	Witoto Indian Creator	Columbia	
Humena *Hinku*	god-in-sky, "my little spirit"	Cubeo Indians on Vaupas River, Columbia	
tzitsim*ine*	malevolent spirit	Aztec	
Chat*ino*	an ethnic group	Oaxaca, Mexico	
Ta*ino*	Indians	Caribbean	
Ipur*ina*	Indians	Arawakan	
Ahahnee*nin*	"White Clay People"	Gros Ventre (Plains Indian)	
*Ini*skim	shaman's magical buffalo rock	Great Plains	used in rituals
*Ini*pi	rite of purification	Lakota	"sweat lodge"
Kac*hina*	surrogate deities	Hopi	
*Hai*nit Yunenkit	He who made the Sun	California Mission Indians	
Hast*shin*	the First Beings	Apache	
Tlast*iin*	First Man	Navajo	
Hino	(a) beneficent god (b) thunder god/ "grandfather"	Wyandot Iroquois	link to the "Land of the Little People"

Name	Meaning	Location	Comment
Mt. Nisir	place where ark landed	Sumer	
Nidaba	goddess of writing	Sumer	first Literatti
Nin	Queen, Goddess	Mesopotamia	"Great Lady"
Ninazu	patron deity	Eshnunna	god of healing
Ninlil	mother of Ninazu	Sumeria	spouse of Enlil
Ningiszida	son of Ninazu	Sumeria	
Ninsutu	consort of Ninazu	Sumeria	
Ninshubar	chief messenger of the gods	Sumeria	faithful to Inanna
Ninsun	Divine Mother	queen of Uruk	famed for her wisdom
Ninkhursag	mother goddess of Ur	Sumeria	The Noble queen
Ninurta	god of agriculture	Sumeria	"Farmer of Enlil"
Ninisinna	tutelary deity of Isin	Sumeria	a weeping goddess
Ninkurra	deity engendered by Enki	Dilmun	
Ninmug	deity engendered by Enki	Dilmun	
Ningal	wife of Nanna, moon god	Sumer	
Ningirsu	God of Lagash	Sumeria	his temple: EnINNU
Ninkasi	goddess of beer		
Nis	a type of sprite	Sweden, etc.	
Nix	legendary sprite	Europe	
Nibelung	race of dwarfs	Norse	
manikin	"little man"	Holland	
Niscute	place with dwarf architecture	Mexico	
Nisqualli	Indians of Washington	U.S.	with little people nearby
Nima	a leader	Maya	
Ni	deity of the Pacific Ocean	Chimu	

Name	Meaning	Location	Comment
*Ni*merigar	Native American sprite	Wyoming	
*Ni*kwasi	mound of the little people	North Carolina	
*Ni*cotani	priestly dynasty	Cherokee	
*Ni*ttevo	atavistic pygmies	Ceylon	
*Ni*addi	Negritos of Cochin	India	
*Ni*hoa	a Menehune enclave	Hawaii	

The Word *Men* from the Proto-Historical World

Men/Min: The small-size aristocrats of the protohistorical world actually gave us the word "men," which (as it varies with min), also gave the language numerous words for "little": diminish, miniature, minute, mini-, minus(cule), mince, minor(ity), minimize, minnow, and so on. The first real men, (i.e., progenitors of the modern type) are locked up in the Hindu name for Noah: Menu. The Ojibwa Noah, is *Min*abozho, while *Mini*-sinoshkwe were the priestly forefathers of their sacred society of mysteries. In Mayan society: We Ah-Men = shamans, or guardians of the mystery tradition (We = old, Ah = earth, Men = the elect). (*Min*nesota, Minetaren Indians, Menomini, Minneganewashaka may share in this provenance).

These **priestly ancestors** were deified, becoming, in Egypt, the Earth gods, remembered perhaps in village names like Fide*min*, *Min*ieh, and so forth. Later, King *Men*es built the temple of Memphis, which is the city of Ptah, the dwarf creator-god. Probably of similar origin are pharaohs Menkaure and Amenhotep, as well as Menes, eldest son of Sargon, the first Akkadian king, and Menelik, the son of the (Ethiopian) wise man. We include also the ruler of Europe's first civilized race: King *Min*os of Crete, and Menedemus, a legendary Cretan hero. Recalling those remarkably carved gems of the Minoans and the supremacy of the dwarf race in the *min*ing arts, it seems that even "mine," "mineral," and the stone "menhir" may share a common root, ultimately attesting to the little men and women who civilized the Old World. The earliest Greeks, the *Min*yans, with their tholoi and *Min*erva, goddess of wisdom, were also culture-bearers for barbarian Europe.

In Brittany's region of *Mené*, the little fées were seen up till the nineteenth century. The small white founders of Hawaii also bear the old name: *Mene*hune, while *meni,* among the Kenta means "white"; other Negritos carry the name tribally—Menik, Mincopie, Mindoro, Minh-Cam. Kuli*min*a is the **Arawak goddess** who created women. These Venuses are Ihin women (see chapter 9) the Irin "goddesses."

Man, Megafauna, and Mastodons in the Mesolithic

In the far north, huge woolly mammoths, with broad curving tusks, roamed the Siberian steppes up to 10,000 BP, along with enormous felines, steppe bison, sloths, and tapirs; Scythian goldwork shows the struggle between hunters and great saber-toothed tigers.

Well over a hundred New World sites offer human artifacts in situ with megafauna remains. In Mexico, numerous architectural motifs suggest the features of the mammoth. It is the same in South America where a pottery design at Tiahuanaco, Bolivia, shows a toxodon, supposedly extinct for millions of years! At the Marcahuasi plateau in Peru, rock cliffs are carved into huge representations of lions, camels, and something resembling stegosaurus. Mastodon, giant sloth, armadillo—all have a confirmed date in Venezuela and Chile of 18,000 BP.

In America's Southwest, Pueblo legend recalls monsters and animals of prey with claws and terrible teeth—today's mountain lion is "but a mole in comparison to them." In Oklahoma, the acclaimed Lenape Stone answers to Indian traditions of a tremendous quadruped called Father of Oxen; the battle scene depicted on the Stone certainly raises questions about the mammoth in America. There is no doubt that in the Mesolithic, the bison, bear, wolf, and elk were of extraordinary size, as were many other quadrupeds of the Pleistocene, with its teeming faunal life.

MAN AND MASTODON

- Giant mastodon bones unearthed by paleontologists came from "behemoths that terrorized the moundbuilders."
- In America, starting in the 1830s, mastodon remains were found in association with axes and spears.
- Folsom, New Mexico, points for hunting bison and mammoth, with delicate and accurate flaking, have been dated to 17,000 years ago. Sandia points have been dated to 18,000 BP (some were even older: 22,000 years old).
- Points in association with mammoth bones have been uncovered in Alaska, New Mexico, Colorado, and Arizona. In Arizona a chance flood revealed the skeleton of a mammoth alongside eight typical Clovis fluted points and four flint knives. At Havasupi Canyon, Arizona, a rock picture more than 12,000 years old depicts a mastodon.
- In the ruins of ancient homes in Nevada are fossil remains of mastodon and saber-toothed tiger as well as utensils made of ivory.

Notes

PREFACE

1. Vaillant, "A Bearded Mystery," 243.
2. Jones, *Antiquities of the Southern Indians,* 192. See also Wilkins, *Mysteries,* 131.
3. Stewart, "Negrito and Negrillo," available at http://stewartsynopsis.com/Synopsis%206.htm (accessed July 24, 2012).
4. Flower, "The Pygmy Races of Men," 11.
5. Eiseley, *The Immense Journey,* 106.
6. Kramer, *History Begins at Sumer,* 256.
7. Vallee, *Passport to Magonia,* 73 (quoting David MacRitchie).

CHAPTER 1. THE OLD ONES

1. Leeming, *A Dictionary of Creation Myths,* 146.
2. Reported in *Science Digest* in October 1960 (62–63) as well as in *The Interamerican,* November, 1960.
3. Gorner, "Tiny-Human Find Becomes Huge News," A10.
4. Quatrefages, *Pygmies,* 26.
5. Turnbull, *The Forest People,* dedication page.
6. Quoted in Evans, *The Negritos of Malaysia.*
7. Campbell, *The Masks of God: Primitive Mythology,* 350.
8. Wabschall, personal communication.
9. Hayden, *American Journal of Science,* 1862, 2:34: 57–66.
10. Dubois, *The Great Encyclopedia of Faeries,* 12.

11. Ellis, *Polynesian Researches,* 122.

12. Jones, *Exploring the Aboriginal Remains in Tennessee.*

13. Graves, *The White Goddess,* 432.

14. Wagner, "The Elusive Little People," available at http://paranormal.about .com/od/othercreatures/a/little-people.htm (accessed July 24, 2012).

15. H. S. Olcott, *People from the Other World.*

16. Eno, *Gods, Ghosts, and Destiny,* 193.

17. Evans, *Negritos,* 102.

18. This and other entries taken from Oahspe, Book of Saphah's word lists.

19. Oahspe, First Book of God 23:20.

20. Oahspe, Book of Saphah 6:13, 38 (S'ang).

21. Evans, *Negritos,* 46.

22. Oahspe, The Lords' First Book 1:75.

23. Ibid.

24. Heindel, *Rosicrucian Cosmo-Conceptions,* 292.

25. Oahspe, Book of Divinity 11:13.

26. Oahspe, The Lords' First Book 1:75.

27. Fawcett, *Lost Trails, Lost Cities,* 268.

28. Ibid.

29. Wilkins, *Mysteries.*

30. Steiger, *Monsters among Us,* 72.

31. Oahspe, Book of Inspiration, chapter 6.

32. Ginzburg, *Legends of the Jews,* 124.

33. Oahspe, Book of Wars 29:4; see footnote.

34. Briggs, *The Vanishing People,* 180, 88.

35. Keightley, *World Guide,* 81.

36. Doyle, *On The Edge of The Unknown,* 126.

37. Keightley, *World Guide,* 175.

38. Adams, *Prehistoric Mesoamerica,* 217.

39. Oahspe, Book of Aph and Lika 22:15.

40. Oahspe, Book of Wars 7:9.

41. Oahspe, Book of Osiris, 11:7.

42. Wilson, *Apologies to the Iroquois,* 205.

43. Oahspe, Book of Osiris 10:10.

CHAPTER 2. WHERE ARE THE LITTLE PEOPLE?

1. Kramer, *History Begins at Sumer,* 92.

2. Adams, *Prehistoric Mesoamerica,* 243.

3. Brinton, *The Myths of the New World,* 200.

4. Lee, *Folk Tales of All Nations,* 324.

5. Graves, *The White Goddess,* 207.

6. Van der Post, *Lost World,* 30.

7. Vallee, *Magonia,* 66.

8. Carpenter, *Tales of a Basque Grandmother,* 116.

9. Valentine, *The Great Pyramid,* 61.

10. Campbell, *Primitive Mythology,* 428.

11. Coon, *Living Races,* 50; 8.

12. Oahspe, Book of Fragapatti 40:2–4.

13. Graves, *Goddess,* 50.

14. Graves, *Goddess,* 51.

15. Cerve, *Lost Continent,* 256–58.

16. Lubbock, *Pre-historic Times,* 241.

17. Vallee, *Magonia,* 72.

18. Churchward, *The Lost Continent of Mu,* 123.

19. Campbell, *Primitive Mythology,* 378.

20. Vallee, *Magonia,* 18.

21. Wollaston, *Pygmies and Papuans,* 303.

22. Coon, *The Living Races of Man,* 154.

23. Durrani, "Egyptian Dwarfs," available at www.world-archaeology.com/news/egyptian-dwarfs (accessed July 25, 2012).

24. Keightley, *World Guide,* 406.

25. Oahspe, Book of Fragapatti 39:12.

26. Churchward, *The Children of Mu.*

27. Jones, *The Lost Data on the Chariots of the Elohim,* 64–66.

28. Vallee, *Magonia,* 73.

29. Photograph available at http://en.wikipedia.org/wiki/File:Stele_Naram_Sim_Louvre_Sb4.jpg (accessed July 25, 2012).

30. Brion, *The World of Archaeology.*

31. Stewart, "Negrito and Negrillo," available at www.stewartsynopsis.com/Synopsis6.htm (accessed July 25, 2012).

32. Charroux, *The Mysteries of the Andes,* 100–1 and Childress, *Lost Cities of*

North and Central America, 538. Both books present material on Kun-Lun that ties it to the lost continent of Mu, or Pan.

33. www.stewartsynoppsis.
34. Gladwin, *Men Out of Asia,* 43.
35. Flower, "The Pygmy Races of Men," 10.
36. Lee, *Folk Tales,* 141.
37. Brinton, *The Myths,* 226.
38. Jones, *Mythology of the American Nations,* 60.
39. Churchward, *The Lost Continent of Mu,* 75.
40. Bahn, *100 Great Archaeological Discoveries,* 192.
41. Berlitz, *World of the Incredible but True,* 76.
42. Vallee, *Magonia,* 55.
43. Turnbull, *The Forest People,* 73.
44. Oahspe, The Lords' Third Book 1:17.
45. Schebesta, *The Negritos,* 282.
46. Mooney, *History, Myths, and Sacred formulas of the Cherokee,* 333.
47. Donnelly, *The Antediluvian World,* 145.
48. Hitchcock, *American Antiquities,* 16: 209–11.
49. Corliss, *Ancient Man,* 661.
50. Carpenter, "Tumuli in Southwestern Pennsylvania."
51. Adams, *Prehistoric,* 25.
52. Gladwin, *Men Out of Asia,* 157.
53. According to Charles Jones, *Antiquities,* 9.
54. Wilson, *Apologies,* 204–5.
55. Jones, *Antiquities,* 217.
56. Wilkins, *Mysteries,* 138, identifies the Shoshone as the earliest basketmakers and canal builders in North America, just as Oahspe mentions Shoshone among the first holy tribes of Indians.
57. Flower, "The Pygmy Races of Men," 18.
58. Spence, *The Myths of Mexico and Peru,* 234.
59. Brinton, *The Myths,* 24.
60. Mack, "Mexico's Little People," 40.
61. Verrill, *Old Civilizations of the New World,* 138.
62. Churchward, *The Lost Continent of Mu,* 225–27.
63. Ibid., 20.
64. Verrill, *The American Indian,* 47.
65. Mack, "Mexico's Little People," 39.

66. Verrill, *Indian,* 406.

67. Marsh, *White Indians of Darien,* 190.

68. Verrill, *Indians.*

69. Dunbar, "Immune to Cancer: The Astonishing Dwarf Community in Ecuador Who Could Hold the Key to a Cure."

70. Fawcett, *Lost Trails, Lost Cities.*

CHAPTER 3. LEGEND OF THE SCARLET HAT

1. Dubois, *Faeries,* 18, 118.

2. Higgins, *Anacalypsis;* taken from Oahspe Commentary, 862, 872, 877, 883.

3. Described in Oahspe, Book of Saphah.

4. White, *Pole Shift,* 278.

5. Moses ceremonies in Oahspe, Book of Saphah: Tablet of Biene, verse 22. "Sacred" and "Secret" probably have the same derivation; see The Lords' Fourth Book 1:20.

6. Oahspe, First Book of God 49:4.

7. Ibid., 27:24.

8. National Geographic Society, *Mysteries of Mankind,* 126.

9. Van der Post, *Lost World,* 24.

10. Oahspe, Book of Thor 1:6.

11. Oahspe, Book of God's Word 18:22.

12. Oahspe, First Book of the First Lords 3:24.

13. Oahspe, The Lords' Fifth Book 3:7.

14. Oahspe, Book of Bon, chapter 20.

15. Oahspe, God's Book of Eskra 10:10.

16. Oahspe, Book of Saphah, Tablet of Biene, verse 22.

17. Oahspe, Book of Saphah, Semoin Interpretation, verse 19.

18. Gladwin, *Men Out of Asia,* 270.

19. Frobenius, *The Childhood of Man,* 51.

20. Ebon, *True Experiences with Ghosts,* 66–67, goes into details of the ghost-seeing of a medium born with the caul.

21. Holland, "Having a Drink with the Fairies," available at www.uncannyuk .com/183/having-a-drink-with-the-fairies (accessed July 25, 2012).

CHAPTER 4. THE PARAGON

1. Turnbull, *The Forest People,* 276.
2. Oahspe, Book of Wars Against Jehovih 21:7.
3. Oahspe, Book of Saphah, Semoin Interpretation, verse 6.
4. Oahspe, First Book of God 27:21; Book of Sethantes 6:18.
5. Oahspe, Book of Saphah: Semoin Interpretation, verses 51–53.
6. Oahspe, Book of Ah'shong 8:10.
7. Thomas, *The Harmless People,* 223.
8. Keightley, *World Guide.*
9. Dubois, *Faeries,* 126.
10. See Mithen, *After the Ice,* 474, and Goodman, *The Genesis Mystery.* Both authors discuss the trance dancing, dreams, visions, and shamans portrayed in rock painting throughout the world.
11. Oahspe, Book of Aph 12:8.
12. Brinton, *The Myths,* 226. The Babylonian Flood story was also told in song—twelve songs or cantos of about three hundred lines each.
13. Campbell, *Primitive Mythology,* 319.
14. Churchward, *The Children of Mu,* 28
15. Oahspe, God's Book of Eskra 10:12.
16. James, *The Hopi Indians,* 106.
17. Endicott, *Batek Negrito Religion,* 109.
18. Stewart, *Pygmies and Dream Giants,* 98.
19. Thomas, *Harmless,* 21.
20. Keightley, *World Guide.*
21. Wilkins, *Mysteries,* 29.
22. Dubois, *Faeries,* 13.
23. Oahspe, The Lords' Fifth Book 4:10.
24. Keightley, *World Guide,* 495.
25. Clark, *Indian Legends.*
26. Quoted in Adams, *Prehistoric Mesoamerica,* 39.
27. Oahspe, The Lords' Fourth Book, The Lords' Fifth Book.
28. Oahspe, First Book of the First Lords 2:19.
29. Oahspe, The Lords' Third Book, 1.
30. Brinton, *The Myths,* 185.
31. Clark, *Indian Legends.*
32. Melham, "Puzzles of the Plains," 121.

33. Further references for the reader who is curious about Mesolithic cities: Oahspe Synopsis 1:21; The Lords' First Book, chapter 2; The Lords' Fifth Book, chapter 5.

34. Connelley, *Indian Myths,* 62–65.

35. Jones, *Antiquities,* 94.

36. Childress, *Lost Cities,* 193.

37. Verrill, *The American Indian,* 466.

38. Bahn, *100 Great,* 201. James Churchward goes back as far as 17,000 years to date the medicinal knowledge of the Uighurs, our Tua Git.

39. Endicott, *Batek.*

40. See a recent, excellent photo of a Thai Negrito of the Mani tribe (scroll down for the image) available at www.andaman.org/BOOK/chapter36/text36.htm (accessed July 26, 2012).

41. Dubois, *Faeries,* 14.

42. Ibid., 50.

43. Mithen, *Ice,* 35.

44. Van der Post, *Lost World,* 57.

45. Many more intriguing passages of this sort, for the curious reader: Book of Aph 13:12, Commentary: 859, The Lords' First Book 1:61, First Book of the First Lords 3:3, The Lords' Second Book 1:4, The Lords' Third Book 2:6, The Lords' Fourth Book 1:5 and 2:5, First Book of God, chapter 5.

46. Oahspe, Book of Divinity 11:3.

47. Dubois, *Faeries,* 12.

48. Oahspe, The Lords' Fourth Book 2:16.

49. Endicott, *Batek,* 126.

50. White, *Pole Shift,* 278.

51. Verrill, *Old Civilizations of the New World,* 88.

52. Goodman, *Mystery,* 218–19.

53. Wilkins, *Mysteries,* 133.

54. Hancock, *Fingerprints of the Gods,* 194.

55. Corliss, *Ancient Man,* 234.

56. Stuart, *Discovering Man's Past in the Americas,* 191.

57. Childe, *The Most Ancient East,* 28.

58. For evidence of prehistorical lenses and microscopes, see Tomas, *We Are Not the First,* 117–18; Oahspe, Book of Wars 5:3, and Book of Fragapatti 2:16. At Oas (in Persia) "the mirrors and lenses . . . were so constructed

that the stars could be read as well in the day as at night." See also Wilkins, *Mysteries of Ancient South America*, 189.

59. Vallee, *Magonia*, 27.

60. Van der Post, *Lost World*.

61. Mithen, *Ice*, 74–75.

62. Roux, *Ancient Iraq*, 353.

63. Von Daniken, *Chariots of the Gods*, 88.

64. Goodman, *Mystery*, 12–13.

65. See Charroux, *The Mysteries of the Andes*, 17, 22, 119.

CHAPTER 5. HIS FLESH WAS WHITE AS SNOW

1. Briggs, *Vanishing*, 167.

2. Goodman, *American Genesis*, 98.

3. Churchward, *Lost Continent*, 99.

4. Keightley, *World Guide*, 175.

5. Bahn, *100 Great*, 84.

6. Wollaston, *Pygmies and Papuans*, 312. Quatrefages, *Pygmies*, 30, also speaks of the Papuan Negritos "whose feet and hands are remarkably small."

7. James, *The Hopi Indians*.

8. Wilkins, *Mysteries*, 95.

9. Jerome Clark, *Unexplained!*

10. Oahspe, First Book of the First Lords, chapter 2.

11. Oahspe, Book of God's Word 26:16.

12. Wilkins, *Mysteries*, 46, 51.

13. Lee, *Folk Tales of All Nations*, 735.

14. Graves, *Goddess*, 207.

15. Keightley, *World Guide*, 351.

16. Oahspe, Book of Saphah: Tablet of Biene, verse 8; Kadeth Iz.

17. Lee, *Folk Tales*, 808.

18. Dubois, *Faeries*, 118.

19. Verrill, *Old Civilizations*, 331.

20. Graves, *Goddess*, 241.

21. Young, *2013: The Beginning is Here*, 144–45.

22. Deloria, *Red Earth, White Lies*, 212.

23. Endicott, *Batek*, 181.

24. Graves, *Goddess*, 207.

25. Radcliffe-Brown, *The Andaman Islanders,* 265.

26. Churchward, *Lost Continent,* 204.

27. Ellis, *Polynesian Researches,* 340.

28. Wilkins, *Mysteries,* 95.

29. Brinton, *The Myths,* 200.

30. *Indians of South America,* quoted in Gladwin, *Men Out of Asia,* 343.

31. Ellis, *Polynesian,* 122.

32. Gladwin, *Men Out of Asia,* 234.

33. Ellis, *Polynesian,* 123.

34. Quoted in Stemman, *Atlantis and the Lost Lands.*

35. Wilkins, *Mysteries,* 185.

36. Jones, *Mythology of the American Nations,* 182.

37. Adams, *Prehistoric Mesoamerica,* 398.

38. Jones, *The Lost Data on the Chariots of the Elohim,* 239.

39. Verrill, *The American Indian,* 2, 446.

40. Verrill, *Old Civilizations,* 12–13.

41. Campbell, *Primitive Mythology,* 209.

42. Von Daniken, *Chariots of the Gods,* 92.

43. Honore, *In Quest of the White God,* 188.

44. Verrill, *The American Indian,* 46.

45. Wilkins, *Mysteries,* 51.

46. Ibid., 59.

47. Corliss, *Ancient Man,* 701.

48. Marsh, *White Indians of Darien,* 26.

49. Verrill, *The American Indian,* 433.

50. Wilkins, *Mysteries,* 116–17.

51. Charroux, *Man's Unknown History,* quoting Garcilasco de la Vega, "Comentarios reales de los Incas 1609–17."

52. Oahspe, The Lords' First Book 1:18.

53. Gladwin, *Men Out of Asia,* 199.

54. Brinton, *The Myths,* 30.

55. Wilkins, *Mysteries,* 59, 178.

56. Churchward, *Lost Continent,* 81, 204, 233.

57. Brinton, *The Myths,* 188; Brinton notes that *wanb* mean "white" and *naghi* means "ancestors."

58. Jones, *Antiquities,* 85.

59. Wilkins, *Mysteries,* 59.

60. Brinton, *The Myths,* 200.

61. Ibid., 195.

62. Ibid.,189.

63. Ibid.

64. Spence, *The Myths of Mexico and Peru,* 24.

65. Hesiod, *Theogony.*

66. The ancient Hebrews "had blond and curly hair, uncommon to other eastern peoples" according to Solas Boncompagni, "L'Antico del Giorni," *Clypeus* 30, Anno VIII, No. 5/6.

67. "White Immigrants in Polynesian Tradition," *Nature* 125(1930): 614.

68. Wollaston, *Pygmies and Papuans,* 48, 110.

69. Eiseley, *The Immense Journey,* 96–102.

70. Van der Post, *Lost World,* 6.

71. Evans, *Negritos,* 294.

72. Steiger, *Monsters,* 37.

73. Wilkins, *Mysteries,* 118, 184.

74. See Zar ceremonies in Crapanzano, *Case Studies in Spirit Possession,* especially pages 25–26, 177, 190, 194; referring to the *wuqabi* cult of Ethiopia.

75. Oahspe, First Book of the First Lords, chapter 1 and 4.1.

76. Oahspe, The Lords' First Book 2:16.

CHAPTER 6. THE NIGHT OF TIME

1. Turnbull, *The Forest People,* 16.

2. Stewart, *Pygmies and Dream Giants,* 73.

3. Berlitz, *Mysteries from Forgotten Worlds,* 151–52.

4. Wilkins, *Mysteries,* 19.

5. Coon, *Origin,* 534.

6. Charroux, *The Mysteries of the Andes,* 106.

7. Ginzburg, *Legends of the Jews,* 60.

8. Oahspe, First Book of the First Lords 4.6.

9. Oahspe, Book of Apollo 14:4.

10. Oahspe, Synopsis of Sixteen Cycles: Sixteenth cycle.

11. Reader, *Missing Links,* 232.

12. See Apollo's mission to correct the monstrosities in *Oahspe,* Book of Apollo, chapter 5.

13. Oahspe, Book of Apollo 3:16.

14. Eiseley, *The Immense Journey,* 105.

15. Oahspe, The Lords' Fifth Book 5:8–11.

16. Vallee, *Magonia,* 73.

17. Wilkins, *Mysteries,* 59.

18. See Wilkins, *Mysteries,* 17–18, on additional legends from the Amazons of the time of darkness.

19. Molten heat falls. See Oahspe, Book of Sethantes 16:4–5.

20. Oahspe, The Lords' Fifth Book 5:8. About 3,000 years ago: "great darkness on the earth"; Velikovsky expands on this theme as does the Book of Ben in Oahspe.

21. Oahspe, The Lords' Fourth Book 4:23–24.

22. Oahspe, God's Book of Eskra 9:3, 9:13 and Book of Divinity; see Martinez, *Time of the Quickening,* chapter 4 for information on these spells of darkness.

23. Mithen, *After the Ice,* 87.

24. Verrill, *The American Indian,* 406.

25. Wilkins, *Mysteries,* 58.

26. Oahspe, The Lords' First Book 2:4.

27. Keightley, *World Guide.*

28. Oahspe, The Lords' First Book 1:25, 1:32.

29. Oahspe, Book of Sethantes 11:27–8; The Lords' First Book 1:25.

30. Oahspe, The Lords' Fifth Book 4:4, 4:8.

31. Ginzburg, *Legends of the Jews,* 125.

32. Lee, *Folk Tales,* 92.

33. Vallee, *Magonia,* 55; Silverberg, *Mound Builders of Ancient America,* 33.

34. Evans, *Negritos,* 278.

35. Schebesta, *The Negritos of Asia,* 159.

36. Ibid., 274.

37. Flower, "The Pygmy Races of Men," 5.

38. Evans, *The Negritos of Malaya,* 17, 33.

39. Flowers, "The Pygmy Races of Men," 10.

40. Lubbock, *Pre-historic Times,* 53.

41. Oahspe, The Lords' Fifth Book 1:14.

42. Van der Post, *Lost World of Kalahari.*

43. Ibid., 52.

44. Turnbull, *Forest People,* 247.

45. James, *The Hopi Indians,* 56–58.

46. Vallee, *Magonia,* 73, 76.
47. Van der Post, *Lost World of Kalahari,* 44.
48. Keightley, *World Guide,* 4.

CHAPTER 7. MOUNDS OF MOUNDS

1. Silverberg, *Moundbuilders of Ancient America,* 69, quoting Caleb Atwater, in *Archaeologia Americana.*
2. Verrill, *The American Indian,* 21.
3. Oahspe, footnote to The Lords' Fifth Book 5:7.
4. Oahspe, First Book of God 24:3.
5. Ceram, *Hittites,* 246.
6. Oahspe, Book of Saphah: Agoquim 11.
7. Wilkins, *Mysteries,* 123. "Lost Civilizations Found in the Jungle," by Will Hunt, on the Archaeology Beat at *Discover* magazine (March 20, 2011, page 19) informs us that the Amazon was once densely populated and graced with earthworks that "could only have been built by large, coordinated populations"—perhaps as large as 9 million souls.
8. Stuart, *Discovering Man's Past in the Americas,* 158.
9. Brinton, *The Myths,* 29, 80; Childress, *Lost Cities,* 278, informs us that a ceramic of the Aztec god of agriculture is found in a Texas burial.
10. Silverberg, *Moundbuilders.*
11. Coe and Diehl, *In the Land of the Olmec.*
12. Lubbock, *Pre-historic Times,* 273.
13. James, *Hopi,* 36.
14. Oahspe, The Lords' Third Book, footnote.
15. Churchward, *Lost Continent,* 224; *The Children of Mu,* 21.
16. Adams, *Mesoamerica,* 326.
17. Kolosimo, *Timeless Earth,* 216.
18. Lubbock, *Pre-historic,* 259, 519.
19. Sherratt, *The Cambridge Encyclopedia of Archaeology,* 374.
20. Brinton, *The Myths,* 92.
21. Ibid., 31, 141.
22. Ibid., 92.
23. Oahspe, First Book of God 24:9.
24. Oahspe, God's Book of Eskra 10.
25. Adams, *Prehistoric Mesoamerica,* 29.

26. Ritchie, *Sketches of Rabun County History,* 5.

27. Jones, *Antiquities,* 134.

28. Brinton, *The Myths,* 273.

29. Lubbock, *Pre-historic,* 281.

30. A seventeenth-century work on Scotland's elves and fairies, the *Sleagh Maith,* quoted by Vallee, *Magonia,* 64.

31. Oahspe, Synopsis of Sixteen Cycles 1:21.

32. Ibid., 3:9 and 2:6.

33. Goodman, *Mystery,* 269–70.

34. Mithen, *Ice,* 53–54.

35. Jones, *Chariots,* 152.

36. Mithen, *Ice,* 33–34, 36, 43.

37. Goodman, *Mystery,* 6.

38. Oahspe, Book of Osiris 9:15.

39. Campbell, *Primitive Mythology,* vii.

40. Sherratt, *The Cambridge Encyclopedia of Archaeology,* 324–25.

41. See chapter 4.

42. Jones, *Antiquities,* 176, 162.

43. Jones, *Mythology of the American Nations,* 226.

44. Quoted in Savoy, *Antisuyo,* 191. Note that Zara is the Peruvian word for maize (see chapter 5 on zar-); there is a tradition that the originators of Peruvian culture came in boats bringing plants never seen before, no doubt including corn, for there is no wild corn pollen found in the ancient records—only the cultivated variety.

45. Sherratt, *Cambridge Encyclopedia,* 370.

46. Cremo, *Forbidden,* 143.

47. Oahspe, The Lords' First Book 2:13.

48. Verrilll, *The American Indian,* 314.

49. Oahspe, The Book of Aph and First Book of the First Lords 3:4, 3:6.

50. Adams, *Prehistoric Mesoamerica,* 109.

51. Childress, *Lost Cities,* 158.

52. Vallee, *Magonia,* 77.

53. Van der Post, *Lost World,* 19.

54. Mithen, *Ice,* 92–93.

55. Lubbock, *Pre-historic,* 53–54.

56. Oahspe, The Lords' First Book, chapter 2.

57. Oahspe, Synopsis of Sixteen Cycles 1:21.

58. Sherratt, *Encyclopedia,* 360, 402.

59. Oahspe, The Lords' Third Book 1:6.

60. "Pygmies," *Gentleman's Magazine,* 182.

61. Oahspe, First Book of God. footnote to v. 14 in chapter 5.

62. Oahspe, Book of Aph 13:3; druks were the first to slay the little people. See First Book of the First Lords 1:14.

63. Silverberg, *Moundbuilders,* 199.

64. Oahspe, The Lords' Second Book 2:11.

65. Wilson, *Apologies,* 206.

66. Oahspe, First Book of the First Lords 3:25.

67. The last six quotes are from Oahspe: The Lords' First Book 1:29; The Lords' Second Book 2:10–13; The Lords' Second Book; First Book of the First Lords 3:24; The First Book of God 14; First Book of the First Lords 3:23; The Lords' Third Book 2:18; megafauna was not killed off for food ("overkill" theories), hunted to extinction, but simply eliminated as a menace.

68. Jones, *Antiquities,* 424–25.

69. Thompson, *Tales of the North American Indians,* 101.

70. Oahspe, Book of Saphah: Agoquim, v. 8.

71. Oahspe, First Book of the First Lords 3:3–4.

72. In the mounds: from Mithen, *Ice,* 65. At Gobekli—perched on a hilltop, "circular structures that had been sunk into the hill the create what looked like cellars in the earth."

73. Oahspe, The Lords' Fifth Book 3:19.

74. Maspero, *The Dawn of Civilization,* 350.

75. Herodotus, *Histories,* 274.

76. Detailed by Jones, *Chariots,* 185–86, 189, 191, 205.

77. Stuart, *Discovering Man's Past,* 151.

78. Oahspe, The Lords' Third Book 1:14.

79. Atwater, "Antiquities Discovered in the State of Ohio," vol 1.

80. Silverberg, *Moundbuilders,* 83.

81. Adam Clarke, LLD, quoted in Silverberg, *Moundbuilders,* 69.

82. Oahspe, Book of Apollo 14:10.

83. Childress, *Lost Cities,* 442.

84. Oahspe, Book of Cosmogony and Prophecy 11:13.

85. Brave Bird, *Ohitika Woman,* 104–5.

86. Oahspe, Book of Wars 7:6.

87. Oahspe, The Lords' Fifth Book 6:35; Book of Wars 21:4.

88. Ibid.

89. Lubbock, *Pre-historic,* 271.

90. Ibid.

91. Ibid.

92. Sprague de Camp, *The Ancient Engineers,* 289.

93. Brinton, *The Myths,* 286.

94. "Colorado Solar Hogan Demonstration," www.dennisrhollowayarchitect .com/html/SolarHoganaa.html (accessed August 6, 2012).

95. Oahspe, Book of Saphah: "When the drouth destroyeth, let the faithful hold [Eswin] on the mountain-tops, and the rains will I send from heaven."

96. Oahspe, Book of Wars 7:9.

CHAPTER 8. TALL TALES AND SHORT SUBJECTS

1. Wickland, *Thirty Years Among The Dead.*

2. Goodman, *American Genesis,* 87.

3. Marsh, *White Indians,* 213.

4. "A New Tribe of Light-Skinned Natives in New Guinea," 16–18.

5. Gladwin, *Men Out of Asia,* 235.

6. Adams, *Prehistoric Mesoamerica,* 168.

7. Graves, *White Goddess,* 213.

8. Eiseley, *The Immense Journey,* 106.

9. Mithen, *Ice,* 405.

10. Darwin, *Descent,* 49.

11. Mithen, *Ice,* 310.

12. Coon, *Origin,* 112.

13. Wollaston, *Pygmies,* 312.

14. Lemonick, "Bones of Contention," available at www.time.com/time/maga zine/article/0,9171,985306,00.html (accessed August 8, 2012).

15. "Life History trade-offs explain the evolution of human pygmies." Proceedings of the National Academy of Science.

16. Quatrefages, *Pygmies,* 85.

17. "More Little People Fossils Found," available at www.world-science.net/ othernews/080310_micronesia (accessed August 8, 2012).

18. In Oahspe, The Lords' Third Book 2:2; and Book of Apollo 5:2, we learn

of the Ongwees, an Ihuan-Ihin hybrid that "came suddenly into the world
. . . in one generation, behold, a new race is born."

19. Fagan, *World Prehistory,* 65–67.

20. Ibid., 75–76.

21. Verrill, *Old Civilizations,* 43, 59.

22. Wilkins, *Mysteries,* 151.

23. Hibben, *The Lost Americans,* 8.

24. Evans, *Negritos of Malaysia,* 9.

25. Leach, *The Beginning,* 142–44.

26. Van der Post, *Lost World,* 30.

27. Coon, *The Living Races of Man,* 176.

28. Ibid., 206.

29. Corliss, *Ancient Man,* 700.

30. Wollaston, *Pygmies,* 174.

31. Stewart, *Pygmies and Dream Giants,* 129.

32. Turnbull, *Forest People,* 18.

33. Van der Post, *Lost World,* 52.

34. Campbell, *Primitive Mythology,* 378.

35. Gladwin, *Men Out of Asia,* 45.

36. Van der Post, *Lost World,* 24, 30.

37. Childe, *The Most Ancient East,* 22.

38. Van der Post, *Lost World,* 24–25, 45.

39. Tomas, *We Are Not the First,* 33.

40. Von Daniken, *Chariots of the Gods,* 64, 76.

41. Honoré, *In Quest of the White God,* 120, 126.

42. Hancock, *Fingerprints of the Gods,* 38.

43. Verrill, *Old Civilizations,* 247.

44. Roux, *Ancient Iraq,* 131, both quotes.

45. Ellis, *Polynesian Researches,* 121.

46. Wilkins, *Mysteries,* 196, dates the "pre-cataclysmic age" to 25,000 years ago.

47. Ibid., 187.

48. Hardaker, *The First Americans,* 10, 26, 127.

49. Mithen, *Ice,* 215.

50. Goodman, *American Genesis,* 98, 209.

51. Bahn, *100 Great Archaeological Discoveries,* 64.

52. Gladwin, *Men Out of Asia,* 7.

53. Ceram, *The Secret of the Hittites,* 312.

54. Campbell, *Primitive Mythology,* 15, 146, 274.

55. Coon, *Origin,* 656; Mithen, *Ice,* 314.

56. Mithen, *Ice,* 361–3.

57. Cremo, *Forbidden Archaeology,* 183.

58. Brinton, *The Myths,* 112.

59. Oahspe, Synopsis of Sixteen Cycles 3:28.

60. Goodman, *American Genesis,* 95.

61. Adams, *Prehistoric Mesoamerica,* 24.

62. Ibid., 49, 80–82, 94.

63. Goodman, *Genesis,* 127.

64. Gladwin, *Men Out of Asia,* 44.

65. Wilkins, *Mysteries,* 82.

66. Bahn, *100 Great Archaeological Discoveries,* 187.

67. Campbell, *Primitive Mythology,* 444.

68. Gladwin, *Men Out of Asia,* 234.

69. Churchward, *The Lost Continent,* 81.

70. Campbell, *Primitive Mythology,* 208.

71. Gladwin, *Men Out of Asia,* 45.

72. Churchward, *The Lost Continent,* 34.

73. Oahspe, Synopsis of Sixteen Cycles 3:27.

74. Ibid., 27:24.

75. Oahspe, First Book of God 25:1.

76. Brinton, *The Myths,* 14.

77. Wilkins, *Mysteries,* 146–48.

CHAPTER 9. MEN AND MANIMALS

1. Brinton, *The Myths,* 239.

2. Lee, *Folk Tales,* 81.

3. Oahspe, Book of Divinity 11:13.

4. Brinton, *The Myths,* 226.

5. Ibid., 238.

6. Dubois, *Faeries,* 13.

7. Jim Dennon, "Removing Oahspe's Enigmas," 7.

8. Endicott, *Batek,* 88.

9. Oahspe, Book of Saphah: Tablet of Biene v. 14; see also Oahspe, Book of Jehovih 7:1.

10. Oahspe, Book of Jehovih 6:18.

11. Goodman, *American Genesis,* 91.

12. See also Oahspe, First Book of First Lords 1:2–3.

13. Drake, *Gods and Spacemen of the Ancient Past,* 99.

14. Oahspe, First Book of the First Lords 1:3 and 8.

15. Oahspe, Book of Sethantes 8:8.

16. Ibid., 8:9.

17. Oahspe, The Lords' Fifth Book 1:14 and chapter 3.

18. Oahspe, First Book of the First Lords 1:10.

19. Johnson, *Scroll of the Great Spirit,* 26:21.

20. Ibid.

21. Oahspe, Lords' First Book 1:19.

22. Oahspe, The Lords' Second Book 1:18–19.

23. Oahspe, Book of Divinity 11:13; Book of Jehovih 7:21.

24. Pike, *Morals and Dogma,* 599.

25. Verrill, *Indians,* 397.

26. "Orang Pendek," available at www.monstropedia.org/index.php?title= Orang Pendek (accessed August 9, 2012).

27. Steiger, *Monsters Among Us,* 2, 53, 56.

28. Coleman, *The Field Guide to Bigfoot, Yeti and Other Mystery Primates Worldwide,* 98.

29. Eiseley, *The Immense Journey,* 133.

30. Oahspe, The Lords' Fifth Book 1:19.

31. Ibid., 1:21.

32. Fell, *America B.C.,* 232.

33. Maspero, *The Dawn,* 171.

34. Spence, *The Myths of Mexico and Peru.*

35. Genesis 5:5–31, 9:29. Adam, Seth, Enosh, Kenan, Jared, Methuselah, and Noah all lived for hundreds of years.

36. Oahspe, Synopsis of Sixteen Cycles 2:13 and 1:22.

37. Steiger, *Monsters,* 94; Wilkins, *Mysteries,* 194.

38. Oahspe, Synopsis of Sixteen Cycles 1:25–61 (11th cycle).

39. Coon, *Origin,* 583, 609.

40. Jones, *Antiquities,* 9.

41. Oahspe, First Book of God 24:4.

42. Churchward, *Lost Continent,* 37.

43. James, *Hopi,* 37.

44. Steiger, *Monsters,* 37.

45. Campbell, *Primitive Mythology,* 314, 325.

46. Goodman, *Mystery,* 141.

47. National Geographic Society, *Mysteries of Mankind,* 24.

48. Briggs, *Vanishing,* 164.

49. Kelly, *Irish Folk and Fairy Tales,* 301.

50. Wilkins, *Mysteries,* 191.

51. Kramer, *History Begins at Sumer,* 107.

52. Ibid., 84.

53. Ibid., 299.

54. Ibid., 142.

55. Adams, *Prehistoric,* 401.

56. Campbell, *Primitive Mythology,* 413.

57. Kramer, *Sumer,* 285–87, 291.

58. "The ur [Ur] and Harran Latitudes, and Gobekli Tepe," available at http://jqjacobs.net/blog/gobekli_tepe.html (accessed August 9, 2012), and "Gobekli Tepe—Eden, Home of the Watchers," available at www.andrewcollins.com/page/articles/Gobekli_Tepe_interview.htm (accessed August 12, 2012). Similar temples of the same age are being explored at Karahantepe, Sefertepe and Hamzantepe, all antedating the Neolithic.

59. Wilkins, *Mysteries of Ancient South America,* 98.

60. Verrill, *Old Civilizations,* 88.

61. Adams, *Prehistoric,* 29.

62. Kennedy, "Early Man in the New World."

63. Goodman, *American Genesis,* 95.

64. Cremo, *Forbidden,* 579

65. http://news.nationalgeographic.com/news/2007/01/070116-neanderthals.html (accessed September 13, 2012).

66. Cremo, *Forbidden,* 683.

67. Skorjenko, "Oahspe Study: Ancient Races of Man," available at http://oahspestandardedition.com/OSAC/AncientRacesofMan.html (accessed August 9, 2012).

68. Cremo, *Forbidden,* 704.

69. Deloria, *Red Earth,* 110.

70. Goodman, *Genesis,* 175.

71. Goodman, *Mystery,* 215, 219.

72. Mithen, *Ice,* 227.

73. Goodman, *Mystery,* 199.

74. Montagu, *Man and His First Two Million Years,* 70.

75. Bahn, *100 Great Archaeological Discoveries,* 139.

76. Ibid., 187.

77. Oahspe, First Book of the First Lords 4:19.

78. Oahspe, The Lords' Fourth Book 4:10.

79. Goodman, *The Genesis Mystery,* 132, 144, 162, 184, 198, 207. *Homo habilis,* too, showed more modern traits than his supposed successor *Homo erectus.*

80. Wilkins, *Mysteries,* 117.

81. Fagan, *Prehistory,* 75–76.

82. Goodman, *Mystery,* 179–80.

83. Hardaker, *The First,* 250, 253.

84. Timmer, "Human Sequence Cropping Up in Neanderthal Genome," available at http://arstechnica.com/journals/science.ars/2007/10/15/human-Sequences-cropping-up-in-neanderthal-genome (accessed August 9, 2012).

Bibliography

Adams, Richard E.W. *Prehistoric Mesoamerica*. Norman, Okla.: University of Oklahoma Press, 1996.

Adovasio, James M., and Jake Page. *The First Americans: In Pursuit of Archaeology's Greatest Mystery*. New York: Random House, 2002.

Arrowsmith, Nancy. *A Field Guide to the Little People*. New York: Wallaby Books, 1977.

Bahn, Paul G. *100 Great Archaeological Discoveries*. New York: Barnes and Nobel Books, 1995.

Bartram, William. *Travels through North and South Carolina*. London: N.p., 1792.

Berlitz, Charles. *Mysteries from Forgotten Worlds*. New York: Doubleday and Co., 1972.

Brave Bird, Mary. *Ohitika Woman*. New York: Harper Perennial, 1993.

Briggs, Katharine. *The Vanishing People*. New York: Pantheon Books, 1978.

Brinton, Daniel G. *The Myths of the New World*. Blauvelt, New York: Multimedia Publishing Corp., 1976.

Brion, Marcel. *World Archaeology*. New York: Macmillian, 1962.

Bullfinch, Thomas. *Bullfinch's Mythology*. New York: Laurel Publishing, Laurel Classic, 1959.

Campbell, Joseph. *The Masks of God, vol. 1, Primitive Mythology*. New York: Penguin Books, 1987.

———. *The Masks of God, vol. 2, Oriental Mythology*. New York: Penguin Books, 1962.

Carpenter, Edmund S. "Tumuli in Southwestern Pennsylvania." *American Antiquity* 16 (1951): 329–46.

Carpenter, Frances. *Tales of a Basque Grandmother.* New York: The Junior Literary Guild, 1930.

Carter, Mary Ellen. *Edgar Cayce on Prophecy.* Portland, Ore.: Hawthorne Books, 1968.

Ceram, C. W. *Gods, Graces and Scholars.* New York: Alfred A Knopf, 1967.

———. *The Secret of the Hittites.* New York: Alfred A. Knopf, 1956.

Cerve, Wishnar S. *Lemuria: The Lost Continent of the Pacific.* San Jose, Calif.: The Rosicrucian Press, 1931.

Charroux, Robert. *The Mysteries of the Andes.* New York: Avon Books, 1974.

Childe, V. Gordon. *The Most Ancient East.* Hertford, Great Britain: Stephen Austin and Sons, Ltd., 1928.

Childress, David Hatcher. *Lost Cities of North and Central America.* Stelle, Ill.: Adventures Unlimited Press, 1993.

Churchward, James. *The Children of Mu.* New York: Paperback Library, Inc., 1931.

———. *The Lost Continent of Mu.* New York: Paperback Library, Inc., 1931.

Clark, Ella. *Indian Legends of the Northern Rockies.* Norman, Okla.: University of Oklahoma Press, 1966.

Coe, Michael D., and Richard A. Diehl. *In the Land of the Olmec.* Austin, Tex.: University of Texas Press, 1980.

Coleman, Loren, and Patrick Huyghe. *The Field Guide to Bigfoot, Yeti, and Other Mystery Primates Worldwide.* New York: Avon Books, 1999.

Connelley, William E. *Indian Myths.* Chicago: Rand McNally and Co., 1928.

Coon, Carleton. *The Living Races of Man.* New York: Alfred A. Knopf, 1965.

———. *The Origin of Races.* New York: Alfred A. Knopf, 1962.

Corliss, William. *Ancient Man.* Glen Arms, Md.: The Sourcebook Project, 1978.

Cottrell, Leonard, Ed. *The Concise Encyclopedia of Archaeology.* New York: Hawthorne Books, 1960.

Cremo, Michael, and Richard Thompson. *Forbidden Archaeology.* Los Angeles, Calif.: Bhaktivedanta Book Publishing Co., 1998.

Crapanzano, Vincent. *Case Studies in Spirit Possession.* Hoboken, N.J.: Wiley, 1977.

Crow Dog, Mary, and Richard Erdoes. *Lakota Woman.* New York: Harper Perennial, 1991.

Curtin, Jeremiah. *Creation Myths of Primitive America.* Santa Barbara, Calif.: ABC-CLIO, 2002.

Darwin, Charles. *The Descent of Man.* New York: Penguin Books, 2004.

Deloria, Vine, Jr. *Red Earth, White Lies.* New York: Scribner, 1995.

Donnelly, Ignatius. *Atlantis: The Antediluvian World*. New York: Gramercy Publishing Co., 1949.

Doyle, Arthur Conan. *On the Edge of the Unknown*. New York: G. P. Putnam's Sons, 1930.

Drake, Raymond. *Gods and Spacemen of the Ancient Past*. New York: A Signet Book, 1974.

Dubois, Pierre. *The Great Encyclopedia of Faeries*. New York: Simon and Schuster, 1999.

Dunbar, Polly. "Immune to Cancer: The Astonishing Dwarf Community in Ecuador Who Could Hold the Key to a Cure" (August, 2008). www.dailymail.com.uk (accessed September 13, 2012).

Durrani, Nadia. "Egyptian Dwarfs." *World Archaeology* 15 (January 2006). www.world-archaeology.com/news/egyptian-dwarfs (accessed July 25, 2012).

Ebon, Martin. *True Experiences with Ghosts*. New York: Signet, 1968.

Ellis, William. *Polynesian Researches*. Rutland, Vt.: Charles E. Tuttle Co, 1969.

Endicott, Kirk. *Batek Negrito Religion*. New York and Oxford, England: Clarendon Press, 1979.

Eiseley, Loren. *The Immense Journey*. New York: Time Reading Program Special Edition, 1957.

Evans, Ivor Hugh Norman. *The Negritos of Malaya*. Cambridge: Cambridge University Press, 1937.

Fagan, Brian M. *World Prehistory. A Brief Introduction*. New York: Longman, 1999.

Fell, Barry. *America B.C.* New York: A Demeter Press Book, 1977.

———. *Saga America*. New York: Times Books, 1980.

Flower, William Henry. "The Pygmy Races of Men." Royal Institution of Great Britain, Weekly Evening Meeting Lecture, 1888.

Frazer, James G. *The Golden Bough*. New York: Gramercy Books, 1981.

Frobenius, Leo. *The Childhood of Man*. London, England: Seeley and Co. Ltd., 1909.

Ginzburg, Louis. *Legends of the Jews*. Philadelphia, Penn.: Publications Society, 2003.

Gladwin, Harold S. *Men Out of Asia*. New York: McGraw-Hill Book Co., 1947.

Goodman, Jeffrey. *American Genesis*. New York: Summit Books, 1981.

———. *The Genesis Mystery*. New York: Times Books, 1983.

Gorner, Peter. "Tiny-Human Find Becomes Huge News," *Orlando Sentinel*, Nov. 4, 2004, A10.

Gould, George M., and Walter L. Pyle. "Anomalies and Curiosities of Medicine." http://etext.lib.virginia.edu/toc/modeng/public/GouAnom.html.

Graves, Robert. *The White Goddess.* New York: Farrar, Straus and Giroux, 1988.

Grimm, Jacob. *Grimm's Fairy Tales.* New York: Barnes and Noble Classics, 2003.

Hancock, Graham. *Fingerprints of the Gods.* New York: Three Rivers Press, 1995.

Hardaker, Christopher. *The First Americans.* Franklin Lakes, N.J.: New Page Books, 2007.

Heindel, Max. *Rosicrucian Cosmo-conception.* New ed. Oceanside, Calif.: Rosicrucian Fellowship, 1997.

Hibben, Frank. *The Lost Americans.* New York: T.Y. Crowell and Co., 1968.

Hitchcock. *American Antiquities* 16: 209–11.

Holland, Richard. "Having a Drink with the Fairies." www.uncannyuk.com/183/having-a-drink-with-the-fairies.

Honore, Pierre. *In Quest of the White God.* New York: G. P. Putnam's Sons, 1964.

Howells, William. *Getting Here: The Story of Human Evolution.* Washington, D.C.: Howells House, 1997.

Irwin, Constance. *Fair Gods and Stone Faces.* New York: St. Martin's Press, 1963.

James, Harry. *The Hopi Indians.* Caldwell, Idaho: Caxton Printers, 1956.

Johnson, Brice. *Scroll of the Great Spirit.* Tiger, Ga.: Essene Faithists, 1992.

Jones, Alison. *Larousse Dictionary of World Folklore.* New York: Larousse Kingfisher Chambers, Inc., 1995.

Jones, Charles C., Jr. *Antiquities of the Southern Indians.* New York: D. Appleton and Co., 1873.

Jones, David M., and Brian L. Molyneaux. *Mythology of the American Nations.* London: Hermes House, 2004.

Jones, Martha Helene. *The Lost Data on the Chariots of the Elohim.* www.lulu.com/contents/5532143, 2008.

Keightley, Thomas. *The World Guide to Gnomes, Fairies, Elves and Other Little People.* New York: Avenel Books, 1978.

Kelly, Sean, ed. *Irish Folk and Fairy Tales.* New York: The Rutledge Press, 1982.

Kennedy, G. E. "Early Man in the New World." *Nature* 255 (May 22, 1975): 274–75.

Kolosimo, Peter. *Timeless Earth.* New York: Bantam Books, 1975.

Kramer, Samuel Noah. *History Begins at Sumer* 3rd edition. Philadelphia: University of Pennsylvania Press, 1981.

Layard, John. *Stone Men of Malekula.* London: Chatto and Windus, 1942.

Leach, Maria. *The Beginning.* New York: Funk and Wagnalls Co., 1956.

Lee, F. H. *Folk Tales of All Nations.* New York: Tudor Publishing Co., 1930.

Leeming, David Adams. *A Dictionary of Creation Myths.* New York: Oxford University Press, 1994.

Lemonick, Michael D., and Dan Cray. "Bones of Contention." *Time,* October 14, 1996. www.time.com/time/magazine/article/0,9171,985306,00.html.

"Life History Trade-offs Explain the Evolution of Human Pygmies." *Proceedings of the National Academy of Science* 104, no. 51 (December 18, 2007): 20216–20219.

Lossiah, Lynn King. *Cherokee Little People.* Cherokee, N.C.: Cherokee Publishing, 1998.

Lubbock, Sir John. *Pre-historic Times.* New York: D. Appleton and Co., 1872.

Mack, Bill. "Mexico's Little People." *Fate.* August, 1984: 38–40.

Marsh, Richard Oglesby. *White Indians of Darien.* New York: G. P. Putnam's Sons, 1934.

Maspero, Gaston. *The Dawn of Civilization. Vol. I & II.* London: Society for Promoting Christian Knowledge, 1894.

Mayell, Hillary. "Hobbit-like Human Ancestor Found in Asia," *National Geographic News* (online), Oct. 27, 2004. http://news.nationalgeographic.com/news/2004/10/1027_041027_homo_floresiensis.html

Melham, Tom. "Puzzles of the Plains," in National Geographic Society *Mysteries of Mankind.*

Mithen, Steven. *After the Ice.* Cambridge, Mass.: Harvard University Press, 2003.

Mooney, James. *History, Myths and Sacred Formulas of the Cherokee.* Asheville, N.C.: Historical Images, 1992.

"More 'Little People' Fossils Found." Public Library of Science, March 11, 2008. www.world-science.net/othernews/080310_micronesia.

National Geographic Society. *Mysteries of Mankind.* Washington, D.C.: National Geographic Society, 1992.

"A New Tribe of Light-Skinned Natives in New Guinea." *Science* 85 (March 6, 1937): 16–18.

Oahspe. New York and London: Oahspe Publishing Association, 1882.

Pike, Albert. *Morals and Dogma.* Charleston, S.C.: The Supreme Council of the 33rd Degree of the Southern Jurisdiction of the United States, Kessinger Publishing, 1946.

Prorok, Count Byron de. *In Quest of Lost Worlds.* New York: E. P. Dutton and Co., 1936.

"Pygmaioi." www.theoi.com/Phylos/Pygmaioi.html.

"Pygmies." *Gentleman's Magazine* 3:8 (1837).

Quatrefages, Armand de. *The Pygmies.* New York: D. Appleton and Co., 1895.

Radcliffe-Brown, A. R. *The Andaman Islanders.* Cambridge, England: Cambridge University Press, 1922.

Reader, John. *Missing Links.* Boston, Mass.: Little, Brown and Co., 1981.

Reader's Digest Association. *Man and Beast.* Pleasantville, New York: Reader's Digest, 1993.

Reed, William Allan. *Negritos of Zambales.* Manila: Bureau of Public Printing, 1904.

Richardson, Emeline. *The Etruscans.* Chicago and London, England: The University of Chicago Press, 1976.

Ritchie, Andrew Jackson. *Sketches of Rabun County History.* Clayton, Georgia: Rabun County Historical Society, 1948.

Roux, Georges. *Ancient Iraq.* New York: Penguin Books, 1992.

Sarfati, Jonathan D. *Refuting Evolution.* Green Forest, Ark.: Master Books, 1999.

Savoy, Gene. *Antisuyo. The Search for the Lost Cities of the Amazon.* New York: Simon and Schuster, 1970.

Schebesta, Paul. *The Negritos of Asia, Vol. 2.* Human Relations Area File, 1962.

Scheerer, Otto. *The Nabaloi Dialect.* Manila: Bureau of Public Printing, 1905.

Sherratt, Andrew, ed. *The Cambridge Encyclopedia of Archaeology.* New York: Crown Publishers Inc., 1980.

Silverberg, Robert. *Mound Builders of Ancient America.* Greenwich, Conn.: New York Graphic Society, 1968.

Skorjenko, Ruth. "Oahspe Study: The Ancient Races of Man." http://oahspestandardedition.com/OSAC/AncientRacesofMan.html.

Spence, Lewis. *The Myths of Mexico and Peru.* New York: Dover Publications, 1994.

Sprague de Camp, Lyon. *The Ancient Engineers.* New York: Ballantine Books, 1963.

Steiger, Brad. *Monsters Among Us.* New York: Berkley Books, 1989.

Stemman, Roy. *Atlantis and the Lost Lands.* London: Aldus Books, 1976.

Stewart, Kilton. *Pygmies and Dream Giants.* New York: W. W. Norton and Co., 1954.

Stewart, M. "Stewart Synopsis." http://stewartsynopsis.com/Synopsis%206.htm.

Stuart, George E. *Discovering Man's Past in the Americas.* Washington DC: The National Geographic Society, 1973.

Thomas, Elizabeth Marshall. *The Harmless People.* New York: Alfred A. Knopf, 1959.

Thompson, Stith. *Tales of the North American Indians*. Mineola, N.Y.: Dover Publications, 2000.

Time-Life Books, Eds. *Barbarian Tides*. Fairfax, Va.: Time-Life Books, 1987.

Timmer, John. "Human Sequence Cropping Up in Neanderthal Genome." *Ars Technica,* October 15, 2007. http://arstechnica.com/journals/science. ars/2007/10/15/human-Sequences-cropping-up-in-neanderthal-genome.

Tomas, Andrew. *We Are Not the First*. New York: G. P. Putnam's Sons, 1971.

Turnbull, Colin. *The Forest People*. New York: Simon and Schuster, 1968.

Tylor, Edward Burnett. *Researches into the Early History of Mankind*. Chicago: University of Chicago, Phoenix Books, 1964.

Vaillant, George C. "A Bearded Mystery." *Natural History* 31 (1931): 243–52.

Vallee, Jacques. *Passport to Magonia*. Chicago: Henry Regnery Co., 1969.

Van der Post, Laurens. *The Lost World of the Kalahari*. San Diego: Harcourt Brace and Co., 1958.

Verrill, A. Hyatt. *The American Indian*. New York: The New Home Library, 1927.

———. *Old Civilizations of the New World*. New York: New Home Library, 1943.

Von Daniken, Erich. *Chariots of the Gods*. New York: Bantam Books, 1973.

Wagner, Stephen. "The Elusive Little People." http://paranormal.about.com/od/ othercreatures/a/little-people.htm.

Waters, Frank. *Book of the Hopi*. New York: Penguin Books, 1977.

White, John. *Pole Shift*. New York: Doubleday, 1980.

Wichman, Frederick. *Kauai Tales*. Honolulu: Bamboo Ridge Press, 1985.

Wickland, Carl. *Thirty Years among the Dead*. Hollywood, Calif.: Newcastle Publishing Co., 1974.

Wilkins, Cary, ed. *The Andrew Lang Fairy Tale Treasury*. New York: Avenel Books, 1979.

Wilkins, Harold T. *Mysteries of Ancient South America*. Kempton, Ill.: Adventures Unlimited Press, 1947.

Wilson, Edmund. *Apologies to the Iroquois*. New York: Farrar, Strauss and Giroux, 1960.

Wollaston, Alexander Frederick Richmond. *Pygmies and Papuans*. New York: Sturgis and Walton Co., 1912.

Young, Jim. *2013: The Beginning is Here*. Alresford, England: John Hunt Publishing, Ltd., 2011.

Index